“This book reveals the most significant elements of Europeanisation that have occurred in Croatia over the last ten years. As such, it will become a key reference work for scholars in the field.”

Will Bartlett, *London School of Economics and Political Science*

“Ten years of Croatia in the EU has got a book that rigorously and thoroughly looks at different aspects of institutional and policy responds of Croatian politics to EU membership. A reader will find nicely written chapters and documented analyses of what and how has been changed in comparison to the accession period.”

Goran Čular, *Faculty of Political Science, University of Zagreb*

Crisis Era European Integration

The year 2023 marked the tenth anniversary of Croatia's membership of the European Union, the last acceding country to the EU, and thus represents a fitting opportunity to explore the political, economic and social dimensions of this tremendous transformation. This book examines how Croatia has changed over the last ten years and looks at the driving forces as well as the obstacles on its post-accession path of Europeanisation.

The book argues that the Croatian case has special importance given that the last decade of European integration has arguably been the most challenging one yet. It started with the Eurozone-wide sovereign debt crisis and ended with the economic hardship caused by the COVID-19 pandemic and Russia's aggression on Ukraine. Such demanding circumstances where agenda was often defined in an ad hoc way posed a huge test for Croatia's governmental capacity. The book provides answers to the question of how successful Croatian policymakers were in dealing with the crises-related challenges and other needed adaptations. The book explores how EU membership has affected the design and implementation of selected national public policies, the functioning of governing institutions and patterns of cooperation between main social actors. Expert contributors analyse the impact of the EU membership in two principal areas: political and economic, with individual chapters addressing relevant topics.

The book is intended for researchers, academics and students interested in these issues, as well as policymakers, entrepreneurs and lobbyists concerned with European integration.

Jakša Puljiz is Head of the Department for European Integration at the Institute for Development and International Relations (IRMO), Zagreb, Croatia.

Hrvoje Butković is a senior research associate in the Department for European Integration at the Institute for Development and International Relations (IRMO), Zagreb, Croatia.

Routledge Studies in the European Economy

65 **The European Union Digital Single Market**
Europe's Digital Transformation
Edited by Łukasz Dawid Dąbrowski and Magdalena Suska

66 **Economic Wellbeing and Household Debt**
Agnieszka Wałęga, Grzegorz Wałęga and Ryszard Kowalski

67 **Transition Economies in Central and Eastern Europe**
Austrian Perspectives
Edited by Alicja Sielska

68 **The Silver Economy**
An Ageing Society in the European Union
Agata Niemczyk, Katarzyna Szalonka, Anna Gardocka-Jałowiec, Wioletta Nowak, Renata Seweryn, Zofia Gródek-Szostak

69 **Knowledge Cohesion**
Uniting Europe Through Research Networks
İbrahim Semih Akçomak, Umut Yılmaz Çetinkaya, Erkan Erdil and Müge Özman

70 **Financial Stability, Economic Growth and Sustainable Development**
Edited by Marc Baudry, Sławomir Ireneusz Bukowski and Marzanna Barbara Lament

71 **Crisis Era European Integration**
Economic, Political and Social Lessons from Croatia
Edited by Jakša Puljiz and Hrvoje Butković

For more information about this series, please visit www.routledge.com/series/SE0431

Crisis Era European Integration

Economic, Political and Social Lessons from Croatia

Edited by Jakša Puljiz and Hrvoje Butković

Routledge
Taylor & Francis Group
LONDON AND NEW YORK

First published 2025
by Routledge
4 Park Square, Milton Park, Abingdon, Oxon OX14 4RN

and by Routledge
605 Third Avenue, New York, NY 10158

Routledge is an imprint of the Taylor & Francis Group, an informa business

British Library Cataloguing-in-Publication Data
A catalogue record for this book is available from the British Library

ISBN: 978-1-032-49480-7 (hbk)
ISBN: 978-1-032-49483-8 (pbk)
ISBN: 978-1-003-39401-3 (ebk)

DOI: 10.4324/9781003394013

Typeset in Times New Roman
by Newgen Publishing UK

Contents

Figures

Tables

Contributors

Zdenko Babić is Full Professor at the University of Zagreb, Faculty of Law, Department for Social Policy. His research interests include social policy, labour market and social economy and social entrepreneurship. That is documented in his publications and research projects. He is currently engaged as a Croatian national expert for the European Commission funded project European centre of expertise in the field of labour law, employment and labour market policies ("ECE"). He is also Croatian national expert for the European Commission in European social policy expert network-ESPN network. He was also leading consultant on several UNICEF, UNDP and World Bank projects in Croatia.

Nika Bačić Selanec holds the Jean Monnet Module on "EU Constitutional Law and Methodology" at the University of Zagreb – Faculty of Law, Department of European Public Law. She obtained her LLM degree at the University of Michigan Law School in 2014 as Hugo Grotius Fellow (with merit) and obtained her PhD in Zagreb in 2019 (summa cum laude). She is the Executive Editor of the *Croatian Yearbook of European Law and Policy* and the President of the "Croatian European Union Studies Association". Her academic interests and expertise include EU constitutional law, judicial methodologies and theories of adjudication, EU citizenship and migration law.

Predrag Bejaković took his doctorate at the Economics Faculty in Zagreb and worked full time as a member of permanent staff in the Institute of Public Finance, Zagreb. He publishes in scientific and professional journals and he is author and co-author of a number of books from the areas of the economy, pension system, education (particularly VET and adult education), policy planning, public finance and labour economics. He received a yearly prize for contribution in social science by the Republic of Croatia in 2009. His main fields of interests are labour economics, health economics, pension system, public administration and education.

Paško Bilić is a senior research associate at the Department for Culture and Communication, Institute for Development and International Relations. He has co-edited, with Thomas Allmer, the book titled *Critical Sociology of Media and Communications: Theoretical Contributions to a Disconnected Field,* which is expected to be published by Brill in 2024. He has also authored a book, along with Toni Prug and Mislav Žitko, titled *The Political Economy of Digital Monopolies*, published by Bristol University Press in 2021. In addition to this, he has authored a book in Croatian titled *Sociology of Media: Routines, Technology, and Power* (Jesenski i Turk, 2020) and has edited, along with Jaka Primorac and Bjarki Valtysson, the book titled *Technologies of Labour and the Politics of Contradiction* (Palgrave Macmillan, 2018).

Ivana Biondić is a research assistant at the Institute for Development and International Relations in Zagreb. She earned her Master's degree from the Faculty of Economics and Business at the University of Zagreb in 2017 and has been enrolled in a doctorate program at the joint program at University of Innsbruck and University of Linz since 2019. Her research interests include examining the impact of EU policies, with a particular emphasis on EU Cohesion policy, on the national public policies of member states and other countries engaged in the enlargement process. Additionally, her interests encompass regional and local development.

Ana-Maria Boromisa, PhD, is a Head of Department for International Economic and Political Relations at IRMO. Boromisa has extensive research and consulting experience relating to economic and financial analysis, environmental financing, decarbonisation, energy and climate. The clients include international and European organisations (such various UN bodies, the World Bank, WTO, the European Commission, the European Parliament, CINEA), national and regional governments. Ana-Maria Boromisa also teaches (at Master and PhD level) at the University of Zagreb and the University of Yantai (China). She currently serves as a chair of the Zagreb Mayor's advisory council for citizens' energy. Previously she was a member of IRMO management board 2006–2012 and the president of Scientific Council (2013–2017). In the period 2001–2005 she served as a Commissioner at the Croatian Energy Regulatory Council.

Hrvoje Butković is a senior research associate at the Department for European Integration of the Institute for Development and International Relations (IRMO) Zagreb. He defended his doctorate in 2010 at the Faculty of Political Sciences of the University of Zagreb. He participated in the implementation of many international scientific projects that analysed various aspects EU integration and industrial relations in the new EU member states. Since 2018 he writes contributions on Croatia for the *Yearbook of European Integration* published by the IEP Berlin. The topics of his primary scientific interest are the EU affairs, democratic political institutions and processes and industrial relations in an internationally comparative perspective.

Tihomir Cipek, PhD, a political scientist, is a full-time professor in tenure at the Faculty of Political Science in Zagreb. He won twice the Croatian National Award for Science. He served as the president of the Croatian Political Science Association. He was a visiting professor and researcher at the universities in

Austria, Brazil, Germany, Slovakia and Slovenia, as well at IWM Institute in Vienna. He was a member of the International Editorial Board of *The International Encyclopaedia of Political Science* published by APSA. The subjects of his research interests are political ideologies, comparative politics and European studies.

Nevenka Čučković, PhD, is a senior research fellow in permanent position at the Institute for Development and International Relations (IRMO), Zagreb, Croatia. Her research expertise and interests are particularly directed to EU economic and institutional convergence processes, global value chains, restructuring and competitiveness of the enterprise sector with a focus on SME policy and entrepreneurship development, innovation and R&D policies, and labour skills. She has been a team leader and researcher of a number of international research projects financed by research grants including those of Horizon 2020, FP7, FP6, World Bank, OECD, EBRD and London School of Economics. Her work was published in refereed scholarly journals and books in both Croatia and abroad.

Marina Funduk is a research associate in the Department for Resource Economics, Environmental Protection and Regional Development at the Institute for Development and International Relations (IRMO), Zagreb. She holds a PhD in Comparative Politics from the Faculty of Political Science, University of Zagreb (2015). Her research interests include topics like environmental policy, sustainable development, nature protection, water management and bioeconomy.

Iris Goldner Lang is a Jean Monnet Professor of EU Law, Head of the Department of European Public Law and Vice Dean at the University of Zagreb – Faculty of Law. She is the holder of the UNESCO Chair on Free Movement of Persons, Migration and Inter-Cultural Dialogue and a partner in the Volkswagen Foundation project "Algorithmic Fairness for Asylum Seekers and Refugees" and in the Horizon project "Protecting Irregular Migrants in Europe". She is the President of Croatian Society for European Law; Vice-Chair of the Board of Trustees of the Academy of European Law (ERA); member of the Odysseus Network; and member of Editorial Boards of Croatian Yearbook of European Law and Policy and of European Foreign Affairs Review.

Krešimir Jurlin was born 1964 in Zagreb Croatia where he received PhD at the Faculty of Economics (2000). Since 1992, he has been employed at the Institute for Development and International Relations, currently as scientific associate. From 1995 to 2003, he was a member of the Council of the Agency for the Protection of Market Competition. He participated in two major World Bank projects on accession of Croatia into the EU, as well as on national and regional competitiveness, supported by UNDP. Recently he participated in research on institutional quality, labour market, regional development, culture and tourism and sustainable development.

Maroje Lang is a Chief Advisor at the Croatian National Bank and Deputy President of the Croatian Fiscal Policy Commission. He served as Assistant Minister of Finance from 2012 to 2015, overseeing macroeconomic and fiscal analysis, financial system, and international and EU relations. During this period, he was also National Authorising Officer and a member of the EU Economic and Financial Committee. Maroje holds a PhD in Economics from the University of Zagreb and an MSc in Economics from the LSE, and he was a visiting scholar at MIT. His research interests include monetary policy, fiscal policy and climate change.

Iva Lopižić, PhD, is an assistant professor at the Department of Administrative Science, Faculty of Law, University of Zagreb. She is an author of more than 30 scientific and professional papers in the area of decentralisation and local self-government, inspection supervision, comparative public administration and human resources management. She is a member of the Institute of Public Administration, Central Eastern European Society of Administrative Sciences, and the Croatian Academy of Legal Sciences. She won the Eugen Pusić Award for the scientific paper of the best young scientist in 2019.

Sanja Maleković holds a PhD in Economy from the University of Zagreb (1997). She is engaged as a scientific advisor in the Institute for Development and International Relations in Zagreb. Her main research interests are local and regional development, EU cohesion policy, Croatian regional policy, governance, program evaluation, regional competitiveness and strategic development planning. Sanja has also been engaged as consultant in Croatia and South-east Europe as key expert and team leader of national- and EU-funded projects, as program evaluator and advisor. Sanja holds courses on several graduate and post-graduate courses and is co-head of the university post-graduate study: "Preparation and Implementation of EU projects".

Romea Manojlović Toman, PhD, is an associate professor at the Department of Administrative Science, Faculty of Law, University of Zagreb. She is the author of more than 50 scientific and professional papers dealing with areas such as public management, human resources management, comparative public administration and evaluation studies. She is the member of the Croatian Academy of Legal Sciences, the Institute for Public Administration, and the Scientific Council for Government, Judiciary and the Rule of Law of the Croatian Academy of Sciences and Arts. She is the assistant editor-in-chief of the scientific journal *Croatian and Comparative Public Administration.* She is currently leading the project "Attracting and Retaining People in Croatian Public Administration".

Gordana Marčetić, PhD, is a full-time professor in permanent position, head of the Department of Administrative Science, Faculty of Law, University of Zagreb. She has published 2 scientific monographs, 7 co-authored books, more than 80 scientific and professional works in books and scientific journals dealing with human potentials management and development, civil service legislation, ethics and integrity of public administration, comparative public administration and post-socialist transition. She has presented at about 60 international and domestic conferences and participated in 18 scientific and research projects in the field of public administration. She was the head of the Public Administration Study, president of the Ethics Committee for Civil Servants of the Republic of Croatia, president of the Expert Council of the State School of Public Administration, head of the postgraduate specialist study Public Law and Public Administration, deputy president of the Council for the Implementation of the Code of Conduct of State Officials in Executive Authorities and performed many other functions. She is also a member of numerous professional bodies, editorial boards, working groups and commissions.

Željko Mrnjavac is a Full Professor at the University of Split, Faculty of Economics, Business and Tourism, Croatia, where he teaches labour economics and economic policy. He is faculty member for 30 years and in that period main field of his interest are labour market and public policies. He is author and co-author in a number of publications, reviewer in scientific journals, member of conference program committees and the member of Croatian Expert Committee for the monitoring and analysis of the minimum wage trends. He was a member of Eurofound's Advisory Committee on Labour Market Change and of European Commission's Expert Group on Gender and Employment (EGGE).

Davor Petrić is a Lecturer and postdoctoral researcher at the University of Zagreb Faculty of Law, Department of European Public Law. He earned his LLM degree at the University of Michigan Law School. He defended his doctoral dissertation (summa cum laude) at the University of Zagreb Faculty of Law. As a visiting researcher, he has stayed at Saarland University, Vrije Universiteit Amsterdam, Hertie School in Berlin and University College Dublin. His research interests include the EU judicial system, constitutional aspects of European integration and jurisprudence.

Jakša Puljiz is a senior research associate and Head of the Department for European Policies of the Institute for Development and International Relations (IRMO) Zagreb. He earned his PhD degree at the Faculty of Economics in Split in 2009. He is author and co-author of a number of journals and books from the areas of the regional and local development, EU Cohesion policy and competitiveness. He served as the Deputy Minister at the Ministry of Regional Development and EU Funds and economic advisor to the Prime Minister. As an expert he has been engaged in numerous technical assistance projects funded by domestic and international organisations, mainly in areas of Cohesion policy, regional development and economic governance.

Domagoj Račić is Lecturer in Management in the Social Sector at the Faculty of Law of the University of Zagreb and Director of the Knowledge Network. Since 1998, he has worked as a researcher, project consultant and author of analytical papers, feasibility studies, reports and evaluations for international organisations, government institutions and private sector companies. In the area of education, employment and labour market policies, Domagoj Račić has worked on various projects for the national authorities, European Commission and the World Bank. He has (co-) authored more than 100 research and professional publications (journal papers, book chapters, conference papers, reports, etc.).

Senada Šelo Šabić is a senior research associate at the Institute for Development and International Relations in Zagreb, Croatia. She holds PhD in Political and Social Sciences from the European University Institute in Florence, Italy, and has earned two Master's degrees – in International Relations from the University of Zagreb and in Peace Studies from the University of Notre Dame, USA. Her research interests are European affairs, Balkans, migration and international security. She is a representative of Croatia in the Standing Working Group on Gender in Research and Innovation at the European Research and Innovation Committee, a chair of the Development Cooperation Projects Approval Committee of the City of Zagreb and a member of the European Council on Foreign Relations.

Sanja Tišma holds a PhD in Economics from the University of Zagreb and is the Director of the Institute for Development and International Relations (IRMO) Zagreb as well as the Head of Resource Economics, Environmental Policy and Regional Development Department. Ms. Tišma has 34 years of professional experience as a scientist, project manager, particularly in the field of sustainable development, environmental economics and environmental policy. She is the author of numerous articles and studies in the field of environmental protection. She is a specialist in the development of cost-benefit analysis (CBA) of environmental impact projects. She is also an expert in regional and local strategic planning policy development. Ms. Tišma also works as evaluator of development programmes and projects.

Igor Vidačak is a Full Professor at the Faculty of Political Science, University of Zagreb, Croatia. He holds a PhD in Comparative Politics from the University of Zagreb and an MA in European Political and Administrative Studies from the College of Europe Natolin. He leads courses on the European Union political system, interest groups and lobbying in the EU, and EU enlargement. He published the first book on lobbying in the Croatian language (Lobiranje – Interesne skupine i kanali utjecaja u Europskoj uniji, 2007). As an international consultant, he has around 20 years of experience in supporting better governance and civil society policy engagement in EU enlargement and neighbouring countries.

Valentina Vučković is an Associate Professor at the Department of Economic Theory, Faculty of Economics and Business, University of Zagreb. She previously worked at the Institute for Development and International Relations (IRMO) in Zagreb at the Department for International Economic and Political Relations. She teaches Principles of Economics, Microeconomics, Political

Economy of Globalisation, Competitiveness Analysis in Modern Economies and Stakeholder approach to the Firm. She authored and co-authored around 60 scientific and professional papers and participated in the realisation of 11 research projects. Her research interests include the political economy of reform, competitiveness analysis, entrepreneurship development and innovation.

Foreword

This book has been written around the ten-year anniversary since Croatia joined the EU, at a crucial time of change and stress for the EU itself. As its newest member state, the Croatian experience has much to tell us about the EU's approach to meeting the challenge of new developments, and about its capacity for future further enlargement to the Western Balkans and beyond, to Moldova and Ukraine. It was a long road from Croatia's independence from former Yugoslavia in 1991 to attaining EU membership in 2013. This 22-year period covered an independence war fought against the forces of former Yugoslavia. It was also a period of political turmoil under the nationalist leadership of Franjo Tudjman, and a period of economic transition from self-managed socialism to "crony capitalism", as Croatian economists dubbed the results of the privatisation process of the 1990s.

My involvement with IRMO dates back to a visit I made to Zagreb in 1994 during a time of ongoing conflict. I found a city full of troops in the middle of an economic recession, inflation and a currency conversion to the Croatian kuna (now abandoned in favour of the Euro – another transition!). This was when I first met the researchers from IRMO, and I recall how impressed I was with the independent research being carried out by the Institute. This led to several joint research activities and publications over subsequent decades. Reading this book, I am delighted to see how far the capacity of IRMO researchers has developed over this time and it is a great pleasure for me to write the foreword to it.

At the time of my visit, Croatia was far from envisaging EU membership. However, within a relatively short space of time I find myself in the paradoxical situation in which my Croatian friends have become EU citizens while I, due to Brexit, no longer have that status. What a turn-around! These events show that no international political arrangement is cast in stone, and we can only expect further changes in the future. Croatian researchers should certainly bear this in mind, and never fall into complacency over the stability of the international and European systems, especially in times that appear to threaten the "rules based international order" which has been the bedrock of international relations over the last 30 years, but which now appears to be under threat as global events undermine long-held assumptions. I am glad to be able to say that none of the authors in this book have fallen into this trap and have all presented critically minded analyses of Croatia's experience within the EU over the last decade. Their analyses are consistently relevant for Croatia's path within the EU over the coming decade. Indeed, the claim made by Jean Monnet – that the EU is built on the basis of the sum of its crises – is well explained in the introductory chapter to the book and forms a unifying theme for the sectoral and policy analyses set out in each chapter.

Croatia applied for membership of the EU 20 years ago under the government of Ivica Račan of the Social Democratic Party (SDP) in February 2003 and was accepted by the EU as a candidate country under the government of Ivo Sanader (Croatian Democratic Union – HDZ) in June 2004. The EU was seen as the only viable path forward by both main political parties, although it remains somewhat of a paradox that the state chose to leave one cross-national union only to join another soon afterwards. On the ten-year anniversary of that latter choice, this book takes stock of the challenges of EU accession and the progress that has been made since. Croatia's accession took place in the midst of the Euro-zone crisis, and the economy was immediately entered into the EU's "excessive deficit procedure" which imposed a deflationary limit of the budget deficit, prolonging the recession until later in the decade. The Croatian economy was hit hard by the Euro-zone crisis and did not recover its pre-crisis levels of economic activity for several years. This was undoubtedly a difficult time for the country with inevitable reflections on the wisdom of EU membership. Nevertheless, the country has recovered from this difficult period and weathered other crises including the Agrokor scandal in which one of the country's largest private company went bust, the COVID pandemic, the ongoing war in Ukraine. Despite that, the country has established itself as a fully accepted and valued contributor to the EU's European integration process. As the introductory chapter explains, this has involved both bottom-up and horizontal processes of Europeanisation, which have complemented the previous focus on top-down Europeanisation – the hallmark of the accession period. These changes in policy orientation have enabled the country to overcome some of the constraints to economic growth related to the multiple challenges surrounding the rule of law, the role of the institutions of local self-government, public administration reform, media pluralism, relatively high levels of individual and regional inequality, social policy reforms, migration, climate change, and the institutional constraints limiting the development of entrepreneurship. Additionally, Croatia benefits from a beautiful coastline and large revenues from tourism, a productive agriculture in the east of the country, and a science and innovation base that is fast developing its capacity.

The book covers all these issues in a thoroughly readable and informative way. It reveals the most significant elements of Europeanisation that have occurred over the last ten years, not least of which is a greater openness to the role of civil society in the policy process. The book also makes an important contribution towards enabling a better understanding of the opportunities and challenges facing Croatia as a member state of the EU. As such, it will become a key reference work for scholars in the field. I hope that any successor to this book, ten years hence, will be able to report further substantive progress in Croatia's economic and social development, and that with her status as an established EU member state, she will be able to guide and assist the current candidates on their path to membership and act as a friend and guide for them if and when they become EU members too.

William Bartlett
Research Affiliate and past Deputy Director
Research on South East Europe
European Institute
London School of Economics and Political Science
UK

Preface

The scholarly literature has seen European integration as a transformative process in which the EU acts as the indispensable catalyst and engine of change and modernisation in the countries aspiring to EU membership. Furthermore, European integration can also be described as an effort to promote the diffusion of ideas based on both hard and soft law across Europe. The tenth anniversary of Croatia's EU membership represents the occasion for exploring the political, economic and social dimensions of this tremendous change in the country, which is still the latest newcomer to the EU.

The Croatian case of EU membership is especially interesting given that the last decade of European integration has arguably been the most challenging yet. For more than a decade, the EU has been in a crisis mode. This meant that it often produced a heavy-handed executive overload, and that agenda was defined in an ad hoc way. This unique background sets Croatia apart from other member states that started their membership in the more conventional circumstances. Therefore, the contributions in this book address various questions that explore the national-level adaptations to functioning as part of a supranational political system which operates under enormous external pressures. The contributions in this volume consider whether the ambition of becoming an active EU player brought results. In other words, whether Croatia completed its transformation from the policy taker to the policymaker. With that in mind, the authors consider possible changes in the country's political goals, legislative framework, administrative organisation and policy-making processes. While focusing on Croatia, this book also produces some general insights into the impacts of Europeanisation in the EU's member states. In that way, it makes a broader contribution to understanding the post-accession political and economic realities.

The book is thematically divided into two principal parts. The first one, from Chapters 2–7, focuses on political and normative developments, while the second part, from Chapters 8–13, explores economic and social issues. Although our initial goal was to include all essential topics and policy areas in this volume, we needed to be selective not to depart from conventional norms in publishing edited books. Therefore, we acknowledge that there are other relevant EU-related topics which we didn't manage to include. We would like to thank the contributors to this volume for their professionalism, enthusiasm and willingness to engage in this project. Special thanks go to external academic reviewers who were engaged for each book chapter. With their suggestions and comments, these reviewers helped the authors improve the quality of their final texts.

We trust that this book will help those engaged in research, teaching and learning about EU integration and Europeanisation in particular, but also to national and supranational policymakers who work on adaptations aimed at achieving optimal functioning within the political system of the European Union.

Jakša Puljiz and Hrvoje Butković
December 2023

Abbreviations

AGS	Annual Growth Survey
ALMPs	Active Labour Market Policies
ARM	Alert Mechanism Report
AROP	At-Risk-of-Poverty
AROPE	At-Risk-of-Poverty or Social Exclusion
AVMS	Audio-Visual Media Services
AVMSD	Audio-Visual Media Services Directive
CAP	Common Agricultural Policy
CBS	Croatian Bureau of Statistics
CDA	County Development Agencies
CE	Circular Economy
CEAP	Circular Economy Action Plan
CES	Croatian Employment Service
CF	Cohesion Fund
CIS	Community Innovation Survey
CJEU	Court of Justice of the European Union
CMPF	Centre for Media Pluralism and Media Freedom
CODEF	Central Office for Development Strategy and Coordination of EU Funds
CODS	Central Office for Development Strategy
CoR	Committee of Regions
CP	Convergence Programme
CRTA	Croatian Radiotelevision Act
CSR	Country-Specific Recommendation
DG ECFIN	Directorate-General for Economic and Financial Affairs
DVB-T	Digital Video Broadcasting Terrestrial
EA	Euro Area
EAC	European Affairs Committee
EAFRD	European Agricultural Fund for Rural Development
EAS	European Administrative Space
EaSI	Employment and Social Innovation
EC	European Commission

EDP	Excessive Deficit Procedure
EED	Energy Efficiency Directive
EESC	European Economic and Social Committee
EFC	Economic and Fiscal Committee
EGD	European Green Deal
EIP	Excessive Imbalances Procedure
EIZ	Institute of Economics Zagreb
EMA	Electronic Media Act
EMFF	European Maritime and Fisheries Fund
EMU	Economic and Monetary Union
ENP	European Neighbourhood Policy
EPBD	Energy Performance of Buildings Directive
ERDF	European Regional Development Fund
ERM2	European Exchange Rate Mechanism II
ESA	European System of National and Regional Accounts
ESF	European Social Fund
ESF+	European Social Fund+
ESI	European Structural and Investment
ESIF	European Structural and Investment Funds
EU	European Union
EU ETS	EU Emission Trading System
EUI	European University Institute
F2F	Farm to Fork
FEAD	Fund for European Aid to the Most Deprived
GAPA	General Administrative Procedure Act
GFC	Global Financial Crisis
GMB	Guaranteed Minimum Benefit
GOL	Government Office for Legislation
HDZ	Croatian Democratic Union
HRD OP	Human Resource Development Operational Programme
HRT	Croatian Radio-television
ICTY	International Criminal Tribunal for the Former Yugoslavia
IDR	In-depth Review
IMD	Institute for Management Development
IPA	Instrument for Pre-Accession Assistance
ITI	Integrated Territorial Investments
JAP	Joint Assessment Paper
JIM	Joint Inclusion Memorandum
JNA	Yugoslav National Army
JTM	Just Transition Mechanism
LCPGEA	Law on Cooperation between Parliament and the Government on EU Affairs
LTRS	Long Term Buildings Renovation Strategy
LULUCF	Land Use, Land Use Change and Forestry
MA	Media Act

MEPs	Members of the European Parliament
MI	Minimum Income
MINURSO	Peacekeeping Operations in Western Sahara
MIP	Macroeconomic Imbalance Procedure
MJPA	Ministry of Justice and Public Administration
MPM	Media Pluralism Monitor
MRDFEU	Ministry of Regional Development and EU Funds
MS	Member States
NDS	National Development Strategy
NECP	Integrated Energy and Climate Plan
NGEU	NextGenerationEU
NMS	New Member States
NRP	National Reform Program
NRRP	National Recovery and Resilience Plan
nZEB	Nearly Zero Energy Building
OPCC	Operational Programme Competitiveness and Cohesion
OPEHR	Operational Programme Efficient Human Resources
PEP	Pre-accession Economic Program
PMR	Product Market Regulation
PPP	Purchasing Power Parity
PPWD	Packaging and Packaging Waste Directive
R&D	Research and Development
RES	Renewable Energy Sources
RIA	Regulatory Impact Assessment
RRF	Recovery and Resilience Facility
RRP	Recovery and Resilience Plan
RVC	Regional Value Chains
S3	Smart Specialisation Strategy
SAA	Stabilisation and Association Agreement
SAP	Stabilisation and Association Process
SCF	Structural and Cohesion Funds
SGP	Stability and Growth Pact
SII	Summary Innovation Index
SLAPP	Strategic Lawsuits Against Public Participation
SMEs	Small and Medium Enterprises
SOA	Security and Intelligence Agency
SOEs	State-owned Enterprises
SSM	Single Supervision Mechanism
SURE	Support to Mitigate Unemployment Risks in an Emergency
SWD	Services Working Document
TFEU	Treaty on the Functioning of the European Union
TPF	Total Factor Productivity
TSCG	Treaty on Stability, Coordination, and Governance
TWFD	Television without Frontiers Directive
UNIFIL	Peacekeeping Operations in Lebanon

UNMOGIP	Peacekeeping Operations in India and Pakistan
VAT	Value-added Tax
WB	World Bank
WEF	World Economic Forum
WFD	Waste Framework Directive
WGI	Worldwide Governance Indicators
YEI	Youth Employment Initiative
ZEB	Zero Energy Building

1 Setting the Scene

Post-accession Europeanisation of Croatian State and Its Public Policies

Hrvoje Butković and Jakša Puljiz

1.1 Introduction

This book examines how Croatia adapted its institutions and policies due to its ten years of EU membership. The contributions ask how Croatia's polity (national institutions) and policy (the content of politics) adapted to pressures that produced the EU accession. There are good reasons for making a clear differentiation between the pre- and post-accession phases because formal EU membership, in many ways, changes the situation of a country by granting it influence over the supranational policy-making process as well as increased funding opportunities (see Czarnecki and Riedel, 2021). Furthermore, most Europeanisation studies focusing on Croatia's post-accession period have been carried out relatively early after the 2013 accession. As such, many of these works were premature because numerous effects of Europeanisation occurred later. Against such background, this book offers insights into post-enlargement realities in Croatia, which, as a country, still represents the most recent newcomer to the EU.

Our primary research question is how the EU membership has affected the design and implementation of selected public policies, the functioning of some core state institutions and patterns of cooperation among main political and social actors. Our contributions examine the extent to which Croatia overcame weak state capacity that was characteristic of the country before its EU accession (see Petak, 2019). Secondly, the book examines to what degree engagement with the EU led to a convergence in governance patterns between Croatia and the rest of the EU. Therefore, contributions assess the scale of political, functional and socio-economic adaptations among Croatian political institutions and policy-making actors. They intend to determine if the EU-caused adaptations led to permanent or temporary transformation of the policy-making processes.

The book addresses several specific questions: What were the main developments in the post-accession period in particular policy areas? What were the patterns of adaptation of national institutions to impulses and stimulations coming from the EU level? What kind of trends can be observed, and what does the comparison to the main peers in the EU reveal? What has been the main characteristic of the policy approach, and which factors were decisive in shaping it? Where and why, during ten years of its EU membership, Croatia fell short of its capacities or could

DOI: 10.4324/9781003394013-1

not seize the opportunities of EU membership? Did the EU membership transform Croatia from a policy taker to a policy-maker in specific policy fields and institutional settings? What are the prospects given the experience of its first decade as a member state? With that in mind, contributions in this book consider possible changes in the countries' political goals, legislative framework, administrative organisation and policy-making processes.

The analytical approach in this book is actor-centred. The contributions offer an empirical assessment of the impact of the EU accession. The understanding of the EU's impact on polity and policy relies on the analysis of the available secondary sources such as the EU and national legislation, strategic and policy documents, academic writing, media sources and court decisions, but also on the interview data which provide additional information about actor behaviour and preferences. In order to describe and interpret different themes, the authors of different chapters rely primarily on qualitative research methods such as qualitative content analysis and interviews. To a lesser extent, quantitative content analysis is applied.

Methodologically, the content of this introductory chapter could be classified as descriptive research aimed at shedding light on selected phenomena and processes crucial for a better understanding of the post-accession. The EU accession process is commonly viewed as an instrument of democratisation and a unique model based on a top-down approach where reforms are demanded from the acceding states in exchange for the benefits of EU membership (see Maldini and Pauković, 2015). With that in mind, we start this introduction by reviewing principal milestones on Croatia's route to EU membership. After that, we present some prominent theoretical conclusions about the effects of the crisis on the EU integration processes. These observations are essential for this book because a context of interchanging economic and political crises marked Croatia's ten-year membership in the EU. The following segment presents different definitions and views of Europeanisation. This exercise aims to understand better this complex process, which is the focus of all book contributions. We then introduce the parts of this book, providing an overview of each chapter and its contribution towards enhancing our understanding of the post-accession realities. Last but not least, the chapter concludes on its core topics.

1.2 Croatia's Road to EU Membership

At the beginning of the 1990s, in parallel with the crisis of the Yugoslav model of socialist self-management, pro-European sentiment strengthened in Croatia. At the same time, Croatian political elites perceived Croatia as a country that, based on its history and determination, would automatically join the EU already in the first wave of expansion towards post-communist transition states (see Grubiša, 2023). This, however, did not materialise due to war and post-war circumstances, which negatively impacted the quality of democratic governance at that time.

The Croatian accession process started with the change of government in 2000 when the Zagreb Summit brought together leaders of the EU member states and five Western Balkan countries who endorsed the objectives of the EU's Stabilisation and

Association Process (SAP). The SAP's aim was to provide support to strengthen democracy, promote the rule of law and market economy and foster regional cooperation. The Summit started negotiations on the Stabilisation and Association Agreement (SAA) between Croatia and the EU, which was signed in 2001. The SAA was a prelude to the accession process as it was focused on domestic reforms and marked the beginning of the alignment of domestic legislation with the EU's *acquis* (Taylor et al., 2013). Croatia and all the EU member states needed to ratify the SAA, which took several years until it came into operation on 1 February 2005.

Instead of taking a cautious step-by-step approach, the country decided to be ambitious and applied for EU membership in 2003, even before its SAA had been ratified. This worked to Croatia's advantage because, in April 2004, the country received a favourable *Avis* from the Commission and, two months later, a candidate status. Soon afterwards, in October 2005, Croatia opened accession negotiations with the EU. After opening negotiations, screening Croatian existing legislation took more than one year. Upon its finalisation, a substantive phase of chapter-by-chapter negotiations began focusing on the conditions under which Croatia was obliged to adopt and implement the EU's *acquis*.

The Negotiating Framework with Croatia established 35 negotiation chapters, or 4 chapters more than for the Central and Eastern Europe (CEE) enlargement. It contained a suspension clause which allowed the EU to suspend negotiations in case of a severe breach of the principles of liberty, democracy, respect for human rights and the rule of law. The EU also introduced the safeguard clause, which allowed more stringent implementation monitoring, particularly after the temporary closure of the negotiation chapter. Still, the most important innovation was the introduction of Chapter 23, "Judiciary and Fundamental Rights", which did not exist as a separate chapter in the previous enlargement rounds (see Butković and Samardžija, 2014).

However, it is unfortunate that Chapter 23, "Judiciary and Fundamental Rights", and Chapter 24, "Justice, Freedom and Security", were both opened late in the negotiation process even though they were related to the implementation of numerous reforms and generally difficult to negotiate (Goldner Lang, 2012). Other difficult chapters were opened in the advanced stage and closed at the very end of the negotiation, such as Chapter 8, "Competition Policy", Chapter 11, "Agriculture", and Chapter 22, "Regional Policy". The late opening of Chapter 8, "Competition Policy", was particularly sensitive as restructuring in the crucial fields of shipbuilding and steel production was almost at the end of negotiations (Samardžija, 2014). Learning from these experiences, the EU adopted a practice concerning future accession negotiations whereby Chapters 23 and 24 need to be opened early. Furthermore, in the event of delayed progress within these chapters' recommendations to open or close other chapters may be withheld (Grubiša, 2023).

Croatia's negotiations were more demanding than previously because the EU applied a new negotiation methodology based on extensive legal, institutional and track-record benchmarks, which the country had to meet before the opening and closing of individual chapters. Although using benchmarks was often helpful in implementing reforms, it also caused the so-called front-loading of conditionality because chapters could not be opened and worked upon before compliance with the opening benchmarks (see Butković and Samardžija, 2014). An additional difficulty stemmed from the fact that Croatia, unlike the CEE states, had to negotiate on a greater volume of legislation and with an increased number of member states, which made negotiations more complex and generally slowed down the entire process (ibid.).

Bilateral problems negatively affected the length of Croatia's negotiations. From December 2008 to September 2009, Slovenia blocked Croatia's EU accession negotiations due to a dispute over the maritime border in the Gulf of Piran and the land border in some micro-locations. Therefore, due to the Slovenian veto, many negotiation chapters could not be opened or closed during that period. Ultimately, the solution to this blockade was found when both countries agreed to accept the future ruling of an international mediation over final border demarcation.

In June 2011, after almost six years of negotiations, the Commission recommended the closure of the accession negotiations, which the June 2011 European Council approved. Subsequently, on 9 December 2011, Croatia signed the Treaty of Accession, becoming the 28th member state by 1 July 2013. Strict requirements for the closure of newly introduced Chapter 23, "Judiciary and Fundamental Rights", allowed Croatia to avoid the establishment of post-accession controlling mechanisms for the monitoring of anticorruption, the fight against organised crime and judiciary reforms, which were previously established for Bulgaria and Romania (Taylor et al., 2013). The decision for Croatia to join the EU was verified through a national referendum, which took place in January 2012.

The period after accession showed that Croatia was successful in harmonising legislation and institution-building in some areas but much weaker concerning economic structural reforms, which remained unfinished (Butković and Samardžija, 2014). Furthermore, some analysts note that during accession negotiations, the Croatian government missed the opportunity to define national interests and priorities which would strengthen the state's institutional capacity. Therefore, Croatia still faces problems related to underdeveloped inter-ministerial coordination, insufficient policy monitoring instruments and low levels of actors' involvement in the policy process (see Maldini, 2015; Petak, 2019).

1.3 The Wider Context Marked by Crisis

Croatia's EU accession happened after a financial crisis, and many different crises marked the entire decade of the country's EU membership. This sets Croatia apart from other more established EU member states, which started their membership in more conventional circumstances. It also obliges us to look closely at some of these crises and their effect on the European integration process.

The crisis corresponds to the extraordinary moment of urgency that challenges the proper functioning in the given domain. Nevertheless, the crisis simultaneously activates specific response modes and policy-making patterns (Ferrara and Kriesi, 2022). Such circumstances are likely to increase interdependence among EU member states and produce intense demands for policy coordination

(Schimmelfennig, 2018). As Jean Monnet, a founding father of European integration, predicted in his memories, "Europe would be built through crisis, and it will be the sum of their solutions" (Monnet, 1978, p. 417).

For Kai Enno Lehmann, the EU has yet to have a productive dialogue about its strategic objectives in the evolving situation. Today, in continuous crisis circumstances, it indulges in incoherent patterns of self-organisation and does whatever generates the least resistance rather than necessary (2018). This state of affairs is caused mainly by its enormous complexity and differences, inevitable in a community of 27-member states (ibid.). Similarly, it is often claimed that many of the problems facing the EU followed from the institutional asymmetries in the political economies of its member states (see Hall, 2016). Other authors are less pessimistic, arguing that the EU has made undeniable progress in how European institutions responded to various crises. For example, since Russia invaded Ukraine, the scope of the European Defence Fund has been enlarged from financing only research and development projects to now also covering the costs of joint purchases of military equipment (Joannin, 2023).

Theories of European integration have developed implicit or explicit alternative perspectives on the causes, process and outcomes of the integration crisis. The liberal intergovernmentalism views integration as the outcome of constellations of the member state preferences and bargaining power (see Rittberger et al., 2017). According to Frank Schimmelfennig, liberal intergovernmentalism predicts that in the crisis, the member state governments will revert to intergovernmental conflict about distributing burdens of the crisis. Contrary to this conceptualisation, neofunctionalism and post-functionalism assume that integration is subject to feedback processes that kick in when the crisis occurs. Neo-functionalism focuses on positive feedback processes of spillover and path dependence that produce more integration than intergovernmentalism would expect. By contrast, post-functionalism emphasises the backlash driven by the mass politicisation of integration, ultimately resulting in less integration (2018, p. 3).

There have always been debates about what the model of European integration means within and outside the EU. In other words, there have always been different interpretations of how far the European integration should go (see Nugent, 2010). Nevertheless, historically, there was always a strong consensus around the EU's overriding purpose, which moved the organisation forward (Lehmann, 2018). This situation has changed with the 2010 Euro crisis, a direct consequence of the 2008 financial crisis. Namely, this particular crisis generated profound differences at the strategic level between those who argue that the crisis is a sign that integration has gone too far and those who argue that it has not gone far enough (ibid., p. 7). Moreover, the Euro crisis showed that a crisis can represent a very different reality at a local and national level than in Brussels. The rise of the populist parties in Greece and Spain arguably represents a direct response to austerity being perceived differently at the national and European levels (ibid., p. 8).

For Frank Schimmelfennig, crises, which are the focus of this book, are open decision-making situations. In the context of EU integration, they manifest a significant probability of disintegration but may also trigger reform activities, leading to more integration (2018). The author noted that while the Euro crisis has brought about a significant deepening of integration, the Schengen (migration) crisis has not. He argues that transnational actors and linkages were strong in the Euro crisis since financial market interdependence increased considerably after introducing the euro. By contrast, transnational interdependence was weak in the Schengen crisis because the EU agencies active in the border and asylum regime have low supranational competencies (ibid., p. 2).

While examining the crisis pressures on European integration, Federico Maria Ferrara and Hanspeter Kriesi distinguish between high- and low-competence areas. In other words, between areas where the EU can independently mobilise resources to execute problem-solving and those where the Union and supranational institutions have lower capacity to tackle the crisis (Ferrara and Kriesi, 2022). A second key distinction by these authors differentiates between symmetrical and asymmetrical crisis pressures. When crisis pressures are distributed symmetrically, the crisis usually catalyses an empathy logic, lowering national identity politicisation. Instead, when the crisis pressures are asymmetrical, the crisis usually catalyses an identity logic that heightens European integration's politicisation and generates greater dissensus across EU member states (ibid.).

Applying this categorisation to the recent most important EU crisis, the authors conclude that the Euro area crisis, where the EU competence was high and crisis pressures asymmetrical, resulted in a decision-making scenario enabling dissensus. The Brexit crisis, where the EU competence was high and crisis pressures symmetrical, ended with permissive consensus. The migration crisis, where the competence of the EU was limited and crisis pressures asymmetrical, brought about a decision-making scenario of constraining dissensus. Finally, the Covid-19 crisis, where the competencies of the EU were also limited but where the crisis pressures were symmetrical, resulted in an enabling consensus (ibid., pp. 1361–1362).

Examining the EU's response to various crises, Stefan Lehne notes that the Euro and Covid-19 crisis demonstrated the evolution of the EU's stance from a greater diversity of views towards greater unity (2022). In the case of the Euro crisis, despite the asymmetric impact of the crisis, all member states faced the common threat of a breakup of the Eurozone, which would have had devastating consequences for all of them. Therefore, despite their division, member states agreed on the far-reaching innovations in the EU's financial architecture. Similarly, during the Covid-19 crisis, the EU achieved significant breakthroughs in public health policy. Although the competencies in this area remain mainly with the member states, the EU agreed on the joint vaccine procurement programme (ibid., p. 3).

By contrast, the author notes that there are cases where the crisis does not lead towards greater unity. Such an example is the Russian invasion of Ukraine, where divisions between member states are more pronounced. Most countries in the northern and eastern parts of the EU view Russia's aggression as a direct threat to national security and push towards tougher sanctions and more military support for Ukraine. In the southern and western parts of the EU, there is less fear of Russia and more worries about the war's impact on energy security (ibid., p. 4).

1.4 The Core Concept of Europeanisation

The concept of crucial importance in this book is that of Europeanisation, defined by Radaelli as a process of construction, diffusion and institutionalisation of formal and informal rules, procedures, policy paradigms and norms, which are first defined and consolidated at the EU level and then incorporated in the logic of domestic discourse, identities, political structures and public policies (2003, p. 30). Other authors note that accession to the EU entails participation in a new policy-making environment characterised by distinctive rules, norms and values, which, in the process of Europeanisation, became gradually internalised and had an impact on the member states' domestic, political, social and economic contours (Czarnecki and Riedel, 2021). On a similar line of thinking, Europeanisation is defined as the emergence and development at the European level of distinct structures that formalise interactions among the actors and of policy networks specialising in creating authoritative European rules. From this perspective, participants must agree on common goals in order to be able to develop institutional arrangements as instruments for policy implementation (Risse et al., 2001).

Europeanisation is also defined as "an incremental process of re-orienting the direction and shape of politics to the degree that EU political and economic dynamics become part of the organisational logic of national politics and policy-making" (Ladrech, 1994, p. 69). Andersen and Sitter distinguish between European integration, which they view as creating community institutions and policies, and Europeanisation, which defines the variation of national impact of integration (2006, p. 315). Some scholars conceive Europeanisation as combining up-loading (top-down) and down-loading (bottom-up) processes. Up-loading is concerned with constructing EU governance and down-loading with adjusting its domestic impact on the state. The candidate and accession states are subject to a far greater degree of up-loading or top-down Europeanisation than the member states, which have more room for balancing these two Europeanisation processes (Börzel, 2003). For Matei and Matei, Europeanisation is conceived as a three-dimensional process. The first dimension is top-down, focusing on the member states reactions to exogenous pressures coming up from the EU. The second is bottom-up, exploring how the member states influence the policy-making process at the supranational level. Finally, the third is horizontal, through which different administrations tend to converge through comparing different practices (2010).

For Johan Olsen, Europeanisation is understood as a political project aimed at deepening the integration of the European continent. Therefore, within this concept, great importance is attached to the study of change as a process of mutual adaptation and co-development of institutions (2003). The author also argues that different definitions of Europeanisation are complementary and not exclusive. Europeanisation is slow in some respects, such as the internalisation of values and norms, but fast in others, such as changes in structures and processes (Taylor et al., 2013, p. 74). It cannot be equated with policy or institutional convergence because it may also produce divergence. Similarly, it cannot be equated with harmonisation, which may result in regulatory competition (Ladrech, 2010).

Europeanisation entails a significant change in the architecture of the polity reflected in a move towards a more diffuse distribution of power. For example, the EU's sound governance principles strive towards greater democracy, transparency, subsidiarity and improved policy impact, which redistributes the power. This new architecture is based on the exchange of resources and bargaining for mutual gains, as no single actor can dominate or achieve outcomes without the cooperation of others (Taylor et al., 2013, p. 209). Considering the distribution of power, the contributions in this book examine the extent to which the policy-making patterns and power in Croatia have become more horizontal and pluralised and more inclusive towards various interest groups, subnational governments and civil society organisations. The evidence from other countries indicates that the norms governing the policy-making patterns change with time from a grudging acceptance of civil society involvement to an acceptance that their participation offers the prospect of better policy (ibid., 210).

Multilevel governance is essential for a better understanding of Europeanisation since it builds on a predisposition that decision-making competencies are shared by actors at different levels of decision-making rather than monopolised by state executives. It further entails that the political arena at the subnational, national and European levels is interconnected rather than nested (Hooghe and Marks, 2001). As such, multilevel governance opposes liberal intergovernmentalism, which views Europeanisation primarily through the national state's lenses. Liberal intergovernmentalism argues that Europeanisation strengthens states and nations through interaction between states, which ultimately retain control over supranational institutions and processes (Moravcsik, 1994). Proponents of the multilevel governance view of Europeanisation argue that successful state-building by the EU member states requires the creation of effective multilevel governance based on horizontal and vertical networks and resource exchange between actors. Although it may operate at the expense of conventional political representation, it remains anchored in territoriality (see Bartolini, 2005).

Europeanisation may help overcome the resistance of domestic veto players that would otherwise block the policy reform process due to the adjustment costs. In other words, it can break the path dependence, often reinforcing suboptimal outcomes (Héritier, 2005). Learning and diffusion of ideas are critical dimensions of Europeanisation, essential in those areas where the EU does not work as a law-making system but as a convergence platform (Bulmer and Radaelli, 2004). This is the case with the open method of coordination, which pertains to policy areas previously impenetrable to Europeanisation, such as asylum or health policy.

Another important concept related to Europeanisation is the sovereignty bargain, which implies that states will voluntarily accept limitations on their sovereignty in exchange for economic and political benefits. The sovereignty bargain is frequently reconfigured due to outside and inner pressures. However, it does not necessarily diminish state sovereignty since losses in one area can become gains in others, such as economic growth (Mattli, 2000). In other words, the EU seeks to enhance Europe's global competitiveness and offer protection against some aspects of globalisation, which results in a parallel process of removing and building various boundaries (Krastev, 2002). Although the sovereignty bargain represents a foundation of the state-EU relationship, securing its benefits depends on the state's ability to translate potential into actual gains (Taylor et al., 2013, p. 17).

Europeanisation is often transmitted through characteristic governance patterns such as positive and negative integration. Positive integration is based on the introduction of an active, supranational policy. Usually, the EU negotiates a policy template, which must be implemented in the member states. Negative integration relates to areas where removing national barriers suffices to create a joint policy (Bulmer and Radaelli, 2004). In the policy areas where the EU is a crucial factor, a decision is always the culmination of the negotiation process. Member state governments are central to this process by being directly seated at the negotiating table or delegating their powers to supranational bodies. By contrast, the primary governance pattern is facilitated coordination in the policy areas where the national governments are the key actors and where the EU is simply an arena for exchanging ideas. This concerns the situations where the policy process is not subject to the EU law or where decisions are bound to unanimity among the governments (ibid.).

The relationship between the EU on one side and the candidate and the accession state on the other is highly asymmetric because membership in the EU is of far greater importance for the aspiring states than for the EU itself. In this asymmetric relationship, the EU disposes of both material benefits of membership and conditionalities derived from the Copenhagen Criteria (see Vachudova, 2005), which are the driving force behind numerous Europeanisation processes. Europeanisation, as such, dramatically changes its dynamics before and after the EU accession. Following the accession, Europeanisation moves beyond the original focus on conditionality as top-down mechanisms and gets complemented by horizontal and bottom-up ones (see Taylor et al., 2013; Czarnecki and Riedel, 2021). This changed and complemented form of Europeanisation represents the core focus of this book.

1.5 Contents of the Book

In the chapter "Impacts of Croatia's EU Membership on the Coordination Patterns within Three Branches of State Power", authored by Hrvoje Butković and Senada Šelo Šabić, the focus of the analyses is on how Croatian EU membership changed the inner procedures and relations between the executive, legislative and judiciary branch of state power. The main research question posed by the authors is to what extent Croatia managed to reduce the executive dominance characteristic for the pre-accession period. The analysis reveals that within the executive branch following the accession, Croatia established an efficient two-layered intra-government coordination system in EU affairs, assuring qualitative and political control of the initially proposed framework positions. The authors note that the Croatian presidency of the Council in the first half of 2020 significantly contributed to the socialisation of Croatian public officials in the EU's multilevel governance system. Supervising the government framework positions within the legislative branch was identified as the most essential parliamentary tool for *ex-ante* scrutiny of the government in EU affairs. This procedure is well codified and regulated by law, but there are shortcomings in its practical application. Finally, the review of the judiciary branch revealed that inter-institutional dynamics in this area primarily concern communication between the national courts and the Court of Justice of the European Union in Luxembourg, which was practically non-existent before the EU accession.

The chapter "Unlocking Influence: Access and Lobbying Strategies of Croatian Interest Groups in the EU Policymaking", authored by Igor Vidačak, analyses the lobbying strategies employed by Croatian interest groups within the EU policy-making processes. Focusing on the ten years following Croatia's entry into the EU, the chapter investigates the types of influence-seeking behaviours (communication activities, participation in public consultations, participation in expert groups etc.) exhibited by Croatian interest groups and the factors influencing their choice between national and EU-level lobbying strategies. It relies on quantitative and qualitative methods to reach its conclusions. The author identifies critical factors influencing lobbying strategies, including issue salience, target audience, available resources, and legal and institutional frameworks. After the EU accession, the access of Croatian interest groups to the national decision-making processes in the area of EU affairs remained limited. However, Croatian business groups and consultancies increasingly use the Croatian Permanent Representation in the EU to influence Croatian framework positions in the Council. This body can intervene with its proposals and suggestions at every stage of preparing the government, i.e., national framework positions.

The chapter "Reform of Croatian Public Administration: Challenges, results and role of the EU" is written by Gordana Marčetić, Romea Manojlović Toman and Iva Lopižić. It provides an overview of EU-induced reforms undertaken within Croatian public administration in five different areas: (i) structures and organisation, (ii) policy-making and implementation, (iii) civil service and human resources management, (iv) transparency and accountability and (v) service delivery and digitalisation. The authors conclude that the most visible progress in Croatian public administration reform during the post-accession period is visible in transparency, where convergence with the European Administrative Space (EAS) standards was substantial. This is followed by the areas of digitalisation and, to a lesser extent, the policy-making where progress is visible, although challenges remain. The lack of institutional capacity caused by the fragmentation of the state system and the system of local self-government is singled out as among the key obstacles in achieving progress in public administration reform. Furthermore, the authors conclude that attracting and recruiting new civil servants into the national civil service represents one of the most significant challenges in the upcoming period.

Authored by Tihomir Cipek the chapter "Croatian Foreign Policy between the EU and the USA", shows how Croatia's EU accession affected its foreign policy. It builds upon the constructivist theory of international relations, which views national identity as one of the key categories in international relations. The chapter argues that Croatia's position towards further enlargement of the EU, as a crucial component of the Union's foreign policy, is ambivalent. On the one hand, the country emphasises that the expansion of the EU to the Southeast of Europe is in its best interest because it would shift it from the periphery to the centre of Europe. On the other hand, at times it seems that Croatia considers the EU enlargement primarily as an opportunity to protect its compatriots in the neighbouring countries and resolve the border issues in its favour. The author underlines Croatia's commitment to the United States because in cases where there is no unified EU foreign policy, Croatia tends to side with the United States. The chapter concludes, among other things, that Croatia still needs to find an area where it could establish itself as the expert and thus affirm its foreign policy role.

The chapter "Media Pluralism and Market Competition in Croatia: Between Expectations and Realities" by Paško Bilić explores Croatia's media policy before and after the EU accession. The chapter relies upon secondary sources and the Media Pluralism Monitor (MPM) findings. This tool comprises 200 legal, economic and social variables that create composite indicators and implementation areas. The MPM involves four areas (fundamental protection, market plurality, political independence and social inclusiveness) with five indicators per area. The author notes that media reforms in Croatia were primarily EU-driven through the transposing of the EU directives. However, since the EU accession, there have been no media reform attempts to strengthen the public service remit or reduce political interference in appointments to key managerial positions. The MPM and other sources confirm that the market in Croatia remains the primary mechanism for allocating publicly relevant information. However, much evidence shows this is becoming an increasingly flawed system for securing plurality in the public sphere. The chapter concludes that Croatia has yet to create a well-coordinated media development strategy with a long-term vision.

The contribution "Rule of law in the EU and the State of Croatian Judiciary" authored by Nika Bačić Selanec, Iris Goldner Lang and Davor Petrić discusses the understanding of judicial independence in Croatia. The authors argue that this understanding needs to be changed because it prevents adequate control of judicial work through checks and balances. Although the current understanding of judicial independence prevents political attacks on the judiciary, it is simultaneously unable to prevent irregularities generated within the judicial system itself. The authors link the shallow public faith in the judiciary system to an incorrect understanding and implementation of judicial independence. They note that proponents of the status quo within the Croatian judiciary system often hide behind arguments of supposed attacks on judicial independence to avert public scrutiny and deny the legitimacy of political or academic criticisms. The chapter also argues that despite the fast-track reforms required during the accession process, the central problems of the Croatian judiciary have never been addressed through systematic reforms.

The chapter "Competitiveness, convergence and Innovation: Assessment of Impacts of the First EU Membership Decade", written by Nevenka Čučković, Valentina Vučković and Krešimir Jurlin, examines how the Croatian economy has adjusted to the EU single market since it acceded to the EU. It discusses how this transformation impacted the competitiveness and development of the Croatian economy. Authors point out that due to the negative impact of a series of economic, health and security crises, the first decade of the membership was highly challenging for the competitiveness of the Croatian economy and its convergence towards the average EU levels of development. Nevertheless, the quantitative and qualitative analysis has confirmed that the Croatian economy's macroeconomic competitiveness and performance substantially improved in the last decade and that the accession to the EU brought generally favourable effects on economic competitiveness, convergence and innovation development. Being part of a larger EU market and having access to EU funding, especially in small and medium-sized enterprises (SME) development and innovations, has contributed much to protecting the Croatian economy in turbulent times. However, as the authors note, at the same time, a lot of thorough transformation and structural economic reforms have been postponed for better times while interventionistic economic crisis management prevailed.

In the chapter "Free Movement of People: Implications for Croatian Labour Market", authors Predrag Bejaković and Željko Mrnjavac analyse the impact of accession into the EU on the labour market, emphasising the main benefits and challenges. Access of Croatian workers to job opportunities in other EU member states has reduced registered unemployment, but it has also resulted in a severe brain drain. Due to the significant differences in income levels between most of the EU member states and Croatia, an influx of foreign workers to Croatia from other EU countries has remained limited. The authors emphasise the advantages of modern technology and appropriate, efficient policy for high-skilled workers, which stimulate them to remain in close contact with domestic actors, thus reducing the negative impact of outmigration. On the other hand, they acknowledge that more young and educated people of both sexes and with entire families are migrating, which increases the danger that the departure is permanent. Given the rapid increase of workers from third countries in Croatia in recent years, the authors emphasise the importance of designing an appropriate immigration policy. This would ensure the efficient immigration of foreign labour force for deficient occupations but also protect the Croatian labour market to a certain extent.

The chapter "From 'Troubled' Newcomer to Euro Area Member: Croatian Integration Success under Brussels Surveillance" investigates the impact of EU economic governance procedures and Brussels surveillance on macroeconomic policies and structural reforms in Croatia. Author Maroje Lang describes how Croatia acceded to the EU when the EU's primary economic policy coordination mechanism was reinforced with a stricter approach to addressing macroeconomic and fiscal imbalances. Shortly after the accession, corrective excessive deficit procedure (EDP) and close monitoring of macroeconomic imbalance procedure (MIP) were launched, which prompted authorities to act swiftly and strengthen the fiscal consolidation efforts. After achieving the necessary consolidation and reducing the deficit below 3% along with a declining debt trajectory, Croatia successfully concluded the EDP in June 2017. However, this achievement was not without sacrifices in terms of the effect of consolidation on short-term economic growth. Adherence to fiscal rules and improving macroeconomic imbalances generated a positive reputation and subsequent support for entry into the Euro area (EA). However, as the author notes, Croatia's determination and ownership of the process were critical factors for admission into EA. The chapter reminds that, unlike fiscal consolidation, implementing structural reforms after the accession to the EU was highly challenging, as the analysis of Country-Specific Recommendations shows. EU's Resilience and Recovery Facility has become a new primary vehicle for structural reforms with its payment system based on the progress in implementing the proposed measures. The chapter concludes with an important note that Croatia has not yet developed strategic solid planning or capacities for integral policy proposals and reforms and, therefore, calls for further strengthening of the coordination framework and development of particular planning institutions.

The authors Ana-Maria Boromisa, Marina Funduk and Sanja Tišma, in the chapter "Croatia and the EU Green Agenda", address the Europeanisation of the green agenda in Croatia. Its main challenges are determined based on identifying the key EU policies, their transposition into Croatian national legislation and implementation. Generally, adopting and implementing key policies in Croatia is slower than planned. Based on the analysis of the situation in critical domains for the EU green agenda, authors see as central challenges a lack of sense of urgency, lack of political will, weaknesses in the strategic planning process, insufficient institutional capacities for the preparation and implementation of policies and investment projects and inadequate financing. Delays in preparing and implementing strategic documents, laws, action plans and project implementation directly decrease absorption capacity for EU funding. As the authors emphasise, the problems related to the weak capacity for policy-making and implementation in main areas related to the green agenda in Croatia have long been known but only partially addressed. More political will and active citizen involvement are required to strengthen the policy-makers' motivation to improve the overall implementation track record.

In the chapter "The Transformative Impact of EU Cohesion Policy in Croatia", Jakša Puljiz, Ivana Biondić and Sanja Maleković study the Europeanisation process stimulated by the EU Cohesion policy. As the authors point out, access to Cohesion policy funds brought significant additional financial resources to encourage development throughout Croatia and profoundly affected domestic policy-making. Due to its vast financial resources and specific implementation rules, the Cohesion policy has become a key driver for domestic public investment policy, bringing both significant and less visible benefits. The impact on domestic institutional and strategic planning was particularly significant. However, the results and effects of the Cohesion policy in Croatia are still limited by the shortcomings of the domestic policy, which leads to the underutilisation of potential benefits. The authors point out that local and regional authorities were among the most important beneficiaries of the Cohesion policy, greatly expanding their investment potential and benefiting from the policy learning process. As in the national-level case, many factors mainly related to various structural weaknesses prevent Cohesion policy instruments' more sustainable and practical contribution to developing local and regional units.

In the chapter "Croatian Social Policy Under the Impact of the European Union", authors Zdenko Babić and Domagoj Račić examine the interrelationship between

Croatian social policy and its EU context. Europeanisation of specific social policy domains in Croatia has been tackled by analysing regulatory frameworks such as the European Semester (which facilitated policy transfer through institutional compliance) and EU funding (which expanded the pool of available resources and affected their distribution). According to the authors, in addition to adopting the *acquis communautaire*, European Semester in general and its Country Specific Recommendations in particular have affected social policy reforms, although often with quite uneven results. The most impact is noted in employment, education and lifelong learning, while the most negligible impact is recognised in pension, health and long-term care. EU policy coordination mechanisms such as the European Semester facilitated policy transfer through institutional compliance or creative appropriation. In contrast, EU funding expanded the pool of available resources and affected their distribution. Authors emphasise that although EU funding has strongly contributed to the resources available for social policy instruments, its impacts have been somewhat limited by the changing needs of beneficiaries, design and implementation issues and other aspects. In many cases, the results and impacts may only be sustainable with further EU co-financing.

1.6 Conclusion

The tenth anniversary of Croatia's EU membership represents the occasion for exploring this tremendous change's political, economic and social dimensions. The contributions in this book analyse how Croatia has changed over the last ten years due to the EU membership and the driving forces and hindering factors behind the country's adaptation to the EU system. The main question in this book is how the EU membership has affected the design and implementation of selected public policies, the functioning of some core state institutions and patterns of cooperation among main political and social actors.

The Croatian EU membership was a significant achievement for the country and the whole SEE region since Croatia was and continues to be the only SAP country that managed to enter the EU. The road to that achievement was long and demanding because of the strengthened EU conditionality. Moreover, Croatia had to negotiate its accession with more member states in the context of an enlarged EU *acquis*. However, the transposition of the *acquis* was easier than implementation, which involved much national-level coordination and generally changed the old simplistic patterns of policy-making. Still, as observed by various scholars, the institutional adaptations need to be completed as Croatia, despite its EU membership, continues to suffer from underdeveloped state capacity.

Many crises marked the decade of Croatia's EU membership. This situation sets the country apart from other more established EU member states. It provides a unique opportunity for analysing functional adaptations to EU membership in a permanent crisis mode of operation. Adaptations in such circumstances are more demanding for a country because the EU tended to expand the scope of its competencies and generally transitioned from greater diversity towards greater unity. This situation had ramifications for national-level decision-making and, as expected, caused opposition from the national actors, which opposed the idea of more integration.

The core theoretical concept of Europeanisation is reflected in all chapters of this book. Most chapters thereby rely on an extensive definition of Europeanisation by Claudio Radaelli (2003), which aims to be comprehensive. Nevertheless, the review presented in this introduction corroborates the insight previously reached by Johan Olsen (2003) that Europeanisation is a complex process challenging to define by a single definition and where different definitions should be viewed as complementary rather than mutually exclusive. As a complex phenomenon, Europeanisation could be observed from different perspectives (EU, national, subnational) and in different stages, i.e., pre- and post-accession. Furthermore, Europeanisation is closely related to other theoretical concepts crucial for its complete understanding, such as the sovereignty bargain, path dependence or multi-level governance.

The contributions in this book can be divided into two sections: one focusing on the political and the other on economic topics. However, in our selection of topics, we needed to be selective not to depart from conventional norms in publishing edited books. Therefore, although all our book chapters are important, this volume has not included all relevant topics. The red thread that connects all chapters is their focus on post-accession Europeanisation in Croatia, which, due to the relatively recent EU accession, still represents a reasonably novel topic.

References

Andersen, S. S. and Sitter, N. (2006) 'Differentiated Integration: What Is It and How Much Can the EU Accommodate?', *European Integration*, 28(4), pp. 313–330.

Bartolini, S. (2023) *Restructuring Europe: Centre Formation, System Building and Political Structuring between the Nation-State and the European Union*. Oxford: Oxford University Press.

Börzel, T. (2003) 'Europeanization: How the EU Interacts with Its Member States', *Political Science Series*, 93. Vienna: Institute for Advanced Studies, pp. 1–22. Available at: https://aei.pitt.edu/1049/1/pw_93.pdf (19.08.2023).

Bulmer, S. J. and Radaelli, C. M. (2004) 'The Europeanisation of National Policy?', Queen's Papers on Europeanisation, 1. Belfast: Queens University Belfast, pp. 1–22. Available at: https://econpapers.repec.org/paper/erpqueens/p0042.htm (19.08.2023).

Butković, H. and Samardžija, V. (2014) 'Challenges of Continued EU Enlargement to the Western Balkans – Croatia's Experience', *Poznan University of Economics Review*, 14(4), pp. 91–108.

Czarnecki, S. and Riedel, R. (2021) 'At the Crossroads of Europeanization and Professionalization: A Cross-Country Policy Analysis of Organised Interests in CEE', in M. Dobbins and R. Riedel (eds.) *Exploring Organised Interests in Post-Communist Policy Making: The "Missing Link"*. London and New York: Routledge, pp. 197–215.

Ferrara, F. M. and Kriesi, H. (2022) 'Crisis Pressures and European Integration', *Journal of European Public Policy,* 29(9), pp. 1351–1373.

Goldner Lang, I. (2012) 'The Impact of Enlargement(s) on the EU Institutions and Decision-Making – Special Focus: Croatia', *Yearbook of European Law*, 31(1), pp. 473–502.

Grubiša, D. (2023) *Povijest europskog ujedinjenja*. Zagreb: Srednja Europa.

Hall, P. A. (2016) 'The Euro Crisis and the Future of European Integration', *BBVA*, pp. 1–22. Available at: www.bbvaopenmind.com/en/articles/the-euro-crisis-and-the-future-of-european-integration/ (19.08.2023).

Héritier, A. (2005) 'Europeanization Research East and West: A Comparative Assessment', in F. Schimmelfennig and U. Sedelmeier (eds.) *The Europeanization of Central and Eastern Europe*. Ithaca, NY: Cornell University Press, pp. 199–209.

Hooghe, L. and Marks, G. (2001) *Multilevel Governance and European Integration*. Boulder, CO: Rowman & Littlefield.

Joannin, P. (2023) 'The European Institutions Dealing with Crisis', Fondation Robert Schuman. The Research and Studies Centre on Europe. Available at: www.robert-schuman.eu/en/european-issues/0668-the-european-institutions-dealing-with-crises (19.08.2023).

Krastev, I. (2002) *The Inflexibility Trap: Frustrated Societies, Weak States and Democracy. Report on the State of Democracy in the Balkans*. Sofia: Centre for Liberal Strategies.

Ladrech, R. (1994) 'Europeanization of Domestic Politics and Institutions: The Case of France', *Journal of Common Market Studies*, 32(1), pp. 69–88.

Ladrech, R. (2010) *Europeanization and National Politics*. Houndmills: Palgrave Macmillan.

Lehmann, K. E. (2018) 'The Crisis of the European Union as a Complex Adaptive System', *Journal of Common Market Studies*, 56(4), pp. 971–988.

Lehne, S. (2022) 'The EU and the Creative and Destructive Impact of Crises', Carnegie Europe, pp. 1–8. Available at: https://carnegieeurope.eu/2022/10/18/eu-and-creative-and-destructive-impact-of-crises-pub-88145 (19.08.2023).

Maldini, P. (2015) 'Croatian Accession to the European Union: EU Democratization Potential and Issues of Democratic Consolidation', in P. Maldini and D. Pauković (eds.) *Croatia and the European Union: Changes and Development*. London and New York: Routledge, pp. 11–32.

Maldini, P. and Pauković, D. (2015) 'Introduction', in P. Maldini and D. Pauković (eds.) *Croatia and the European Union: Changes and Development*. London and New York: Routledge, pp. 1–11.

Matei, L. and Matei, A. (2010) 'The Economic and Social Impact of Public Administration Europeanization', National School of Political Studies and Public Administration (NSPSPA), pp. 1–26. Available at: https://mpra.ub.uni-muenchen.de/24267/1/MPRA_paper_24267.pdf (19.08.2023).

Mattli, W. (2000) 'Sovereignty Bargains in Regional Integration', *International Studies Review*, 2(2), pp. 149–180.

Monnet, J. (1978) *Memories*. London: William Collins.

Moravcsik, A. (1994) *Why the European Community Strengthens the State: Domestic Politics and International Cooperation*. Cambridge, MA: Harvard University, Centre for European Studies.

Nugent, N. (2010) *The Government and Politics of the European Union*. Basingstoke: Palgrave Macmillan.

Olsen, J. P. (2003) 'Europeanization', in M. Cini (ed.) *European Union Politics*. Oxford: Oxford University Press, pp. 333–348.

Petak, Z. (2019) 'Policy Making Context and Challenges of Governance in Croatia', in Z. Petak and K. Kotarski (eds.) *Policy-Making at the European Periphery: New Perspectives on Southeast Europe*. Cham: Palgrave Macmillan, pp. 29–47.

Radaelli, C. (2003) 'The Europeanization of Public Policy', in K. Featherstone and C. Radaelli (eds.) *The Politics of Europeanization*. Oxford: Oxford University Press, pp. 27–56.

Risse, T., Caporaso, J. and Cowles, M. G. (2001) 'Europeanization and Domestic Change: Introduction', in J. Caporaso and T. Risse (eds.) *Transforming Europe: Europeanization and Domestic Change*. Ithaca, NY: Cornell University Press, pp. 1–20.

Rittberger, B., Biermann, F., Guerin, N., Jagdhuber, S. and Weiss, M. (2017) 'Explaining uneven EU integration trajectories: A comparison of the Euro crisis and the Refuge crisis', Paper prepared for the *15th biannual European Union Studies Association (EUSA) Conference*, 4–6 May 2017, Miami. Ludwig Maximilians Universität München. Available at: https://epub.ub.uni-muenchen.de/49165/ (19.08.2023).

Samardžija, V. (2014) 'What Does the EU Membership of Croatia Mean for the Countries of Western Balkans?', in L. Čehulić Vukadinović (ed.) *Yearbook Šipan 2013*. Zagreb: The Atlantic Council of Croatia, Centre for International Studies, pp. 73–84.

Schimmelfennig, F. (2018) 'European Integration (Theory) in Times of Crisis: A Comparison of the Euro and Schengen Crisis', *Journal of European Public Policy*, 25(7), pp. 969–989.

Taylor, A., Geddes, A. and Lees C. (2013) *The European Union and South East Europe: The Dynamics of Europeanization and Multilevel Governance*. London and New York: Routledge.

Vachudova, M. (2005) *Europe Undivided: Democracy, Leverage and Integration after Communism*. Oxford: Oxford University Press.

2 Impacts of Croatia's EU Membership on the Coordination Patterns within Three Branches of State Power

Hrvoje Butković and Senada Šelo Šabić

2.1 Introduction

Croatian membership in the EU was achieved during the lengthy process of negotiations and accession, which lasted 12 years, from entering into force of the Stabilisation and Association Agreement in 2001 to becoming a full member of the EU in 2013. The negotiations proved to be more demanding than previous accession negotiations because the EU applied a new negotiation methodology based on extensive use of benchmarks, which Croatia had to meet before the opening and closing of negotiation chapters. New chapters were introduced, most notably on the judiciary and fundamental rights, and track records for progress were established. In addition, Croatia had to negotiate a greater volume of legislation with more member states. This state of affairs made negotiations more complex and slower than initially expected. Before reaching a common EU negotiating position on any chapter, a lengthy bargaining process between member states and the EU institutions had to be finalised (see Butković and Samardžija, 2014).

From the start in Croatia, there was a broad political consensus among political parties on the importance of achieving EU membership. This was an essential prerequisite for successful accession negotiation because the relationship between the EU and the aspiring states is highly asymmetrical. The economic and political gains from enlargement are much more important for the aspiring states than for the EU (Schimmelfennig and Sedelmeier, 2005). The national governments take centre stage during the membership negotiations. Therefore, previous accession rounds were characterised by an almost exclusive dominance of the EU-state interactions throughout accession negotiations. Moreover, such practice resulted in a one-sided picture of compliance with the EU demands presented by the executive actors (Wunsch, 2018, p. 24).

The relatively marginal role of the Croatian Parliament during the accession negotiation fits very well in the above-described context. Firstly, as a rule, all legislative proposals that had to be harmonised with the EU *acquis communautaire* were not adopted under the ordinary legislative procedure but a summary procedure, which allowed only one reading in the parliament and shorter deadlines for MPs to review the text.[1] Secondly, the monitoring powers of the Croatian Parliament over the accession negotiations were only formal. During this time, the parliament has

DOI: 10.4324/9781003394013-2

set up the National Committee for Monitoring of Accession Negotiations as an *ad hoc* body composed of representatives of all parliamentary political parties and chaired by the political opposition. Although this committee could give opinions and issue guidelines on the government's negotiation positions, its power was advisory and not mandating.[2]

This chapter explores Croatia's Europeanisation of executive government, national legislature and judiciary after its 2013 EU accession. It examines features of the EU coordination within the government (intra-government coordination), between the government and the parliament (the government–parliament coordination) as well as the effects of the EU membership on the practices of the national judiciary. It seeks to contribute to debate about the national EU coordination by providing information on the actual functioning and informal procedures. The main research question is how EU membership influenced the quality of national governance. In other words, to what extent did Croatia reduce the executive dominance characteristic for the pre-accession period?

Methodologically, the chapter is based on the analysis of secondary sources such as the existing academic literature, legislation and official government documents. In addition to these secondary sources, three in-depth semi-structured interviews were conducted, one per each government branch. All interviewed individuals were directly or indirectly (as researchers in the judiciary case) involved in coordinating the EU affairs in Croatia. According to the method of application, in the case of the executive and judicial branches, the interviews were group, while in the case of the legislative branch, an individual interview was made. In order to describe and interpret the theme of this chapter, the authors rely on qualitative research methods such as qualitative content analysis and interviews. To a much lesser extent, quantitative content analysis is also applied. The chapter contributes to the cumulative understanding of the national EU coordination and makes it an accessible point of departure for future research.

Following its introduction, the chapter brings a theoretical section aimed at securing a better understanding of the following analysis. It presents the main patterns and trends in the academic literature on transformations within three branches of state power, i.e. their institutions, caused by the EU membership. The main section of the chapter is divided into three subsections: (i) core executive, (ii) legislature and (iii) judiciary. Each of these parts examines adaptations and specific procedures developed within a particular branch of the state power to meet the demands of the EU legislative processes. The core issues in all three subsections are dynamic relations between various branches of state power and their evolutionary development since the EU accession. The chapter ends with a discussion and conclusion section, which connects insights from the previous parts into one coherent whole and provides conclusions and recommendations.

2.2 Theoretical Background

The joint exercise of sovereignty in the EU incorporates its member states into a complex decision-making system and confronts them with the problem of horizontal coordination within their national negotiation systems (Scharpf, 1993). Furthermore, when national policies are partly supplemented and partly replaced by the EU policies, the latter cannot respect the particular material conditions, actor constellations and historical developments in the member states. Therefore, often they destroy or transform the old structures and lead to sudden changes in power relations between actors which may have evolved over a long historical period (Jachtenfuchs and Kohler-Koch, 1995).

Transformation in power relations at the national level caused by the EU association and membership could first and outmost be detected in a changed balance between legislative, executive and judicial power. In EU affairs, there is a different distribution of power between the government and the parliamentary majority in favour of the government, whereby the parliament loses control over the EU agenda and final decisions (Auel, 2007, p. 429). In this context it is often claimed that national executives have been gaining power in relation to the legislative due to Europeanisation understood as the adaptations made to the domestic political system in order to manage EU affairs (Radaelli, 2003, p. 27; Fink-Hafner, 2014, p. 72). The described disruption of executive–legislative balance is further heightened in times of crisis, which allows the executive to assert greater authority at the expense of the legislature (Bar-Siman-Tov, 2020). The fact that the EU and its neighbourhood were affected by various political and economic crises for the last decade makes relations between branches of state power in post-accession Croatia more critical.

Analysing from the perspective of historic institutionalism, Brigid Laffan notes that the Union's character and governance style place particular demands on central governments. The EU is characterised by dense institutionalisation where different phases of the policy process impose different demands on the national executives (2008, p. 128). The pre-negotiation phase is vital for agenda setting and drafting national positions on the Commission's proposed legislative acts. Subsequently, the decision-making phase involves representatives of the national executives in negotiations within the Council and the European Parliament. Finally, the implementation phase of the policy process obliges the governments to transpose and implement the EC laws and policy guidelines (ibid., p. 129).

There are two critical dimensions concerning national executives' coordination of EU-related issues: centralisation vs. decentralisation and comprehensive vs. selective coordination (Kassim, 2003, p. 93). In the case of the former, a decentralised system is characterised by the fact that no single actor controls the process of aligning domestic positions, whereas, in centralised systems, a unit has overall responsibility for coordination. Concerning later, the focus is placed on the scope of coordination since some member states attempt to agree on all EU-related issues while others tend to be more selective. This kind of classification essentially leads to four coordination types among member states: comprehensive centralisers (e.g. France and Poland); comprehensive de-centralisers (e.g. Germany, the Netherlands, Hungary); selective centralisers (e.g. Ireland, Portugal, Malta); and selective de-centralisers (e.g. Bulgaria, Romania, Estonia) (Gärtner et al., 2011, p. 96).

Centralised systems are more efficient than decentralised ones. Nevertheless, decentralised systems can bear advantages for states that prefer the status quo since enlisting the responsible lead ministry as a domestic veto player can contain the prime minister's bargaining space (Putnam, 1988). The EU coordination systems of the national executives can also be observed from their institutionalisation, i.e. the degree of structuration and routinisation of EU business, where some can be classified as highly institutionalised while others appear weakly institutionalised. In states with a high degree of institutionalisation, the informal processes tend to be subordinate to the formal ones, whereas, in weakly institutionalised systems, the informal is more critical (Laffan, 2008, p. 137).

Still, there needs to be more evidence that Europeanisation of the national executives leads towards increasing uniformity of national EU coordination systems. On the whole, European integration makes the political landscape in the individual member states more diverse and leads to increased complexity. This phenomenon can be explained by the transformative process of EU integration taking place along national paths which have developed in historically different circumstances (Jachtenfuchs and Kohler-Koch, 1995; Laffan, 2008). Therefore, the degree to which the central EU coordination body remains superior to the corresponding units in the respective line ministries varies significantly from country to country (Gärtner et al., 2011, p. 82). Nevertheless, while formal institutional structures highlight resilience, cultural norms, values and officials' identities demonstrate Europe's transformative power (Kassim, 2003).

The common understanding of parliamentary involvement in EU affairs focuses on scrutinising EU draft legislation through specialised procedures. For that to work, attention is placed on the pre-decisional stages of the legislative process, where adequate time needs to be provided to domestic legislatures to conduct their work. Within this process, parliaments need to know more about the ongoing bargaining by being able to demand from the ministers to express their views. Last but not least, such specialised procedures have to grant parliaments sufficient powers and expertise (Rozenberg and Hefftler, 2015). Despite this common understanding, historically, the involvement of parliaments in the EU's legislative and policy cycle has been weak and often reactive (Mittag and Wessels, 2003).

From a broader perspective, such a state of affairs is beneficial. Tight control of governments by the parliaments may prove dysfunctional because it could undermine the bargaining power of governments at the EU level. In order to overcome the control dilemma, parliamentarians have chosen three different strategies: (i) close informal cooperative relations with ministries, (ii) *ex-ante* mechanisms of scrutinising EU legislative proposals in committees, (iii) close direct contact with Members of the European Parliament (MEPs) in order to reduce informational gaps (Benz, 2004; Goetz and Meyer-Sahling, 2008). Parliamentary power in EU affairs scrutiny is undoubtedly dependent on the type of government, with minority governments producing more substantial parliamentary scrutiny than majority coalition governments (Holzhacker, 2005).

The Lisbon Treaty (2009) introduced new instruments that directly involve national parliaments in the constitutional politics of the EU. The first is that representatives of the national parliaments are now involved in preparing the revisions of the EU treaties. In addition, each national parliament is granted a veto in the simplified treaty revision procedure known as the "Passarelle Clause". The second concerns compliance with the principle of subsidiarity, which could be understood as a process by which national parliaments issue advisory opinions based on an assessment of the constitutionality of the EU legislative drafts (Groen and Christiansen, 2015, p. 47). Last but not least, with the advent of the Lisbon Treaty, political dialogue between the Commission and the national parliaments has become a legal requirement for the Commission. As part of this political dialogue, national parliaments can issue opinions on Commission documents or policy areas and receive responses from the Commission (Preising, 2011).

The intersections and interdependences between the legislative and the executive branches underline the importance of having an independent judiciary. Such judiciary must work within the framework of a rationally secured methodological canon and according to the ultimate and penultimate standards of fairness (Häberle, 2002, p. 143). In the context of the EU membership, the task of having an independent and adequately functional judiciary faces even more significant challenges because the EU represents the most developed interplay between national, regional (EU) and international law (Ćapeta and Goldner Lang, 2021).

2.3 National Coordination of EU Affairs after the EU Accession

2.3.1 Core Executive

According to the well-known analogy by Fiona Hayes-Renshaw, the Council may be envisaged as a layered triangle, with the European Council at the top, followed by the Council of Ministers, COREPER and, at the base, a large number of working groups (2002, p. 49). It is helpful to have this analogy in mind when describing the EU coordination systems of the national executives since, otherwise, the complexity could get in the way of creating a clear picture. The Croatian EU coordination system at the national executive level designed for its functioning in the Council was established in 2013 and revised in the following years. It is based on two legal documents: the government's conclusion on the responsibilities of the central bodies of the state administration for participation in the work of the Council and the government's decision on the establishment of the Inter-Sectoral Working Group for EU Affairs (Government of the Republic of Croatia [GRC], 2016, 2019). The former assigns the responsibilities to working groups and committees of the Council, while the latter defines coordination procedures.

The Croatian national EU coordination system is based upon two levels of decision-making: the Intra-Sectoral Working Group for EU Affairs, chaired by the Ministry of Foreign and European Affairs and the Government Coordination for Foreign and European Policy, which is the working body of the government. Members of the Inter-Sectoral Working Group for EU Affairs are 34 coordinators for European affairs in all state administrative bodies, while members of the government coordination are ministries and state secretaries. These two levels of decision-making essentially deliberate upon four types of negotiating positions: (i) positions for the weekly COREPER meetings, (ii) framework positions at the beginning of the legislative process, (iii) positions for the Council of Ministers and (iv) positions for the European Council.

With respect to positions for the weekly COREPER meetings, the envisaged timing is exceptionally tight. This agenda owned by the country presiding over the Council is received by the Ministry of Foreign and European Affairs on Friday afternoon and forwarded to all members of the Inter-Sectoral Working Group for EU Affairs. The responsible ministry and other relevant state bodies will draft a position by Tuesday afternoon. Then, a draft position is presented at the meeting to the Inter-Sectoral Working Group, which determines a final position for the COREPER meeting later in the week. The responsible state bodies are generally well prepared to draft a position for the COREPER meeting despite the tight schedule. This is because immediately after the Commission announces an act or other legally binding document, the responsible state bodies start working on the national tentative position.[3]

The framework positions at the beginning of the legislative process undergo a slightly more complex procedure. The EU act for which it is necessary to draft a framework position is delivered by the Ministry of Foreign and European Affairs to the responsible ministry with the deadline, considering the dynamics of the discussions in the working bodies of the Council. The draft framework position is subsequently forwarded to all Inter-Sectoral Working Group for EU Affairs members, who can make comments within a specific time limit. The draft framework position is also submitted to the Permanent Representation of Croatia to the EU, which can give its comments at any time. With all received comments, the finalised framework position is delivered to the Ministry of Foreign and European Affairs, which forwards it to the Government Coordination for Foreign and European Policy to be discussed and concluded.

For positions for the Council of Ministers, the stages of procedure are the same as for the framework positions. The only difference is timing since positions for the Council of Ministers usually have up to two weeks in order to be composed and adopted.[4] Procedures for the meetings of the European Council differ from those of the Council of Ministers in as much as here, the Office of the Prime Minister assumes the role of the Inter-Sectoral Working Group. Responsible ministries and other relevant bodies submit amendments to the proposed position for the European Council to the Office of the Prime Minister and the Ministry of Foreign and European Affairs. In case they don't express amendments within deadlines, they are considered to have no objections.

The government's decision to establish the Inter-Sectoral Working Group for EU Affairs also describes procedures concerning changes and deviations from the positions for the meetings of the COREPER and the Council of Ministers. In such circumstances, the representative of Croatia is obliged to inform about his/her actions the Ministry of Foreign and European Affairs and the ministry which bears responsibility for the position. In the case of the Council of Ministers meeting, the government also needs to be informed. When an established Croatian position does not exist, the representative of Croatia in the working bodies of the Council can present a principled position or enter a reservation.

One of the most significant challenges facing the Croatian EU coordination system of its national executive is horizontality. At the EU level, there is an explosion of broad topics, such as resilience or climate change, for which it is hard to identify a single responsible state body. Moreover, pandemics require comprehensive involvement and mediation between various state bodies. Last but not least, such extraordinary circumstances disallow the exemption of any ministry from dealing with EU affairs.[5]

Exercising the six-month presidency of the Council has always been an important task. However, demands placed on a presidency state today are much more significant than historically they used to be. This is because the areas of internal and external activity in which the Council is involved have been increased, while negotiations tend to be more conflictual (Hayes-Renshaw, 2002). For smaller states, preceding the Council is even more challenging since they are not used to being listened to with such attention and having a central role in brokering compromises (ibid.). The Croatian presidency of the Council in the first half of 2020 came just a few years after the country's accession, which is unusual and happened only because of Brexit, allowing Croatia to fill the time period initially reserved for the UK. Another aggravating circumstance was presiding over the Council during the global health crisis. Therefore, Croatia had to organise a virtual presidency, which faced technical and organisational challenges as new methods needed to be found to ensure the legal validity of the Council decisions.

The progress of the Croatian presidency in harmonising legislative acts in the regular legislative procedure was not optimal because only about half of what was planned by the European Commission was achieved (Vidačak, 2020, p. 48). Still, part of this lag could be attributed to the crisis circumstances. Furthermore, the fact that, under the Croatian presidency, approximately the same number of meetings of the Council's working groups was held during the previous Finnish presidency demonstrates significant efforts in adapting to emergencies (ibid.). Politically, the presidency could be considered successful since it finalised the Brexit deal and opened accession negotiations with Albania and North Macedonia (Butković, 2020). From a purely national perspective, the Croatian presidency has contributed to further socialisation and adaptation of Croatian public officials within the EU's political system. That way, it strengthened the country's EU coordination at the level of its national executive.[6]

As part of the Croatian Presidency, on 6 May 2020, the EU-Western Balkans Summit was held, where the "Zagreb Declaration" was adopted. In that document, the EU resolutely supports the political, economic and social transformation of the Western Balkan countries and welcomes their determination to respect European values and principles and implement the necessary reforms. The declaration mentions a package of 3.3 billion euros of EU aid to deal with the consequences of the crisis caused by the pandemic. However, it also states that a further increase in aid will depend on the concrete progress of the countries in the ambit of the rule of law and socio-economic reforms (European Council, 2020). The EU-Western

Balkans Summit and adoption of the "Zagreb Declaration" confirmed that the continuation of the EU enlargement represented a highly positioned goal of the Croatian presidency.

In terms of characterising the Croatian EU coordination systems at the national executive level, we tend to agree with Igor Vidačak, who noted that Croatia seems to be the closest to the model of selective centralisers. The author justifies this categorisation with the existence of a central Inter-Sectoral Working Group for EU Affairs, the central government's vital role and the national parliament's limited influence (2022, p. 10). The claim of centralisation could further be supported by the fact that the Croatian coordination system depends on the expertise of the national executive officials who, as the government's employees, work in Brussels. There, they participate in the activities of over 180 working groups, which form the base level of the Council, where the most significant number of issues get resolved.[7]

2.3.2 Legislature

Although most accession-related institutional arrangements ended when Croatia became an EU member state, they left a legacy of considerable expertise significant for developing a Croatian model of parliamentary scrutiny of EU affairs (Butković, 2015). In legal terms, the government–parliament coordination of the EU affairs in Croatia is regulated by the Constitution, the Law on Cooperation between Parliament and the Government on EU Affairs (LCPGEA) and the Standing Orders of the Parliament (Constitution of the Republic of Croatia, 2024; LCPGEA, 2013; Standing Orders of Croatian Parliament, 2020).

At the constitutional level, Article 144 prescribes the participation of the parliament in the European legislative process in accordance with the founding treaties. The LCPGEA enacted in 2013 identifies various forms of indirect and direct participation of the parliament in EU affairs (see Briški and Špiljak, 2014). Indirect participation refers to supervising the government's actions in EU institutions based on national laws and legislation. Such participation primarily refers to (i) supervision of the government's framework positions for the EU acts at the beginning of the legislative process, (ii) supervision of the government's positions for the Council meetings, (iii) supervision of the government's positions for European Council meetings, (iv) supervision of the process of nominating candidates for EU institutions and bodies. Direct participation is based on the provisions of the Lisbon Treaty (2009), which gave national parliaments new powers in the European legislative and regulatory processes. Such participation primarily concerns (i) supervision over compliance with the principle of subsidiarity, (ii) participation in political dialogue with the European Commission, (iii) application of the so-called Passarella clauses and (iv) participation in revision procedures of the EU's fundamental treaties.

The supervision of the government's framework positions for the EU acts at the beginning of the legislative process is arguably the most essential aspect of the government-parliament coordination of the EU affairs in Croatia. The prerequisite for this procedure is the adoption of the Parliament's Annual Work Program which is based on the list provided by the government of proposals for legislative and other acts of the Union expected to arrive on the EU's legislative agenda. All working bodies of the parliament can select proposals for legislative acts of the Union from their competence that they consider legally or politically essential and include them in the Annual Work Program. Therefore, through its Annual Work Program, parliament influences the formation of national priorities in EU affairs.

According to the LCPGEA, the government must deliver it to the parliament immediately after reaching a framework position on an EU act. Likewise, the government must inform the parliament of all crucial changes to its framework position. The government's framework position is forwarded by the European Affairs Committee (EAC) to the relevant sectoral committees, and based on the received inputs, the EAC, in the name of the parliament, can reach a conclusion which is binding for the government. Moreover, such a conclusion could even order the government to change its original framework position. Such strict procedure has led some authors to conclude that Croatia practises a mandatory system for indirect participation of the parliament in EU affairs. In other words, the country has a system which allows the parliament to determine how the government must act in the EU institutions (Briški and Špiljak, 2014; Butković, 2015). The importance of supervising the government's framework positions is confirmed by the fact that this is the only form of indirect participation of the parliament in EU affairs, which provides the MPs with a more extended period to respond. It is situated in the prenegotiation phase of the EU legislative and policy cycle, which is long because years can pass between the initial Commission draft proposal and the finalised EU act. As such, this procedure formally grants the parliament sufficient powers to adequately supervise the government's actions in EU institutions (Rozenberg and Hefftler, 2015, p. 8). In theory, it also allows interested stakeholders to exchange their views with members of the sectoral committees, although, in practice, this opportunity has not been adequately used (Vidačak, 2022, p. 14).[8]

The analysis of framework positions prepared by the government in the 2016–2021 period shows that the parliament's EAC adopted all without any amendments (Vidačak, 2022, p. 16). The more recent check of the database, which stores EU documents considered by the parliament, reconfirms this insight since in the 2021–2023 period such amendments have equally not been adopted (Croatian Parliament, 2023). This state of affairs demonstrates a discrepancy between theory and practice regarding powers assigned to the parliament *vis-à-vis* the government in EU affairs. On paper, Croatia has a mandatory system which allows the parliament to determine the government's actions in EU affairs. However, practice shows that the parliament lacks its own initiative and generally shows a great deal of dependency on the government. Part of the problem may be attributed to the fact that many MPs lack sufficient training in EU affairs today.[9] In addition, the fact that, according to the current legislation, including the sectoral committees in the scrutiny procedures is optional turns off the parliament to affirm itself as a stronger actor. The problem with the inactivity of the sectoral committees is increased because there is no evidence of close informal cooperative relations between the MPs on one side and the ministers or the MEPs on the other (see Goetz and Meyer-Sahling, 2008).

For supervising the government's positions for the Council and the European Council meetings, the written reports enable the parliament's supervision activities. Parliament's conclusions on such reports are not ruled out. The parliament additionally regulated procedures for the occasional and as-needed hearings of the ministers before or after the Council meetings, which, in addition to the EAC, also involved the sectoral committees (Croatian Parliament, 2023). Nevertheless, reporting to the national parliament before and after the Council and the European Council meetings takes the form of information sharing. This is because proposals are finalised at these very high levels of decision-making.[10]

According to the LCPGEA provision for nominating candidates for EU institutions and bodies, the government submits to the parliament a report on the candidate for an EU institution, and the EAC discusses the candidate at the session with that candidate present. After the session, the EAC issues the opinion the government considers when making its final decision. This system gives additional legitimacy to the government's decision on the candidate but has flaws. The main problem here is the fact that within the process of selecting the candidates, the member states are sometimes asked to nominate a candidate for a yet unknown portfolio.[11] In such circumstances, hearing of the candidate in the EAC makes little sense.

Concerning the direct participation of the parliament in EU affairs, the most critical procedure is supervision over compliance with the principle of subsidiarity. The LCPGEA and Standing Orders of the Parliament prescribe that the procedure should be implemented at the EAC. All MPs, groups of MPs and working bodies of the parliament or the government have the right to initiate the surveillance procedure. A proposal to initiate needs to be filed with the president of the parliament within two weeks of receipt of a draft legislative act from an EU institution. The president then delivers the proposal to the EAC, which has seven weeks to implement the procedure. The intention of this type of practice introduced by the Lisbon Treaty was to stop the adoption of acts at the EU level if a certain number of votes given to the national parliaments were to be collected. However, the practice has shown that it is challenging to coordinate national parliaments on this matter and collect one-third or one-half of the votes assigned to them, which then obliges the Commission to reconsider the proposal (Hefftler and Gattermann, 2015).

According to the Croatian Parliament's database, thus far, this institution has issued only two reasoned opinions under its role as a supervisor over the compliance of the principle of subsidiarity. This represents quite a weak result, considering that only in 2021, the General Secretariat of the Council distributed 16 reasoned opinions received within the framework of the subsidiarity check protocol (European Commission, 2022, p. 5). The first reasoned opinion of the Croatian Parliament was issued in 2014 on the proposal of several directives dealing with waste. The second one was issued in 2016 concerning the proposal of the Posted Workers Directive. On both occasions, the initiatives were unsuccessful. In the former case, the national parliaments needed to have managed to collect a sufficient number of reasoned opinions. Later, a sufficient number of opinions were collected, but the Commission opposed it and decided to maintain its original proposal (Ćapeta and Goldner Lang, 2021).

The political dialogue is an even more important aspect of direct parliament's participation in EU affairs than the subsidiarity check because it allows broader and more frequent communication between national parliaments and the Commission. The experience of numerous countries indicates that the national parliaments are far more interested in the content of the Commission's proposals than in questions related to subsidiarity. In less than ten per cent of all positions sent by the national parliaments, the issues were expressed in terms of subsidiarity (Preising, 2011, pp. 151–152). In strictly parliamentary jargon, unlike the subsidiarity check, which enables national parliaments to control European legislation *ex-post*, the political dialogue allows such control *ex-ante* (ibid., p. 152). Since 2013, the Croatian Parliament has sent a dozen opinions as part of the political dialogue and received responses from the Commission (Croatian Parliament, 2023). This situation, similar to the subsidiarity check, is not proof of high or even medium-level activity, considering that only in 2021, the General Secretariat of the Council received 165 opinions issued within the political dialogue framework (European Commission, 2022, p. 5). The weak results of the Croatian Parliament could partly be justified by the fact that, in administrative terms, the institution is under-capacitated. It has 151 MPs and only 240 administrative officials who deal with various issues and cannot provide to the MPs the type of service which is standard in some other member states or the European Parliament.[12]

2.3.3 Judiciary

The EU has two courts, the Court and the General Court, which together form the Court of Justice of the European Union (CJEU). The CJEU, according to Art. 19 of the Treaty of the EU, needs to ensure that the law is observed in the interpretation and application of the EU founding treaties. Nevertheless, responsibility for implementing the Union law rests primarily with the national courts. They are the first to meet the demands of individuals regarding rights concerning areas affected by the Union law. As such, they are the most responsible for its application. They have an interpretive obligation, meaning they must interpret national law to provide the same meaning and ensure the same effects as if an EU norm were directly applied (Ćapeta, 2006).

During the pre-accession phase, the Croatian courts, as building blocks of the judiciary branch of state authority, were bound to interpret the Croatian law following the EU law. However, during the pre-accession period, the practices of Croatian courts concerning the interpretive obligation were rare, inconsistent and sometimes contradictory.[13] Moreover, the Croatian Constitutional Court was not coherent about whether such an interpretation of Croatian law was legally binding for Croatian judges (Ivančin and Petrić, 2019, p. 508). A significant problem at that time was the poor knowledge of Croatian judges and lawyers of the EU law itself.[14]

There are generally three types of cases concerning the EU law in the EU member states: (i) preliminary rulings, (ii) infringement procedures and (iii) proceedings initiated by individuals against EU institutions (see Materljan, 2019, p. 213). In cases where the application of the Union rights is not the clearest, national courts can, and sometimes must, send a request to the CJEU asking for the interpretation. The proceedings initiated based on a request for a preliminary ruling are sent by the national courts and are related to the interpretation of the Union law. The 2019 analysis of Croatian cases sent to the CJEU indicates that the number of requests for preliminary rulings forwarded by the Croatian national courts was relatively small (14). Therefore, the author concludes that Croatian legal practitioners must fully recognise their role in applying the Union law (ibid., p. 264). In most cases, only the first-instance courts referred requests for a preliminary ruling. In addition, a relatively large number of requests did not meet the standards of the CJEU to contain (i) conclusions of the national court on the facts, (ii) a description of the relevant provisions of national law and (iii) the reasons why the interpretation of Union law is necessary (ibid., p. 265).

In a recent publication, Croatian legal scholars showed more optimism, praising that Croatian courts have referred questions to the CJEU, even if they made some mistakes in their formulation. They note that the judiciary's learning process is underway from the early misunderstandings of the newly joined EU legal system and the purpose of preliminary rulings to developing domestic remedies in the case of non-referral (Bačić Selanec et al., 2020, p. 12). They invoke the 2014 case of surrendering to Germany a Croatian citizen based on a political murder charge under provisions of the European Arrest Warrant. Back then, the Zagreb County Court, the Croatian Supreme Court and the Constitutional Court of Croatia refused to refer to the CJEU for interpretation, claiming that interpreting Croatian legislation transposed from the EU directives falls within the exclusive jurisdiction of Croatian courts. Today, they argue, a situation like this would not be possible because the Croatian Constitutional Court has developed a case law which stipulates that in such cases, courts of the last instance are obliged to refer to the CJEU (ibid., p. 13).

One procedurally successful example of a request for a preliminary ruling by a first-instance court in civil matters refers to the case Vodoopskrba II from 2016. In that case, the court, as part of the CJEU, decided on the request for a preliminary ruling by the Municipal Court in Velika Gorica (see Materljan, 2019, pp. 226–227). The defendant in the main proceedings objected to the payment of a fixed part of communal water supply services, which is calculated independently of actual water consumption. The Croatian court took the position that determining the price of water services according to the amount of water consumed is only one of the possible ways to encourage users to use the resources efficiently. It also requested the interpretation of Directive 2000/60/EC of the European Parliament and the Council from 23 October 2000 on establishing a framework for Community action in the field of water policy. For this case, the court examined the documents based on which Directive 2000/60/EC was adopted and its transposition within various national legislations. Based on that analysis, the court ruled that Croatian regulations, which prescribe that the price of water services is determined based on the fixed and variable parts, are under the directive mentioned earlier (ibid.).

One of the reasons why Croatian judges fail to interpret the laws as the EU legislator intended is time. In order to understand whether national legislation correctly transposes an EU directive, it is necessary to enter into the interpretation process, which assumes checking both the original directive and the CJEU practice. Croatian judges often need more time for this kind of research since their efficiency is measured purely by the number of resolved cases.[15] In order to alleviate this problem to a certain extent, some national courts have established special offices whose task is to monitor the case law of the CJEU. Nevertheless, this system has not yet fully come to life because mutual communication and networking between these offices is relatively low.[16]

After the EU accession, the lower-level national courts predominantly started to comply with the interpretative obligation, which empowered these courts in their relationship with the higher-level national courts. The practice has shown that the higher-level courts will avoid getting involved in an infringement procedure for non-compliance with the EU law. Therefore, following the preliminary ruling, the higher-level courts tend to adjust their previous interpretation to the CJEU's (Ivančin and Petrić, 2019). This dynamic process has contributed towards overcoming excessively formalistic reasoning of the courts that was characteristic during the socialist period (ibid.). Nevertheless, the EU law in Croatia will gain much greater significance only when the higher-level courts become dominant in exercising their interpretative obligation. For now, the Supreme and Constitutional Courts' annulment of lower-level courts' judgements for non-compliance with the EU law is still relatively rare.[17]

In the so-called infringement procedure, a member state appears as the defendant. The procedure empowers the CJEU to conduct a judicial review of member states or to control the compliance of the laws of the member states with the EU law (Materljan, 2019). After joining the EU, many infringement procedures were initiated against Croatia. However, when viewed in proportion to population, this number is similar to other member states. The most significant number of infringement proceedings, in the case of Croatia as in other member states, ends with a pre-court settlement. It should be emphasised that all infringement proceedings against Croatia have so far concerned the legislative and executive branches of power and not the judiciary branch. In other words, these cases tackled wrong transposition or implementation of EU acts, while judicial interpretations still need to be addressed.[18]

By announcing the supremacy of the Croatian Constitution over the EU law in 2015, the Constitutional Court has allowed the possibility for the constitutional review of the secondary EU law. However, at this moment, relatively early after the accession, the case law on the domestic constitutional limits of EU integration has not yet started to develop (Ćapeta and Goldner Lang, 2021). The Croatian Constitutional Court seems to have not yet built the essential institutional capacity necessary to remove obstacles to harmonising the national and EU legal order (Selanec, 2021, p. 322). For example, the Croatian Constitutional Court does not have the research mentioned earlier that follows developments in the case law of the CJEU.[19]

According to Tamara Ćapeta and Iris Goldner Lang, the adjudicating culture in Croatia has changed since the EU accession. The old, strictly formalistic view of law is gradually being replaced by a legal culture that recognises the importance of interpretation in law (2021, p. 309). The Croatian Judicial Academy was crucial in this process because it made judges and lawyers familiar with the interpretation-based EU law. The generational factor also played a role, as younger judges and lawyers tend to be more inclined to refer to the provisions of EU law.[20] However, much work remains to be done on raising awareness among legal practitioners and parties in legal proceedings about the importance of the EU law. The inconvenient truth is that the EU law needs to be better addressed in Croatia, similar to other member states.[21]

2.4 Discussion and Conclusions

Following the signing of its Stabilization and Association Agreement with the EU and throughout its accession negotiations, Croatia was faced with the dominance of its executive power branch in EU-related matters. This phenomenon represents nothing new since it was previously observed in all other acceding countries. In that respect, the EU membership represents a chance for gradual normalisation of power relations between the three branches of state power in EU affairs. Nevertheless, regarding EU affairs, some form of executive dominance represents a constant that cannot be fully resolved even after the accession. The reason for this is the dense institutionalisation of the EU, which imposes comparatively greater demands on the national executives (see Laffan, 2008).

After the EU accession, Croatia established a two-layered intra-government coordination system in EU affairs. Its procedures circle around two newly created bodies: the Intra-Sectoral Working Group for EU Affairs, chaired by the Ministry of Foreign and European Affairs, and the Government Coordination for Foreign and European Policy, which is the working body of the government. These bodies manage the EU affairs within the core national executive based on the given phase of the policy-making process, i.e. under the assigned formations of the Council. The position of the Intra-Sectoral Working Group for EU Affairs is more central within the established coordination system since, in terms of content, it contributes the most to creating the various positions. The Government Coordination for Foreign and European Policy is a political level of coordination which usually serves as a final check on the previously established content.

From the point of view of centralisation vs. decentralisation, the established system of intra-government coordination could be considered centralised (see Vidačak, 2022), which means that the responsible lead ministry does not have the role of a potential veto player. Furthermore, it could be considered highly institutionalised since its structure does not allow any dominant role for informal processes. The problems of the established intra-government coordination do not seem to be functional. The system has passed the efficiency test, if not earlier than by 2020 when Croatia relatively successfully presided over the Council in the extraordinary circumstances of the raging health crisis. This coordination's most significant problem seems to be the horizontality of the topics dominating the EU agenda. This often makes it hard to determine a single lead ministry responsible for drafting a national position and, if needed, to coordinate the work of more than one ministry. Nevertheless, this particular problem is experienced by all EU member states equally and should, therefore, at least partly be transnationally resolved.

The government-parliament coordination in the EU affairs established after the accession complements the country's intra-government coordination. This mainly concerns parliament's supervision of the government's framework positions for the EU acts at the beginning of the legislative process, which forms the central part of the parliament's indirect participation in EU affairs. Only this one provides adequate time for implementing an effective *ex-ante* government scrutiny within parliament's indirect participation procedures. This means that the sectoral committees are from the very beginning involved. They can shape the government's framework positions through cooperation or even mandates and, in that way, influence the EU legislation. The only problem is that, for the time being, sectoral committees of the parliament show little readiness to become more deeply involved in the scrutiny process.

Croatian Parliament's direct participation in EU affairs was secured through novel provisions of the Lisbon Treaty, which primarily concern the so-called subsidiarity check and political dialogue. Through these procedures, which establish formal lines of communication between the national parliaments and the European Commission, the former can coordinate their views and directly intervene in the content of the draft EU legislation. The subsidiarity check procedure involved the Croatian Parliament in only two drafts of the reasoned opinions. Such weak results confirm claims that structured formal coordination between various national parliaments is still far from optimal (see Hefftler and Gattermann, 2015). In other words, the technical opportunities provided through the existing platforms for information exchange are insufficient prerequisites for successful coordination. In the ambit of political dialogue, which enables exchange on the content of draft legislation that reaches beyond subsidiarity, the Croatian Parliament marks somewhat better results as more than a dozen such exchanges have been documented. However, to use the political dialogue more strategically, the Croatian Parliament needs to become better capacitated with the administrative officials.

The post-accession coordination patterns within the Croatian judiciary comply with the envisaged role of the national courts, which bear an unambiguous responsibility to implement the EU law. The inter-institutional dynamics in this area primarily concerns communication between the national courts and the CJEU in Luxembourg. The number of requests for preliminary rulings forwarded to the CJEU is small but not insignificant. As a rule, such requests were forwarded by the lower courts, which empowers them in their relationship with the higher-level national courts. Nevertheless, for the EU law in Croatia to take root, the higher-level courts will need to take the initiative in exercising their interpretative obligation. This is because, from these higher-level courts, judicial practice spills over to lower-level ones much faster and easier. The fact that Croatian courts have started to interpret the EU law may be partly attributed to the effects of the government-sponsored education programmes in the area of EU law. Ever since the accession, these programmes have been attended by many judges and legal professionals.

Returning to the research question about the reduction of executive dominance and related increase in governance quality after the EU accession, our analysis shows that Croatia was only partly successful. The EU membership, accompanied by somewhat transformed Europeanisation pressures, affected the functional aspects of the national coordination in the EU affairs by formally strengthening the country's legislature and judiciary. The Croatian Parliament was provided with the legal framework that allows effective *ex-ante* scrutiny of the government in EU affairs. However, the legislature has hardly been up to its task as it rarely questioned the government's positions and restrained from direct participation in EU affairs. In comparative terms, the judiciary could be better evaluated since national judges slowly but indeed started to behave under their interpretative obligation in the domain of EU law, thus ultimately contributing to the reduction of executive dominance.

In order to improve the EU-related coordination patterns within Croatia's three branches of state power, some recommendations could be made. For the executive branch, one of the most prominent issues is finding answers to the horizontality of the contemporary EU agenda. In that sense, the country needs to search for the best operative solutions within its practice and by reviewing experiences from abroad. It would be crucial for the legislature to oblige sectoral parliamentary committees to at least much more active participation in the scrutiny procedures. This kind of action is needed because the EAC needs more expertise. At the same time, the quality of the government's proposals can be improved with additional expert opinions. However, obliging the sectoral committees in that way will only be sufficient if paired with the special education programmes for the MPs. The blueprint for such programmes could be EU law courses available for national judges. Such programmes would enable the MPs to profile their interest in EU affairs and find their specialisations. Finally, the principal recommendation for the national judiciary concerns raising awareness among the higher courts on the importance of their direct engagement with the EU law.

Notes

1 Interview with a representative of Croatian Parliament, 31.01.2023.
2 Interview with a representative of Croatian Parliament, 31.01.2023.
3 Interview with Croatian Ministry of Foreign and European Affairs representatives, 20.02.2023.
4 Interview with Croatian Ministry of Foreign and European Affairs representatives, 20.02.2023.
5 Interview with Croatian Ministry of Foreign and European Affairs representatives, 20.02.2023.
6 Interview with Croatian Ministry of Foreign and European Affairs representatives, 20.02.2023.

7 Interview with Croatian Ministry of Foreign and European Affairs representatives, 20.02.2023.
8 After the EU accession, the ability of the parliament to influence the EU-related legislation in the implementation phase has also been increased. Since the EU accession, most EU acts, such as laws which transpose directives, are adopted through the standard legislative procedure. The pre-accession pattern of adopting such laws through the summary procedure has been abandoned. Since the standard legislative procedure takes about six months, this gives the MPs more time to influence the national laws which originate from the EU acts.
9 Interview with a representative of Croatian Parliament, 31.01.2023.
10 Interview with a representative of Croatian Parliament, 31.01.2023.
11 Interview with a representative of Croatian Parliament, 31.01.2023.
12 Interview with a representative of Croatian Parliament, 31.01.2023.
13 Interview with representatives of Chair for European Public Law, Faculty of Law Zagreb, 03.03.2023.
14 Interview with representatives of Chair for European Public Law, Faculty of Law Zagreb 03.03.2023.
15 Interview with representatives of Chair for European Public Law, Faculty of Law Zagreb, 03.03.2023.
16 Interview with representatives of Chair for European Public Law, Faculty of Law Zagreb, 03.03.2023.
17 Interview with representatives of Chair for European Public Law, Faculty of Law Zagreb, 03.03.2023.
18 Interview with representatives of Chair for European Public Law, Faculty of Law Zagreb, 03.03.2023.
19 Interview with representatives of Chair for European Public Law, Faculty of Law Zagreb, 03.03.2023.
20 Interview with representatives of Chair for European Public Law, Faculty of Law Zagreb, 03.03.2023.
21 Interview with representatives of Chair for European Public Law, Faculty of Law Zagreb, 03.03.2023.

References

Auel, K. (2007) 'Democratic Accountability and National Parliaments: Redefining the Impact of Parliamentary Scrutiny in EU Affairs', *European Law Journal,* 13(4), pp. 487–504.

Bar-Siman-Tov, I. (2020) 'Covid-19 Meets Politics: The Novel Coronavirus as a Novel Challenge for Legislatures', *The Theory and Practice of Legislation,* 8(1–2), pp. 11–48.

Bečić Selanec, N. Ćapeta, T., Goldner Lang, I. and Petrić, D. (2020) 'Croatia', in M. Botman and J. Langer (eds.) *National Courts and Enforcement of EU Law: The Pivotal Role of National Courts*. The Hague: Eleven International Publishing, pp. 115–133.

Benz, A. (2004) 'Path-Dependent Institutions and Strategic Veto Players: National Parliaments in the European Union', *West European Politics,* 27(5), pp. 875–900.

Briški, T. and Špiljak, J. (2014) 'Posredno uključivanje nacionalnih parlamenata u europski zakonodavni process: prioritet Hrvatskog sabora u europskim poslovima', *Suvremene teme,* 7(1), pp. 7–28.

Butković, H. (2015) 'The Croatian Parliament in the European Union: Ready, Steady, Go!', in C. Hefftler, C. Neuhold, O. Rozenberg and J. Smith (eds.) *The Palgrave Handbook of National Parliaments and the European Union*. Basingstoke: Palgrave Macmillan, pp. 462–478.

Butković, H. (2020) Hrvatsko predsjedanje Vijećem EU-a u sjeni pandemije Covid-19. *IRMO aktualno*. No. 7. Available at: https://irmo.hr/wp-content/uploads/2020/06/irmo-aktualno-7.pdf (19.03.2023).

Butković, H. and Samardžija, V. (2014) 'Challenges of Continued EU Enlargement to the Western Balkans – Croatia's Experience', *Poznan University of Economics Review*, 14(4), pp. 91–108.

Ćapeta, T. (2006) 'Interpretativni učinak europskog prava u članstvu i prije članstva u EU', *Zbornik pravnog fakulteta u Zagrebu*, 56(5), pp. 1443–1494.

Ćapeta, T. and Goldner Lang, I. (2021) 'Croatian Constitution and Economic and Monetary Integration in the EU', in S. Griller and E. Lentsch (eds.) *EMU Integration and National Constitutions*. Oxford: Hart Publishing, pp. 305–330.

Constitution of the Republic of Croatia (2024) OG 56/90, 135/97, 133/00, 124/00, 28/01, 41/01, 55/01, 76/10, 85/10, 05/14. *Zakon.hr*. Available at: www.zakon.hr/z/94/Ustav-Republike-Hrvatske (26.03.2024).

Croatian Parliament (2023) 'Pretraživanje dokumenata EU,' in *Croatian Parliament's Information and Documentation Service*. Available at: https://sabor.hr/hr/europski-poslovi/posredno-obavljanje-poslova (19.03.2023).

European Commission (2022) Annual Report 2021 on the Application of the Principles of Subsidiarity and Proportionality and on Relations with National Parliaments. Available at: https://commission.europa.eu/system/files/2022-08/com_2022_366_1_en_act_part1_v2.pdf (19.03.2023).

European Council (2020) Zagreb Declaration. Available at: www.consilium.europa.eu/en/press/press-releases/2020/05/06/zagreb-declaration-6-may-2020/ (14.06.2023).

Fink-Hafner, D. (2014) 'Post-Accession Politicisation of National EU Policy Coordination: The Case of Slovenia', *Public Administration*, 92(1), pp. 39–54.

Gärtner, L., Hörner, J. and Obholzer, L. (2011) 'National Coordination of EU Policy: A Comparative Study of the Twelve "New" Member States', *Journal of Contemporary European Research*, 7(1), pp. 77–100.

Goetz, K. H. and Meyer-Sahling J. H. (2008) 'The Europeanisation of National Political Systems: Parliaments and Executives', *Living Reviews in European Governance*, 3(2), pp. 4–22.

GRC – Government of the Republic of Croatia (2016) 'Odluka o osnivanju Međuresorne radne skupine za europske poslove. OG 43/2016', *Government of the Republic of Croatia*. Available at: https://narodne-novine.nn.hr/clanci/sluzbeni/2016_05_43_1118.html (19.03.2023).

GRC – Government of the Republic of Croatia (2019) 'Zaduženja središnjih tijela državne uprave i drugih tijela za sudjelovanje u radu radnih skupina i odbora Vijeća Europske unije', *Government of the Republic of Croatia*. Available at: https://mfin.gov.hr/UserDocsImages/dokumenti/hr_i_eu/Zakljucak_Zaduzenja%202019.pdf (19.03.2023).

Groen, A. and Christiansen, T. (2015) 'National Parliaments in the European Union: Conceptual Choices in the EU's Constitutional Debate', in C. Hefftler et al. (eds.) *Palgrave Handbook of National Parliaments and the European Union*. Houndsmills / Basingstoke: Palgrave Macmillan, pp. 43–59.

Häberle, P. (2002) *Ustavna država*. Zagreb: Politička kultura.

Hayes-Renshaw, F. (2002) 'The Council of Ministers', in J. Peterson and M. Shackleton (eds.) *The Institutions of the European Union*. Oxford: Oxford University Press, pp. 47–70.

Hefftler, C. and Gattermann, K. (2015) 'Interparliamentary Cooperation in the European Union: Patterns, Problems and Potential', in C. Hefftler, C. Neuhold, O. Rozenberg and J. Smith (eds.) *The Palgrave Handbook of National Parliaments and the European Union*. Basingstoke: Palgrave Macmillan, pp. 94–115.

Holzhacker, R. (2005) 'National Parliamentary Scrutiny Over EU Issues: Comparing the Goals and Methods of Governing and Opposition Parties', *Journal of Legislative Studies*, 11(3–4), pp. 428–445.

Ivančin, A. and Petrić, D. (2019) 'Are Croatian Courts Prepared for the Interpretive Obligation?', *Review of Central and East European Law*, 44, pp. 493–526.

Jachtenfuchs, M. and Kohler-Koch, B. (1995) 'The Transformation of Governance in the European Union', *Arbeitspapiere Working Papers*; *Mannheimer Zentrum für Europäische Sozialforschung*. Available at: www.mzes.uni-mannheim.de/publications/wp/wp3-11.pdf (18.03.2023).

Kassim, H. (2003) 'Meeting the Demands of EU Membership: The Europeanization of National Administrative Systems', in K. Featherstone and C. M. Radaelli (eds.) *The Politics of Europeanization*. Oxford: Oxford University Press, pp. 84–111.

Laffan, B. (2008) 'Core Executives', in P. Grazioano and M. P. Vink (eds.) *Europeanization: New Research Agendas*. Chem: Palgrave Macmillan, pp. 128–140.

LCPGEA – Law on Cooperation between the Parliament and the Government in the European Affairs. (2013) OG 8/13. *The Croatian Parliament*. Available at: www.sabor.hr/hr/o-saboru/vazniji-propisi/zakon-o-suradnji-hrvatskoga-sabora-i-vlade-republike-hrvatske-u-europskim (19.03.2023).

Materljan, I. (2019) 'Hrvatski predmeti na sudovima Europske unije', *Godišnjak akademije pravnih znanosti Hrvatske*, 10(1), pp. 211–271.

Mittag, J. and Wessels, W. (2003) 'The One and the Fifteen? The Member States between Procedural Adaptation and Structure Revolution', in W. Wessels, A. Maurer and J. Mittag (eds.) *Fifteen into One? The European Union and Its Member States*. Manchester: Manchester University Press, pp. 413–454.

Preising, C. (2011) 'Der Umgang nationaler Parlamente mit den neuen Rechten des Verlags von Lissabon – die Perspektive der Europäischen Kommission', in G. Abels and A. Eppler (eds.) *Auf dem Weg zum Mehrebenenparlamentarismus?: Funktionen von Parlamenten im politischen System der EU*. Baden-Baden: Nomos Verlagsgesellschaft, pp. 149–156.

Putnam, R. D. (1988) 'Diplomacy and Domestic Politics: The Logic of Two-Level Games', *International Organization*, 42(3), pp. 427–460.

Radaelli, C. (2003) 'The Europeanization of Public Policy', in K. Featherstone and C. Radaelli (eds.) *The Politics of Europeanization*. Oxford: Oxford University Press, pp. 27–56.

Rozenberg, O. and Hefftler, C. (2015) 'Introduction', in C. Hefftler, C. Neuhold, O. Rozenberg and J. Smith (eds.) *The Palgrave Handbook of National Parliaments and the European Union*. Basingstoke: Palgrave Macmillan, pp. 1–39.

Scharpf, F. W. (1993) 'Versuch über Demokratie im verhandelnden Staat', in R. Czada and M. G. Schmitt (eds.) *Verhandlungsdemokratie, Interessenvermittlung, Regierbarkeit*. Opladen: Festschrift für Gerhard Lehmbruch, pp. 25–50.

Schimmelfennig, F. and Sedelmeier, U. (2005) 'Introduction: Conceptualizing the Europeanization of Central and Eastern Europe', in F. Schimmelfennig and U. Sedelmeier (eds.) *The Europeanization of Central and Eastern Europe*. Ithaca, NY: Cornel University Press, pp. 1–28.

Selanec, G. (2021) 'Uloga Ustavnog suda u provedbi prava Europske unije u okviru pravnog poretka Republike Hrvatske', in T. Čapeta and I. Goldner Lang (eds.) *Pravo unutarnjeg tržišta Europske unije*. Zagreb: Narodne Novine, pp. 293–323.

Standing Orders of Croatian Parliament. (2020) OG 81/13, 113/16, 69/17, 29/18, 53/20, 119/2020, 123/20. *The Croatian Parliament.* Available at: https://sabor.hr/hr/pristup-informacijama/vazniji-propisi/poslovnik-hrvatskoga-sabora-narodne-novine-broj-81/2013-113 (19.03.2023).

Vidačak, I. (2020) 'Analiza uspješnosti hrvatskog predsjedanja Vijećem Europske unije', *GONG*. Available at: www.gong.hr/media/uploads/20200909_analiza_hrvatskog_predsjedanja.pdf (19.03.2023.)

Vidačak, I. (2022) 'The Role of Organised Interests in Shaping Croatia's Negotiating Positions in the Council of the EU', *East European Politics*. Available at: www.tandfonline.com/doi/full/10.1080/21599165.2022.2120474?scroll=top&needAccess=true&role=tab (19.03.2023).

Wunsch, N. (2018) *EU Enlargement and Civil Society in the Western Balkans: From Mobilisation to Empowerment*. Chem: Palgrave Macmillan.

3 Unlocking Influence

Access and Lobbying Strategies of Croatian Interest Groups in the EU Policymaking

Igor Vidačak

3.1 Introduction

In 2023, Croatia marked ten years of European Union (EU) membership and 20 years since the application for entry into the Union was submitted. Since the beginning of the European integration process, it was clear that the adjustments to the EU accession requirements affect not only government bodies and public policies but also various interest groups and their relations with public authorities at all levels. The effects of Europeanisation substantially alter the nature of the domestic policymaking process, with an increasing number of legislative and policy initiatives originating from the EU level (Radaelli, 2003; Töller, 2010). Such a changed environment puts national interest groups under increasing pressure and contributes to the gradual shift in their behaviour towards developing dual or multi-level strategies, promoting their interests before domestic and EU institutions (Beyers, 2002; Klüver, 2010) while often trying to maintain relations with local governments and their constituencies or beneficiaries.

In the post-socialist context of EU member states from Central and Eastern Europe, the EU accession process provided various incentives for the transformation of patterns of interest representation in the policymaking processes, affecting also styles of governance but also influence-seeking behaviour of national interest groups (Hafner-Fink et al., 2016; Novak and Lajh, 2019; Petak et al., 2019; Pérez-Solórzano Borragán, 2004; Vidačak, 2007).

As has been the case both in new and old EU member states, European integration further strengthens the national executive in contrast to interest groups and national parliaments (Fink-Hafner, 2014; Vidačak, 2023). The sources of information about the emerging patterns of behaviour of national interest groups and the use of different channels of influence on EU policymaking have been developing over the years. The establishment of the EU Transparency Register has been crucial in that regard as it contains relevant information on the lobbying costs, the number of staff involved in lobbying, involvement of interest groups in different EU-level working bodies, public consultations on draft EU legislative and policy initiatives to which the groups contributed, the structure of financing etc.

DOI: 10.4324/9781003394013-3

This chapter analyses the lobbying strategies that Croatian interest groups employ in the EU policymaking processes. Focusing on the ten years following Croatia's entry into the EU, the study investigates the types of influence-seeking behaviours exhibited by these interest groups and the factors influencing their choice between national and EU-level lobbying strategies. Through quantitative and qualitative methods, this chapter sheds light on the evolving lobbying strategies of Croatian interest groups in the EU decision-making processes. Quantitative analysis of data from the EU Transparency Register reveals patterns and trends in lobbying activities and provides insights into the tactics employed. Furthermore, qualitative analysis, including interviews with representatives from selected interest groups, provides additional information on motivations and challenges in using national and EU-level strategies. The research is expected to contribute to a better understanding of Croatian interest group lobbying in the EU. The findings have implications for interest groups and policymakers, especially regarding enhanced transparency in managing EU affairs and improved access to information.

3.2 Theoretical Background

With an increasing spectrum of competencies being transferred to the EU level, the EU impact or Europeanisation analysis has emerged as a significant phenomenon in the realm of EU studies. It has been widely acknowledged that the concept of Europeanisation generally encompasses the construction, diffusion and institutionalisation of formal and informal rules, procedures, policy paradigms and norms as a transformative process wherein these elements are initially formulated and consolidated at the EU level, subsequently permeating the logic of domestic discourse, identities, political structures and public policies (Radaelli, 2003).

Nowadays most political decisions are made at the European level, while national governments lost monopoly in shaping public policies at the member-state levels. Therefore, national interest groups are under growing pressure to develop new multi-level influence strategies. (Beyers, 2002; Binderkrantz and Rasmussen, 2015; Klüver, 2010). Therefore, in recent years, scholarly attention has increasingly turned towards understanding the Europeanisation of national interest groups and their strategies in EU policymaking. As intermediaries between societal actors and political institutions, interest groups play a crucial role in shaping policy outcomes and influencing decision-making processes. With its complex multi-level governance structure, the EU provides a unique arena for these interest groups to engage in advocacy and lobbying activities.

The analysis of the type of channels used by national interest groups to influence EU decisions is usually done based on two contrasting theoretical views. The first approach is conceptualised as a system of multi-level governance which argues that there are many interacting authority structures at the EU level, spreading vertically between many levels of government and horizontally across multiple quasi-government and interest groups (Marks 1993; Hooghe and Mark, 2001; Jordan, 2001; Marks et al., 1996; Stephenson, 2013). This theoretical concept corresponds well with the neo-functionalist view of EU integration, which focuses on the feedback processes of spillover and path dependence, which, over time, produce more integration (Schimmelfenning, 2018). On the other hand, liberal intergovernmentalism views the EU primarily as a two-level interstate negotiation system (Moravcsik, 1993, 1998. These two theoretical views have different implications for the relevance of domestic politics and the interaction between public institutions and interest groups. The literature on multi-level governance argues that national governments no longer monopolise public policymaking, and the articulation and aggregation of interests occur at different policy levels and, increasingly, at the EU level. On the other hand, the liberal intergovernmental approach affirms that interests are primarily articulated domestically and that national governments play a crucial role in aggregating interests and shaping national preferences mainly through the interactions between the state (government) bodies and organised social and economic interests.

Despite the prevailing assumption that interest groups with multi-level strategies would inherently experience tremendous success, political engagement at the EU level is one of many channels of inclusion in EU policymaking. Direct engagement with Brussels or a European channel of influence involving direct contact with EU-level policymakers represents just one approach. Another avenue is indirect participation through EU-level umbrella organisations or lobbying activities via national actors, known as the "national route" (Beyers, 2002; Vidačak, 2007).

The research on the European federations of interest groups in different sectors questioned, among others, whether the emergence and the impact of Euro-level associations lead to a declining relevance of domestic policymaking processes. Besides, it has been shown that the successive enlargements of the EU have led to a heterogeneous representation within European federations, often limited to the lowest common denominator of national interests. Consequently, some domestic interest groups started to extend their lobbying activities to the European level, often lobbying directly and bypassing their EU-level sectoral federations. The previous analysis of the EU lobbying strategies of interest groups has demonstrated the wide range of inside and outside strategies (De Bruycker and Beyers, 2019), while some authors discuss the level of anticipation and active approach of interest groups and distinguish negative, defensive, reactive and proactive strategies (Geuguen, 2007).

However, not all national interest groups engage in EU-level lobbying activities, which raises questions about the factors influencing this choice (Eising, 2008). While the institutional context at the national level is widely recognised as an important factor, there is ongoing debate regarding how it affects some interest groups' choice of European strategies, with two predominant types of approaches. The first emphasises the correlation between access at the national level and the development of the European strategy of interest groups, suggesting that interest groups with considerable access at the national level are more likely to Europeanise their lobbying activities. The second argues that interest groups compensate for their lack of domestic access by pursuing lobbying directly at the European level. Such an approach emphasises the degree of fit between national and European modes of interest intermediation, indicating that interest groups embedded in national systems resembling EU-level patterns of interest intermediation may find it easier to Europeanise their lobbying activities (Klüver, 2010).

These approaches also suggest that the supposed Europeanisation of domestic interest associations may be substantially stimulated or constrained, on the one hand, by the degree to which they are embedded in domestic policy networks and, on the other, by the constituencies they represent. Other factors affecting the choice of lobbying strategies discussed in the literature also deal with resource availability, professional staff and expertise, policy sector relevance, the openness and accessibility of national institutional venues to interest groups and transparency of the management of EU affairs (Dür and Mateo, 2012; Pritoni, 2019; Binderkrantz, 2005).

Despite the growing interest in the Europeanisation of interest groups, there remains a relative lack of empirical research focused on specific national contexts, especially in new member states from Central and Eastern Europe. Examining the impact of EU membership on the lobbying strategies of interest groups from Croatia can provide interesting insights due to the country's new democracy, socialist past, modest resources and established standards and structures of dialogue between government and civil society.

In the context of experiences of Central and Eastern European (CEE) countries such as Croatia, the applicability of the liberal intergovernmental model has been contested. Namely, contrary to Moravcsik's expectations, it has been shown that economic and societal interests do not have primacy in influencing national preference formulation in some post-communist EU member states (Rybar, 2011; Vidačak, 2023).

This is primarily due to the legacy of the EU accession process of post-communist countries, weak oversight and accountability mechanisms and largely non-inclusive management of EU affairs. Instead, the "path dependence" approach (Pierson, 2000) provides a more appropriate theoretical framework for understanding. Namely, some CEE governments' non-inclusive coordination and management system of EU affairs in the post-accession has proved path-dependent. This means that decisions about specific organisational configurations and "ways of doing things" (especially the "hurry-up atmosphere" around the adoption of national positions on the EU acts) taken early in the post-communist transformations, at the beginning of the EU accession negotiations, tend to last until the present (Dimitrova and Toshkov, 2007; Vidačak, 2023). This is particularly important for explaining the challenges related to using national channels of influence and Croatian interest groups' choice of EU-level strategies.

3.3 Structure and Resources of Croatian Interest Groups Engaged at the EU Level

Regarding interest groups at the EU level, Croatia is relatively comparable to other smaller and newer EU member states from CEE, which face similar challenges of the socialist heritage and lack of tradition of involvement of interest groups in policymaking. In general, there are several differences in the extent of engagement

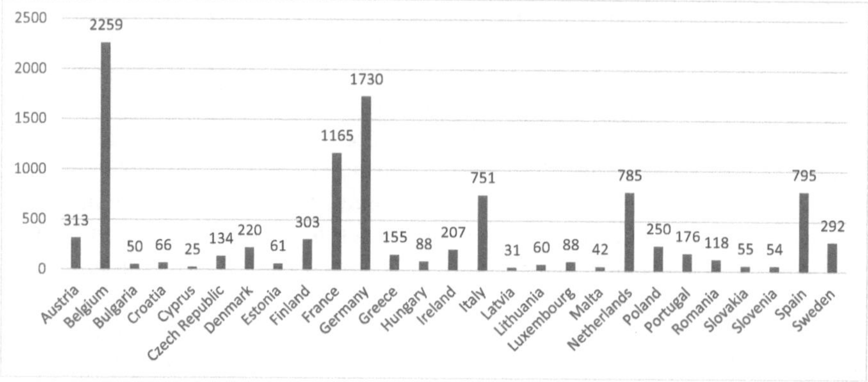

Figure 3.1 Number of interest groups from EU member states in the EU Transparency Register in October 2023.

Source: Ec.europa.eu (2023).

of interest groups from various EU member states in the EU-level policymaking processes, as indicated by the findings of the previous research on the size and scope of the EU interest group population (Dur and Mateo, 2014; Wonka et al., 2009, p. 6).

Limited research on the interest groups from Central and Eastern Europe shows that it is still rare for interest groups from these newer EU member states to enter the Brussels arena (Hafner-Fink et al., 2016; Novak and Lajh, 2019). Interest groups from older as well as bigger member states are present in the Brussels arena in a much greater number, as seen in Figure 3.1.

The types of engagement of Croatian interest groups in EU policymaking can be partly traced through the EU Transparency Register, which gathers data on interest representatives – natural or legal persons, formal or informal groups, associations or networks that engage in different communication activities to influence the formulation or implementation of policy or legislation or the decision-making processes of EU institutions, bodies, offices and agencies.

In October 2023, 66 organisations from Croatia were registered in the EU Transparency Register, with business actors (companies, professional consultancies, business associations) being the most numerous registered entities, followed by NGOs and trade unions.

The structure of representation of interests at the EU level generally mirrors their level of representation at the national level, as seen from recent trends in the participation of interest groups in national e-consultations on draft legislative and policy initiatives (Vidačak, 2022), where companies and NGOs largely dominate the national policymaking arenas. This seems to confirm the assumption of some authors about the correlation between interest associations' domestic embeddedness (i.e., their success in gaining access to domestic public actors) and their strategies for seeking access to European decision-making processes. On the other hand, the fact that the EU Transparency Register contains several organisations that are largely absent from domestic policy networks and rarely get involved in working groups/consultative bodies for drafting of national public policies or national public consultations indicates that some interest groups seek to compensate for their lack of domestic access by pursuing lobbying directly at the European level.

Out of the 66 Croatian interest groups registered in the Transparency Register, 39 organisations indicate their operations at the European level. The availability of resources and professional staff predominantly affects the choice of lobbying strategies and, more particularly, makes EU-level lobbying more demanding. The relatively low number of Croatian interest groups registered in the EU Transparency Register indicates they face challenges.

The most significant number of Croatian interest groups registered in the Transparency Register (20) state that they have one staff member engaged in lobbying but with different percentages of working time dedicated to lobbying activities at the EU level. There are 11 interest groups with 2 staff members, 13 interest groups with 3 staff members, 5 interest groups with 4 members, 4 interest groups with 5 members, 3 interest groups with 6 members, 1 interest group per 7 members, 1 with 8 members, 1 with 9 members, 1 with 10, 1 with 11 and finally 2 registered entities lists as many as 12 staff members engaged in communication with EU institutions. However, in some cases, from the explanation, it is visible that staff members work on EU project management and are only partly involved in influence-seeking and other communication activities towards EU institutions. Of the 66 Croatian interest groups registered in the Transparency Register, only six have members accredited to access the European Parliament building – two NGOs and four companies (professional consultancies).

Based on the analysis of the number of full-time equivalent employees engaged in EU lobbying activities (Table 3.1), there is a similarity in the human resources

Table 3.1 Structure and human resources of Croatian interest groups registered in the EU Transparency Register in October 2023

Category of interest group	*Number of entities in the EU Transparency Register*	*Number of full-time equivalent employees engaged in the EU lobbying activities*
Companies	19	19.2
Professional consultancies	7	10.7
Business associations	7	10.3
NGOs	23	28.7
Trade unions	3	0.4
Cooperatives	1	0.2
Professional associations	1	0.2
Universities	1	2
Research institutes	1	0.3
Public entities	3	10.1
Total	66	80.1

Source: Ec.europa.eu (2023).

available for this purpose in companies (including professional consultancies) and NGOs. This is contrary to traditional expectations about the disbalance of resources as one of the main factors of the lack of access to EU decision-makers between business actors and NGOs.

When it comes to financial resources, the Transparency Register provides the analysis of financial resources of the registered interest groups at four different levels: (i) estimated annual costs attributable to activities covered by the Register (for registrants that promote their interests or the collective interests of their members), (ii) estimated total annual revenue generated attributable to activities covered by the Register (for registrants that advance interests of their clients), (iii) total budget (for registrants that do not represent commercial interests) and (iv) total amount of EU grants in the current and most recent closed financial year.

The majority of Croatian interest groups have a limited annual budget for EU lobbying activities. For example, 21 out of 66 groups assessed their annual EU lobbying budget at lower than 25,000 EUR. In comparison, only six registered groups have a lobbying budget of more than 100,000 EUR and, therefore, have more substantial resources available for lobbying strategies at the EU level. These six groups with the most significant financial resources for EU lobbying include three companies, one business association, one sports NGO and one public agency dealing with EU project management. Besides, 15 Croatian interest groups reported the receipt of EU grants in the recent closed financial year. Among these recipients of EU grants, there are seven NGOs, three companies, two business associations, one trade union, one university and one regional public agency dealing with EU project management.

3.4 EU-Level Strategies of Croatian Interest Groups

This section explores the lobbying strategies Croatian interest groups use to achieve their goals based on data from the EU Transparency Register. Analysing the level of access of interest groups to the EU institutions, as a necessary precondition to influence, is rather demanding (Dür, 2008) and requires, among others, the systematic recording of the engagement of groups in different levels of decision-making but also formulating the preferences and goals of lobbying at the beginning of the process.

The achievement of lobbying strategies is generally linked with the ability of organisations to formulate lobbying goals. Therefore, it is essential to first look into the clarity of formulated goals of EU-level activities of Croatian interest groups, their primary areas of interest and the main legislative proposals on which lobbying is directed.

Most Croatian interest groups (35) state the goals for which the organisation was founded. However, these goals cannot be linked to the need for lobbying on the EU level (for example, "promoting the principles of sustainable development in all segments of society, at the local, regional and national level"). A smaller number of Croatian interest groups (28) state the objectives of lobbying, that is, the objectives for which it was founded and for the achievement of which it is necessary to lobby at the level of EU institutions. However, even those interest groups that list EU-level lobbying goals do not formulate these goals in a way that could be considered specific, measurable, achievable, realistic or time-bound.

Four of 66 interest groups state only one area of interest, while the other 62 groups list two or more areas of interest. The most common area of interest cited by Croatian interest groups is the environment. As many as 34 interest groups list the environment as one of the areas of interest, which is in line with the EU Green Deal priorities, which have been among the most prominent policy priorities of the EU in recent years.

In addition, the majority of Croatian interest groups (39) do not list specific legislative proposals (acts) in the adoption of which they participated or plan to participate by lobbying but only general policies or activities targeted by lobbying (for example, cohesion policy, environmental policy, standard agricultural policy, single market, artificial intelligence, health, tourism, sustainable development and climate change). A total of 32 Croatian interest groups list specific legislative proposals. However, no interest group specifies the proposal they want to push through or the provision they want to change or cancel. The lack of mention of specific EU legislative files they lobby for – by the majority of registered groups might confirm the assumption that most interest groups use the EU Transparency Register only as a source of reputational boosts and an incentive for better positioning itself in domestic policymaking arenas.

Although the Register itself does not explicitly state which lobbying strategies are used by interest groups, the following activities undertaken by interest groups when carrying out lobbying are listed: communication activities (events, campaigns, publications etc.) related to the EU policies, meetings with the European Commission, contributions to the EU-level public consultations on draft legislative initiatives, participating in the EU-level structures and platforms, inter-groups and unofficial groups in the European Parliament, expert groups of the Commission and other EU bodies, participation in other forums and platforms with the EU support.

Communication activities are used and specified in the Transparency Register by 35 Croatian interest groups. Various events, campaigns, publications, projects, conferences, round tables, panel discussions, posts on social networks, workshops, grassroots initiatives, networking, etc., are mentioned. One environmental NGO elaborated on its advocacy effort within the EU Nature Alert campaign, which brought together NGOs from EU countries to fight against the revision of EU rules on the protection of European nature (the Habitats Directive and the Birds Directive). It also stated that, after 1,161 days of persuasion, the European Commission agreed that the directives were reasonable and that they just needed to be better implemented. The action was supported by more than 520,000 people who, during the public consultation, supported a petition against changing the directives. This is an example of more specific data on lobbying activities entered in the Transparency Register.

As many as 30 interest groups do not report any data on communication activities, and six interest groups report data that can hardly be considered relevant to

EU-level communication efforts (for example, only a link to their websites or general support to the production of audiovisual activities).

Data on holding meetings with the European Commission, i.e., with commissioners, members of their cabinets or directors-general, is provided by only nine interest groups – one NGO (listing seven meetings with the European Commission), five companies (one listing five meetings with the European Commission, one listing two meetings and three mentioning one meeting each), two consultancy agencies (mentioning one meeting each) and one business association (mentioning two meetings with the European Commission) (Table 3.2). The other 57 interest groups provided no information on holding the meetings. Regarding the policy areas addressed at the meetings, energy and digital policies largely dominate. This can be explained by the substantial funding focused on the EU green and digital transition. Five of nine interest groups have held meetings with EC commissioners, cabinet members and directors general.

Regarding the meetings of Croatian interest groups with members of the European Parliament (MEPs), these are more difficult to track since the Transparency Register does not contain these data, and almost half of MEPs still do not publish their meetings with interest groups. However, it is based on the information available on the online platform Integrity Watch,[1] managed by Transparency International. Fifteen interest groups from Croatia reported meetings with various MEPs. Half of these meetings were held with Croatian NGOs, which indicates that the European Parliament is a more favoured channel of influence for civil society organisations compared to the European Commission. The meetings with NGOs were predominantly related to migration and human rights issues.

The data mentioned above about the meetings of Croatian interest groups with the European Commission and European Parliament confirm the findings and theoretical expectations from previous research, which build on Bouwen's basic exchange model of access (Bouwen, 2002) and expand it to various private and public interest groups (Michalowitz, 2004). Namely, technical expertise and information are assumed to grant business entities/private interest groups better access to the European Commission, and "expertise about the national situation" is assumed to be translated as more access to the Council of the EU for national firms (Michalowitz, 2004; Chalmers, 2013). On the other hand, NGOs and other actors of organised civil society (public interest groups) are expected to possess information about "public support" and are mainly focused on Parliament, but usually cannot generate technical and expert information and are constantly appealing to general principles which makes their informational contribution to EU institutions less valuable (Chalmers, 2013; Dür and de Bievre, 2007).

The next lobbying strategy used by Croatian interest groups is sending written contributions within the framework of public consultations on draft legislative and policy initiatives. Only 13 interest groups provide information about giving answers within the framework of public consultations (seven from the category of NGOs, two from the category of enterprises, one from the category of trade and business associations, one from the category "other organisations, public or mixed subjects", one from the category of academic institutions and one from the category

Table 3.2 Meetings of Croatian interest groups with the European Commission officials

Interest group	*Category*	*Number of meetings with EC*	*Number of EC officials attending meetings*			*Policy areas discussed*
			Commissioner	*Cabinet Member*	*Director General*	
Youth Sports Games – Association for Sport, Recreation and Education	NGO	8	5	4		Youth, sports
Infobip	Company	5	1	3	1	Digital policy
Croatian Employers' Associations	Business association	2	2			Industry, green transition, demography
Končar Elektroindustrija d.d.	Company	2	2	2		Energy, environment
EuroNavigator Public Affairs	Professional consultancy	2		3		Agriculture, energy
Rimac Technology d.o.o.	Company	1	1	1		Smart transport and mobility
Aircash	Company				1	Financial services, capital markets
Project 3 Mobility	Company			1		Smart mobility
Vlahovic Group	Professional consultancy			1		Energy

Source: Ec.europa.eu (2023).

Note: Meetings between December 2014 and October 2024.

of associations and networks of public authorities). Although generally considered one of the most frequent EU-level lobbying strategies, participation in the EU-level public policy consultations was not mentioned by 53 Croatian interest groups. Even a smaller number of groups take part in the initial phase of consultations on draft roadmaps on concepts of EU policies where only two interest groups (one from NGOs and another from business associations) confirmed their involvement at that stage of policymaking.

Besides, none of the interest groups that had access to meetings with the European Commission's officials (as a more direct lobbying strategy) have submitted any written contributions to public consultations. This indicates that the use of public consultations as a lobbying channel may be perceived as a "weapon of the week" or strategy used mainly through stakeholders with less potential for access to the highest officials in the European Commission during the policy formulation process.

The following technique used by Croatian interest groups is joining or becoming members of various EU-level consultative bodies or platforms where they have more privileged access to policymakers. Only one business association stated the use of that strategy.

In this context, it is essential to mention two EU advisory bodies as relevant institutional channels for interest groups to formally get engaged in the EU legislative and policy processes: the European Economic and Social Committee (EESC) and the Committee of Regions (CoR). There are nine representatives of Croatian socio-economic organised interests in the EESC – three from each group – employers/business associations, trade unions and various Civil Society Organisations (CSOs). Similarly, the interests of local and regional government associations are formally represented in the EU CoR, where associations of municipalities, cities and counties, altogether have nine representatives (three per group). Previous research indicates that the influence of these two advisory bodies is still somewhat limited, primarily due to their focus on consensus-building and lack of use of own-initiative opinions in the earliest stage of policymaking. Therefore, they are used chiefly as indirect channels of pressure when more direct and efficient venues of access and influence are not available (Munta, 2017; Tatham, 2015).

A less formal channel of influence – the participation in inter-groups and other unofficial meetings of the European Parliament – is used by a total of 18 groups – 1 academic institution, 9 NGOs, 4 companies, 1 consultancy agency, 1 trade union, 1 professional association and 1 association of public authorities. It is essential to mention that only interest groups registered in the Transparency Register can participate in inter-group activities or other unofficial activities organised on the premises of the Parliament, for example, by attending meetings or events of inter-groups or other unofficial groups, providing support for events or participating as hosts.

One of the most prominent EU-level channels of influence of interest groups is the participation in expert groups of the Commission and other similar entities in the earliest phase of drafting the documents by the European Commission services or monitoring the implementation of different acts and, therefore, influencing also the evaluation reports with proposals of reformulation of EU-level policies. A total of nine groups list the participation in the EC expert groups – one academic institution, two NGOs, two companies, one trade union and one professional association, two associations and networks of public authorities.

The European networking or membership in different EU-level associations, confederations, unions or networks is indicated by 57 groups, indicating that EU-level networks are still considered a vital channel of influence by Croatian interest groups. This is also confirmed by one of the interviewees who specifically stressed the reliance on the EU networks for timely access to EU decision-makers, primarily due to the lack of financial and human resources for direct lobbying of EU institutions.[2]

3.5 Limitations of the Interest Groups' Use of National Channels for Influencing EU Policymaking

The access of Croatian interest groups to the national decision-making processes regarding the formulation of national positions in the Council of the EU is generally considered to be limited ever since the start of the EU accession process of Croatia (Vidačak and Škrabalo, 2014). It has remained such during the first ten years of EU membership.

To gain more in-depth insights into the factors influencing the role and level of access of organised interests to the process of formulation of national preferences in the Council of the EU, additional primary data was collected from 15 qualitative semi-structured interviews. These concerned representatives from Croatian government bodies, members of the Parliament and representatives of interest groups acting as permanent external members to relevant parliamentary committees. The author conducted the interviews in May 2021.

Croatian ministries do not organise any consultations on draft national positions on acts in the procedure in the Council and have never tried to use the existing, well-functioning central government e-consultation portal for that purpose. The explanation for this lack of inclusiveness in managing EU affairs can be found in the official government clarification after each government session, where national positions in the Council are discussed behind closed doors. In short, the government states that positions are still to be negotiated with other member states and, therefore, can be changed, which makes them not susceptible to more comprehensive public consultations.

This approach reflects the same attitude used by the government during the pre-accession process. It illustrates the path-dependency of the choices taken before the accession and also in the post-accession period. A somewhat different perspective is provided by an interviewed government representative, who states that the lack of human resources and reluctance to do additional work prevents ministries from the proactive, timely publication of positions and organising structured dialogue with interested stakeholders.[3]

As regards the Croatian Permanent Representation in the EU, based on the published list of meetings of the Head/Deputy Head of Representation with interest groups,[4] it is visible that only business interest groups use this specific national channel of direct influence on Croatian positions in the Council. Namely, from October 2019 until October 2023, five Croatian companies and one business association met with the Head or Deputy Head of Permanent Representation. Since the Permanent Representation can intervene with its proposals and suggestions at every stage of preparing national positions, this can be considered an alternative access point for more experienced and resourceful interest groups already registered in the EU Transparency Register. However, such a limited number of meetings with Croatian interest groups indicates their low interest and capacity for using this channel.

Without formal consultation mechanisms between Croatian government bodies and interest groups on draft national positions on EU acts, the main possible national channel of influence remains the Croatian Parliament. According to the Law on Cooperation between Croatian Parliament and Government in managing EU affairs (Croatian Parliament, 2013), the Parliament Committee for European Affairs reviews the selected national positions of the government in the Council and can request the government to conduct and include an impact assessment for the EU act in the Parliament Annual Work Programme for Considering Positions of the Republic of Croatia, in line with the Law on Regulatory Impact Assessment. However, since the entry of Croatia into the EU, the Parliament has never used this provision to question the possible financial, economic, social, environmental and other costs or benefits of the future implementation of planned EU acts in Croatia (Vidačak, 2023).

Based on the Rules of Procedures of the Croatian Parliament, 24 parliamentary committees have 116 permanent external members from various organised interests – NGOs, trade unions, employers' associations, universities, media etc.

Representatives on these committees are selected from the public and receive modest monthly compensation for their work in committees. This practice was introduced in 2008 based on an initiative of civil society organisations and has been considered a significant achievement during the EU accession process of Croatia (Vidačak and Škrabalo, 2014, p. 176). The external members have direct access to discussions on national framework positions on EU acts discussed in the Council of the EU – within their competence in the relevant committee. In addition, the sessions of the parliamentary committees where these national positions are discussed can be attended by other interested parties (guests) – based on requests sent to the responsible parliamentary committee and reviewed prior to attendance. Table 3.3 provides an overview of organised interest categories represented by external members of the Croatian Parliament.

Based on an interview with an external member of the European Affairs Committee of the Croatian Parliament, one of the main obstacles to the effective use of parliamentary committees for influencing the national positions of the government lies in how these representatives are chosen and their closeness to the ruling party. Besides, there is an awareness that the preparation of amendments to national positions of the government requires additional severe expert efforts from external members of interest groups. In contrast, the representatives of government bodies often create the impression that the positions they are presenting to the Parliament

Table 3.3 Overview of interest groups represented in parliamentary committees serving as accountability forum in developing national positions in the Council of the EU

Category of interest groups	*Number of external members of parliamentary committees*
Business associations, chambers of commerce/crafts	5
Companies/consultancy firms/law firms	13
Professional associations	2
Trade unions	2
Non-governmental organisations	20
Academic institutions, think tanks and research organisations	37
Organisations representing churches and religious communities	2
Organisations representing local, regional and municipal authorities, other public or mixed entities etc.	11
Self-employed consultants, individual (non-affiliated) experts	18
Media	6

Source: Vidačak (2022).

are already finalised and that there is no time for amending their content.[5] A representative of an NGO active in the Parliamentary Environment Committee pointed out that the materials for the sessions of the Parliamentary Committee are usually submitted relatively late, not leaving adequate time for studying materials for the session and mobilising relevant expertise within associations/groups that have nominated their representative in the committee.[6]

Overall, the government's non-transparent management of EU affairs, the lack of time and human resources in ministries for organising proper consultations and the weak accountability mechanisms in the Parliament contribute to the low use of national channels of influencing EU policymaking by Croatian interest groups.

3.6 Conclusions

The complex and competitive environment for interest representation in the EU policymaking puts national interest groups under growing pressure to change their behaviour and develop dual or multi-level strategies, promoting their interests before domestic and EU institutions. However, ten years after the entry of Croatia into the EU, the level of engagement of Croatian interest groups in the EU policymaking processes is still very low, and they still do not adequately use a variety of access points offered by the EU multi-level governance system.

The data gathered from the EU Transparency Register indicates that a minimal number of Croatian groups recognise the need for developing EU-level strategies of lobbying regarding the EU policy initiatives from their areas of work. Even a smaller number of registered entities indicates the use of available EU-level channels of influence, such as meetings with EU policymakers or engagement in the EU public policy consultations on draft legislative and policy initiatives. This might be related to the lack of human and financial resources for EU-level lobbying, as seen from the data on the number of involved staff and the minimal budget of the majority of registered entities.

Regarding the national channels of influence, the situation is even more challenging, primarily due to the Croatian government's non-transparent management of EU affairs and the lack of access to national positions in the Council of the EU. Even the existing oversight mechanisms by the Croatian Parliament are not adequately used. During the first ten years of Croatian membership in the EU, both parliamentary deputies and interest groups engaged as external members of parliamentary committees have not demonstrated their capacities to suggest any amendments or changes to Government national positions discussed in these committees. In other words, the government enjoys considerable autonomy in managing EU affairs, and the role of the Parliament and broader civil society is marginalised in this regard. These findings from the Croatian case largely contest the validity of theoretical assumptions of liberal intergovernmentalism. They can have broader implications for the study of the socio-economic interests in the national preference formulation in the EU institutions in other post-communist EU member states.

In general, the lack of open communication and consultation mechanisms on EU affairs in Croatia may only contribute to increasing the feeling of distance between EU institutions and citizens, which can also be manifested through the low turnout in European elections. Besides, the lack of use of any mechanisms for the impact assessment of the implementation of the planned EU acts in Croatia may contribute to increasing the costs of EU membership in the medium and long term.

Notes

1 The list of meetings of Croatian interest groups with MEPs can be searched via the Integrity Watch online platform: www.integritywatch.eu
2 Interview with a representative of the Association of Trade Unions, 18.5.2021.
3 Interview with a representative of the Croatian government, 25.5.2021.
4 The list of meetings can be accessed at: https://mvep.gov.hr/predstavnistvo-94070/transparentnost/sastanci/180023
5 Interview with a representative of a professional consultancy firm, 21.5.2021.
6 Interview with a representative of an environmental NGO, 29.5.2021.

References

Beyers, J. (2002) 'Gaining and seeking access: The European adaptation of domestic interest associations', *European Journal of Political Research*, 41(5), pp. 585–612.

Binderkrantz, A. (2005) 'Interest group strategies: Navigating between privileged access and strategies of pressure', *Political Studies*, 53(4), pp. 694–715.

Binderkrantz, A. S. and Rasmussen, A. (2015) 'Comparing the domestic and the EU lobbying context: Perceived agenda-setting influence in the multi-level system of the European Union', *Journal of European Public Policy*, 22(4), pp. 552–569. DOI: 10.1080/13501763.2015.1008553

Bouwen, P. (2002) 'Corporate lobbying in the European Union: The logic of access', *Journal of European Public Policy*, 9(3), pp. 365–390. DOI: 10.1080/13501760210138796

Chalmers, A. W. (2013) 'Trading information for access: Informational lobbying strategies and interest group access to the European Union', *Journal of European Public Policy*, 20(1), pp. 39–58.

Croatian Parliament (2013) *Law on the Cooperation of the Croatian Parliament and the Government of the Republic of Croatia in European Affairs*. Available at: www.sabor.hr/en/information-access/important-legislation/act-co-operation-croatian-parliament-and-government (21.11.2023).

De Bruycker, I. and Beyers, J. (2019) 'Lobbying strategies and success: Inside and outside lobbying in European Union legislative politics', *European Political Science Review*, 11(1), pp. 57–74.

Dimitrova, A. and Toshkov, D. (2007) 'The dynamics of domestic coordination of EU policy in the new and candidate member-states: Impossible to lock-in?', *West European Politics*, 30, pp. 961–986.

Dür, A. (2008) 'Measuring interest group influence in the EU: A note on methodology', *European Union Politics*, 9(4), pp. 559–576.

Dür, A. and de Bièvre, D. (2007) 'Inclusion without influence? NGOs in European trade policy', *Journal of Public Policy*, 27(1), pp. 79–101.

Dür, A. and Mateo, G. (2012) 'Who lobbies the European Union? National interest groups in a multi-level polity', *Journal of European Public Policy*, 19(7), pp. 969–987. DOI: 10.1080/13501763.2012.672103

Dür, A. and Mateo, G. (2014) 'The Europeanization of interest groups: Group type, resources and policy area', *European Union Politics*, 15(4), pp. 572–594. Available at: https://doi.org/10.1177/1465116514532556 (21.11.2023).

Ec.europa.eu (2023) *Transparency Register*. Available at: https://ec.europa.eu/transparencyregister/public/homePage.do?redir=false&locale=en#en (21.11.2023).

Eising, R. (2008) 'Interest groups in EU policy-making', *Living Reviews in European Governance*, 3(4), pp. 4–23.

Fink-Hafner, D. (2014) 'Post-accession politicisation of national EU policy coordination: The case of Slovenia', *Public Administration*, 92(1), pp. 39–54.

Gueguen, D. (2007) *European Lobbying*. Brussels: Europolitics,

Hafner-Fink, M., Novak, M., Fink-Hafner, D., Eising, R., Daniel, R. and Rozbicka, P. (2016) 'Giants and dwarfs: The multi-level lobbying strategies of national interest organisations', *Teorija in Praksa*, 53(3), pp. 605–624.

Hooghe, L. and Marks, G. (2001) *Multi-Level Governance and European Integration*. Lanham, MD: Rowman and Littlefield.

Jordan, A. (2001) 'The European Union: An evolving system of multi-level governance… or government?', *Policy and Politics*, 29(2), pp. 193–208. DOI: 10.1332/0305573012501305

Klüver, H. (2010) 'Europeanization of lobbying activities: When national interest groups spill over to the European level', *Journal of European Integration*, 32(2), pp. 175–191. DOI: 10.1080/07036330903486037

Marks, G. (1993) 'Structural policy and multi-level governance in the EC', in A. Cafruny and G. Rosenthal (eds.) *The State of the European Community: The Maastricht Debate and Beyond*. Boulder, CO: Lynne Rienner, pp. 391–411.

Marks, G., Hooghe, L. and Blank, K. (1996) 'European integration from the 1980s: State-centric v. multi-level governance', *Journal of Common Market Studies*, 34(3), pp. 341–378. DOI: 10.1111/j.1468-5965.1996.tb00577.x

Michalowitz, I. (2004) *EU Lobbying – Principals, Agents and Targets. Strategic Interest Intermediation in EU Policymaking.* Münster: LIT Verlag.

Moravcsik, A. (1993) 'Preferences and power in the European Community: A liberal intergovernmentalist approach', *Journal of Common Market Studies*, 31(4), pp. 473–524. DOI: 10.1111/j.1468-5965.1993.tb00477.x

Moravcsik, A. (1998) *The Choice for Europe: Social Purpose and State Power from Messina to Maastricht.* Ithaca: Cornell University Press.

Munta, M. (2017) 'Europski gospodarski i socijalni odbor: Kula od karata ili utvrda civilnog društva?', *Politička Misao*, 54(3), pp. 30–63.

Novak, M. and Lajh, D. (2019) 'Entering the Brussels arena: Slovenian interest groups and the pursuit of a dual strategy', *Southeast European and Black Sea Studies*, 19(2), pp. 315–331. DOI: 10.1080/14683857.2019.1568665

Pérez-Solórzano Borragán, N. (2004) 'EU accession and interest politics in central and Eastern Europe', *Perspectives on European Politics and Society*, 5(2), pp. 243–272. DOI: 10.1080/15705850408438887

Petak, Z., Vidačak, I. and Dvorny, D. (2019) 'Interest groups in Croatia: Institutional development, strategies, and influence', *Journal of Public Affairs*, 19(2), pp. e1718. Available at: https://onlinelibrary.wiley.com/doi/10.1002/pa.1718 (21.11.2023).

Pierson, P. (2000) 'Increasing returns, path dependence, and the study of politics', *The American Political Science Review*, 94(2), pp. 251–267.

Pritoni, A. (2019) 'Preferring Rome to Brussels: Mapping interest group Europeanisation in Italy', *South European Society and Politics*, 24(4), pp. 441–462. DOI: 10.1080/13608746.2020.1728958

Radaelli, C. (2003) 'The Europeanization of public policy', in K. Featherstone and C. Radaelli (eds.) *The Politics of Europeanization.* Oxford: Oxford University Press, pp. 27–56.

Rybář, M. (2011) 'National determinants of international preferences in post-communist Europe: The case of Slovakia in the European Union', *Communist and Post-Communist Studies*, 44(3), pp. 161–171. DOI: 10.1016/j.postcomstud.2011.06.001

Schimmelfenning, F. (2018) 'European integration (theory) in times of crisis: A comparison of the euro and Schengen Crisis', *Journal of European Public Policy*, 25(7), pp. 969–989.

Stephenson, P. (2013) 'Twenty years of multi-level governance: 'Where does it come from? What is it? Where is it going?'', *Journal of European Public Policy*, 20(6), pp. 817–837. DOI: 10.1080/13501763.2013.781818

Tatham, M. (2015) 'Regional voices in the European Union: Subnational influence in multilevel politics', *International Studies Quarterly,* 59(2), pp. 387–400.

Töller, A. E. (2010) 'Measuring and comparing the Europeanization of national legislation: A research note', *JCMS: Journal of Common Market Studies*, 48, pp. 417–444. Available at: https://doi.org/10.1111/j.1468-5965.2009.02058.x (21.11.2023).

Vidačak, I. (2007) *Lobiranje i kanali utjecaja interesnih skupina u proširenoj Europskoj Uniji: mogućnosti i izazovi za Hrvatsku.* Zagreb: Planetopija

Vidačak, I. (2022) 'Beyond usual suspects? Inclusion and influence of non-state actors in online public consultations in Croatia', *Social Sciences*, 11: 436, pp. 1–15. DOI: 10.3390/socsci11100436

Vidačak, I. (2023) 'The role of organised interests in shaping Croatia's negotiating positions in the Council of the EU', *East European Politics*, 39(2), pp. 345–365. DOI: 10.1080/21599165.2022.2120474

Vidačak, I. and Škrabalo, M. (2014) 'Exploring the effects of Europeanization on the openness of public administration in Croatia', *Croatian and Comparative Public Administration*, 14(1), pp. 149–187.

Wonka, A., Baumgartner, R., Mahoney, C. and Berkhout, J. (2009) 'Measuring the size and scope of the EU interest group population', Paper prepared for *the 5th ECPR General Conference, Potsdam, Germany, 10–12 September 2009*, pp. 1–20. Available at: https://fbaum.unc.edu/papers/ECPR-2009-IG-Population.pdf (27.04.2024).

4 Reform of Croatian Public Administration

Challenges, Results, and Role of the EU

Gordana Marčetić, Romea Manojlović Toman and Iva Lopižić

4.1 Introduction

In the aftermath of the collapse of socialism and gaining independence in 1991, Croatia began rebuilding its public administration system as part of a democratic and economic transition. Following a War of Independence (1991–1995) and post-war institution-building focusing on reducing war's political, economic, and social consequences, the EU integration process was initiated in 2000. The EU had a decisive role during the pre-accession period when reform measures were required to comply with EU accession criteria. In the post-accession period, this pressure has lessened, but the role of the EU remains strong. Nowadays, the EU exerts its impact through annual reports and recommendations on public administration within the European semester, financial assistance through EU funds, and financial assistance for realising projects planned in the National Recovery and Resilience Plan. The chapter aims to assess how the Croatian public administration has responded to EU demands, what reform measures have been undertaken and the results thereof, and what challenges remain.

After a brief overview of the European Union's impact on the public administration systems of its member states, the chapter describes the reform measures implemented in Croatia due to the Europeanisation process in five crucial areas: (i) structures and organisation, (ii) policymaking and implementation, (iii) civil service and human resources (potentials) management, (iv) transparency and accountability, (v) service delivery and digitalisation. These reform areas follow the EU categorisation of the most crucial public administration topics (Koprić, 2018a). The analysis of the results, challenges, and the role of the EU in these areas are given in the last part of the chapter.

Methodologically, the chapter relies on primary and secondary sources. The primary sources are the interviews with seven persons: five high-level civil servants from the Ministry of Justice and Public Administration (MJPA), one civil servant from the Government Office for Legislation (GOL), the first Information Commissioner in Croatia (2013–2018).[1] Furthermore, the personal insides of one of the authors, Gordana Marčetić, who performed the function of the first president of the Ethical Committee (2009–2015) and performs the function of deputy president of the Council for the Implementation of the Code of Conduct for State Officials

DOI: 10.4324/9781003394013-4

in Executive Bodies (from 2023), were also important. The interviews were semi-structured around five thematic areas – main developments in the respective administrative area, the evaluation of the EU and national impact on these developments, the administrative capacities, and remaining challenges. The secondary sources are the official reports and scientific papers written mainly by Croatian public administration scientists – members of the Chairs of Administrative Sciences at the Faculty of Law in Croatia.

4.2 European Union and Croatian Public Administration

The EU enlargement has enriched the discussion about the concept of European Administrative Space (EAS), which is defined as a "set of values and social and citizens' expectations, governance principles and standards of public administration organisation and functioning defined by law, whose application is supported by the appropriate procedures and accountability mechanisms" (Koprić, 2017, p. 31). The principles and standards of the EAS, most notably the principles of the rule of law, openness and transparency, responsibility, efficiency and effectiveness, proportionality, subsidiarity, coherence, and participation (Koprić et al., 2012, pp. 140–141), have become the essential prerequisites for the EU accession and basic principles according to which the public administration of all member states should function. The EAS principles were created by different European actors, most notably EU institutions (the Court of Justice of the European Union, the European Parliament, European Council, the Council of the European Union, the European Commission), facilitated by civil servants' contacts, learning, and exchanges, and supported by the expectations of the European citizens (Kovač, 2017, p. 9; Koprić et al., 2012, p. 143). In transitional countries, the recognition of EAS principles and standards and their implementation in domestic public administration was greatly supported by the work of SIGMA, established in 1992 as a joint initiative of the EU and OECD. SIGMA has prepared several reports and papers, including Paper n. 27, which contains and explains the main EAS principles (SIGMA, 1999). The Council of Europe also has a vital role in forming EAS.

The EU suffers from an implementation deficit since it must rely on the public administration of the member states to carry out the EU policies coherently. This fact makes the administrative capacities of national member states an essential prerequisite for ensuring compliance with the EAS principles and standards. In the broadest sense, administrative capacities are understood as the capability of public administration to participate and implement EU policies, to implement the European *acquis communautaire*, and to accept standards regarding the civil servants' system. The strengthening of administrative capacities requires legal, organisational, functional, personal, and other types of changes in the public administration of a single country (Koprić et al., 2012, pp. 166–171). Since the European Council meeting in Madrid in 1995, administrative (institutional) capacities have become a precondition for EU accession.

The idea of the EAS is harmonising and converging member states' public administrations towards a standard model. However, in practice, it has been proved that complete convergence is impossible to achieve (Musa, 2006, pp. 139–142). According to Pollitt (2002, cited in Koprić et al., 2012, p. 139), there are four different phases of convergence: talk – when a specific concept is widely discussed among member states; decision – when specific procedures, and methods, organisational forms, and structures are being formally accepted; action – when particular new method, technique, or procedure is being implemented in practice; and results – when there is convergence in the obtained results. The existence of different phases of convergence explains why there are differences in the degree of Europeanisation across member states or certain reform areas (Koprić et al., 2012, p. 68; Musa, 2014, pp. 243–256). The effects of Europeanisation were, at first sight, more substantial in the new EU member states because they had to transform their public administration structures and procedures to meet the conditions of joining the EU. In reality, the level of convergence in these countries mostly stops at the phases of talk and decisions – specific measures are being formally accepted but not implemented as they should have been. This represents a so-called shallow Europeanisation in which the states formally reform a particular area by accepting new laws, practices, or structures as one of the EU requirements. However, there is no more profound transformation of the institutions (Koprić et al., 2012, p. 68; Musa, 2014, pp. 243–256).

Croatia signed the Stabilization and Association Agreement in 2001. After a decade of negotiation, the accession treaty was signed on 9 December 2011, and Croatia became a member state on 1 July 2013. In its 2012 Report, the EU Commission stated that "further efforts are needed to improve the professionalism of the public service" and that "taking into account the additional responsibilities related to EU membership, Croatia should address without delay the administrative capacity constraints" (EC, 2012, p. 3). In its 2013 Monitoring Report on Croatia's accession preparations, the EC (2013, p. 14) has concluded that "Croatia is generally meeting the commitments and requirements arising from the accession negotiations, in all chapters". Nevertheless, a pre-accession period represented a "legislative tsunami" period in which numerous legislative changes have been made. However, the question is whether these changes were sufficient to increase the administrative capacities in all the areas.

4.3 Reform Areas

4.3.1 Development of Croatian Public Administration before EU Accession

Croatian public administration has undergone a few significant reform phases (Koprić et al., 2021a, pp. 386–408), of which the EU had influenced the last two. In the first foundation phase (1990–1993), the structures from the previous socialist period remained unchanged. However, the personal structure of civil service changed according to the political preferences of the leading party (ibid., p. 387). In the second consolidation phase (1993–2001), the foundations of the Croatian public administration model were set by adopting legislation on the organisation of state and local self-government systems in 1993 to ensure a centralistic model of state governance. The system of local self-government was transformed, with the previous 100 communes transformed into more than 500 municipalities and towns and 20 counties established as second-level units with dual functions as self-governing and state administration units. The system of state administration was transformed as well. Central state administration consisted of state ministries, ministries, and state administration organisations that took over the majority of tasks previously exercised by the communes. Relying on the figure of the county governor as state territorial representative and dense network of deconcentrated state administration, the central state heavily controlled all processes in local self-governing units (Koprić, 2001). This period was characterised by nationalisation, centralisation, politicisation, and authoritarian political leadership (Koprić et al., 2021a, p. 387). In 1994, the first law on civil servants and state employees was passed. The law introduced significant elements of the career system – regular salary promotion and advancement in titles for civil servants (three to five years), which was later replaced by the position-based system. However, there was legal chaos in local self-government because there was no similar law for local and regional public servants; instead, the provisions of the Law on Administration (1978) from the socialist period were applied in an "appropriate" way (Marčetić, 2005, pp. 302–305).

In 2000, the Europeanisation phase began with the change in the ruling party from the right to the centre-left wing coalition and the signing of the Stabilization and Association Agreement. In this phase, some necessary reforms took place. Concerning structures and organisation, the position of local self-government units was improved by the adoption of a new Law on Local and Territorial (Regional) Self-Government, legislative changes of sectoral legislation that enabled the decentralisation of education, health, and social services in 2001, and complete ratification of the European Charter of Local Self-Government in 2007. The role of county governors as state territorial representatives was abolished, and counties became solely second-level self-governing units. Some rationalisation measures in deconcentrated state administration accompanied this process. Despite certain progress in democratising the territorial dimension of the Croatian public administration, the fragmentation of state and local structures that hindered both vertical and horizontal coordination remained unaddressed.

On the contrary, the fragmentation was further accelerated by the proliferation of ministerial branch offices as well as agency types of organisations as a direct result of the Europeanisation process. Europeanisation has also pushed the regionalisation process, with statistical regions being formed and the first Act on Regional Development adopted in 2009. However, these legislative changes needed to be stronger to incite structural changes and simplifications or to increase counties' capacities for coordinated implementation of regional policies.

As for policymaking and implementation, the most important steps were introducing the regulatory impact assessment (RIA) process and public consultations. The RIA was first introduced in 2005 on the influence of the World Bank's Programmatic Adjustment Loan, while the Code of Practice on Consultation with Interested Public in the Process of Adopting Laws, Other Regulations and

Policies was adopted in 2010. A special Office for RIA was established in 2007. However, the Office did not produce results, and the media attacked its work, so it was abolished in 2009 (Koprić, 2018b, p. 52). With the new RIA Act of 2011, all the RIA tasks were assigned to the GOL. However, Croatia has entered the EU with limited capacities for policy planning and deficiencies in the spheres of public consultations and RIA, with a limited number of consultations undertaken and a limited number of acts undergoing the RIA procedure.

In civil service and human potential management, the most important is adopting the new Civil Servants Act in 2006 due to the EU-financed CARDS 2001 project (Marčetić and Musa, 2013). The Act set up common rules for recruitment procedures, which was considered a significant novelty. However, some basic institutes of human potential management (HPM), such as the classification of jobs, promotions, salaries, and remunerations, were left to different by-laws, some of which had never been enacted (Marčetić, 2007, p. 289). Due to deficiencies in HPM and the civil service system, the Human Potential Development Strategy for the 2010–2013 period was adopted. The Strategy should have been a qualitative framework for attracting and promoting highly competent, professional, dedicated, and motivated individuals in civil service (see more in Marčetić and Prelec, 2011). Nevertheless, the Strategy was too ambitious, so its goals were never achieved. Two positive steps forward in this period were the establishment of the State School for Public Administration (2010, OG 144/10, 62/12, 112/12, 72/15, 84/18) with a task to provide programmes for professional training and development for civil and public servants, and the setting up of the central payroll system and database for all central level civil and public servants.

The developments in transparency and accountability started with the first Act on Access to Public Sector Information, adopted in 2003 and amended in 2010. In 2006 the first Code of Ethics for Civil Servants was adopted, but only at the declarative level. Tangible steps were taken two years later when a new Code of Ethics for civil servants was adopted as part of the Anti-corruption Strategy. This step established an institutional framework for reporting unethical behaviours and strengthening ethical principles. The Code of Ethics for civil servants set up ethics commissioners in all state bodies and an independent second instance body – the Ethics Committee, as the primary mechanisms for determining unethical behaviour by civil servants. Unfortunately, the new Code of Ethics that entered into force in 2011 reduced the powers of the Ethics Committee. In the meantime, some state and public organisations have adopted their codes (Marčetić, 2013, pp. 11–12). The work on anti-corruption is presented as permanent tasks, although the results are still unsatisfactory. The first National Plan for Fight Against Corruption was adopted in 2002, followed by different Strategies for Combat Corruption adopted in 2008 and 2015. To fulfil the EU accession criteria in 2003, the first Act on the Prevention of Conflicts of Interest was adopted.

In 2009, as the result of the EU-financed CARDS project, the new Law on General Administrative Procedure Act (GAPA) was adopted to modernise administrative procedures that the more than 50-year-old GAPA regulated. However, the new GAPA has allowed for continuing with the old practices (Đulabić, 2009). In parallel, in 2010, the administrative justice system was transformed, and except for one, four first instances, administrative courts, and one high administrative court were established. The first steps towards digitalisation of Croatian public administration were set by the GAPA in 2009, which enabled electronic communication with public law bodies in numerous phases of administrative procedure. However, this was not fully functional in the pre-accession period, and proper development in this area mainly started in the post-accession period.

4.3.2 Reforms after the EU Accession

4.3.2.1 Organisation and Structures

The fragmentation of state and local structures in Croatia has been one of the main criticisms in EC reports on Croatia (EC, 2018, p. 51). This problem has also been acknowledged during the interviews with MJPA civil servants, who stated that even though the EU acquis does not directly influence central state administration and local self-government structures, domestic political actors considered EU criticism in shaping their political agenda and put rationalisation of administrative structures as one of the national priorities in government strategies.[2]

In this period, some cosmetic changes were introduced in state administration and local self-government system, officially proclaimed as measures aimed at its rationalisation but without natural effect on the simplification of state and territorial structures. In 2019, the new State Administration Act was adopted, and central state offices as a type of state administration bodies and county state administration offices as first-instance state administration bodies were abolished. The number of central state administration bodies was reduced from 32 to 28. These changes failed to achieve the proclaimed goals of rationalisation. Firstly, central state offices have not been abolished but only reclassified to the group of state administration bodies. Secondly, the abolition of 20 county state administration offices has yet to lead to the rationalisation of deconcentrated state administration since its fragmentation arises from a dense network of ministerial deconcentrated units whose number has been constantly increasing, reaching the number of 1464 in 2018. Also, rationalisation through reducing the number of state civil servants is not feasible since these civil servants were transferred to county self-government or got high severance pay (Lopižić and Manojlović Toman, 2019, pp. 860–861). However, rationalisation in the state administration system was realised by merging 17 business inspections under the State Inspectorate in 2019 that were previously organised under eight-line ministries. Since 44 inspections were operating before its establishment, this measure significantly reduced fragmentation in the inspection supervision and rationalised the organisation of inspection services in territorial units (Džinić and Lopižić, 2022, p. 183).

As for the local self-government system, two measures aimed at its rationalisation were introduced. The first relates to reducing the number of deputy executive leaders by 92% and the number of local councillors by 10% and limiting their remuneration. The planned savings represent only about 4.4% of local expenditures, so the real significance of this change is questionable (Đulabić, 2021). The second measure relates to the introduction of financial incentives for local units' cooperation or their merger. This government's policy has faced serious shortcomings as only 23 municipalities (4%) responded to a public call in September 2022 and applied for financial incentives for inter-municipal cooperation (joint administrative department or joint company). Furthermore, not a single municipality showed interest in an actual merger.

However, specific steps towards rationalisation were introduced in the area of regulatory agencies, whose number was reduced from 87 in 2009 to about 70 by the end of 2017. However, since there is no unique act regulating the Croatian agency system that would be the basis for its reorganisation, efforts for further rationalisation of the agency system have stalled halfway (Musa, 2017, pp. 41–43). Additionally, some measures aimed at improving the coordination of territorial policies were introduced by the new Act on Regional Development, adopted in 2014 and amended in 2018 and 2019. The Act foresaw implementation of the principles of partnership and cooperation through regulating partner councils' work, introducing development agreements, differentiated urban categories areas, and setting foundations for more transparent regional development through monitoring, evaluation, and reporting provisions. However, the Act failed to regulate essential issues (e.g., planning areas), and some of its provisions are not applied in practice (Đulabić and Čepo, 2017, p. 556).

4.3.2.2 Policymaking and Implementation

According to the interviewee,[3] the Europeanisation process, EAS standards, and different projects financed by the EU and international organisations pushed Croatian public administration to pursue some good practices in policymaking and implementation faster than it would have been if relying on national political actors' programmes.

The first phase of the policy and law-making process (preparatory phase) has seen considerable improvements. Strategic planning has been recognised as crucial for the proper implementation of EU funds and for coherent and harmonised policymaking. An important step forward was made in 2017 when the new Act on Strategic Planning and Development Management System of the Republic of Croatia was adopted. This Act tries to amend long-term problems in the strategic planning system, especially the non-coordinated enactment of strategic acts and the uneven approach to enactment, implementation, and evaluation (GRC – Government of the Republic of Croatia, 2017, p. 1). The new Act establishes long-term, middle-term, and short-term strategic documents and requires coordination. The National Development Strategy until 2030 is prepared as the umbrella document. Despite improvements, problems continue to exist. Notably, there needs to be more capacity for strategic planning (especially on the level of local and regional units) and evidence-based policymaking (MJPA, 2022, pp. 29–30). Additionally, there is a coordination problem since the coordinating role is left to the Ministry of Regional Development and EU funds. However, it is questionable if this ministry is politically strong enough to carry out this role or if this should be done by the Centre of Government (EC, 2022, p. 2).

Croatia has also improved public consultations and RIA. The 2013 Right to Access Information Act introduced the legal obligation of all public bodies to conduct public consultations for their primary and secondary legal acts, while its amendments in 2015 introduced the "E-consultation" website. These improvements constitute the direct results of EU principles of openness and participation (Đurman, 2020, pp. 409–410). The evidence from practice indicates an increase in the use of this instrument: the number of e-consultations grew from 366 in 2015 to 1031 in 2019, with a continuing growth in the number of comments as well (Đurman, 2021, p. 7). Around 20% of the comments are accepted by the public body. However, since 43% of comments are addressed by "note taken", the participants do not know whether and in what way their comments will be incorporated into the document (Public Information Commissioner, 2022, p. 108), which gives the perception that public consultations in Croatia are just a formality (State Ombudsman, 2022, p. 25).

The same can be said for the RIA process. In 2017, the new RIA Act was adopted, requiring the government to prepare an annual legislative plan containing data on the number of laws expected to undergo the RIA procedure. In 2021, 145 laws were planned in total. However, only 85 (58.62%) of them were adopted. The RIA was planned for 20 laws but carried out only in eight cases (GOL, 2022, p. 5). Apart from the *ex-ante* evaluation, which is the basis of the RIA, there is also the *ex-post* evaluation for laws excluded from the RIA. In 2021, 11 *ex-post* evaluations were carried out (GOL, 2022, pp. 11–12). Although there are considerable improvements in this area, RIA is still conducted only for a limited number of laws. The unplanned legislative acts, common in Croatia (29% in 2021 and more than 60% in 2019 and 2020 see Škarica, 2022, p. 5), are excluded from it. This situation is partly due to the lack of personnel in the GOL and the lack of competencies necessary for policy analysis in the central state bodies (Škarica, 2022, p. 4).

The implementation and evaluation phases of the policy and law-making process show fewer improvements. One of the crucial problems in implementation is the lack of inter-ministerial coordination with the existence of a strong "silo" among the ministries (MJPA, 2022, p. 30) and the non-existence of a strong centre of government (Giljević, 2015). The evaluation of public policies and laws is weak and primarily present in the scientific literature (Koprić, 2018b, p. 56). Additionally, evidence-based law-making is lacking (cf. Lalić Novak et al., 2021). As the interview suggested,[4] the main challenge in policymaking and implementation is forming a pool of experts in analytics within each central state administration body that would be specialised and focused exclusively on analytical issues.

4.3.2.3 Civil Service and Human Resources (Potentials) Management

The HPM is "the weakest link" in Croatian public administration (MJPA, 2022, p. 28). In the interviewees' opinion, the legislative framework for HPM was significantly improved and laid down the foundations for modern HPM.[5] However, in practice, its implementation is deficient due to insufficient personal and organisational capacities of Croatian public administration.

The problems with HPM existing in the pre-accession period were repeated in Strategy of Public Administration Development 2015–2020. Again, eight ambitious goals were stated (competency model development, improvements in the in-service training, creation of the efficient and transparent selection system, career development for employees in public administration, new pay system in public administration, rationalisation in the number of employees, ethical principle respecting, development of education for public administration). However, the analysis of the Strategy implementation (Koprić et al., 2021b, pp. 5–8) showed that none of the goals has been achieved totally or even half-heartedly and that in most of them, no progress has been made.

The 2019 State Administration System Act introduced measures to depoliticise the central state administration. As stated by the interviewees,[6] these measures were directly influenced by the EU. In the 2011–2019 period, assistant ministers, who were politically appointed, directed the work of internal organisational units within the ministries and other central state bodies. As of 2019, these positions are given to top senior civil servants. The government appoints them upon public competition that requires only the interview with the minister or other politically elected head of the organisation, with no other testing. Thus, their position is still under political influence and real depoliticisation and professionalisation of state administration have yet to be realised.

In its 2018 Report, Koprić (2018a, pp. 132–134) stated that the level of professionalisation, one of the essential European standards, has declined compared to 2012. Among others, the reasons are the influence that politics has in the appointment of top senior civil servants, lack of progress in the education of senior civil servants, no results in the in-service training of civil servants, no coherent performance management system that could motivate civil servants, and a general formalistic and legalistic approach that impedes changes. The MJPA (2022, pp. 24–29) acknowledges additional problems, such as the inexistence of a proper advancement system, lack of possibilities for horizontal mobility, lack of possibility for salary promotions which lead to the creation of unnecessary managerial positions as the only way to award good civil servants, lack of performance management which impedes to distinguish the best civil servant and to manage talents in public administration effectively, the problem of unsystematic in-service training without clear criteria which civil servants are taking part in it, lack of competency evaluation as the basis for the recruitment and advancement of civil servants, as well as the problem of objectivity, validity, and organisation of state professional exams. The interviews particularly point to the lack of any retention system that should help to award the best people and guarantee their remaining in the service.[7] These are long-standing problems which are getting more pronounced with public administration losing its attractiveness. The 2020 Report (Marčetić et al., 2020, pp. 10–11) shows that the civil service was not perceived as an attractive employer. The situation has worsened, and the civil service is now facing problems in filling the vacancies. As a result, in 2022, the Civil Servants Act (CSA) had to be changed to allow civil servants to work until 67 years of age to avoid the situation in which a too high number of older civil servants would leave the service without having their replacements.

Some critical projects have reform potential, but it is still early to assess the impact they will have. The project "Development of the Competency Framework for Employees in the Public Administration" has resulted in a competency framework for public administration, which should be the basis for other HPM processes such as recruitment, performance appraisal, advancement, and in-service training. To implement the competency framework in practice, the State School of Public Administration conducted training for trainers (one course), managers (five courses), and staff of HPM departments in public organisations (five courses) during 2022 and 2023. In addition, a project dealing with the centralised recruitment system in civil service is underway, as well as preparation of the Act on salaries in public administration, which are all part of the National Recovery and Resilience Programme 2021–2026, financed through the EU's Recovery and Resilience Facility.

4.3.2.4 Transparency and Accountability

Transparency is the most visible progress in Croatian public administration in the post-accession period. As stated by the interviewee, the EU was the key catalyst for introducing principles of transparency and openness, among the main ones of the EAS.[8]

In 2013, the new Act on Access to Public Sector Information was adopted, and changes in strengthening the anti-corruption mechanisms were introduced. The Parliament elected the first Public Information Commissioner in 2014. In 2022, the Act was amended to transpose the EU directive on open data and reuse of information and specify the 14 groups of documents and data that must be proactively available on public bodies' web pages. As said by the interviewee, all these changes make this law "among the best in the world".[9] In 2021, 18,576 requests for information access were made (Public Information Commissioner, 2022, p. 8), while in 2011 and 2012, the number was higher than 50,000 requests (Koprić, 2018b, p. 47). The reduction in the number of requests shows that more information is made available and there is less need to use the right to information access. In 2020, an additional step was made, with the amendments to the Law on Local and Regional Self-Government requiring local units to publicly publish the spending of the resources, allowing this information to be easily accessible and searchable.

The Code of Ethics for Civil Servants (from 2011) did not change in the post-accession period. The number of complaints made to the Ethics Commissioners in central state bodies has continuously dropped from 425 complaints in 2015 to 276 in 2019. It is not known whether the lower number of complaints is caused by the reduction of unethical behaviour in the civil service, wrongly directed complaints that were dismissed, or the applicant's disbelief in the positive outcome of the procedure. Worryingly, there were around 25% of complaints in 2019 whose foundation could not be determined, which shows that Ethics Commissioners, which are the first instance body, are not educated enough and do not have adequate capacities to carry out the process which affects citizens' rights and diminishes the trust in ethical complaints as a reliable remedy (Marčetić and Manojlović Toman, 2022, p. 159). On the local level, the codes of ethics for local public servants are not universally adopted. There is a lack of understanding of their role (Marčetić and Vukojičić Tomić, 2016), but recently (2021), the Law on Prevention of Conflicts of Interest, following anti-corruption strategic documents, prescribed an obligation for representative bodies in local and regional self-government to adopt ethical codes to regulate the behaviour of their members, so the majority of local/regional units have done so. After different recommendations from the European Commission and Greco, the Code of Conduct for State Officials in Executive Bodies was finally adopted in 2022. The Council for monitoring its implementation was established in January 2023. The Council will also train officials on the issues the code covers. The first education for the prime minister and ministers was held at the beginning of July 2023.

The first Strategy for Combat Corruption was adopted in 2008, then in 2015, and the latest Strategy for Combat Corruption for the period 2021–2030 is presently in force. Despite these anti-corruption documents and various implementation measures they prescribe, Croatia is still lagging behind other European countries (with only Bulgaria, Hungary, and Romania having a higher corruption perception than Croatia) and struggling with low trust in government and a high corruption perception index (Grubišić and Zrinščak, 2022, pp. 78–79).

4.3.2.5 Service Delivery and Digitalisation

The digitalisation of public administration is one of the most critical tasks. However, it takes place with many challenges, primarily due to extensive fragmentation and the tendency to subject digitisation to existing processes in the organisational "silos" (MJPA, 2022, p. 20). The EU reports on the digitalisation of Croatia show that Croatia insufficiently exploits the potential of ICT to provide public e-services and other public services. Similarly, one of the interviewees concluded that the digitalisation of Croatian public administration is thriving when it comes to digitalisation, primarily due to the COVID-19 pandemic. However, some old practices and formalities (for example, using an official seal instead of just an electronic signature) have yet to vanish, which impedes the broader use of digital technologies.[10]

Digitisation of public administration is on the agenda of all government programmes and is recognised as a strategic priority in both sectoral (e.g., 2012–2020 National Health Care Strategy and Digital Maturity Schools Development Programme) and cross-sectoral (e.g., Public Administration Strategy 2015–2020, National Plan on Public Administration Development 2022–2027) national strategic documents. Additionally, some national strategic documents related to digitisation were adopted. In 2017, the e-Croatia 2020 Strategy was adopted following directives from the European Union, primarily from the Digital Agenda for Europe (EC, 2020). The Digital Croatia Strategy for the period to 2032 was adopted in 2022. The digitisation process was also encouraged by the establishment of a central state administration body specialised in digitisation issues (Central State Office for Digital Society Development) and the Council for National Information Infrastructure in 2015.

In 2014, the Act on State Information Infrastructure was adopted, aimed at defining the rights, obligations, and responsibilities of competent public sector bodies regarding establishing, developing, and managing the state information infrastructure system and the system of public registers. The 2021 amendments to GAPA broadened electronic communication in administrative procedures (initiation of administrative proceedings, disposition of administrative requests, examination procedure, delivery) (Đanić Čeko and Guštin, 2022, pp. 797–799). Consequently, different legislation enabled and facilitated further digitalisation in different areas of state activity (see EC, 2020, p. 9). In 2021, the execution of all office operations in electronic form was allowed, and the obligation on data exchange was introduced, with the parallel development of electronic services, such as e-signature and e-stamp (integration of 33 public institutions and local self-government units) (CSODSD, 2022).

The most remarkable step in the digitalisation of Croatian public administration is the introduction of digital one-stop-shop e-citizens in 2014. In 2014, 14 e-services were available to citizens. The number of e-services is constantly increasing and reaching more than 100 services used by more than 1.59 million citizens, which increased by almost 25% in the past year. In 2021, the portal was redesigned to meet the needs and ways citizens use their digital identity (CSODSD, 2022, p. 36). From 2021 onwards, the e-business portal, as an addition to the e-citizens platform, aims to offer different public services for business users in one place and has been developing (CSODSD, 2022). As for back offices that enable the realisation of the "only once principle" in citizens' interaction with public administration bodies, a big step was made by forming the Centre for Shared Services in 2019. The programme ensures the standardisation of digital services, better base connection data in all state administration bodies, the economy of the entire ICT system, safety data storage, and centralised data management. It is used by 300 public institutions (ministries, other state bodies, hospitals, etc.) (ibid.).

Even though the area of digitisation shows improvements, according to the EU (DESI, 2022), Croatia seriously lags behind other countries in some digitalisation components (low broadband speeds and high broadband prices; deficient use of interconnected registers that allow application of "only once principle"; narrow scope of digital public services available for businesses; low use of iED, eDocuments, authentic sources, and digital post).

4.4 Results, Challenges, and Role of the EU

Overall, looking at the results obtained in different reform areas, the data presented in the previous chapter and Table 4.1 show that Croatian public administration has progressed in most reform areas. However, the results still need to be improved. The area of transparency shows the best results and adherence to EAS standards. The areas of policymaking show improvements, particularly in the areas of public consultations

Table 4.1 Main results in different reform areas in the post-accession period

Reform area	*Results*
Structures and organisation	Modest progress in rationalisation of state administration (reduced number of state agencies, establishment of State Inspectorate, abolition of first-instance state administration bodies). Improvements in coordination of territorial policies (adoption of new Act on Regional Development in 2014). Cosmetic rationalisation measures in the local self-government system (reduction in number of deputy executive leaders and local councillors). All of them are not substantial reform measures.
Policymaking and implementation	Progress made in the area of strategic planning (adoption of the Act on Strategic Planning and Development Management System of the Republic of Croatia in 2017). Progress has been made in policy formulation with the 2013 Right to Access Information Act and the 2017 Regulatory Impact Assessment Act. There has been no considerable progress in the area of implementation and evaluation.
Civil service and human resources (potential) management	Legislative changes to the Civil Servants Act and numerous by-laws. Formal depoliticisation of the central state administration. No significant implementation results.
Transparency and accountability	Considerable progress in the area of transparency (introduction of Public Commissioner institution in 2014, amendments of Law on Local and Territorial (Regional) Self-Government in 2021, and Act on Access to Public Sector Information in 2022, increase in the availability of public data and proactive role of the Public Information Commissioner). Development of ethical infrastructure in civil service (adoption of Code of Conduct for State Officials in Executive Bodies in 2022 and establishment of Council for monitoring its implementation in 2023, publication of information about the officials, and the work of the Council on the official website of the MJPA). Development of ethical infrastructure in local and regional self-government (adoption of codes of ethics for members of municipal, city, and county councils, which are publicly announced). Legislative improvements in the area of anti-corruption with the adoption of the Strategy for Combat Corruption for the period 2021–2030.
Service delivery and digitalisation	Improvements with the 2014 Act on State Information Infrastructure, 2021 amendments to the General Administrative Procedure Act, and other legislation aimed at broader use of digital technologies. Introduction of digital one-stop shops (e-citizens in 2014) and back offices (Centre for Shared Services in 2019).

Source: Authors.

and RIA, but not in the policy implementation and evaluation. Steps forward were made in the area of digitalisation as well. The area of civil service and HPM shows the least progress, and there are only legislative changes which have not produced enough improvements concerning the adherence to the EAS standards. Only limited progress has been obtained in the area of structures as well, with persisting highly fragmented state and local structures hindering coordination and efficient policy formulation and implementation. The lack of progress in the areas of structures and HPM confirms the observation that Croatia, in a responsive but mainly superficial manner, made certain steps forward in adjusting its public administration's legal and institutional framework to European standards, while the core structure and internal procedures remained arguably the same (Škarica, 2018, p. 303).

Based on the last European Semester Country Report on Croatia (2020), National Plan on Public Administration Development 2022–2027, and data presented in Chapter 3, the main challenges presently existing in Croatian public administration are summarised according to the covered thematic areas (see Table 4.2).

Table 4.2 Main challenges in different reform areas

Reform area	*Challenges*
Structures and organisation	• High fragmentation at the local self-government level. • Numerous small municipalities' personnel, financial, and administrative resources do not match their responsibilities and competencies. • Significant regional disparities. • There is no legal framework regulating agency-type organisations.
Policymaking and implementation	• Constrained capacity to design and implement policies and projects and inefficient coordination between ministries. • Modern quality management systems or similar standards of public management have not been applied in public administration, or they have just begun being introduced. • There is a need for more capacity for strategic planning, especially in the local self-government system. • Lack of continuity due to frequent organisational changes, difficult communication, and coordination. • Lack of inter-ministerial coordination and non-existence of a strong centre of government. • Insufficient use of evidence-based instruments in shaping public policies and inconsistent implementation of already adopted goals and measures. • Evaluation of public policies, regardless of their importance, is rarely carried out.
Civil service and human resources (potential) management	• Lack of objective and transparent criteria for recruitment and advancement. • Too long and too complex a recruitment process. • The state administration does not conduct activities that would profile itself as an attractive employer.

(*Continued*)

Table 4.2 (Continued)

Reform area	*Challenges*
	• There is no consistent classification of jobs and work processes in the state administration and local/regional self-government. • The salary-setting framework still lacks consistent criteria across the public administration and public services, resulting in inequality. • The state administration and public services salary system needs to be more competitive. • Inexistence of a proper advancement system. • Lack of possibilities for horizontal mobility. • Deficiency in the performance appraisal system impedes distinguishing the best civil servants and effectively managing talents in public administration. • In-service training and development are not based on a competency framework and are often not tied to achieving strategic, organisational, and workplace goals. • The current system of passing the state professional exam has numerous problems and difficulties concerning the objectivity and validity of the examination and the organisation of the examination itself.
Transparency and accountability	• The level of self-initiated disclosure of information, with its informativenessss and presentation, is still unsatisfactory in terms of structure, visibility, and ease of searching. • Education for public servants and citizens and special education for public information officials and those coordinating consultations with the public are not continuous. • Training on the code of ethics and the ethical behaviour of civil servants is focused only on ethical commissioners, is primarily normative, and does not deal with practical application. • Specific education programmes on corruption, conflict of interest, and other unethical behaviours for state officials in executive bodies have not yet been developed.
Service delivery and digitalisation	• Digital technologies and the application of digital solutions still do not play a significant role in increasing the quality and efficiency of public administration work. • Croatia still does not have a satisfactory level of digitisation compared to other member states of the European Union and insufficiently exploits the potential of ICT to provide e-public services. • Existing networks of state information infrastructures do not meet the needs of public administration bodies.

Source: Authors based on the National Plan for the Development of Public Administration in the 2022–2027, European Semester Country Report on Croatia (2020) and interviews.

In his analysis, Koprić (2008, 2016) has systematised four problems in Croatian public administration. These are orientational problems (problems in the strategic approach and policymaking with the lack of evidence-based policymaking, which leads to problems in the law-making process), organisational problems (fragmentation of local self-government and overall weak capacities of counties, with the not-rational organisation of central state administration), motivational problem (politicisation of civil service, lack of motivational mechanisms for civil servants, lack of adequate education for public administration which lead to inadequate level of professionalisation and authoritarian administrative culture), and implementation problem (non-complete compliance with the EU standards in policy implementation, low ethical standards and perception of corruption, resistance to change, and underdeveloped public management). The present analysis shows that in 2023, most of the problems identified by Koprić in 2008 and 2016 continue to exist.

Some progress was made only in the sphere of orientation. Organisational, motivational, and implementational problems, to a greater extent, however, remained unresolved. The last two are becoming even more problematic due to demographic changes and decreased available workforce. The interviews with MJPA representatives confirmed that the EU accession increases the workload of national public administration and requires specific competencies from most civil servants.[11] However, motivational problems lead to the need for more adequate personnel capacity, a precondition for proper implementation of any reform measures and EU policies. Looking at the examined reform areas, the conclusion is that the problems existing in the civil service, HPM, and structures generate problems in other areas – the lack of institutional capacities produced by the fragmentation of the state and local structures and the lack of civil servants' competencies produced by the deficiencies in HPM and civil service legislation lead to the problems in policymaking, accountability, service delivery and digitalisation, openness and transparency decelerating the positive effects of Europeanisation in these areas.

The pre-accession period is characterised by more numerous reform measures than the post-accession one, primarily due to the conditionality mechanisms according to which the accession is conditioned upon fulfilment of the EU requirements. The more profound effects of these reform measures are questionable since the crucial problems of the Croatian public administration in structure and organisation, and HPM continue to persist during the post-accession period. Other areas show some progress, although not uniform.

In the post-accession period, the EU exerts its influence formally through the legislative and judicial activity of EU institutions and its financial power, mainly through EU funds, to condition the member states to implement changes in the areas where financial assistance is needed. However, the influence is also informal. In interviews[12] they have shown that contacts among civil servants and formal and informal networks (for example, the EUPAN network) act as platforms for experience and good-practice exchange. This situation points out the importance of these informal, secondary EAS-creating factors. It requires greater attention to them since they have a high progress-building potential.

The role of the EU is thus a crucial factor in undertaking different reform measures. According to some interviewees, "it would come to that, but the question is when. It is an inevitable consequence of globalisation and global changes".[13] Others state that "without the EU, there would be no progress",[14] and "If there would be no European semester, National reform programmes and stability or convergence programmes, I do not know how that would work. We would be far behind what we have now".[15] The role of the EU prevails in reform areas where the EU has a direct influence (such as transparency and openness), indicating its overall positive effects on changes and progress in Croatian public administration.

The dissimilarities in progress in different administrative areas could be explained by various intervening domestic factors, such as political, societal, and economic ones. While there is a broad political consensus on the need to digitise and make public administration more open and transparent, there is no political will to reorganise Croatian public administration or introduce changes in the civil service system and HPM. On the contrary, no government has shown the political will for a real rationalisation of state and local structures, and reforms have mostly been cosmetic or superficial. This is because such unpopular reforms are related to numerous other problems in the public administration system and society in general, so they cannot immediately give visible positive results, nor can they be implemented during the mandate of one government. So, the same story continues for decades regardless of which political party is in power. Thus, the political factor and the lack of political will impede progress in structure organisation and civil service in HPM.

The societal factor should be included as well. While there is a broad public interest in digitisation, openness, transparency, accountability, and integrity, the issue of territorial fragmentation is not publicly perceived as an essential issue. The voters continue to vote for the same political parties despite their clear intentions not to change anything substantial in that respect. Additionally, there is a negative public perception of the civil service, making it even more difficult for the civil service to attract and retain the best people who are the necessary precondition for any reform.

In the end, there is the economic factor. While changes in areas such as transparency, openness, policymaking, or digitalisation can be obtained by using funds from different domestic and international projects, the changes in the areas of structure and organisation require consensus in the Parliament about the strategic approach, substantial resources, and a complete political dedication to such reform. Since there is no political dedication, there is no possibility for substantial funds to be allocated for that purpose.

4.5 Conclusion

The chapter provides an overview of the reforms in Croatian public administration in five different areas, showing that the EU was the main driving force for most of them. However, the results of the conducted reforms are not uniform. The area of transparency is where the most significant achievements have been made and where the convergence to the EAS standards is not just on the level of talk and decision but also where actual actions and results have been produced. This is followed by the areas of digitalisation and elements of policymaking where progress is visible, although challenges remain. There were primarily legislative changes in accountability and structures with limited progress. In contrast, civil service and HPM remain with almost inexistent improvements made after the EU accession.

These results indicate that the EAS standards have been accepted on the formal level, but Europeanisation has yet to produce more profound changes in many areas. Thus, Croatian public administration does not escape the "shallow Europeanisation". The administrative capacities are still not adequately strong enough to respond to all the demands from the EU membership, mainly because of the deficiency in the HPM and civil service system and the inadequate organisation of central and local level administration.

The results show that the EU, mainly the EU funds, are the main drivers of the reforms. On the one hand, this is positive since it pushes Croatian public administration in the right direction, i.e. towards deeper implementation and incorporation of the EAS standards and principles. On the other hand, this is worrisome since it shows the lack of internal impulse to change, i.e. the lack of political will to undertake deeper reforms and to transform the way public administration functions.

Therefore, the necessary precondition for the fundamental reform of Croatian public administration is the political will to implement changes, particularly in the organisation of the central and local administration and HPM. This also requires the dedication of the necessary economic resources and a sound public campaign which will introduce the citizens, NGOs, and the public to the purpose of the reform, its long-term goals, and expected outcomes. At the moment, the first precondition, political will and political consensus about organisational reform, is absent, which calls for caution.

Notes

1 Mrs Anita Markić, Director of the Department for Political System and General Administration, MJPA; Mr Krešimir Orešković, Head of the Sector for Political System and Central State Administration, MJPA; Mrs Katarina Serdar, Head of the Sector for Local and Regional Self-Government, MJPA; Mrs Sanda Pipunić, Head of the Sector for Civil Servants, MJPA; Mrs Fadila Bahović, Head of the Accountancy Sector, MJPA; Mr Boris Zelenika, Assistant Director of the GOL; and Dr Anamarija Musa, the first Information Commissioner in Croatia. The authors wish to express their gratitude to all the interviewees.
2 Interview with MJPA civil servants, 4 April, 2023.
3 Interview with a civil servant from the GOL, 5 April 2023.
4 Interview with a civil servant from the GOL, 5 April 2023.
5 Interview with the MJPA civil servants, 5 April, 2023.
6 Interview with the MJPA civil servants, 5 April, 2023.
7 Interview with the MJPA civil servants, 5 April, 2023.
8 Interview with the first Information Commissioner in Croatia (2013–2018), 22 April 2023.
9 Interview with the first Information Commissioner in Croatia (2013–2018), 22 April 2023.

10 Interview with a civil servant from the GOL, 5 April 2023.
11 Interview with the MJPA civil servants, 5 April, 2023.
12 Interview with the MJPA civil servants, 5 April, 2023.
13 Interview with the MJPA civil servants, 5 April, 2023.
14 Interview with a civil servant from the GOL, 5 April 2023.
15 Interview with a civil servant from the GOL, 5 April 2023.

References

CSODSD – Central State Office for Digital Society Development (2022) *Strategija digitalne Hrvatske. Predstavljanje analize stanja za izradu Nacrta prijedloga Strategije zainteresiranoj javnosti.* Available at: https://rdd.gov.hr/UserDocsImages/SDURDD-dokumenti/Predstavljanje%20Analize%20stanja%20za%20izradu%20Strategije%20zainteresiranoj%20javnosti.pdf (28.03.2023).

Đanić Čeko, A., and Guštin, M. (2022) 'Digitalizacija hrvatske javne uprave s posebnim osvrtom na sustav socijalne skrbi', *Zbornik radova Pravnog fakulteta u Splitu*, 59(4), pp. 793–821.

DESI (2022) *Digital Economy and Society Index (DESI) 2022. Thematic Chapters.* Bruxelles: European Commission.

Đulabić, V. (2009) 'Novi hrvatski Zakon o općem upravnom postupku kao poluga modernizacije javne uprave', *Hrvatska javna uprava*, 9(2), pp. 307–316.

Đulabić, V. (2021) *Can the Changes in Local Self-Government Regulation Be Considered a Reform?* Available at: https://administratiopublica.wordpress.com/2021/01/ (02.04.2023).

Đulabić, V., and Čepo, D. (2017) 'Regionalism and Sub-Regional Representation: A Guide to the County Transformation of Croatia', *Hrvatska i komparativna javna uprava – Croatian and Comparative Public Administration*, 17(4), pp. 539–568.

Đurman, P. (2020) 'Savjetovanje s javnošću u pripremi propisa u Hrvatskoj', *Zbornik Pravnog fakulteta u Zagrebu*, 70(2–3), pp. 407–444.

Đurman, P. (2021) 'Društvena okolina upravnih organizacija: analiza sudionika e-savjetovanja u Hrvatskoj', *Hrvatska i komparativna javna uprava – Croatian and Comparative Public Administration*, 21(1), pp. 59–87.

Džinić, J., and Lopižić, I. (2022) 'Novo uređenje upravnog i inspekcijskog nadzora u hrvatskoj državnoj upravi: problemi i otvorena pitanja', *Zbornik radova Pravnog fakulteta u Splitu*, 59(1), pp. 173–193.

European Commission (2012) *Comprehensive Monitoring Report on Croatia's State of Preparedness for EU Membership, COM (2012) 601 Final.* Available at: https://neighbourhood-enlargement.ec.europa.eu/system/files/2019-06/hr_rapport_2012_en.pdf (28.03.2023).

European Commission (2013) *Monitoring Report on Croatia's Accession Preparations, COM (2013) 171 Final.* Available at: https://eur-lex.europa.eu/LexUriServ/LexUriServ.do?uri=COM%3A2013%3A0171%3AFIN%3AEN%3APDF (28.03.2023).

European Commission (2018) *Izvješće za Hrvatsku 2018. s detaljnim preispitivanjem o sprječavanju i ispravljanju makroekonomskih neravnoteža.* Available at: https://vlada.gov.hr/ UserDocsImages/00%20Foto%20mobitel/Europski%20semestar/Dokumenti%20i%20publikacije/2018/Izvje%C4%87e%20za%20Hrvatsku%20i%20AGS/CELEX_52018SC0209_HR_TXT.pdf (28.03.2023).

European Commission (2020) *Digital Public Administration Factsheets Croatia.* Available at: https://joinup.ec.europa.eu/sites/default/files/inline-files/Digital_Public_Administration_Factsheets_Croatia_vFINAL.pdf (04.04.2023).

European Commission (2022) *Public Administration and Governance: Croatia.* Luxembourg: Publications Office of the European Union.

Giljević, T. (2015) 'Utjecaj okoline organizacije na upravnu koordinaciju: Ministarstvo uprave kao studija slučaja', *Hrvatska i komparativna javna uprava- Croatian and Comparative Public Administration*, 15(4), pp. 875–908.

GOL – Government Office for Legislation (2022) *Izvješće o provedbi plana zakonodavnih aktivnosti za 2021. godinu.* Available at: https://zakonodavstvo.gov.hr/UserDocsImages//dokumenti//Izvjesce%20o%20provedbi%20PZA%202021%20final.pdf (04.04.2023).

GRC – Government of the Republic of Croatia (2017) *Prijedlog Zakona o sustavu strateškog planiranja i upravljanja razvojem Republike Hrvatske.* Available at: www.sabor.hr/sites/default/ files/uploads/sabor/2019-01-18/081240/PZ_189.pdf (17.10.2023).

Grubišić, K., and Zrinščak, S. (2022) 'Korupcija', in K. Grubišić, G. Marčetić, S. Zrinščak, R. Manojlović Toman (eds.) *Etika i javna uprava.* Zagreb: Pravni fakultet Sveučilišta u Zagrebu, pp. 75–96.

Koprić, I. (2001) 'Uloga županija u hrvatskom sustavu lokalne samouprave i uprave 1990-ih i perspektive regionalizacije nakon promjena Ustava iz 2000. godine', *Hrvatska javna uprava*, 3(1), pp. 63–87.

Koprić, I. (2008) 'Reforma hrvatske javne uprave: problemi, rješenja i zablude', in J. Barbić (ed.) *Hrvatska država i uprava – stanje i perspektive.* Zagreb: Hrvatska akademija znanosti i umjetnosti, pp. 49–65.

Koprić, I. (2016) 'Reforma javne uprave u Hrvatskoj: ni bolni rezovi ni postupne promjene – nužna je nova upravna paradigma', *Političke analize*, 7(26), pp. 3–12.

Koprić, I. (2017) 'European Administrative Space – Myth, Reality, and Hopes', in I. Koprić, P. Kovač (eds.) *European Administrative Space: Spreading Standards, Building Capacities.* Bratislava: NISPACee, pp. 31–54.

Koprić, I. (2018a). *Public Administration Characteristics and Performance in EU28: Croatia.* Available at: https://op.europa.eu/en/publication-detail/-/publication/97f87f51-9608-11e8-8bc1-01aa75ed71a1/language-en (28.03.2023).

Koprić, I. (2018b) 'One Candle, Two Candles… Is There the Third One? Croatian Public Administration Reform before and after the EU Accession', *The NISPAcee Journal of Public Administration and Policy*, 9(1), 41–61.

Koprić, I., Marčetić, G., Musa, A., Đulabić, V., and Lalić Novak, G. (2021a) *Upravna znanost – Javna uprava u suvremenom europskom kontekstu.* Zagreb: Pravni fakultet Sveučilišta u Zagrebu & Studijski centar za javnu upravu i javne financije.

Koprić, I., Musa, A., and Lalić Novak, G. (2012) *Europski upravni prostor*. Zagreb: Institut za javnu upravu.

Koprić, I., Škarica, M., Džinić, J., Giljević, T., Manojlović Toman, R., and Lopižić, I. (2021b) 'Hrvatska javna uprava u 2020. godini', *Special issue of Hrvatska i komparativna javna uprava – Croatian and Comparative Public Administration*, 21(2), pp. 3–22.

Kovač, P. (2017) 'Introduction to European Administrative Space as a Base for Spreading Standards and Building Capacities', in I. Koprić, P. Kovač (eds.). *European Administrative Space: Spreading Standards, Building Capacities.* Bratislava: NISPACee, pp. 9–18.

Lalić Novak, G., Giljević, T., and Manojlović Toman, R. (2021) '(Never)mind the Evidence: Evidence-Based Law-Making in Croatian Regulation on Migration', *Hrvatska i komparativna javna uprava – Croatian and Comparative Public Administration*, 21(2), pp. 205–224.

Lopižić, I., and Manojlović Toman, R. (2019) 'Prethodna evaluacija ukidanja ureda državne uprave u županijama', *Zbornik Pravnog fakulteta u Zagrebu*, 69(5–6), pp. 635–670.

Marčetić, G. (2005) *Javni službenici i tranzicija.* Zagreb: Društveno veleučilište u Zagrebu &Konrad Adenauer Stiftung.

Marčetić, G. (2007) *Upravljanje ljudskim potencijalima u javnoj upravi.* Zagreb: Društveno veleučilište u Zagrebu.

Marčetić, G., (2013) 'Etički kodeksi za državne službenike. Pravna kategorija ili moralna obveza?', *3. Forum za javnu upravu*, Friedrich Ebert Stiftung i Institut za javnu upravu, Zagreb, pp. 29–45.

Marčetić, G., and Manojlović Toman, R. (2022) 'Etički kodeksi i kodeksi ponašanja', in K. Grubišić, G. Marčetić, S. Zrinščak, R. Manojlović Toman (eds.) *Etika i javna uprava.* Zagreb: Pravni fakultet Sveučilišta u Zagrebu, pp. 131–171.

Marčetić, G., Manojlović Toman, R., and Džinić, J. (2020) *Tackling the Challenge of Employment and Retention in the Civil Service. EUPAN Presidency Brief Report Croatia.* Available at: www.eupan.eu/wp-content/uploads/2020/07/EUPAN-Presidency-Report-Croatia.pdf (04.04.2023).

Marčetić, G., and Musa, A. (2013) 'Europeizacija službeničkog prava: usklađivanje hrvatskog zakonodavstva s europskim standardima', *Zbornik radova Pravnog fakulteta u Splitu*, 50(3), pp. 725–756.

Marčetić, G., and Prelec, D. (2011) 'Development of a Human Resources Development Strategy in Croatian Civil Service', *Croatian International Relations Review*, 17(62/63), pp 41–56.

Marčetić, G., and Vukojičić Tomić, T. (2016) 'European Standards for Public Service Codes of Ethics and their Application in Croatian Local Government', in D. Lhomme, A. Musa, S. de la Rosa (eds.) *Good Local Governance: Application of European Standards for Local Public Services in France and Croatia.* Bruxelles: Bruyland, pp. 371–393.

MJPA – Ministry of Justice and Public Administration (2022) *National Plan for the Development of Public Administration in the 2022-2027 Period.* Available at: https://mpu.gov.hr/UserDocsImages/dokumenti/Strategije,%20planovi,%20izvješća/Nacionalni%20plan%20razvoja%20javne%20uprave%20za%20razdoblje%20od%202022_2027.pdf (27.03.2023).

Musa, A. (2006) 'Europski upravni prostor: približavanje nacionalnih uprava', *Hrvatska javna uprava*, 6(1), pp. 123–153.

Musa, A. (2014) *Agencijski model javne uprave.* Zagreb: Pravni fakultet Sveučilišta u Zagrebu & Studijski centar za javnu upravu i javne financije.

Musa, A. (2017) 'Kakva reforma agencija u Hrvatskoj?', in A. Musa (ed.) *Javne agencije- u potrazi za reformom.* Zagreb: Friedrich Ebert Stiftung and Institute of Public Administration, pp. 23–45.

Public Information Commissioner (2022) *Izvješće o provedbi Zakona o pravu na pristup informacijama za 2021.* Available at: https://pristupinfo.hr/wp-content/uploads/2022/03/1.-Izvjesce-o-provedbi-ZPPI-za-2021.pdf?x57830 (27.03.2023).

SIGMA (1999) *SIGMA Paper n. 27. European Principles for Public Administration.* Paris: OECD.

Škarica, M. (2018) *Implementation of Strategy for Public Administration Development in Croatia (2015-2020): A Mid-Term Evaluation?* Available at: www.esd-conference.com/upload/book_of_proceedings/Book_of_Proceedings_esdSplit2018_Online.pdf (27.03.2023).

Škarica, M. (2022) European Public Administration Country Knowledge Country brief 2022: Croatia. Unpublished Report.

State Ombudsman (2022) *Izvješće pučke pravobraniteljice za 2021.* Available at: www.ombudsman.hr/hr/download/izvjesce-pucke-pravobraniteljice-za-2021-godinu/? (27.03.2023).

5 Rule of Law in the EU and the State of Croatian Judiciary

Nika Bačić Selanec, Iris Goldner Lang and Davor Petrić

5.1 Introduction

Over the past few years, the protection of the rule of law has been one of the major concerns in the European Union (EU), primarily due to the political overtakes of the judiciary witnessed in Hungary and Poland (Goldner Lang, 2019).[1] Croatia was, in contrast, never singled out by the EU as a state with such systemic rule of law violations. The European Commission's recent reports monitoring the state of the rule of law in EU Member States have never identified structural problems with independence or systemic corruption of Croatian judiciary. The main challenges of the Croatian judicial system consistently concern problems with efficiency and quality of judicial work, as well as the lack of public trust in the judiciary, leading to the lowest level of perceived judicial independence in the EU. However, despite the public perception, the EU has never accused the Croatian judiciary of the lack of independence *per se*. This chapter does not try to refute the Commission's findings and argue that the Croatian judiciary is not formally independent or is subject to political control of the executive or legislative branches of the government. Instead, this chapter aims to show that within the Croatian context, the understanding of judicial independence has been distorted and turned on the flipside, disabling the requisite level of democratic control over the judiciary through checks and balances and making the Croatian judiciary almost impenetrable from the outside. While this system tends to discourage direct and overt political attacks on judiciary, leading to the rule of law backsliding like the ones in Hungary and Poland, its downside is the practical difficulty in addressing the systemic problems of judicial ineffectiveness, public mistrust, the lack of quality and other irregularities when they are supported and internalised within the system. Croatian "rule of law" problem with independence of judiciary may not be overt but does exist and remains deeply imbedded within its mode of operation.

To support our central argument, this chapter will explore the state of the Croatian judiciary described in a number of pre- and post-accession reports and secondary sources and analyse the relevant jurisprudence of both Croatian courts and the Court of Justice of the EU. The chapter is divided into eight sections. Following the introduction, Section 5.2 briefly portrays the state of Croatian judiciary in the accession negotiations. Section 5.3 turns its attention to the post-accession period

DOI: 10.4324/9781003394013-5

and the Commission's Rule of Law Reports. Section 5.4 elaborates on the misconception of judicial independence in Croatia and explains the consequences of such misconception for both the Commission's understanding of the rule of law standards in the country and the internal modes of judicial operation. Section 5.5 analyses the resulting failures of judicial reforms in the post-accession period, followed by the Croatian judiciary's own perspective on the rule of law issues. Section 5.6 analyses what topics Croatian judiciary currently regards as important rule of law issues. Section 5.7 examines the (potential) use of EU law to protect judicial independence in Croatia. Section 5.8 briefly summarises the main findings and makes the conclusions.

5.2 Croatian Judiciary in the Accession Negotiations

Croatian accession negotiations were rather lengthy and difficult (Goldner Lang et al., 2019). After the initial postponement of the starting date of accession negotiations until the date on which the Chief Prosecutor of the International Criminal Tribunal for the Former Yugoslavia (ICTY) gave a positive assessment of Croatia's full cooperation with the ICTY, the accession negotiations were officially launched on 3 October 2005. However, in December 2008, the accession negotiations were stalled as Slovenia blocked the opening and closing of several negotiating chapters due to a border dispute with Croatia. Upon mediation of the European Commission and political pressure from a number of member states, Slovenia agreed to detach the border dispute from Croatia's accession negotiations and resolve it as a bilateral issue using international arbitration. Accession negotiations continued in September 2009 and were concluded on 30 June 2011, when the last of the 35 negotiating chapters was closed.

Out of the 35 chapters that were negotiated, Chapter 23, on judiciary and fundamental rights, and Chapter 24, on justice, freedom and security, were the most challenging. Both chapters were opened relatively late in the negotiating process. This fact proved to cause difficulties as they were among the most burdensome to negotiate. Chapter 24 was opened on 21 October 2009 and closed late in the negotiating process, on 22 December 2010, while Chapter 23 was opened on 30 June 2010 and was the last to be closed on 30 June 2011. Based on its experience negotiating Chapters 23 and 24 with Croatia, the Union opened these chapters among the first in later accession negotiations with the Western Balkans countries.

The Croatian negotiating working group in Chapter 23, consisting of representatives of the judiciary, ministries and other state institutions, and several academics, had five subgroups: judiciary reform, national war crimes trials, anti-corruption policy, fundamental and minority rights, and return and housing of refugees. The closure of Chapter 23 required Croatia to fulfil ten closing benchmarks (CBMs) in the following four areas: judiciary, combating corruption and organised crime, fundamental and minority rights, and cooperation with the ICTY. Closing benchmarks (CBMs) in the area of judicial reform were to update the Judicial Reform Strategy and Action Plan and ensure effective implementation (CBM 1); strengthen the independence, accountability, impartiality and professionalism of the judiciary (CBM 2); improve the efficiency of the judiciary (CBM 3); and improve the handling of domestic war crimes cases (CBM 4). In the second area of the fight against corruption and organised crime, the closing benchmarks were to establish a track record of substantial results based on efficient, effective and unbiased investigation, prosecution and court rulings in organised crime and corruption cases at all levels, including high-level corruption, and in vulnerable sectors such as public procurement (CBM 5); and establish a track record of strengthened prevention measures in the fight against corruption and conflict of interest (CBM 6). In the third area of fundamental and minority rights, the closing benchmarks were to strengthen the protection of minorities, including through effective implementation of the Constitutional Act on the Rights of National Minorities (CBM 7), settle the outstanding refugee return issues (CBM 8), and improve the protection of human rights (CBM 9). Finally, in the fourth area pertaining to war crimes, the closing benchmark (CBM 10) was to continue full cooperation with the ICTY (European Commission, 2011).

The negotiations of Chapter 23 required Croatia to provide a track record of measures it had undertaken to achieve the required objectives set as benchmarks. This was a novel practice when compared to previous accession negotiations. Certainly, the reforms that were conducted during the accession negotiations had positive effects on the functioning of the judiciary and the fight against corruption. However, the methodology of accession negotiations and the benchmarks that were relied on enabled a limited degree of both quantitative and qualitative improvements in the Croatian judiciary. As the following sections will demonstrate, the pre-accession fast-track reforms have not fulfilled the expectations of creating a modern and efficient judiciary, whose functioning fulfils the rule of law standards set in principle by the EU and whose work is controlled through the system of checks and balances. The reforms failed to tackle some of the pertinent problems of the Croatian judicial system and its operating mode and further unleashed new problems. Additionally, some reforms started were not finalised or were reversed due to opposition in judicial or political circles and the change of political priorities. Despite the efforts in the accession negotiations, the Croatian judiciary did not reach the level of some member states with more mature democracies and more robust constitutional traditions.

5.3 Post-Accession Period and the Rule of Law Reports

A decade since Croatia joined the EU, the problems that have characterised the state of its judiciary during the accession process continued and have not fundamentally changed. The European Commission's reports on the state of the rule of law in Croatia,[2] issued annually since 2020, are informative in supporting this argument. Throughout the past four years, the Commission's reports have continuously identified two central problems (or features) of the Croatian justice system. First, the Croatian judiciary experiences "serious efficiency and quality challenges", and second, "the level of perceived judicial independence" in Croatia is very low, effectively the lowest in the EU (European Commission, 2020, p. 1; 2021, p. 1;

2022a, p. 1; 2023, p. 1). There are no startling novelties in those two conclusions for anybody loosely familiar with the state of judiciary in the EU's most recent addition: problems with *efficiency* and *quality*, and *public perception*.

The system's *inefficiency* is mainly tied to excessive backlogs and the length of proceedings, which, despite some recent progress, are still "amongst most considerable in the EU" (European Commission, 2020, p. 7; 2023, p. 11).[3] The closures during the pandemic and massive earthquakes in certain Croatian regions in 2020 further worsened the numbers and contributed to the country's last place in the EU Justice Scoreboard (European Commission, 2021, p. 8). But even if we take all these external adverse effects aside, the latest trends show remarkable resilience and even further accumulation of backlog or increased length of proceedings at first-instance courts, while certain albeit limited decrease has been witnessed in cases pending before second and final instance courts (European Commission, 2022a, p. 10; 2023, p. 10).

As for *quality* concerns, the Commission's reports primarily identify procedural formalities that pertain to, for example, limited use of electronic communication and case management tools, which – despite some increase in use in recent years – leave much "room for improvement"; or complications with postal delivery of judicial documents (European Commission, 2020, p. 5; 2021, p. 7; 2022a, p. 8; 2023, p. 6). In addition to the slow responses to digitalisation challenges, a significant concern also pertains to very low levels of online publication of judgements of Croatian courts, placing Croatia at the bottom of the list in the EU (European Commission, 2020, p. 6). The only remaining challenges identified in the reports concern shortages of financial and human resources, in particular shortages of administrative staff in the State Judicial Council (European Commission, 2021, p. 7), and the lack of financial and material conditions which do not correspond to the importance of the judiciary. The Commission expressed concerns that such shortages could have a negative impact on the judiciary's responsibility to preserve democratic governance (European Commission, 2023, p. 9).

The lack of resources and administrative support continuously serves as an excuse for the lack of jurisprudential quality in a country which, paradoxically, has one of the most massive judicial systems in the EU. Compared to other member states, only Slovenia has a higher number of judges per capita than Croatia, which has 44 judges per 100,000 inhabitants, and the same high numbers apply to non-judicial staff (Bratković, 2021, p. 177).

The size of the system, combined with inadequate maintenance and investment in the quality of personnel and overall working conditions of Croatian judiciary, recently proved its unsustainability. In mid-2023, pressured additionally by inflation, the judicial system came to a breaking point which led to a country-wide strike of both judicial and non-judicial staff. The "white" strike of the judiciary, postponing all but urgent hearings for two weeks in May 2023, was soon followed by an eight-week-long strike of non-judicial staff, which amounted to the longest strike of public servants since the establishment of the Croatian state, making the third branch of Croatian government practically non-accessible for more than two months (European Commission, 2023, p. 9). Ultimately, the strike was resolved with an agreement on a limited-percentage salary increase. However, most of the structural, organisational and quality problems of the Croatian judiciary remained unaddressed, missing yet another opportunity for a meaningful change (Lukić, 2023; Raić, 2023).

The second most important challenge identified in the Commission's yearly reports on the Croatian justice system is the public perception of (the lack of) judicial independence in Croatia. The level of perceived judicial independence in Croatia is the lowest in the EU. In 2020, only 24% of the Croatian general public perceived the judiciary as independent. In 2021, the percentage followed a downward trend, decreasing to 17%, and settling to 20% in 2022 and 22% in 2023. The main cited reason for the lack of trust (of roughly four out of five Croats) in judicial independence has continuously been the "perception of interference or pressure from the Government and politicians", or "from economic or other specific interest" in case of perceptions of private market participants (European Commission, 2020, p. 2; 2021, p. 3; 2022a p. 8; 2023, p. 3).

Yet, despite all these worrying numbers and other steady indicators of ineffectiveness, the lack of quality of judicial outputs, or the corresponding lack of public trust in state institutions, Croatia has never been placed on the EU's rule of law "list of shame". The Commission's reports have not identified structural problems with judicial independence in Croatia or other "systemic rule of law" concerns. In particular, there were no issues that would force the Commission to initiate infringement proceedings based on rule of law violations pertained to the judiciary, as it did in the case of Hungary and Poland.[4]

From all these considerations, it might appear that the central problem with the rule of law in Croatia, as the youngest member state, is simply lagging behind in quality of judicial (and administrative) outputs compared to the "older" member states, with unjustified lack of public trust, while the system does make continuous efforts to improve.

Such an outlook, however, as well as the Commission's overall conclusions on the state of Croatian judiciary in light of the rule of law standards seem far too benevolent and cursory. The true picture is much more complex and disconcerting.

5.4 The Misconception of Judicial Independence in Croatia

As the previous section has demonstrated, the European Commission has never addressed (the lack of) judicial independence as a self-standing rule of law concern in Croatia. Its reports lead us to conclude, quite straightforwardly, that Croatia does not have problems with direct "attacks" on judicial independence coming from the political branches of the government, as is currently the case with Poland and Hungary occupying the Union's limelight. The only problems related to judicial independence in Croatia that are even mentioned in the reports have to do with public perception (or a lack of it), but the independence of judiciary as such is never questioned.

However, in the authors' opinion, all the quality and efficiency problems of Croatian judiciary should not be considered true causes for extremely low public faith in the system or its overall poor state, as the Commission's reports might seem to suggest by identifying these issues as the points of primary concern. This is further demonstrated by the fact that certain improvements in the functioning of the justice system identified by the Commission have not led to the commensurate improvement in the public perception of the system's quality and independence (European Commission, 2023, p. 10).

Rather, all these problems are merely symptoms of another worrisome, chronic disease of Croatian judiciary, which the Commission's reports fail to identify and straightforwardly deal with, representing a much more troubling rule of law concern. The implementation and the understanding of the concept of judicial independence in Croatia remain widely misperceived, particularly within the system itself, which is moreover deeply tied to the operating mode of our judicial culture.

In Croatia, the concept of judicial independence has been turned inwards. Members of the bench do not primarily perceive it as a guarantee of their autonomous decision-making based on the normative strength and legitimacy of the law as a requisite of effective judicial protection central to achieving the high standards of the rule of law. Instead, judicial independence is oftentimes used as a convenient excuse for isolationism of the judicial branch towards all the other actors in the democratic process, resulting in extremely limited possibilities to monitor and control their work through the system of checks and balances. Croatian judiciary operates under a lack of transparency and is alienated not only from the political branches of the government (at least directly) but also from the general society, professional organisations and other participants in the judicial process. Often, the system hides behind arguments of supposed attacks on judicial independence to avert public scrutiny and deny the legitimacy of political or academic criticisms. Instead of supporting it, such absolute separation of the judiciary stands in sharp contrast with the system of checks and balances in democratic governance based on the rule of law, in which a certain level of mutually exercised influence and control of all participants in a democratic process, on an institutional level and towards the society at large (as the system's very purpose and legitimising *demos*), is an absolute necessity to achieve the requisite balance.

In other words, in the Croatian context the independence of judiciary is, from within the system itself, often used as a shield to thwart the requisite level of democratic control. When used to its maximum, such misconception of judicial independence can be perilous for the rule of law, as it can preserve non-transparency, closedness, alienation and self-sufficiency of the judicial system. It can perpetuate the *status quo*, favouring the most powerful judicial interest circles which do not tolerate criticism, which keep closed circles in charge of untransparent judicial management, including judicial appointments, and which can threaten the quality of judicial argument, interpretation and application of the law because its isolationism allows for the normative value of law not to be questioned. This is a major rule of law concern of its own. Such judicial isolationism may be less conspicuous than direct overtakes of the judiciary by political branches, as such attacks are more evident, overt, tangible and more measurable. However, when the lack of democratic legitimacy comes from within the judiciary itself, and the system's aspirations of reform are directed towards further isolationism, the system may be just as far from the ideal of checks and balances as in the case of direct attacks from the outside.

In an academic study of the state of Croatian judiciary, Professor Uzelac, as one of the system's leading observers and critics, recently stressed the primary characteristics and explained the underlying causes of such a state of affairs (Uzelac, 2020a). Claiming that Croatian judiciary still suffers from "transitional diseases", he explained that one of its central problems pertains to, on the one side, dysfunctional self-government and the lack of quality in judicial administration (using the example of a mismatch between the wide extent of powers of the State Judicial Council and its "meagre capacity for their meaningful discharge"). On the other side, there is a lack of quality in judicial outputs, which stems from either "escaping responsibility for final decision-making" by "repetitive striking down and remittals of judgments to lower instances" or from its operating mode of positivistic legal reasoning, shielding the lack of quality in excessive legal formalism. This leads Uzelac to conclude that a high formal level of institutional independence and accountability of Croatian judiciary actually instigates the opposite – "very little real independence and lack of personal integrity in decision-making" (ibid., p. 2).

The lack of judicial accountability for the poor state of affairs is, for Uzelac, not a misplaced accusation but a justified concern as too many "holders of judicial functions" still fail to "act objectively and independently", and the system is still characterised by a "high degree of clientelism, nepotism and even corruption". This condition is also closely tied to the increasing closure of judiciary from the rest of society and avoidance of public criticism, or the overall lack of transparency in how judiciary functions. Uzelac claims that such developments are evident and "increasingly lacking at all levels, from education to recruitment of personnel; from planning legislative reforms to professional training; from monitoring judicial statistics to publishing court decisions and shaping long-term development policies". This lack of transparency and openness of the system moreover facilitates the creation of closed judicial elites, ultimately detrimental not only to the society as a whole, but also to the judiciary itself (ibid., p. 2).

The roots of such a state of judiciary date back to the 1990s and the interim period between the country's war for independence and the beginning of the EU accession process. It was a period of systemic reforms of judiciary and strong interventions to dismantle the pre-existing communist regime. The massive recruitment of judicial personnel that followed was not based on standards of professional independence, impartiality or encouraging "strong individuality" of judicial actors. Instead, the highest levels of judiciary were selected based on their political loyalties. At the same time, a whole layer of judges from the previous regime, even those well-skilled and experienced enough to carry the burden of democratic transformation, was removed from office. The newly appointed personnel often lacked knowledge and expertise and, with inexperience and political obedience, reproduced older modes of operation, which, in turn, resulted in a steady "decline in the legal and technical quality of judicial work", silently upholding the old socialist mindset of preserving "the unity of the government" (Uzelac, 2020a, p. 3).

By the time the new system consolidated in the 2000s, the accession process emphasised the relevance of judicial independence as a precondition for the rule of law required from the aspiring candidate states. The post-transitional system of judicial governance assumed the concept of independence, but turned it inwards, exaggerating its institutional relevance and self-dependence to the point of judicial isolationism. Uzelac reports that during that time, the "judicial elites took over exclusive control of non-judicial processes essential for good administration of justice: judicial administration, education and professional training of judges and state attorneys, and the drafting of legislative proposals that might affect the work of judiciary" (ibid., p. 4). The system turned to absolute separation from the other branches of government, but also all other actors of democratic control, misplacing the required institutional and professional independence of judiciary that still takes meaningful part in collaborative democratic governance based on the system of checks and balances.

5.5 Judicial Reforms in the Post-accession Period

Despite the fast-track reforms required during the accession process, the central problems of ineffectiveness and the lack of quality in Croatian judiciary have never been addressed through a set of systematic reforms that could effectively address the primary points of concern (Bratković, 2019). Quite paradoxically, the reforms that even could have a prospect of changing the *status quo* would have to cut deep – which is impossible given not only the lack of governmental will or political consensus needed to execute it, but also the constitutional requisite of independence of judiciary against encroachments of the political branches.

The past legislative reforms have been patchwork and have not addressed its core rule of law problem. Instead of much needed proactive and comprehensive reforms, the reforms attempted in recent years have mainly been introduced reactively, i.e. to an identified or publicly scrutinised particular issue. In addition, they mostly failed to achieve the desired limited goals and make any profound changes. The Croatian legislature and the overall legal culture thus perpetuated the *status quo* in the judiciary, its lethargy and self-sufficiency.

Take the example of a reform of the State Judicial Council's process in selecting judges. This issue has even been identified by the Commission's Rule of Law Report in 2020 as one of the points of concern. However, the Commission's assessment appears rather superficial, failing to identify and consider the bigger picture lurking in the background of the reform.

The judicial appointment process, led by the Judicial Council, was in principle designed to be merit-based. In the first part of the process, the points are objectively attributed to candidates based on their education and prior performance (either in the National School for Judges or their courtroom, in case of judicial promotions to higher instances). Nevertheless, the final decisions of appointment rely heavily on the Judicial Council's more subjective assessment of a candidate, based on the number of points it awards to a candidate based on a personal interview. These interview-based points could weigh enough to determine the outcome of the appointment, even to the detriment of candidates who received higher scores for their education and prior performance.

In one such occurrence, in 2018, the Constitutional Court (Decision U-III-5074/2017) struck down the Council's appointment decision due to insufficient reasoning for tipping the balance in favour of specific candidates without disclosing criteria and reasons for its decisions. As a result of the decision of the Constitutional Court and the increasing public criticism of the Council's arbitrariness in the scoring process, the legislator sought to amend the law on the State Judicial Council. Aiming to increase the objectivity and transparency of the appointment procedure, the 2018 reform decreased the Council's discretion and reduced the overall number of points that can be assigned to candidates based on interviews.

The Commission's 2020 Rule of Law Report, presumably based on inputs received from national judicial actors during the country visit, criticised those amendments as reducing the Council's powers to distinguish amongst the available candidates and diminishing its role in selecting judges (European Commission, 2020, p. 4). Moreover, the Council reported that after the reform, they "faced challenges in trying to avoid reducing the appointment procedure to a mechanical counting of points" and that they reflected on how to improve the standards of their reasoning by defining more clearly the criteria for awarding interview-based points (ibid.).

After the Commission's criticism, the Croatian legislature obediently responded by amending the procedure again. Only two years after the initial decrease, the legislator re-increased the number of interview-based points the Council can award and re-installed its extensive power in selecting candidates (European Commission, 2022a, p. 5). This demonstrates responsiveness of the Croatian government to the Commission's soft-law recommendations. However, it is questionable how prudent or effective both reforms were in achieving their stated aims. The initial amendment that, on its face, appeared as a lowering of the Judicial Council's independence and authority in selecting judges, from the other perspective, looked more like an attempt to constrain the use of arbitrary decision-making authority by the Judicial Council, which would often be based not on the candidates' merit but on particular interests of individual judges or certain interest circles within the judiciary. Moreover, the consecutive nature of these reforms certainly has not contributed to increasing public trust in the judicial system. Instead, most likely, it achieved the opposite.

Another recent example of a failed and ill-considered attempt at reform deals with introducing periodic security checks for judges. In addition to the existing obligation to subject all judges to a security check before the initial appointment (or allocating a judge to organised crime and corruption cases), the reform of the Law on Courts from 2022 made the security checks of all judges mandatory every five years, with a proclaimed aim of reducing the "high levels of perception of corruption in judiciary" (European Commission, 2022a, p. 6). A decision on the existence of security obstacles in these periodic screenings, much similar to the initial ones, would be issued by a special panel of Supreme Court judges based on the report of the national Security and Intelligence Agency (SOA). Upon its introduction, the reform was subject to harsh and vocal criticisms from the judiciary, in particular the Supreme Court and the Croatian Association of Judges, emphasising concerns for judicial independence and the separation of powers (or the possible "external pressure") given the increased role of the intelligence sector which is under the control of the executive (ibid.).

The reform was also assessed by the Venice Commission, which claimed that it would aggravate rather than alleviate the perception of the lack of judicial independence and "alleged interference or pressure from government and politicians" while ensuring judicial integrity could equally be achieved through mechanisms already in use, such as annual asset declarations by judges and the possibilities of disciplinary and criminal proceedings for judicial misconduct (Venice Commission, 2022, paras. 18, 35–36). The European Commission followed cue in its 2022 report, criticising the increased role of the SOA as the body under executive control and the regular nature of the vetting process. It urged the Croatian government to reconsider the periodic security checks as the only rule of law-related recommendation issued to Croatia at the time, and called for ensuring judicial integrity based on the existing mechanisms, taking into account European standards on judicial independence and the aforementioned opinion of the Venice Commission (European Commission, 2022a, p. 2).

Merely a year after it was introduced in February 2022, the legislative amendments were struck down by the Constitutional Court as violating the constitutional principles of the rule of law and legal certainty, also disproportionately interfering with judges' rights to private life without a detailed regulation and sufficient procedural safeguards (Decision U-I-2215/2022). The Commission's 2023 report referred to this move as "significant progress" in response to the 2022 recommendation (p. 5). However, once again, the reform of the judicial system attempting to promote public faith into the system failed as quickly as it was introduced. The lack of adequate procedural guarantees and poor execution made the reform an easy target.

In the end, the failed attempts just fed into further isolationism of judiciary which successfully prevented yet another attempt on their independence.

5.6 The Judiciary's Perspective on the Rule of Law Issues

So far, we have discussed external perspectives on the rule of law problems that plague the judicial system in Croatia, as they appear in the Commission's reports, attempted legislative reforms and legal scholarship. Now, we turn to the Croatian judiciary itself, to observe more closely what kind of things they regard as important rule of law issues they currently face.[5]

One frequently discussed theme is the material resources judges have at their disposal. They consider their salaries to be insufficient, which makes them less motivated to do their job and, at the same time, deters promising lawyers from entering the service; they complain about the lack of administrative, technical and expert assistance, given that much-qualified staff migrated abroad in search for better-paid jobs; and they are dissatisfied with limited access to the judgements of national courts and a lack of assistance with researching the judgements of European courts, which makes them uninformed about recent developments in the case law. In their view, the key to changing any of this is not in the hands of the judiciary but rather the executive, who controls "the purse". However, it is difficult to represent these concerns as a rule of law issue, absent conscious strategy on the part of other branches of the government to defund the judiciary, make their functioning harder and force them into submission. On the contrary, it may be seen as a reflection of the problems in the Croatian public service in general. Nevertheless, it is true that in a long-term perspective, inadequate material resources, especially those leading to a decrease in human capital, could turn out to be a massive problem for the Croatian judiciary, affecting its efficiency and quality of its decisions, which are among the most important rule of law concerns.

Another more pertinent theme concerns the workload of Croatian courts. They remain among the most burdened in the EU concerning the number of incoming and pending cases per number of inhabitants. This situation has not changed with improvements in tools for electronic communication (European Commission, 2022b, EU Justice Scoreboard, Section 3.1 "Efficiency of justice systems"; European Commission, 2021, p. 8). As one of the leading causes of the malaise, Croatian judges often point to the so-called Framework criteria for the performance of judges. Namely, Article 79(1) of the Law on Courts empowers the Minister of Justice and Administration to set these criteria and determine the number of decisions judges are individually obliged to deliver during a calendar year (Bodul, 2022). Many judges would argue that the thresholds set annually by the minister overburden them and lead to the excessive length of judicial proceedings. In their view, judges who could meet the set requirements before deadline do not have an incentive to do so since, by being on time, they only risk being handed in an additional number of cases by the president of their court. Therefore, these framework criteria arguably enable the executive to exert pressure on the judiciary, which could raise concerns related to the rule of law. If these criteria negatively impact the judicial workload and, by extension, the length of the court proceedings, the result would be less effective judicial protection of the rights of individuals, which is also an essential rule of law issue. On many previous occasions, excessively long proceedings before Croatian courts were found by the European Court of Human Rights to be in breach of Articles 6 and 13 (right to a fair trial and right to an effective remedy) of the European Convention on Human Rights (*Marić v. Croatia*, App. No. 9849/15; *Glavinić and Marković v. Croatia*, Apps. No. 11388/15 and 25605/15). However, there has been no firm evidence, except perhaps anecdotal, that the framework criteria have such a detrimental impact on the courts' caseload or the length of proceedings, although the correlation seems obvious.

A more important cause of the problems with workload and non-expeditious adjudication concerns Croatian procedural law, in particular, the possibility of quashing judgements on appeal an indefinite number of times and referring them back to a lower court for a new decision instead of reversing them by the appellate court and adopting a decision on merits, thus bringing a dispute to an end (Uzelac, 2021, pp. 134–136). This evasion technique is one of the characteristics of the socialist legal tradition, which remains incredibly resilient in Croatia even three decades after the change of socio-political paradigm (Uzelac, 2010). The "ping pong" between lower and appellate courts is reinforced through the rules of evidence that can be abused to drag proceedings endlessly and the availability of all kinds of legal remedies that delay the enforceability of judgements. Related characteristics of Croatian post-socialist legal tradition include bureaucratised judiciary and rigid formalism, seen as a preference for deciding cases on purely formal or procedural grounds to evade final meritorious decisions that would require taking responsibility for making important value and policy judgements.

Moreover, excessive formalism also leaves a visible mark on the style of judicial reasoning (Ćapeta, 2005). Generally, Croatian courts adopt magisterial, impersonal and deductive style of reasoning. Their judgements are often written in abstract and bureaucratic language, referencing almost exclusively formal legal reasons, like legislation or legal principles, and only exceptionally constitutional provisions or case law. In them, judges do not reflect on different possible interpretations of the law or arguments supporting them but rather extensively discuss facts, giving the impression that they are mechanically applying the law and not creatively expounding the law through interpretive choices.

Frequent formalism in the reasoning of Croatian courts is not without important consequences for the rule of law. One of its main requirements is that every exercise of state authority, including by the judiciary, be appropriately justified. From the perspective of individuals, the requirement of proper justification of judicial decisions is a correlative of their right to access justice, to get a fair trial and to have an effective legal remedy at their disposal, which are all essential elements of the rule of law (Bačić Selanec and Ćapeta, 2022). From a systemic perspective, the legitimacy and authority of courts as one of the branches of democratic government depends on the quality of their reasoning. Through justification and argumentation of their decisions, courts fulfil many functions that are essential for a functioning constitutional order based on the rule of law: from instructing the executive and the legislator about the limits of their actions to ensuring uniform application of the law, which is essential for the equality of citizens, to promoting interests of transparency and democracy by openly elaborating the reasons which led to the rulings of extraordinary socio-political weight, to increasing the accountability of deciding judges.

Instrumentalisation of material and procedural law and formalistic judicial reasoning pose significant challenges to several fundamental requirements of the rule of law in a (ideal) liberal-democratic constitutional order. A "vicious circle" of cryptic and untransparent judgements and appellate courts that persistently return them to first-instance courts without taking over the responsibility is a far more critical cause of excessively long judicial proceedings than the number of judgements that have to be delivered by each judge. Slow and inert proceedings negatively impact legal certainty and predictability. Individuals cannot know when and whether a final court decision will vindicate their rights and interests. Such a judicial environment cannot guarantee efficient rights protection and earn public trust. As already discussed, this leads to citizens having so little trust in Croatian courts. These factors better explain the statistics according to which the Croatian judiciary remains at the bottom of the EU regarding the citizens' perception of judicial independence and corruption in the justice sector (European Commission 2022b, EU Justice Scoreboard, Section 3.3 "Independence"). The level of mistrust is equally present in the business sector, arguably resulting in a bad investment climate, thus stifling economic growth.

5.7 EU Law as a Mechanism of Protecting Judicial Independence

It is sometimes considered that the Croatian judiciary has grown so far from any influence, good or bad, of other branches of the government or civil society that it has become "a state within the state" (Orešić, 2021). Nevertheless, we were not left with a modern, efficient, impartial and independent judicial system. Instead, unaccountable and isolated from public criticism, that system perpetuated all the previously mentioned bad traits inherited from the old regime, filtered through a partial democratic, post-conflict transition that followed country's independence. The Croatian judiciary became the resilient guardian of the *status quo*, making it difficult to implement meaningful legislative reforms, positive and constructive or harmful and destructive.

Ironically, this may be one of the key reasons why, in Croatia, we have not seen a complete rule of law "backsliding", like in Poland or Hungary. Political elites would have difficulty trying to "capture" the judiciary because of its isolationism and dysfunctionality. To successfully make an illiberal and autocratic turn in any state, one would need to control the most important levers of power, which, besides political institutions, include courts, media and education institutions. To control them, one would need to staff them with a loyal and capable cadre and provide them with functional tools and mechanisms to bring the plan to life. However, a successful capture becomes much more difficult when one of those essential levers is itself a state within the state and an inefficient and inert state. Political forces cannot wholly hijack the system without taking over the judiciary's fortress.

Of course, although the good thing is not being able to make a sharp turn to illiberal authoritarianism, the bad thing is not being able to make a determined step forward either. Given that other branches of the government cannot effectively threaten the position of the Croatian judiciary, the most significant opportunity for challenging the *status quo* comes from within the system itself, within the judicial ranks. To do so, individual judges rely on mechanisms offered by EU law.

An interesting example concerns a preliminary reference from Croatia pending before the Court of Justice of the EU. It raises the question of judicial independence not vis-à-vis other branches of the government, which was the issue in the previous case law of the Court of Justice (Ćapeta, 2020), but rather internally, i.e. within the national judiciary. In *Hann-Invest/Udruga KHL Medveščak Zagreb* (Joined Cases C-554/21, C-622/21 and C-727/21), the High Commercial Court asked whether Article 40(2) of the Croatian Law on Courts and Article 177(3) of the Croatian

Rules of Procedure of the Courts are in line with the requirements of independence and impartiality of judges under Article 19 of the Treaty on the EU and Article 47 of the Charter of Fundamental Rights of the EU and relevant case law of the Court of Justice.

Article 40(2) of the Law on Courts provides that "legal positions" adopted at the plenary meeting of all judges or sections of Croatian high courts bind individual chambers and judges of those courts or sections. Article 177(3) of the Rules of Procedure of the Courts provides that the decision of a court of second instance is not finalised, i.e. published and delivered to the parties until a judge appointed by the president of that court, the so-called registrations judge, confirms it. The registration judge examines the legal merits of every judgement to ensure the consistency of case law. If they consider that a judgement is based on an erroneous interpretation of the law or departs from the earlier holdings of the same court or section of that court, the registration judge may refer the matter back to the deciding judge or chamber with comments on how the original judgement should be amended. If the deciding judge or chamber disagrees with the registration judge, the latter can refer the issue to the meeting of a relevant section of the court, which can then issue a binding "legal position" under Article 40(2) of the Law on Courts.

These meetings of court sections happen behind closed doors. National procedural rules do not govern them, and the parties to the original proceedings have no insight or say in these meetings. Croatian academia has already criticised the national provisions for not being in line with the principle of judicial independence guaranteed under the national constitution (Uzelac, 2020b, pp. 125–138). In his recent opinion in *Hann-Invest/Udruga KHL Medveščak Zagreb* (Joined Cases C-554/21, C-622/21 and C-727/21), Advocate General Pikamaë considered that such national rules, which aim at ensuring the consistency of case law, do not pose a threat to the standard of judicial independence guaranteed by Article 19(1) TEU. Still, given the high standards employed in its recent case law, it is possible that the Court of Justice will take a different approach and consider these rules contrary to EU law, at least for how they have been employed by Croatian high courts thus far. If this happens and the relevant provisions or judicial practice change, it will undoubtedly lead to an increased standard of judicial independence in Croatia, thanks to the initiative of a couple of national judges who were aware of procedural mechanisms offered by the EU Treaties and case law of the Court of Justice on judicial independence and its importance for the rule of law in the EU (Bačić Selanec and Petrić, 2024).

Other recent examples show how national judges can rely on EU law to push for greater standards of the rule of law regarding judicial independence and adequate protection of individual rights. It is well known how the Court of Justice, in its case law, developed several doctrines – most notably, direct effect and supremacy – that bind national courts when giving effect to EU law in their domestic legal systems, thus turning them into "European judges" (Ćapeta, 2002). These doctrines, in effect, destabilise the judicial hierarchy that existed (and may still exist) in the context of national law by empowering lower national courts over higher courts.

There are indications that some Croatian courts are making full use of these opportunities. For instance, the Split Municipal Court invoked the duty of interpreting national law in conformity with EU law to openly discredit the Croatian Supreme Court's earlier decisions as erroneous. It adopted a different interpretation in line with the relevant case law of the Court of Justice of the EU (Ivančan and Petrić, 2019, pp. 516–519). Similarly, the Zagreb County Court persisted with its preliminary reference to the Court of Justice in a high-profile corruption trial against former Croatian prime minister (Order K-Us-29/15; Order Kv-I-Us-84/17 (K-Us-50/14)), although the Supreme Court two times annulled its order to send reference and instructed it to proceed with the trial, holding that the questions of interpretation of EU law were irrelevant for the trial in question (Decision I-Kž-Us-102/17-4; Decision I-Kž-Us-4/2018-4). Croatian scholars thereby criticised the Supreme Court for disregarding the well-established case law of the Court of Justice on the discretion of national courts to initiate the preliminary ruling procedure (Lukić, 2017). The Court of Justice eventually admitted and replied to the reference of the County Court (Case C-268/17 *AY*), implying that its questions were relevant, hence proving the Supreme Court wrong and exposing its parochial understanding of the preliminary ruling procedure. Following this controversy, the Croatian legislator intervened and amended national procedural rules (Article 18(a) of the Law on Criminal Procedure and Article 213 of the Law on Civil Procedure), which no longer allow for an appeal against a court's decision to stay proceedings and submit preliminary reference to the Court of Justice.

In another example, the Zagreb Municipal Civil Court initiated the preliminary ruling procedure to challenge the compatibility of national law as interpreted by the Croatian Supreme Court with EU law, in particular with Article 47 of the Charter, which guarantees effective judicial protection (Petrić, 2023). This dispute concerned consumer credits in Swiss francs and the Croatian Law on Conversion, which allowed these credits to be switched from francs to euros after unfair terms in original contracts had been annulled by the Supreme Court, in one of the most significant legal proceedings in recent years. In the subsequent "model decision", the Supreme Court issued an authoritative interpretation of the Law on Conversion. However, it failed to refer relevant questions of interpretation of Directive 93/13 on unfair terms in consumer contracts to the Court of Justice without adequately explaining why the preliminary reference was unnecessary. Given that "model decisions" are binding on lower courts, the Municipal Civil Court turned to the Court of Justice to question whether the Supreme Court's decision was in line with EU law on consumer protection and the requirements of Article 47 of the Charter. In its reply, the Court of Justice held the reference to be inadmissible due to a lack of its jurisdiction, given that the contract at issue in the main proceedings before the referring court was outside the material scope of Directive 93/13 (Case C-567/20 *Zagrebačka banka*).

Nevertheless, this episode and earlier examples demonstrate the potential of EU law and especially the far-reaching impact of cooperation with the Court of Justice of the EU for lower courts in Croatia. They can use basic EU law doctrines and the preliminary ruling procedure both as a "shield" – to protect themselves against decisions of Croatian higher courts that are allegedly not aligned with EU law – and as a "sword" – to prompt superior courts to pay greater respect to EU law. By bringing the Court of Justice into play, lower courts in Croatia are "outsourcing" the responsibility to Luxembourg, which makes it easier for them to confront higher courts. This strategy is something that certain voices from within the Croatian highest courts have already called for, for instance, Justices Kušan and Selanec from the Constitutional Court, who encouraged Croatian lower courts to send preliminary references to Luxembourg and thus "leapfrog" Croatian higher courts who are unwilling to do so (Dissenting Opinion to Decision U-III-4150/2019 et al. – *Swiss francs II*). This becomes even more important given the troubled record of Croatian high courts regarding the application of EU law and their attitude towards cooperation with the Court of Justice (Bačić Selanec et al., 2020).

One of the causes of such a problematic treatment of EU law and the preliminary ruling procedure by Croatian courts, which may raise significant issues of judicial independence and the rule of law, is the lack of institutional capacities and knowledge. On the one hand, Croatian courts still do not have the proper resources to catch up with EU (case) law developments. It is true that the Supreme Court recently established a section that follows and studies the case law of the Court of Justice and the European Court of Human Rights, which can communicate its findings to other Croatian courts (Article 44 of the Rules of Procedure of the Supreme Court). However, this service remains understaffed, and it is questionable how efficiently it can operate given the scale of the task.

On the other hand, many judges, especially more senior ones, need to be properly trained and educated in EU law. Although university courses and life-long learning programmes on different aspects of EU law were introduced during the pre-accession period, activities in this area have stagnated following the accession. For instance, in its programmes, the Judicial Academy initially offered several courses on fundamental principles and procedures of EU law. However, for a couple of years now, courses about the most important aspects of EU law are no longer being offered, whereas EU law is being taught in the framework of very specific courses that address issues that are interrelated with national law.

This approach results from an incorrect assumption in the Croatian judicial circles that when it comes to the education of judges, EU law basics have been covered at the beginning, and there is no need to come back to these topics anymore. This attitude is problematic in two respects. First, it marginalises the importance of basic EU law principles and EU legal reasoning, which has significant repercussions for the application of EU law in Croatia, as we saw. Second, it takes a formalistic approach instead of concentrating on the substance. It assumes that the fact that a country has joined the EU means there is no longer a need to continue investing in knowledge about EU matters. As such, it fits into Croatia's overall formalistic approach to EU law. It is considered sufficient to run some educational programmes for judges, no matter how or by whom they are taught. It is considered sufficient to establish a research service that assists courts with EU law, irrespective of how many sit there and whether they are provided with resources to do their job properly. It is considered sufficient to pass a certain number of legislative acts and bylaws to implement EU law without ensuring that there exist people, institutions, procedures and patterns of behaviour that will effectively implement that law in accordance with its purpose. And it is considered sufficient not to have direct interferences in judicial independence by other branches of the government while disregarding other issues that are equally disruptive to the rule of law but come from within the judiciary.

This formalism merely follows practices from the pre-accession period when the rule of law reforms remained superficial and was not coupled with a genuine transformation of legal and political culture (Rodin, 2005). The same is visible not only on the national level but also on the EU's level, as can be seen in the Commission's Rule of Law Reports, a "tick the box" exercise of the things that can be measured and quantified. However, the formalistic approach easily misses many issues that are equally, if not more, relevant to the rule of law, which are substantive and qualitative and cannot be quantified, such as legal culture and tradition, legal values, legal reasoning and legal education – the issues we have placed at the centre of our discussion in this chapter.

5.8 Conclusion

This chapter presented the complex evolution of Croatian judiciary over the past two decades during the accession negotiations and in the post-accession period. It showed that the external imposition of legal and political standards from the EU did not fully achieve the desired aim. This was due to a combination of different reasons. It was partly due to the methodology of accession negotiations, which was more focused on quantitative and formal requirements than on true changes in the legal culture and the internal judicial structure and functioning of the Croatian judiciary. Additionally, the limited success of the reform of the Croatian judiciary also proved that without real commitment and support in the respective member state to carry out and implement the necessary changes and to preserve them after the accession, the reform cannot achieve the desired results.

The effects of maintaining *status quo* in Croatian justice system are self-evident. On the one side, the current impregnability of the Croatian judiciary tends to discourage direct and overt political attacks on the judicial branch, leading to the rule of law backsliding like the ones witnessed in Hungary and Poland. On the other side, the concept of independence is internalised to the point of isolationism, thwarting the requisite level of democratic control over Croatian judiciary necessary to achieve the liberal ideal of the rule of law and preventing judiciary's full participation in collaborative democratic governance based on the system checks and balances. The lack of accountability remains and will remain translated to the lack of efficiency, quality and public trust into the system that predominantly characterise the operating mode of Croatian judiciary. Perhaps recourse to mechanisms available under EU law could provide some positive impact. As was repeatedly shown, any meaningful change can only come from within the system.

Notes

1 The Court of Justice of the EU has, since the 2018 judgement in *Associação Sindical dos Juízes Portugueses* (Case C-64/16), consistently insisted that member states' obligation under Article 19 of the Treaty on the EU to ensure effective judicial review by independent judiciary is "of the essence of the rule of law" (paras 36 and 41). The same position was taken by EU legislature, which listed "endangering the independence of the judiciary" amongst the breaches of the principles of the rule of law in Regulation 2020/2092 on a general regime of conditionality for the protection of the Union budget.

2 The European Commission's annual "rule of law reports" form part of the so-called Rule of Law Mechanism, a political programme of the Commission demonstrating its commitment to monitor the state of the rule of law in the member states and address the rising rule of law concerns within the bloc. The Mechanism is designed as a preventive, transparency-raising and cooperative reporting mechanism resulting in the Commission's annual communication of its findings to other EU institutions through individual country reports.

3 The only slightly positive example of handling backlog was identified in the High Commercial Court, which has assigned most procedural work previously done by judges to court staff.

4 The Commission, likewise, did not identify any judgement of the Court of Justice of the EU which Croatia failed to comply with, which should demonstrate the country's tendencies to violate EU law. For a general discussion about the Commission's use of infringement actions against Croatia, see Carević (2021).

5 The following remarks are based on the authors' participation in the "Roundtable on the Rule of Law", held at the Faculty of Law in Zagreb on 4 November 2022, which brought together legal scholars and judges from several Croatian courts (High Administrative Court, Commercial Court in Zagreb, and County Court in Sisak).

References

Bačić Selanec, N. and Ćapeta, T. (2022) 'The Rule of Law and Adjudication of the Court of Justice of the European Union', in T. Ćapeta, I. Goldner Lang and T. Perišin (eds.) *The Changing European Union: A Critical View on the Role of Law and the Courts*. Oxford: Hart Publishing, pp. 50–75.

Bačić Selanec, N., Ćapeta, T., Goldner Lang, I. and Petrić, D. (2020) 'Report for Croatia', in M. Botman and J. Langer (eds.) *National Courts and the Enforcement of EU Law: The Pivotal Role of National Courts in the EU Legal Order. XXIX FIDE Congress in The Hague, Congress Publications Vol. 1*. The Hague: Eleven International Publishing, pp. 115–132.

Bačić Selanec, N. and Petrić, D. (2024) 'Internal Independence of Judiciary in the EU and the Ghosts From Socialist Past: Why the Court of Justice Should Not Follow AG Pikamäe in *Hann Invest*', *Croatian Yearbook of European Law and Policy*, 20(1), pp. 1–25.

Bodul, D. (2022) 'Nova Okvirna mjerila za rad sudaca. Objektivno provjerljivi parametri ili ne?', *Informator: instruktivno-informativni list za ekonomska i pravna pitanja*, 6717, pp. 1–4.

Bratković, M. (2019) 'Građansko pravosuđe u službi građana', in J. Barbić (ed.) *Europska budućnost hrvatskoga građanskog pravosuđa*. Zagreb: Hrvatska akademija znanosti i umjetnosti, pp. 161–183.

Bratković, M. (2021) 'In Search of Efficiency: Court Structure and Case Management in Croatia', in Peter C. H. Chan and Remco C. H. Van Rhee (eds.) *Civil Case Management in the Twenty-First Century: Court Structures Still Matter*. Singapore: Springer, pp. 169–191.

Ćapeta, T. (2002) *Sudovi Europske unije. Nacionalni sudovi kao europski sudovi*. Zagreb: Institut za međunarodne odnose.

Ćapeta, T. (2005) 'Courts, Legal Culture and the Enlargement of the EU', *Croatian Yearbook of European Law and Policy*, 1(1), pp. 23–53.

Ćapeta, T. (2020) 'Može li Europski sud spasiti vladavinu prava?', in A. Bačić (ed.) *Pravo i politika EU – stara pitanja, novi odgovori*. Zagreb: Hrvatska akademija znanosti i umjetnosti, pp. 57–87.

Carević, M. (2021) 'Caught on the Radar of the European Commission: Croatian Experiences with the Infringement Procedure', *Croatian Yearbook of European Law and Policy*, 17(1), pp. 279–305.

European Commission (2011) *Interim Report from the Commission to the European Parliament and the Council on Reforms in Croatia in the Field of Judiciary and Fundamental Rights (Negotiation Chapter 23), COM (2011) 110*. Available at: https://eur-lex.europa.eu/legal-content/EN/TXT/PDF/?uri=CELEX:52011DC0110 (27.03.2024).

European Commission (2020) *Staff Working Document: 2020 Rule of Law Report, Country Chapter on the Rule of Law Situation in Croatia, SWD(2020) 310.*

Available at: https://eur-lex.europa.eu/legal-content/EN/TXT/PDF/?uri=CELEX:52020SC0310 (27.03.2024).

European Commission (2021) *Staff Working Document: 2021 Rule of Law Report, Country Chapter on the Rule of Law Situation in Croatia, SWD(2021) 713.*

Available at: https://eur-lex.europa.eu/legal-content/EN/TXT/PDF/?uri=CELEX:52021SC0713 (27.03.2024).

European Commission (2022a) *Staff Working Document: 2022 Rule of Law Report, Country Chapter on the Rule of Law Situation in Croatia, SWD(2022) 511*. Available at: https://eur-lex.europa.eu/legal-content/EN/TXT/PDF/?uri=CELEX:52022SC0511 (27.03.2024).

European Commission (2022b) *The EU Justice Scoreboard, COM(2022) 234*. Available at: https://commission.europa.eu/system/files/2022-05/eu_justice_scoreboard_2022.pdf (27.03.2024).

European Commission (2023) *Staff Working Document: 2023 Rule of Law Report, Country Chapter on the Rule of Law Situation in Croatia, SWD(2023) 811* . Available at: https://commission.europa.eu/system/files/2023-07/27_1_52610_coun_chap_croatia_en.pdf (27.03.2024).

Goldner Lang, I. (2019) 'The Rule of Law, the Force of Law and the Power of Money in the EU', *Croatian Yearbook of European Law and Policy*, 15(1), pp. 1–26.

Goldner Lang, I., Đurđević, Z. and Mataija M. (2019) 'The Constitution of Croatia in the Perspective of European and Global Governance', in A. Albi and S. Bardutzky (eds.) *National Constitutions in European and Global Governance: Democracy, Rights the Rule of Law*. The Hague: T. M. C. Asser Press/Springer, pp. 1139–1177.

Ivančan, A. and Petrić, D. (2019) 'Are Croatian Courts Prepared for the Interpretive Obligation?', *Review of Central and East European Law*, 44(4), pp. 493–526.

Lukić, S. (2017) 'Profesorica s Pravnog fakulteta u čudu: "Odluka Vrhovnog suda u slučaju Ina-Mol protivna je europskom pravu" ', *Jutarnji list*, 6 October. Available at: www.jutarnji.hr/vijesti/hrvatska/profesorica-s-pravnog-fakulteta-u-cudu-odluka-vrhovnog-suda-u-slucaju-ina-mol-protivna-je-europskom-pravu-6619758 (22.05.2023).

Lukić, S. (2023) 'Skroman uspjeh službenica, zatečena i uplašena čelnica sindikata, bully iz bazena, šutnja sudaca i odvjetnika', *Jutarnji list*, 28 July. Available at: www.jutarnji.hr/vijesti/hrvatska/skroman-uspjeh-sluzbenica-zatecena-i-uplasena-celnica-sindikata-bully-iz-bazena-sutnja-sudaca-i-odvjetnika-15359916 (08.08.2023).

Orešić, B. (2021) 'Četiri prijedloga za reformu pravosuđa: Kako promijeniti sustav koji je postao država u državi', *Jutarnji list*, 25 April. Available at: www.jutarnji.hr/globus/politika/4-prijedloga-za-reformu-pravosuda-kako-promijeniti-sustav-koji-je-postao-drzava-u-drzavi-15068031 (22.05.2023).

Petrić, D. (2023) 'The Application of Article 47 of the Charter in Croatia: Happening by Accident?', in M. Bonelli, M. Eliantonio and G. Gentile (eds.) *Article 47 of the EU Charter and Effective Judicial Protection – Volume 2: The National Perspective*. Oxford: Hart Publishing, pp. 29–48.

Raić, A. (2023) 'Ugledni profesori pravnih fakulteta tvrde da je štrajk sudaca posve nezakonit: "Ovo što rade je nakaradno"', *Telegram*, 9 May. Available at: www.telegram.hr/politika-kriminal/ugledni-profesori-pravnih-fakulteta-tvrde-da-je-strajk-sudaca-posve-nezakonit-ovo-sto-rade-je-nakaradno/ (08.08.2023).

Rodin, S. (2005) 'Discourse and Authority in European and Post-Communist Legal Culture', *Croatian Yearbook of European Law and Policy*, 1(1), pp. 1–22.

Uzelac, A. (2010) 'Survival of the Third Legal Tradition?', in J. Walker and O. Chase (eds.) *Common Law, Civil Law and the Future of Categories*. Toronto: LexisNexis, pp. 377–396.

Uzelac, A. (2020a) *Judiciary in Croatia 2020. Current Situation, Causes of Crisis and Possible Reform Measures*. Available at: www.alanuzelac.from.hr/pubs/C04_Judiciary_in_Croatia_preprint.pdf (04.07.2023).

Uzelac, A. (2020b) 'Jedinstvena primjena prava u hrvatskom parničnom postupku: tradicija i suvremenost', in J. Barbić (ed.) *Novine u parničnom procesnom pravu*. Zagreb: Hrvatska akademija znanosti i umjetnosti, pp. 111–168.

Uzelac, A. (2021) 'Accountability and Transparency in Civil Justice: Some General Remarks and a View from Croatia', *Revija Kopaoničke škole prirodnog prava: časopis za pravnu teoriju i praksu*, 3(1), pp. 121–146.

Venice Commission of the Council of Europe (2022) *Opinion No. 1073/2021 on the introduction of the procedure of renewal of security vetting through amendments to the Courts Act, CDL(2022)005*.

6 Croatian Foreign Policy between the EU and the United States

Tihomir Cipek

6.1 Introduction

This chapter tries to show how Croatia's entry into the European Union has affected its foreign policy. The central question is whether Croatia went from a country that was the subject of the European Union's foreign policy to one that, at least partially, shaped it, or rather, how Europeanisation affected Croatian foreign policy. Europeanisation is defined as the effect that the policies of the EU have on its members or, rather, the process in which EU dynamics affect the political dynamics and policy choices of its members. It is about transforming European rules, procedures and even paradigms into the logic of the domestic discourse, identity, political structures and public policies of its member states (Radaelli, 2003, p. 30). So, the assumption is that the EU has clear and effective policies. However, that is not always the case with its foreign policy. The EU has difficulty establishing a unified foreign policy because it has trouble creating its own identity (Bretherton and Vogler, 2006; Guérot and Ritz, 2022; Kekeleire and Delreux, 2022). Member countries are guided by their interests and identities. This also applies to the EU's enlargement policy, which has proven to be a powerful instrument of its foreign policy. Since Croatia has experience negotiating the accession to the EU, it could assert itself as an expert on EU enlargement to the Western Balkans. This expertise could be a potential "niche" for affirming Croatian foreign policy. Nevertheless, is this something that Croatia even wants? Namely, the entire process of joining the EU was interpreted as Croatia's departure from the Balkans. In order to address this question, the chapter uses the constructivist theory of international relations, which emphasises how national identity is understood. Its starting point is that political subjects act according to how they understand themselves. The main founding myth of the independent Croatian state is the Homeland War, in which the country defended itself against Serbian aggression. An important assistance in the defence of the country and the preservation of its territorial integrity was provided by the United States. That is the reason why, in cases where there is no unified European foreign policy, Croatia usually sides with the United States. Croatia has learned from its own experience that the United States leads the West and that American policies significantly influence processes in Southeast Europe. This lesson became even more

DOI: 10.4324/9781003394013-6

urgent after the Russian aggression against Ukraine. Croatia is considered a part of the West, so it has joined the policy of defending Ukraine, led by the North Atlantic Treaty Organization (NATO) alliance or the United States. Croatian foreign policy has still not found a special "niche", meaning a topic through which it could assert itself. This niche could be found in the support for the EU enlargement to the Balkans, but since there is no unified EU policy on this issue, Croatia is also hesitant. It is declaratively in favour of the enlargement, but it is also aware that member states can block the entry of new countries into the Union. Croatia seems to have doubts about how to position itself towards the EU enlargement policy. On the one hand, it is aware that EU enlargement to the southeast would "move" Croatia towards the centre of the Union and protect it from the thankless position of being the EU's periphery and border. On the other hand, however, one of Croatia's foreign policy goals is to support ethnic Croats in the neighbouring countries, which leads it to pursue a policy of blocking the entry of its neighbours into the EU. After all, it has unresolved border issues with these countries. That is why Croatia has still not found an area where it could establish itself as an expert and thus affirm its foreign policy role. The indecisiveness of Croatian foreign policy does not stem solely from its doubts but primarily from the fact that even the European Union has not established itself as an independent factor in global politics. This thesis will be presented through four chapters. The first one – *Globalisation and Foreign Policy* – provides an insight into the global challenges faced by the European and Croatian foreign policies and defines a theoretical approach to the examined phenomena. The second chapter, *Three Phases of Croatian Foreign Policy*, establishes a connection between the defining of the Croatian national identity, the goals of its foreign policy and the process of Europeanisation. The third chapter, *Rearrangement of Foreign Policy Goals during the Integration into International Alliances*, outlines the development of the dynamics between Croatian and European foreign policy through which Croatia wanted to complete its Europeanisation process fully. It also shows how the membership in the NATO alliance and US policy influence Croatian foreign policy. The fourth chapter, entitled *New Goals of Croatian Foreign Policy*, examines the country's foreign policy goals in the most recent period. It bears repeating that the relationship between Croatian foreign policy and the process of Europeanisation is examined based on the constructivist theory of international relations, which states that national identity is one of the key categories. This chapter attempts to answer whether a small country like Croatia, after completing the processes of Europeanisation, will even be capable of leading an independent foreign policy. That is not only a question of understanding its own identity but to call on the realist theory of international relations, real power relations.

6.2 Globalisation and Foreign Policy

The globalisation of world politics has brought with it new challenges for the foreign policies of individual countries. It has shown that even the most powerful countries have to make alliances and that, in international politics, individual countries are dependent on each other and compelled towards cooperation (Keohane and Nye, 2000; Milner and Moravcsik, 2009). Countries cannot ensure their security without creating regional and even global alliances. This thesis has been proven by the Russian aggression against Ukraine (Krickovic and Sakwa, 2022). It has been shown that European states can only build foreign and defence policies if they create a system of alliances in the security field. Without its army and defence policy, the European Union must rely on the NATO alliance, in which the United States plays the central role. The reason why the European Union has yet to manage to shape itself into a solid and independent subject of global politics, however, lies in more than just the dominance of the United States as the undisputed leader of the West. The absence of a single European foreign policy stems from its member states' different interests and ideas about EU policy in general.

Furthermore, the EU does not meet a formal prerequisite for a robust global role – it is not represented as a unit in the United Nations (UN). Out of all European countries, France yields the most significant power in international politics and is also a permanent member of the UN Security Council. Germany, the most significant European economic power, does not have the same status in global politics. Nevertheless, it has managed to direct the policy of the European Union together with France.

Russia's aggression against Ukraine has exposed all the weaknesses of the EU security policy and clearly showed that the decisive voice in that area belongs to NATO and the United States as the alliance leader. Moreover, the distinction between foreign and security policy has disappeared, as foreign policy has been reduced to defending Ukraine, which is presented as the defence of the West. It appears that the goal of European politics is to use the protracted war to economically and militarily exhaust Russia or even destroy it while at the same time turning the NATO alliance under American leadership into a leading political instrument. Of course, knowing how the war will end and its consequences on international relations is impossible. However, it can be noted that the strength of the transatlantic alliance led by the United States prevails over the capacity of the European Union to develop an independent foreign policy. The Union should build such a policy by considering some other circumstances that are specific to it. Namely, the EU has not realised that its periphery is seeing "the emergence of a bipolar or multipolar order" (Jović, 2018, p. 376).

It also ignored that Russian geopolitics does not acknowledge a Europe separate from Asia but talks about Eurasia (Boban and Cipek, 2017, p. 278). This term has been used by a part of the new Russian nationalist elite to show that Russia is an independent country and a distinct civilisation whose culture represents the essence of the Eurasian civilisation. Instead of paying attention to new geopolitical interpretations and signals within Russian foreign policy (Cipek, 2018), the EU chose to embrace liberal optimism or adhere to the thesis that the whole world wanted to adopt liberal values. This slightly arrogant attitude has also prevailed when it came to the European Union enlargement policy. The Union likes to think that integration and membership in the EU is the only right path for all European countries.

It still likes to see itself as the only legitimate power in Europe, which should also play a decisive role on the global level.

> Such an understanding of Europe has something imperial or at least neo-imperial about it. It defines Europe as an ideal, a higher goal, a final destination and a model that drives the transformation of countries and societies in its surroundings – through the enlargement policy and even through the European Neighbourhood Policy or its Eastern Partnership.
>
> (Jović, 2018, p. 376)

This attitude is still dominant today even though the power of the EU is declining, and it is proving to be inferior to the United States. Indeed, asking whether the EU can lead an independent and efficient foreign policy is justified. Is such a policy even possible or necessary? Current circumstances prove that authors such as Jović (2018) were right in referring to Asle Toje, who said that the European Union is a small power which, despite its size and economic strength, will continue to play a relatively modest role in international politics (Toje, 2011). Of course, the leaders of EU member states are also aware of this, which is why each member state leads its independent foreign policy. The issue, therefore, is the need of each country – in light of the EU's deficient foreign policy profile (or regardless of it) – to confirm its sovereignty, or rather its identity, in international politics. However, the European Union member states try to contribute to the international political order in some specific respect simply because they understand a certain international context or policy in a particular region better or differently than other members. This principle also applies to the foreign policy of small countries, such as Croatia. In the analysis, we start from the thesis that small states are not defined exclusively by the power they possess. However, concerning the context of their actions, "smallness is defined through the relationship between the state and its external environment" (Steinmetz and Wivel, 2016, p. 7). Therefore, *smallnes*s is a comparative concept. Considering how to find their way in the external political environment, small states can become small powers and realise their interests. "This brings to our attention a particular set of policy problems and foreign policy dilemmas and allows us to distinguish between issue areas, where the notion of small state is relevant, and issue areas, where it is not" (Steinmetz and Wivel, 2016, p. 7).

However, the question that should be asked is how small countries, including Croatia, act when the EU still needs a unified foreign policy. Are they more inclined to support proposals coming from the core of the European Union, i.e. proposals that weigh France and Germany behind them, or do they favour the United States' foreign policy? To wit, the US foreign policy has great power, which leads it to try and bring international organisations under its control and instrumentalise them to realise its national interests. On the other hand, Croatia, as a small country that does not possess economic, military or political power with which it could significantly influence international relations,[1] has several possibilities. Hill lists the following: (i) foreign policy that is focused on preservation or survival; (ii) multilateralism as a form of bulwark/shelter in international relations; (iii) foreign policy that is focused on one specific task or specialisation, the so-called niche; and (iv) foreign policy of silence (quietism). Since Croatia most certainly belongs among small countries, the strategies offered in the second part of Hill's article seem appropriate. The orientation of Croatian foreign policy towards membership in the European Union and NATO is a typical example of the strategy of "multilateralism as a form of shelter in international relations" (Hill, 2003, p. 247). For large countries, the EU can represent an attempt at "directed multilateralism", in which leading countries try to use EU institutions to achieve their national or corporations' interests (Streeck, 2021). Of course, Croatia is also trying to do that, but its power sources are limited, and it does not have its own commercial companies. Croatian politics thus depends on the relations within the European Union, especially its economic policy and the expansion policy to the southeast of Europe. In this environment, Croatian foreign policy tries to orient itself according to its self-understanding and position within the European Union. After all, its entry into the European Union was also primarily treated as a question of identity – a "return to Europe" or "departure from the Balkans". Croatia's politics saw the European Union primarily as a shelter from the problems coming from Southeast Europe.

6.3 Three Phases of Croatian Foreign Policy

The politics of national identity also determined the European path of Croatian politics. The accession into Europe was framed as a matter of returning to Croatia's true identity.

> Croatian Europhilia is determined more negatively than positively: Croats are passionately trying to prove to foreigners that they are Europeans in order to highlight their difference from the "deep Balkans", and less because of any real positive sense of belonging to and understanding of the European integration processes around them.
>
> (Nobilo, 2000, p. 69)

Most of the Croatian public thought of it as a process in which EU institutions should recognise that the Croatian identity is a European one because Croatian history, architecture, painting, music and even landscape are an integral part of Europe, not the Balkans. However, once they realised that it was not about that but about the process of negotiating the fulfilment of the conditions for membership, the public started to become increasingly sceptical. Nationalists began to decry a loss of state independence that had been dearly won during the war. A liberal interpretation tried to oppose this, claiming that Euroscepticism developed because people were not sufficiently informed. That thesis, however, was utterly wrong.

On the contrary, the French and Dutch public was well informed about the European Constitution and still rejected it through referendums. It has been shown that an informed public can do the exact opposite of what the political elites expect and that citizens are willing to put national identity before economic interests (Fukuyama, 2018). Brexit made this clear. Disappointment over EU accession became even more significant because it was not really about a process of negotiations "but rather about feigning negotiations to cover up the acceptance of fixed and a certain number of variable conditions for joining the EU". "The sovereignty of European countries is still too dangerous to be allowed in any meaningful way. Sovereignty thus becomes nominal and symbolic, and not real in a political sense" (Jović, 2018, p. 379).

The entry into the EU was thus presented as Croatia's historical goal; once it was finally achieved and Croatia became a member of the Union, it would mark a kind of end of history. This begs the question of whether a country can conduct an independent foreign policy after the end of history after its main goal has been achieved. The constant emphasis on the "shared values" of Europe shows that these values are abstract and shaped by the European "global class" (Dahrendorf, 2002). After all, Wolfgang Streeck was right to wonder why the so-called shared European values were more important than, say, Dutch, Bavarian, Greek, Croatian or other values (Streeck, 2021, pp. 132–134). Thus, Croatian foreign policy is strongly connected with identity politics in which Europe is defined as an ideal. Entry into the European Union represents a definitive separation of Croatia from the Balkans and a change in Croatian public policies. The constructivist approach is the most appropriate for analysing Croatian foreign policy. That does not mean interpretations derived from the realist and liberal approaches do not explain some features of Croatian foreign policy. It is a given that Croatia also starts from its real power, which is not significant, but its membership in the Union gives it additional sway. There is also a clear need for economic and political modernisation of the country through EU membership. However, what is questionable is the liberal thesis that peace and prosperity will prevail once liberal democracy spreads all over the world.

Moreover, this idea leads to global conflicts. So, we will advocate the thesis that international relations cannot be fully explained through the category of power and democracy. A country's foreign policy is also a cultural phenomenon, and how a country and a nation understand themselves significantly impacts their foreign policy. In this analysis, we thus start from the idea "that people act not only to win things but also to defend a certain conception of who they are". Furthermore:

> We act, that is, not only because there are things we want to have, but also because there are persons we want to be. This latter kind of action must be the more fundamental since it is only as someone we can be interested in something. Without this "someone", there would not be anyone around for whom something could or could not be an interest. Actions undertaken to establish this someone are thus the more basic, and they cannot be redescribed in rationalistic terms – calculations of utility gains and losses can make no sense until they can be attached to a certain person.
>
> (Ringmar, 1996, p. 3)

How someone defines themselves and how they define others is therefore crucial.

Namely, the principle of identity – that A = A because A is not B – also applies to foreign policy. Accordingly, Croatia is Europe because it is not the Balkans. This distinction still significantly determines Croatian foreign policy. Do the Others constitute a threat? Should they be helped or stopped on their way to the European Union? The answers to these questions shape the direction of Croatian foreign policy. The exact identity matrix also determines the second goal of Croatian foreign policy, which is to influence the status of Croats in neighbouring countries. It should thus be concluded that identity issues have significantly determined the main features of Croatian foreign policy.

Croatian foreign policy was significantly shaped by its experience with EU accession negotiations. However, as was already mentioned, these negotiations are not negotiations in the complete sense of the word but more checks to see whether a country meets the conditions for membership. Moreover, since Croatian political elites have declared that joining the EU was the only path Croatia should take, the public did not perceive that outcome as an act of freedom. Croatia's experience of joining the EU was like driving in a predetermined direction, where every deviation from the path meant defeat. Countries that accept the terms of entry into the European Union lose part of their sovereignty. However, the question is whether, after the experience of joining the EU, which clearly shows that the path to the EU is a one-way and entirely determined one, a small country like Croatia can even develop an independent foreign policy. Or, better yet, do Croatian elites have the ideas, knowledge and energy to lead an independent foreign policy? What is their perception of the benefits and resources at Croatia's disposal after joining the European Union? These were influenced not only by the experience of negotiations and joining the Union but also by the fact that Croatia had been building a foreign policy aimed at a single clear, primary goal. This process went through three phases (Vukadinović, 2000). In the first phase, the goal of Croatian foreign policy was to gain international recognition for the newly proclaimed Republic of Croatia; in the second one, it was to gain international support in order to defend itself against the Great Serbian aggression supported by the JNA (Yugoslav National Army) and ensure its territorial integrity and freedom. In the third phase, the goal was to join the NATO alliance in 2009 and the EU in 2013 (see Table 6.1).

Croatia's Foreign policy experiences before joining the EU had significantly determined its foreign policy as an EU member. In the first phase, it became obvious that Croatia's international recognition was first met with hesitation and later with

Table 6.1 Three phases of Croatian foreign policy

Phase	*Goals*	*Results*
First	International recognition of the country	22 May 1992 – Croatia was admitted as a member of the United Nations
Second	Ensuring territorial integrity	5 August 1995 – Operation *Storm;* 12 November 1995 – The Erdut Agreement
Third	Entry into NATO and the EU	1 April 2009 – NATO member; 1 July 2013 – EU member

Source: Compilation of the author according to Vukadinović (2000).

division within the EU. The Union first tried to solve the crisis in Yugoslavia by accepting the entire Yugoslavia to the EU to prevent its disintegration and civil war. After the JNA attack on Slovenia and the beginning of the Serb rebellion in Croatia, which was encouraged and organised by Serbia under the leadership of Slobodan Milošević, the EU abandoned the policy of preserving Yugoslavia's unity and, at Germany's incentive, decided to grant Slovenia and Croatia's requests to recognise their independence. This decision later received support from influential members of the UN – United States, China and Russia, which further encouraged other member countries to recognise Croatia as an independent country and admit it to UN membership. However, although German politics claimed that the recognition of the new countries would stop the war and force Milošević to come to terms with the new international situation, which did not happen. The aggression against Croatia continued. It turned out that the EU could not stop the war, not only because it did not have its military forces but because it had proved difficult to reach an agreement on foreign policy goals. Croatian politics learned its lesson and began relying on the United States to strengthen its international position and liberate the country. Davorin Rudolf, the then Croatian Minister of Foreign Affairs, wrote

> For me, the United States of America has always been the most important and decisive foreign policy actor in resolving the Yugoslav state crisis. Simply put, for more than fifty years, since the end of the Second World War, the Europeans have failed to act as a "united force". When I was serving as the Croatian Minister of Foreign Affairs, I personally tried my hardest to gain the trust and support of the Americans.
>
> (Rudolf, 1999, p. 323)

It also became evident that, within the Union, parties gathered within the European People's Party provided stronger support than those connected with social democrats or other political factions (cf. Granić, 2005). The support of the United States proved to be crucial. After the military Operation Storm, it was US support and organisation that led to the signing of the Erdut Agreement, which integrated back into Croatia the areas in Eastern Slavonia, Baranja and Western Syrmia that had been forcibly separated and united into the Republic of Serbian Krajina, with headquarters in Knin. The Erdut agreement resulted in the unification of the territory of the Republic of Croatia and the establishment of a single legal, political and economic system. During the second phase, Croatia thus secured its territorial integrity (Jović, 2018). In the third phase, the focus was on its national security and the development of liberal democracy and market economy. Croatia's leadership tried to achieve the first goal by joining the NATO alliance. This issue enjoyed the consensual support of centrist parties. Both the main HDZ party (Croatian Democratic Union) and the social democrats considered NATO membership to be beyond dispute. There was some initial scepticism among several smaller parties. However, they also agreed to support the country's entry into the NATO alliance if public opinion polls showed that most citizens supported it. Of course, it was not a firm imperative on their side more of an excuse to change their mind and side with the majority. Stronger resistance came from the student left, whose nucleus comprised students of the Faculty of Humanities and Social Sciences of the University of Zagreb. However, their attempts to collect enough signatures for a referendum on Croatia's membership in NATO were unsuccessful. Nevertheless, their activity pointed to a clear and strong connection between domestic and foreign politics. It also became clear that NATO membership could be used to block the entry of new countries into the alliance. As Turkey is currently making it difficult for Sweden to join NATO, Croatia had a similar problem with the Slovenian nationalist right, gathered around Janez Janša's Slovenian Democratic Party. We cannot know what was going on behind the curtain. However, we can assume that the US pressure on Janez Janša was so strong that he was forced to give up. The necessary two-thirds majority in the Parliament of the Republic of Slovenia eventually supported Croatia's entry into the NATO alliance. This case showed that thanks to their membership in international organisations, even small countries like Slovenia could gain blackmail power. The power to block others from joining an international organisation is a key fact and a challenge for the politics of small countries. Thanks to this, a small country has the power leverage that exceeds its real strength and can turn it into a country that influences international relations. In such situations, a small country becomes a small power. Can Croatia resist this temptation? Will its EU membership be used to block the entry of candidate countries into the Union? These questions will be addressed further in this chapter.

6.4 Rearrangement of Foreign Policy Goals during the Integration into International Alliances

6.4.1 On the Path of Euro-Atlantic Integrations

The previous chapter has shown that Croatia's path to NATO and the EU depended on the decision of the political elites. In the Croatian context, the leading role was played by the president of the country, Franjo Tuđman; his political doctrine was centred on the idea of state sovereignty. He originated the so-called Tuđman's fortress, a constitutional provision to defend Croatian sovereignty. Article 141 of the 1997 Constitution of the Republic of Croatia states that a decision to join an international alliance needs to be reached through a referendum "with the majority of the total number of voters in the country". This provision made it difficult for Croatia to enter all international associations, including the EU. This is unsurprising because, in his "sovereignism", Tuđman was also sceptical of the EU. Tuđman's advisor for foreign policy, Anto Nobilo, has said that "The ruling party, including Tuđman himself, were largely Europhobic and suspicious of liberal European ideas, which dissolve the identities of small nations through these integrations". During the 1990s, Tuđman said, "The EU is not the first European community, and the previous 'empires' also fell apart".

Furthermore, "This reflected his virulent historicist approach to a modern process. Tuđman also saw the UN membership as a status symbol, a final confirmation of sovereignty, and less as a mechanism for Croatia's integration into modern global trends" (Nobilo, 2000, p. 236). While Franjo Tuđman was the President of Croatia, joining the European Union was not a priority of Croatian politics. The situation changed when a coalition of social democrats, liberals and other left-centre parties came to power in 2000. Only after their victory did Croatian political elites' principal foreign policy goal become an entry into NATO and the European Union, as a project that would definitively separate Croatia from the Balkans, "return it to Europe", and guarantee its security and economic development. This was the goal on which the two leading Croatian parties – the centre-right HDZ and the centre-left SDP – reached a consensus, supported by almost the entire economic and cultural elite. In 2001, the Republic of Croatia signed the Stabilization and Association Agreement (SAA) with the European Union. It applied for EU membership in 2003 and was granted the official status of a membership candidate by the European institutions in 2004. The negotiations began in 2005 and, despite the initial blockade by Slovenia – which tried to use this issue to resolve its border dispute with Croatia – they were successfully concluded on 30 June 2011; the Treaty of Accession was signed on 9 December of the same year. When the negotiations finally ended after ten years, Croatia's reason for entering the EU was not apparent anymore, especially since the Union was also experiencing a significant economic crisis and a crisis of its legitimacy. The referendum on EU accession was held on 22 January 2012; the turnout was 43.5%, of which 66% voted in favour of joining the Union and 33.1% were against it (SECRC - State Electoral Commission of the Republic of Croatia, 2024). A good definition of the attitude of the Croatian public towards the European Union was provided by Dejan Jović, who described it as "Euro-indifference". This means that the majority of the public was neither for nor against the European Union but considered their country's entry into the EU an inevitable process they could not influence.

> The results of the referendum on the European Union show that Croatia is first and foremost a Euro-indifferent country, not particularly Eurosceptic nor Euro-enthusiastic. In this, it is increasingly similar to current EU members and many candidates and potential candidate countries.
>
> (Jović, 2013, p. 165)

Many citizens know that their countries are not or could be active subjects of international politics. That is why they accept EU accession as a process entirely in the hands of the EU, which cannot be influenced by the policies of the countries of which they are citizens. As mentioned, Croatia's entry into the EU was primarily perceived emotionally, not rationally, and in the light of understanding its national identity, not material interests (cf. Šelo Šabić, 2014). This attitude of Croatian citizens was attributed to, among other factors, the government's campaign for EU accession, which targeted emotions and did not highlight the country's interest in joining the EU. Also counterproductive were the messages that Croatia would be threatened with economic ruin if it did not become an EU member. Today, the Croatian public believes that the EU is divided into a core that profits from the Union and a periphery that must submit to the interests of the core. However, despite this, most Croatian citizens support membership in the EU, which can be seen from the election results for the European Parliament, in which Eurosceptic parties fare poorly.

6.4.2 Prominent Influence of the United States

Croatia already uses the European Union as a shelter under which it can more easily withstand the challenges of international politics. But what if that cover does not work? This happens when the European Union has no clear and unified foreign and security policy. We should, therefore, examine how Croatia's foreign policy behaves when it is left without European protection, which we can do on the example of Croatia's decision-making during the 2012 vote in the UN Assembly. At the global level, Croatia often sides with the United States and votes against the majority of EU members, or rather, it sides with those Union members who follow American foreign policy. This came to the fore during the vote on the position of Palestine in the UN. Although it seemed that Croatia would recognise Palestine as an associate member of the UN, this did not happen. Namely, the session of the Council for Foreign Affairs in Brussels revealed that member states had different positions on this issue. The Croatian delegation at the UN abstained during the vote on Palestine's status as an associate member of the UN, thus clearly siding with the minority that followed the US lead. In the UN General Assembly vote, the principle that the Palestinian people have the right to independence and statehood was supported by 138 member states, which resulted in the Palestinian self-government becoming an observer to that international body. Croatia's decision to abstain from the vote caused much criticism and showed that there were two standpoints on Croatian foreign policy. The first thought that foreign policy should be based on principles, while the second one believed that Croatia, as a small country, should either side with the more substantial powers or be restrained in the face of challenges. The first position was defended by Budimir Lončar, a long-time diplomat and adviser to the former President Stipe Mesić. In an interview with the *Jutarnji* newspaper, Lončar explicitly criticised Croatia's abstaining:

> The recognition of Palestine is a moral issue, and the decision for Croatia to abstain is a mistake. One could understand that Germany abstained because of its role in the Holocaust. However, Croatia was founded on anti-fascism, and there was no reason not to support Palestine, just as more than half of European countries did. After all, it is precisely because of our past, in which the Croatian people did not have the right to their state for a long time and had to shed much blood in the nineties for that right, that we have sympathy for people like the Palestinians.

On the other hand, the decision of the Croatian diplomacy received support from Mate Granić, who served as a Minister of Foreign Affairs for seven years:

> The fact is that the Palestinians have the right to a state, but we must not forget that the main representative of the Palestinian people is Hamas. Hamas does not recognise Israel and wants to destroy it, and even denies the existence of the Holocaust, which is unacceptable. Finally, Croatia has to keep track of its close allies, primarily America, so when everything is considered, our UN representatives reacted correctly.
>
> (Bajruši, 2012)

The statements of Mate Granić and Budimir Lončar show two different understandings of the principles that should guide Croatian foreign policy and two different interpretations of the principles on which international relations should be based. This dilemma between respect for principles and an appreciation of someone's strength is not specific to Croatia but also takes place in other countries as a discussion on a unilateral or multipolar world. A similar situation was repeated during the 2017 vote on Jerusalem as the capital of Israel. Croatia was one of six EU states that did not vote for the UN General Assembly resolution calling the United States to withdraw its recent recognition of Jerusalem as Israel's capital. Besides Croatia, the resolution was rejected by the Czech Republic, Hungary, Poland and Romania, while Latvia was absent during the vote. All other members of the European Union were in favour of the resolution. Croatia proved itself to be a loyal American ally. Despite strong opposition from the United States, the resolution was adopted with 128 votes in favour, 9 against, 21 absentees and 35 abstentions (United Nations [UN], 2017). This episode revealed Croatia's belief that the United States plays a decisive role in international relations and that, in cases where the EU does not have a clear, unified position, it should support the United States. This episode can also be interpreted as agreeing with what Hill calls the politics of quietism (2003, p. 249).

6.5 New Goals of Croatian Foreign Policy

New foreign policy goals of Croatian politics also start from an understanding of its own identity. With an apparent air of self-satisfaction, the Croatian Ministry of Foreign Affairs has asserted that

> Croatia is a sovereign Central European, Danubian, Adriatic and Mediterranean country that independently shapes its strategies and policies intending to achieve its national interests and goals, economic, political and social development, the safety of its citizens, and the protection of its national identity and fundamental values determined by the Constitution.

And further:

> Since achieving independence, defence and liberation of its territory in the Homeland War, the Republic of Croatia has developed into a free, democratic

> and responsible country. Membership in the North Atlantic Treaty Organization (starting now: NATO) and the European Union marked the achievement of important foreign policy and security goals and created conditions that allow Croatia additional economic, political and security development opportunities. (Narodne novine, 2017)

"Additional opportunities" mean that Croatia is allowed to fully integrate into the European Union and become a "real" European country. In Croatian self-understanding, this also implies a definite distancing from the Yugoslav past, which, together with the Balkans, represents a kind of spectre that constantly hovers over Croatian politics. This means a totally icy attitude towards the non-aligned countries in foreign policy. This policy could not even be changed by Radovan Vukadinović (1993), a respected expert on international relations, who warned that it was not good to leave the relations with non-aligned countries to Belgrade because the influence of non-aligned countries in the UN should not be ignored. Of course, Croatian politics was aware of this, but the identity pressure to escape the Balkans and Yugoslav history, in which non-alignment played an important role, was stronger than pragmatic interests.

As these official goals listed in the documents of the Croatian government and the Ministry of Foreign Affairs reveal, Croatia's politics is determined by how it understands its national identity (see Table 6.2). This also produced the only specific goal of Croatian foreign policy: to support Croats in the diaspora and primarily to protect the Croatian ethnic population in Bosnia and Herzegovina (Vlada RH, 2020). After all, if one looks at how some other countries have used their membership in the EU, it becomes clear that they also start from the interpretation of national identity. Thus, Greece challenged Macedonia's right to its name and blocked its negotiations on EU accession. After the Macedonian government changed the country's name to North Macedonia under pressure from the EU, the independence of the Macedonian national identity and the accession negotiations have been challenged by Bulgaria.

On the other hand, Slovenia blocked Croatia's entry into the EU over a state border issue. It is thus clear that the new member states from Southeast Europe have been using their EU membership to block the entry of neighbouring countries

Table 6.2 New goals of Croatia foreign policy

Goals	*Achieved*
Full integration into the European Union	1 January 2023 – Entry into the eurozone and the Schengen Area
Protecting Croats in Bosnia and Herzegovina	2 October 2022 – Changing the Bosnian electoral law and the Constitution of the Federation of Bosnia and Herzegovina
Assisting the process of EU and NATO enlargement to Southeast Europe	So far, no results

Source: Created by the author.

with whom they have disputes over national identity, borders or even just identity symbols. One has to wonder why Croatia would not act from the same position and block the negotiations and entry into the EU of its neighbouring countries, with which it has similar disputes.

As a member of the European Union, Croatia has thoroughly followed all the policies advocated by the European Commission. Moreover, its foreign policy is based on the belief that a state should be fully integrated into the European Union. This belief has meant replacing the national currency with the euro, that is, becoming a member of the eurozone and becoming a reliable guardian of EU borders by entering the Schengen area. At the same time, the ruling coalition led by the HDZ encountered resistance from a part of the public who believed that Croatia should not give up its national sovereignty and the possibility of conducting its own monetary as well as economic policy (Eurobarometer, 2022).

However, the Croatian government firmly believed in the advantages of the European Union. It is interesting that, in the debates in the Croatian parliament, hardly anyone referred to the example of Greece and its unsuccessful attempt, led by the left-wing Syriza party, to resist the Union and pursue an independent economic policy. It was precisely the example of Greece that demonstrated the weakening power of nation-states. It showed that public policies are defined at the level of the European Union, while the political remains at the level of individual countries. Political dynamics thus take place within the framework of the states, but important policy decisions are made at the level of the European Union. This also applies to foreign policy. Political elites are aware of this, as are the Croatian ones, and this results in foreign policy turning into a policy of pursuing goals that come "from above". These decisions are the only possible expert solutions backed by "European values". It is a phrase that has been repeated so much that it has become an *empty signifier*. The same goes for "democracy", "liberalism" and the "free market"; all of them have had and still have the function of magic words used to denote some European utopia. For most of the politicians of Southeast European countries, it was a utopia they were striving for. For the leading politicians of Montenegro, Bosnia and Herzegovina, North Macedonia and Serbia, it was a positive utopia, a goal to strive towards. Whether Croatia will use its new power as an EU member to help or prevent its entry into the Union remains to be seen. The programme of the Croatian government currently emphasises that

> The Republic of Croatia remains committed to the Euro-Atlantic perspective and the future of the countries of Southeast Europe, and strongly supports the enlargement processes of the European Union and NATO. The Republic of Croatia is determined to provide further support and encouragement in their Euro-Atlantic integrations and reform processes in general, using the experience and knowledge from its accession processes, which it will offer to these countries, including assistance in building and strengthening their capabilities so that they can respond to security challenges and threats on their own.
>
> (Vlada RH, 2020)

A quote from the Ministry of European and Foreign Affairs programme shows that Croatia is a dedicated supporter of the EU enlargement policy. However, one has to wonder whether Croatia, like Slovenia and Greece, will resort to a policy of blocking, which can be surmised from the statement that candidate countries should fulfil all the conditions. Of course, these are political processes that cannot be fully predicted. However, it can be assumed that Croatia's behaviour will depend on the policy of the European Union; if the EU takes a decisive and unified position on its expansion to the southeast of Europe, Croatia will not be able to oppose it for long, even if it wants to.

It should be noted that during its presidency of the EU Council in the first half of 2000, Croatia listed support for EU enlargement as a priority of its policy. At the Zagreb Summit held on 6 May of the same year via a video link, the President of the European Commission, Ursula Von der Leyen, said that the meeting was proof of the importance that the Union attaches to the Balkans because Western Balkans undoubtedly belonged to the EU. At the same time, she stressed the need for these countries to follow the EU's foreign policy and not get too close to Russia and China. Croatian Prime Minister Andrej Plenković confirmed that the meeting was the highlight of Croatia's six-month mandate at the head of the EU. Nevertheless, hovering over the summit was the shadow of Brexit. Namely, the United Kingdom's withdrawal from the EU destroyed the legitimacy myth, according to which the Union was admittedly flawed, but not to the extent that anyone would decide to leave it. Brexit shattered that myth and opened up a series of political and legal questions on how that withdrawal would be carried out. That is why, during the Croatian presidency of the EU Council,

> an orderly Brexit was agreed upon with the adoption of the Withdrawal Agreement, based on which the United Kingdom ceased to be a member of the EU on 1 February 2020. The agreement regulates numerous aspects of Brexit, including a transition period that ensures the application of EU law in Great Britain until the end of 2020. Another success of the presidency as well as the wider efforts was the start of negotiations on the future partnership between the EU and United Kingdom later in March.
>
> (Butković, 2020, p. 2)

The enlargement policy to the southeast of Europe should have been one of the priorities of the EU's foreign policy. This policy is entirely in the hands of the EU and clearly shows its power. The enlargement policy was found to be the natural arena of European foreign policy. This was also recognised by Croatia, during whose presidency, in March 2020, the European Council decided to open accession negotiations with North Macedonia and Albania. The EU's commitment to its enlargement to the Western Balkans was emphasised in the Zagreb Declaration on 6 May 2020. The Declaration states that the EU is

> determined to intensify its engagement at all levels further to support the region's political, economic and social transformation and welcomes the pledge of the

> Western Balkans partners to uphold European values and principles and to carry out necessary reforms thoroughly and vigorously. Increased EU assistance will be linked to tangible progress in the rule of law and socio-economic reforms, as well as on the Western Balkans partners' adherence to EU values, rules and standards.
>
> (European Council and Council of the European Union, 2020)

However, the EU was not decisive enough on this issue, and now, these negotiations could last forever. It has been shown that the individual accession of each country would be very complex because it would open up the problem of unresolved relations between a particular country and its neighbours. This is why the idea is emerging of accepting the entire Western Balkans into the EU at once. It remains to be seen how the initiative of France and Germany on the regulation of relations between Serbia and Kosovo, which is supported by other EU members and, most importantly, the United States, will play out. This is the main challenge because EU accession has less and less public support in Serbia, and the state recognition of Kosovo is a fundamental political issue.

Croatia's foreign policy related to support for EU enlargement needs to be more decisive. Declaratively, Croatia favours enlargement but is doing nothing to enable it. It has yet to resolve open border issues with the neighbouring countries. The situation with the border with Slovenia is on hold. There are no negotiations, not even an initiative to open negotiations on border issues with Serbia, Montenegro, and Bosnia and Herzegovina, although everyone knows that resolved border issues are one of the conditions for admission to EU membership. Croatia does not have the strength to take on such a responsibility.

Nevertheless, in light of the war in Ukraine, which has led to a deterioration of relations between the US-led West on the one hand and Russia and China on the other, the EU has decided to suppress the influence of Russia and China in the southeast of Europe. The best instrument for this job is precisely the enlargement. Thus, the Union is expected to strengthen its enlargement policy because geopolitical reasons will be more important than the candidate countries' fulfilment of conditions. This is where Croatia could play an important role. However, it hesitates and cannot rule out the possibility of resorting to the blockade policy. The Croatian foreign policy is split into two currents on this issue. The first emphasises that the expansion of the EU to the southeast of Europe is in Croatia's interest because it would shift it from the periphery to the centre of Europe. The second group is also not opposed to the expansion. However, it considers it primarily an opportunity for Croatia to protect its compatriots in the candidate states and resolve border issues in its favour.

Croatia has proven itself active in NATO and European Union peacekeeping missions. The Government of the Republic of Croatia considers the "missions and operations under the auspices of the EU's Common Security and Defence Policy to be an important instrument of this policy". According to the Ministry of Foreign Affairs data, since 1999, Croatia has participated in 19 UN peacekeeping missions with about 1,500 members of its armed forces. Croatia is part of three

UN peacekeeping operations in Asia, Africa and the Middle East today. These are peacekeeping operations in India and Pakistan (The United Nations Military Observer Group in India and Pakistan), in Western Sahara (The United Nations Mission for the Referendum in Western Sahara) and Lebanon (The Unated Nations Interim Force in Lebanon) (UN Peacekeeping, 2024). The Croatian military is well-integrated into NATO (Bilandžić, 2008). This is the result of Croatia's national security policy, which believes that the alliance with the West and membership in the NATO alliance guarantee both Croatian and European security (Tatalović et al., 2017). After the Russian attack on Ukraine, Croatia joined the European Union in providing Ukraine with humanitarian and military assistance. It has been doing this consistently and decisively, so it has found itself on the list of Russian enemies (Wikipedia, 2024). However, the policy of military support to Ukraine also confronts structural and institutional problems of Croatian foreign policy. The issue lies in a constitutionally determined division of responsibility for conducting foreign policy, which is split between the prime minister and the state president. Foreign policy is blocked if these two people differ in their views or cannot suppress their personal intolerance. The president and the prime minister need to agree on appointments to high diplomatic posts, and their recent disagreement has resulted in the fact that Croatia has not appointed many ambassadorial posts. However, a far greater challenge to foreign policy is the ideological conflict between pro-European and pro-Atlantic factions and sovereignists on the other. The former believes that Croatia should fully integrate into the politics of the EU and NATO. In contrast, the latter believes Croatia should pursue its national interests and emphasise its sovereignty. The first position is represented by Prime Minister Andrej Plenković, who is a convinced European, and the second by President Zoran Milanović, who is a Eurosceptic and emphasises the democratic deficit of the European Union. Milanović also believes that aid to Ukraine should be accompanied by efforts to start peace negotiations. He thinks the EU plan of unconditional support to Ukraine until its final victory is too risky. He is extremely critical of EU policy:

> This stupid policy of the European Union has not been in Croatia's interest from day one. It is not even in Germany's interest, but they dare not say so. The European Union cannot jointly help in the energy crisis caused by the war in Ukraine. We allow ourselves to be swayed by those who are louder than us and drown headlong into something we cannot control. In the end, every country will take care of itself. I guarantee it.
>
> (Slobodna Dalmacija, 2023)

However, despite this harsh statement, Milanović does not question Croatia's obligations as a member of NATO and the EU. The structural conflict between the two agents of Croatian politics has continued during discussions about the next goal of Croatian foreign policy – concern for the position of Croats abroad, especially in Bosnia and Herzegovina (Program, 2020). In this matter, the president and the prime minister differ in political tactics. The prime minister relies on the support of the European Union and believes that Croatia has it. At the same time, the president claims that the support never materialised and that the Union is humiliating Croatia (HRT Vijesti, 2022). There is no doubt that pro-Europeans and Eurosceptics also differ in their assessment of Croatian and European foreign policy towards Croats in Bosnia and Herzegovina. This is not just about the conflict between the two leading figures of Croatian foreign policy but about a general rift that has appeared in Croatian society. There is a fear that the nation could disappear or become extinct, which is also present in other Southeast European countries. To those who share this fear, the policy of the Croatian government seems excessively subject to the policy of the European Union, which is why they demand that Croatia conduct its foreign policy independently from the European policy. The conflict between sovereignists and pro-Europeans has also spilt over to the demands on Croatian foreign policy. But it seems that, in principle, neither side has anything against the Europeanisation of Southeast Europe. This fact is crucial because Russian aggression against Ukraine has encouraged the expansion of the West towards that part of Europe that is still not part of the EU and NATO. It should be assumed that the enlargement policy will, therefore, be one of the important goals of the European Union's policy in the coming period.

6.6 Conclusion

Croatian foreign policy is primarily determined by its understanding of the national identity. The prevailing narrative is that Croatia is a European, not a Balkan country. This dominant narrative encouraged Croatian processes of Europeanisation and entry into the European Union. The Croatian example, however, reveals the paradox of Europeanisation. The more European rules and procedures are adopted by a small country, the lower its ability to design and implement an independent policy. Europeanisation, therefore, has two faces. It contributes to the effectiveness of introducing global market principles transferred by the United States to the EU and, thus, to the member states. However, at the same time, it narrows the possibility of an independent action of EU member states and the EU as a whole. However, as a small country, Croatia cannot significantly influence international relations, so it has decided to seek refuge in international alliances. Considering itself part of the West, Croatia has found shelter in membership in the NATO alliance and the European Union. Even after joining the EU, it continued striving for complete Europeanisation, achieved by joining the Eurozone and the Schengen zone. Nevertheless, in its foreign policy, Croatia did not find a particular "niche", an area in which it would assert itself in foreign politics. There was a chance for Croatia to establish itself as an expert on Southeastern Europe. However, it has failed to do so, probably because it was too involved in the region in terms of its interest and identity. Most of those countries still have Croatian communities of various sizes living there. Croatian politics claims that it will encourage the expansion of the EU to the southeast of Europe. Still, there is always a possibility that, due to border issues, it will be guided by its own experience of having its accession blocked by Slovenia and take advantage of EU membership blocking others in turn.

Furthermore, even though Croatia is fully integrated into the European Union, if there is no unified European policy, the country will side with the United States in the UN, even if most European countries decide otherwise. It should be noted that Euro-indifference has recently been accompanied by an increasing Euroscepticism. Part of the public believes that most benefits from the EU are enjoyed by the countries in its centre and that Croatia, being on the Union periphery, is neglected. Nevertheless, none of this influences Croatia's foreign policy centred on the idea that the country belongs to the West and that it should, therefore, follow the policies of the EU and the NATO alliance. It is thus to be expected that Croatia will be encouraged to help the expansion of the West into Southeast of Europe. Still, the prerequisite is to define clear relations between the two agents who lead foreign policy in the country, the president and the prime minister. Although they may disagree over understanding Croatian foreign policy's tasks, explicit legal provisions regulating their relations could reduce potential conflict. Croatia also needs to show its support for EU enlargement policy more clearly by offering its assistance to the Western Balkans countries in the negotiation process. This would open up the possibility of establishing coordination between candidate countries, in which Croatia could play a significant role. It is of the utmost importance that Croatian foreign policy wholeheartedly supports the enlargement policy. This is not currently the case because of a fear that Croatia as a truly European country could end up in the Balkans again. Therefore, there can only be a genuine will to help the enlargement once the decision-making centres embrace the attitude that the Union's expansion to the Southeast of Europe would mean that Croatia would cease to be the outer periphery of the European Union and move closer to its centre. Still, the prerequisite for this is that the entire EU foreign policy returns to the policy of pragmatic compromise, which is the basis for a successful international policy.

Note

1 The status of Croatia as a small country is evident in the fact that out of 10,000 meetings with lobbyists that European Parliament members have registered since July 2020, not one included members from Croatia (Net.hr, 2020).

References

Bajruši, R. (2012) 'Suzdržanost Hrvatske zbog Palestine. Diplomati i bivši ministri: Palestince volimo, ali SAD i Izrael su Hrvatskoj važniji', *Jutarnji list*. Available at: www.jutarnji.hr/vijesti/hrvatska/diplomati-i-bivsi-ministri-%E2%80%98palestince-volimo-ali-sad-i-izrael-su-hrvatskoj-vazniji%E2%80%99-1367745#:~:text=Brojne%20Kritike (23.03.2023).

Bilandžić, M. (2008) 'Hrvatska vojska u međunarodnim odnosima', *Polemos: časopis za interdisciplinarna istraživanja rata i mira*, 11 (2), pp. 11–27. Available at: https://hrcak.srce.hr/file/65472 (23.03.2023).

Boban, D. and Cipek, T. (2017) *Politički sustav Rusije*. Zagreb: Plejada.

Bretherton, C. and Vogler, J. (2006) *The European Union as a Global Actor*. London: Routledge.

Butković, H. (2020) 'Hrvatsko predsjedanje Vijećem EU u sjeni pandemije Covid 19', IRMO – *aktualno*, 7, pp 1–7. Available at: https://irmo.hr/wp-content/uploads/2020/06/irmo-aktualno-7.pdf (23.03.2023).

Cipek, T. (2018) 'Russia and the European Union: What Remains of the Partnership?', *Journal of Balkan and Black Sea Studies*, 1(1), pp. 11–29. Available at: https://dergipark.org.tr/en/pub/balkar/issue/41667/463567 (23.03.2023).

Dahrendorf, R. (2002) *Die Krisen der Demokratie. Ein Gespräch*. München: Verlag C. H. Beck.

Eurobarometer (2022) *Croatia after the Euro Changeover*. Available at: https://europa.eu/eurobarometer/surveys/detail/3013 (23.03.2023).

European Council and Council of the European Union (2020) *Zagreb Declaration*. Available at: www.consilium.europa.eu/media/43776/zagreb-declaration-en-06052020.pdf (23.03.2023).

Fukuyama, F. (2018) *Identity: The Demand for Dignity and the Politics of Resentment*. New York: Farrar, Straus and Giroux.

Granić, M. (2005) *Vanjski poslovi – iza kulisa politike*. Zagreb: Algoritam.

Guérot, U. and Ritz, H. (2022) *Endspiel Europa. Warum das politische Projekt Europa gescheitert ist und wie wir wieder davon träumen können*. Frankfurt am Main: Westend.

Hill, C. (2003) 'What Is to Be Done? Foreign Policy as a Site for Political Action', *International Affairs*, 79(2), pp. 233–255. Available at: www.jstor.org/stable/3095819 (23.03.2023).

HRT Vijesti (2022) *Milanović o rezultatima izbora u BiH: Fijasko i sramota za Hrvatsku*. Available at: https://vijesti.hrt.hr/hrvatska/predsjednik-milanovic-na-14-konferenciji-o-odrzivom-razvoju-9958785 (23.03.2023).

Jović, D. (2013) 'Hrvatski referendum o članstvu u Europskoj uniji i njegove posljedice za smanjeni Zapadni Balkan', *Anali Hrvatskog politološkog društva*, 9(1), pp. 163–182. Available at: https://hrcak.srce.hr/file/146972 (23.03.2023).

Jović, D. (2018) 'Europa izvan Europske unije? Nove dileme pri definiranju europskog identiteta', *Revija za sociologiju*, 48(3), pp. 359–394. Available at: https://hrcak.srce.hr/file/317596 (23.03.2023).

Kekeleire, S. and Delreux, T. (2022) *The Foreign Policy of the European Union*. Edition 3. Basingstoke: Palgrave Macmillan.

Keohane, R.O. and Nye, J.S. Jr. (2000) 'Globalisation: What's New? What's Not? (And So What?)', *Foreign Policy*, 118, pp. 104–119. Available at: https://doi.org/10.2307/1149673 (16.10.2023).

Krickovic, A. and Sakwa, R. (2022) 'War in Ukraine: The Clash of Norms and Ontologies', *Journal of Military and Strategic Studies*, 22(2), pp. 89–109.

Milner, H.V. and Moravcsik, A. (eds.) (2009) *Power, Interdependence, and Nonstate Actors in World Politics*. Princeton: Princeton University Press.

Narodne novine (2017) *Strategija nacionalne sigurnosti Republike Hrvatske*. Available at: https://narodne-novine.nn.hr/clanci/sluzbeni/2017_07_73_1772.html (23.03.2023).

Net.hr (2020) *Nismo zanimljivi europskim lobistima: Održali su 10000 sastanaka s europarlamentarcima, ali niti jedan s našima*. Available at: https://net.hr/danas/hrvatska/nismo-zanimljivi-europskim-lobistima-odrzali-su-10-000-sastanaka-s-europarlamentarcima-ali-niti-jedan-s-nasima-02be12f4-b1c6-11eb-8b91-0242ac13002d (16.10.2023).

Nobilo, M. (2000) *Hrvatski Feniks: Diplomatski procesi iza zatvorenih vrata 1990–1997*. Zagreb: Globus.

Radaelli, C. (2003) 'The Europeanization of Public Policy', in: K. Featherstone and C. Radaelli (eds) *The Politics of Europeanization*. Oxford: Oxford University Press Roberts, pp. 27–56.

Ringmar, E. (1996) *Identity, Interest and Action: A Cultural Explanation of Sweden's Intervention in the Thirty Years War*. Cambridge: Cambridge University Press.

Rudolf, D. (1999) *Rat koji nismo htjeli. Hrvatska 1991*. Zagreb: Globus.

SECRC - State Electoral Commission of the Republic of Croatia (2024) *Referendum o pristupanju Republike Hrvatske Europskoj uniji*. Available at: www.izbori.hr/site/UserDocsImages/484 (28.03.2024).

Šelo-Šabić, S. (2014) 'Croatian Fast-Forward Foreign Policy. From Yugoslavia to the EU', in S. Keil and B. Stahl (eds.) *The Foreign Policies of Post-Yugoslav States*. New York: Palgrave Macmillan, pp. 69–93.

Slobodna Dalmacija (2023) *Što je sve Milanović pričao o ratu u Ukrajini zadnjih 365 dana: 'Solidarni smo i to je to. Dalje od toga ne'*. Available at: https://slobodnadalmacija.hr/vijesti/hrvatska/sto-je-sve-milanovic-pricao-o-ratu-u-ukrajini-zadnjih-365-dana-solidarni-smo-i-to-je-to-dalje-od-toga-ne-1267547 (23.03.2023).

Steinmetz, R. and Wivel, A. (2016) *Small States in Europe. Challenges and Opportunities*. London/New York: Routledge.

Streeck, W. (2021) *Zwischen Globalismus und Demokratie. Politische Ökonomie im ausgehenden Neoliberalismus*. Berlin: Suhrkamp.

Tatalović, S., Mikac, R. and Jakešević, R. (2017) 'Croatia' in H-P. Bartels, A.M. Kellner and U. Optenhogel (eds.). *'Croatia. Strategic Autonomy and the Defence of Europe – On the Road to European Army?* Bonn: Verlag J.H.W. Dietz Nachf. GmbH, pp. 103–115.

Toje, A. (2011) *The European Union as Small Power: After the Post-Cold War*. Basingstoke: Palgrave Macmillan.

United Nations (UN) (2017) *General Assembly resolution ES-10/19*. Available at: www.timesofisrael.com/full-text-of-un-resolution-rejecting-jerusalem-recognition/ (23.03.2023).

UN Peacekeeping (2024) *Where we operate*. Available at: https://peacekeeping.un.org/en/where-we-operate (23.03.2024).

Vlada RH (2020) *Program Vlade Republike Hrvatske 2020 – 2024*. Available at: https://vlada.gov.hr/UserDocsImages/ZPPI/Dokumenti%20Vlada/Program%20Vlade%20Republike%20Hrvatske%20za%20mandat%202020.%20-%202024..pdf (23.03.2023).

Vukadinović, R. (1993) 'Vanjska politika Republike Hrvatske', *Politička misao: časopis za politologiju*, 30(3), pp. 124–141. Available at: https://hrcak.srce.hr/file/164325 (23.03.2023).

Vukadinović, R. (2000) 'Hrvatska vanjska politika – novo vrijeme i nove zadaće', *Međunarodne studije*, 1(1), pp. 1–20. Available at: https://hrcak.srce.hr/file/414250 (23.03.2023).

Wikipedia (2024 *Unfriendly Countries List*. Available at: https://en.wikipedia.org/wiki/Unfriendly_Countries_List (23.03.2024).

7 Media Pluralism and Market Competition in Croatia

Between Expectations and Realities

Paško Bilić

7.1 Introduction

Liberalising media markets marked the Croatian path to EU accession. It arrived at the time of deepening internal market and monetary union, the convergence of European economic and social models (Nölke, 2021) and the stagnant eastward expansion. The liberalisation process was conditioned in the negotiations, as evident in Progress reports which emphasised more market liberalisation for audio-visual broadcasting (Bilić and Švob-Đokić, 2016). Commercial media serve as an outlet for stimulating consumption and demand through advertising. At the same time, they can provide and withdraw legitimacy to social actors. They exercise soft political power, which cannot replace the law and state administration but can sway public opinion in different directions, significantly affecting political processes (Habermas, 1996). The normative role of media in democratic societies is defined through freedom of expression and media pluralism, aiming that no single media outlet should have too much influence on shaping public opinion. Media pluralism can be external in the form of different organisations operating in the market and internal in the sense of diverse views offered by individual organisations.

After EU accession, the country needed to balance private media and public goals, external and internal pluralism. Few media reforms enacted in the last ten years were primarily EU-driven, mainly through transposing EU directives such as the Audio-Visual Media Services Directive (AVMSD) (Official Journal of the European Union (2018). The country has yet to create a media development strategy, meaning that all media reforms lack long-term visions and are sporadic and uncoordinated. In most media policy interventions, the explicit and implicit expectation was that markets would secure media pluralism and that the state should minimise interventions in the media sector. Interventions were usually directed at the media industry, for example, in the case of state funding during the COVID-19 pandemic. Similar mechanisms were not extended towards the struggling third media, non-profit sector.

There are many ways of seeking media pluralism in democratic societies beyond the argument that market behaviour paradigmatically represents freedom (Karppinen, 2013). In Croatia and most member states, securing pluralism of opinion through market plurality is the most challenging task, as evident in the

DOI: 10.4324/9781003394013-7

high-risk scores for that domain in the Media Pluralism Monitor (MPM) project (CMPF, 2022), funded by the European Commission since 2014. Furthermore, while the past 30 years of media restructuring in Croatia delegated most control over the mediated public sphere to private actors, direct political power remains in appointments to the public service broadcaster and the central media authority (Bilić et al., 2022; European Commission, 2022a).

This chapter takes a diachronic, political economy of the media perspective to understand how Croatian media reforms were enacted in the pre- and post-accession balancing of EU media policies and national specificities. It focuses on media pluralism, a complex construct with many dimensions. It includes diversity of media supply, use and distribution, ownership and control, media types and genres, political viewpoints, cultural expression, and local and regional interests (KU Leuven, 2009). Due to the complexity and multi-dimensionality of the concept, we will focus on the operationalised definition of media pluralism within the MPM project. In particular, we will focus on the market plurality domain to assess risks to media pluralism related to the economic context in which relevant market players operate. We will use industry data on media market structure and MPM reports for Croatia (Bilić et al., 2015, 2016, 2017; Bilić, 2020; Bilić, Valečić, et al., 2021; Bilić et al., 2022).

One of the critical issues for media pluralism in member states is the friction which may occur between horizontal EU policies of the internal market and competition enforcement and public service objectives and cultural considerations primarily delegated to the (sub)national policy level (Donders and Pauwels, 2008; Michalis, 2014; Nowak, 2014; Nyberg, 2021; Ungerer, 2014). While the current EU approach to media policy seems to ease economic considerations in favour of transnational coordination of media freedom, pluralism and public goods, Croatia is still treading the path of self-correcting markets and minimal state intervention. Without proper consideration of national specificities, media policies inspired primarily by European institutions will likely shift the mediated public sphere away from public control and responsibility. To remedy the poor track record of freedom of expression, increasing numbers of strategic lawsuits against public participation (SLAPP) directed towards journalists (Bilić et al., 2022) and the weak rule of law (European Commission, 2022a), the country needs to do more to improve media pluralism than wait for EU initiatives. The following text aims to reveal lessons from critical junctures (McChesney, 2008) in the past ten years.

7.2 European Media Policy Actors, Instruments, Interests

The European media policy between 1945 and 1980/90 was primarily shaped by national, socio-political and public service considerations over economic interests (van Cuilenburg and McQuail, 2003). Early liberalisation through satellite and cable technology began in the 1970s (Donders, 2012, p. 13). Starting from 1980/90, governments opted for policies of breaking monopolies and privatising. Much of the first decade of the twenty-first century was dominated by economic considerations, with one of the main policy guidelines being that 'competition rules should be the prime vehicle for regulating the electronic communication market' (van Cuilenburg and McQuail, 2003, p. 199). Central and Eastern European countries followed the same, well-trodden path in their accession.

The European media policy is best described as a complex maze of actors, regulatory instruments and interests (Donders et al., 2014).[1] Liberalisation of broadcasting markets in the European Union was coordinated by the Television without Frontiers Directive (Official Journal of the European Union, 1989) with the general aim to 'ensure the free movement of broadcasting services within the internal market and at the same time to preserve certain public interest objectives, such as cultural diversity, the right of reply, consumer protection and the protection of minors'. The TWFD was adopted in 1989, amended in 1997 and radically overhauled in 2007. Even though market liberalisation was initiated in Italy, the UK, France, and Germany before the Television without Frontiers (TWF) (Michalis, 2014, p. 133), the Directive has ended national broadcasting sovereignty and instilled a more commercial logic into European broadcasting (Katsirea, 2014, p. 297).

The TWF Directive went hand-in-hand with competition policy and state aid regulation rules in Articles 106 and 107 of the Treaty on the Functioning of the European Union (Official Journal of the European Union, 2012). Article 107 states that

> same as otherwise provided in the Treaties, any aid granted by a Member State or through State resources in any form whatsoever which distorts or threatens to distort competition by favouring certain undertakings or the production of certain goods shall, in so far as it affects trade between the Member States, be incompatible with the internal market.

The reasons behind such a strong emphasis on competition policy were the arrival of advertisement-based television and pay-television channels at the start of the 1990s and new media platforms after 2000. These developments led to new business models and a race towards building gatekeeper positions (Ungerer, 2014, p. 405). State aid rules were a tool for harmonising the internal market and reducing state subsidies, tax reductions and other interventions in areas that could harm competitive markets. With a vital public service broadcasting model in most European countries, some funding arrangements, such as dual financing from a license fee and advertising, can be deemed anti-competitive. The Treaty of Amsterdam, nonetheless, recognised the public service remit and allowed member states to organise national public media without interference, so long as they did not influence competition between member states (Official Journal of the European Union, 1997).[2]

On the normative side, there is an apparent conflict between economic interests and cultural considerations embedded in the public service remit for social inclusiveness, plurality, and diversity. In reality, this conflict was only sometimes interpreted to the detriment of public media and has often led to legislative changes at the national level not induced by the European Commission (Donders and Moe, 2014, p. 438). The TWF Directive was revised in 2007 and again in 2018 under the Audio-Visual Media Services (AVMS) Directive to include non-linear and streaming services. Although classified as a law of minimum harmonisation, technological developments and the liberalising approach of European law have been the main impetus for breaking down borders for audio-visual services. Throughout this process, consideration for freedom of expression for AVMS' role seemed tertiary (Micova, 2021, p. 265).

Competitiveness remains high on the European media policy agenda, as evident from the Digital Services Act package targeting digital platform markets (Official Journal of the European Union, 2022a; Official Journal of the European Union 2022b). However, faced with the spread of disinformation and hate speech, freedom of expression violations, and poor protection of journalists, the EU media policy seems to be seeking a different kind of balance between market liberalisation principles and cultural and democratic considerations. One of the reasons for this shift is the destabilisation of news production and advertising markets, as well as media literacy and access to media content in the new ecosystem dominated by transnational platforms. The state's role is increasingly emphasised in media policies worldwide (Flew et al., 2016). There is an increasing need to re-consider and re-imagine the concept of media pluralism in the EU (Brogi et al., 2021). New media policy mechanisms, e.g. European Democracy Action Plan and European Media Freedom Act (European Commission, 2020; European Parliament, 2024), are searching for ways to better harmonise media pluralism and freedom of expression at the EU level. However, judging from the fact that previous harmonisation policies did not lead to unified outcomes (e.g. Becker et al., 2021; Nölke, 2021), we can expect that this round of policy-making will also result in many national specificities and exceptions.

7.3 Croatian Media Policy Pre- and Post-Accession

Broadcasting has a long history in Croatia. Radio Zagreb started transmitting in 1926, and Television Zagreb in 1956. Unlike European countries that started breaking up national monopolies in the 1980s, Croatia maintained a state-owned radio-television broadcasting monopoly until the early 2000s. During the 30 years of the post-socialist transition, the media underwent successive stages of privatisation, liberalisation and commercialisation (Car and Bilić, 2023). They were reshaped by new laws, ownership, technology, journalistic norms and audience habits at each critical juncture. Local radio and television stations started appearing in the 1990s but only in 2000 and 2003 were the first national broadcasting licenses granted to private companies (Nova TV and RTL). At the same time, in the early 2000s, Croatian Radio-television (HRT) was reformed from a state-owned medium to a public service medium. Management was opened to civil society representatives, and political interference was reduced. While the liberalisation process created more external plurality through a diversity of owners, it also created unintended consequences by reducing internal plurality in the broadcasting space. The HRT slowly moved towards popular and trivial topics in competition for audiences with commercial providers (Perišin, 2008). The process has not been recognised by the primary policy actors or public service media (PSM) management structures. Over time, politicised appointments, dismissals of the Director and management, and political bias towards ruling parties led to increasing political interference in the operation of the HRT (Bilić et al., 2022).

Croatia signed the Stabilisation and Association Agreement in 2001 and negotiated for EU membership between 2005 and 2011. Formally, the accession was completed in July 2013. Broadcasting liberalisation in the early 2000s was shaped by the scarcity of the radio frequency spectrum and the political will to displace the national monopoly. At the same time, a more advanced stage occurred during the EU negotiation process. It was defined by technological developments such as the digital video broadcasting terrestrial (DVB-T) switchover in 2010, the rise of cable, IPTV, and pay TV and further liberalisation conditioned in the EU negotiation process. The result of these reforms, especially regarding DVB-T, was an expansion of universally available commercial channels. The HRT struggled with internal crises and management changes before setting up its specialised news and culture channels (HTV3 and HTV4). Chapter 10 (Information Society and the Media) was not problematic in the negotiation process and was closed in 2009.

Post-EU accession, imitative media policy and copy-pasting EU mechanisms, characteristic of many central and eastern European member states (Jakubowicz, 2008; Splichal, 2000), continued in Croatia. More often than not, local specificities needed to be considered more. There were no significant media reforms between 2013 and 2023, apart from the mandatory transposition of the 2018 AVMSD, which occurred through an overhaul of the Electronic Media Act (EMA) in 2021 (OG 111/21). There were no initiatives to foster an internal plurality of the mediated public sphere by reforming public subsidies or stabilising the HRT by removing political interference. Moreover, the Ministry of Culture withdrew specific funding mechanisms for non-profit media in 2016. The allocation of other funding mechanisms (e.g. from the European Social Fund) was stalled for years, creating an unfavourable position for the fragile third media sector (Bilić, 2020).

7.3.1 The State of the Media Market

Most media markets in Croatia are highly concentrated. For print dailies, two companies dominate sales and advertising. Styria media, an Austrian-based company, owns '24 sata' and 'Večernji List'. Hanza media, a Croatian company, owns 'Jutarnji List' and 'Slobodna Dalmacija'. Sales and advertising have been dropping for more than a decade. Between 2018 and 2021, circulated copies for all daily newspapers decreased from 60,426,858 to 37,236,988 (AZTN, 2022). Total advertising expenditure on all print media (dailies, weeklies and other formats) in 2021 was 19 million euros (HURA, 2023). Some companies introduced subscription-based models and paywalls for their online outlets. In 2022, there were around 10,000 subscribers to online outlets owned by Styria, Hanza Media, and Telegram Media Grupa – a digitally native news company (DZNAP, 2023). However, subscription numbers are still too low to provide viable revenue sources beyond advertising.

Television viewership is dominated by HTV1, HTV2 and HTV4 and two private companies with their general and specialised channels, 'Nova TV' and 'Doma TV' owned by the United Group, 'RTL' and 'RTL 2' owned by Central European Media Enterprises (AEM, 2023). Two pay TV providers dominate the market. 'Max TV' is owned by Hrvatski Telekom, a Croatian company majority-owned by Deutsche Telekom. 'A1' is owned by A1 Telekom Austria Group. In terms of news sources, television (through a TV set) was the primary source (39.9%) for citizens and internet users in 2021, followed by online newspapers (16.4%), web portals (15%) and social media (13.8%) (Vozab and Peruško, 2021). Television is the dominant medium for advertising, capturing 108 million euros in 2021 (HURA, 2023).

Unlike other media, radio is fragmented and highly regional and local. In terms of audiences, the most listened stations in the fourth quarter of 2022 were 'Bravo!', 'Otvoreni radio' and 'HR2' with national broadcasting licenses, followed by 'Radio Kaj' and 'Radio Dalmacija' with regional licenses (De facto, 2022). Commercial and private radio stations dominate the broadcasting space, co-funded mainly by the Council for Electronic Media (Mučalo, 2020). In general, radio attracts the smallest amount of advertising. In 2021, it captured 16 million Euros (HURA, 2023).

The digital news media space is a mixture of traditional print and television news media outlets (e.g. '24sata.hr' by Styria or 'Dnevnik.hr' by Nova TV) and digital native websites such as 'Index.hr', 'Net.hr' and 'Telegram.hr' competing for audiences and advertising. Websites with the highest reach are 'Index.hr', '24 sata.hr' and 'Jutarnji.hr' (Peruško, 2022). In 2021, the internet advertising market (without search and social) attracted 55 million euros (HURA, 2023). At the same time, total internet advertising investments are much higher and dominated by Google and Facebook, which capture more than half of the market (Bilić and Primorac, 2018).

Economic growth in Croatia is directly tied to consumption, and the media play an essential role in stimulating demand. The biggest advertisers in 2018 were primarily transnational or foreign-owned companies such as T-Hrvatski Telekom, LIDL, TELE 2,[3] Konzum, Kaufland, Procter & Gamble, The Coca-Cola Company, and Ferrero (Lider, 2019). Private media have little incentive to change business practices of attracting audiences and selling attention to advertisers. Global financial crashes, economic downturns during the pandemic, technological changes and the dominance of transnational tech conglomerates all affect media markets, sharpening competition for advertising revenue. Commercial considerations highly influence the mainstream media in Croatia in their editorial policies or under strong political interference in the HRT. The first ten years of EU membership were shaped by hyper-liberalisation and *laissez-faire* regulation, primarily online. In parallel, there is an overall erosion of the journalistic profession into commercialisation and tabloid-style reporting (Grbeša and Volarević, 2021; Mučalo, 2020) as well as pressures on journalists from various interest groups (Ivanuš, 2021). Given the unique characteristics of media products, such trends can be characterised as market failures for allocating public information in a highly liberalised market.

7.3.2 Market Competition and Media Pluralism in National Law

Freedom of expression can be understood as either freedom *from* state and commercial influences or freedom *to* exercise certain rights (Tambini, 2021, pp. 15–17). Freedom of expression should naturally lead to media pluralism, given that societies are shaped by ethnic, social, religious, regional, local and other groups. Media freedom and pluralism are 'crucial corollaries of the right to freedom of expression' (Council of Europe, 2018). Various mechanisms support media pluralism in Croatia through negative ('freedom *from*') and positive ('freedom *to*') obligations.[4] These include, for example, ownership restrictions from too much commercial media influence and special market competition rules for the media, the public service media remit defined by law, and state subsidies such as the Fund for the Promotion of Pluralism and Diversity of Media.

Ownership transparency requirements are defined in the Media Act (MA) and the EMA. Media service providers must submit data on the legal entity and registered office, i.e. name, surname and residence of all legal and natural persons who are directly or indirectly holders of shares or business stakes in a media service provider, with information on the percentage of shares or business stakes. The Croatian Chamber of Commerce manages the ownership register for print media and the Council for Electronic Media for radio, television, electronic publications (i.e. digital news media), and other electronic media. Still, the ultimate individual owners can sometimes be hidden from the public through different legal and business entities. The EMA defines the dominant position in the market (40% of the annual revenue), preventing dominant companies from acquiring new licenses or establishing electronic publications. The MA and EMA define thresholds in terms of capital shares for horizontal concentration and capital shares and the number of printed copies for cross-media concentration. Cross-media concentration includes ownership limitations between print, electronic media (local, regional and national) and advertising agencies. It contains no thresholds for electronic publications. There are no specific competition rules for the digital news media market.

Audience reach for all media types is not a benchmark in law for determining concentration in media markets. At this point, it is essential to note that private media ownership and concentration restrictions aim to secure external plurality or a plurality of different organisations operating in the market. However, as the former Deputy Director General of DG Competition at the European Commission stated

> [g]iven that the application of competition law cannot have a direct impact on 'internal plurality', there remain important problems when member states establish specific media laws that do not ensure this plurality, made possible by the lack of a European framework.
>
> (Ungerer, 2014, pp. 410, 411)

A traditional way to establish internal plurality through media policy is with public service media, a relatively stable institution in most EU member states, even though decades of commercialising broadcasting space or complete political control in some member states such as Hungary are evident (Batorfy et al., 2022). In Croatia, the public service remit is defined in the Croatian Radio-television Act (CRTA) through specific program principles (articles 5–8) and the definition of content and function of the HRT's public service (articles 9–15). Article 9 states that the program commitments of the HRT should meet the democratic, social and cultural needs of Croatian society and guarantee pluralism, including cultural and language diversity. The HRT is funded by a monthly license fee, a maximum of 1.5% of a monthly net salary in Croatia. Advertising is also allowed, representing a minor share of the annual revenue. The number of advertising minutes per hour was reduced during the EU negotiation process due to the EU state aid rules, which declared the license fee as a form of mandatory tax, and hence a form of state aid, which affected competition between commercial audio-visual broadcasters in the country (Bilić and Švob-Đokić, 2016).

In addition to the HRT, an essential element for securing internal plurality is the community media, which are poorly defined by Croatian law. Community media can be understood as media with regional and local licenses, minority media or non-profit media in Article 55 of the EMA, which is closest to the definition set forth by the European Parliament (European Parliament, 2008). Non-profit media services and non-profit providers of electronic publications in Article 55 can be domestic and foreign associations and their foundations, institutions, art organisations, chambers, trade unions, employers' associations and all other legal entities whose primary goal of the operation is not to acquire profit. Non-profit media compete for different national and EU subsidies. The crucial source in Croatia is the Fund for Promoting Diversity and Pluralism, managed by the Council of Electronic Media. The Fund is financed by 3% of the monthly license fee collected by the HRT. It supports public interest projects, programs and content, which include the right to be informed, cultural diversity and heritage, education, science, arts, language diversity, national minorities, people with disabilities, gender equality and other social inclusiveness topics. In practice, funds are mainly allocated to private, local radio and television, often seen as buying political influence at the local level. The non-profit media, especially digital non-profit media, compete for a small percentage of available funds (5%) based on the Allocation rules of the Fund (OG 84/22). There are no must-carry obligations for distributing non-profit media content on the HRT channels or pay-tv distributors.

Since the EU accession, there have been no media reforms or attempts to strengthen the public service remit or reduce political interference in appointments and dismissals of the Director and key management positions. In addition, the third media sector has yet to be considered necessary for securing internal pluralism. The only reforms that occurred were related to the mandatory transposition of EU directives. The market is the primary mechanism for allocating publicly relevant information. However, as evidence from EU research projects such as the MPM shows, the market is becoming an increasingly flawed system for securing plurality in the public sphere.

7.3.3 Findings from the Media Pluralism Monitor

The MPM is a tool funded by the European Union, coordinated by the Centre for Media Pluralism and Media Freedom (CMPF) at the European University Institute (EUI) in Florence and implemented in all member states. The pilot implementation started in 2014 and 2015, and since then, it has been fully implemented in 2016, 2017, 2020, 2021 and 2022.[5] The tool comprises 200 legal, economic and social variables that create composite indicators and implementation areas. Currently, the tool involves four areas (Fundamental Protection, Market Plurality, Political Independence and Social Inclusiveness) with five indicators per area. Variables composing the indicators are weighed, and risk scores are allocated per indicator and implementation area.[6]

Consistent implementation and quantified risk calculation allow comparisons between member states. For example, if a country scores low risk in the fundamental area, it would imply high legal standards of freedom of expression, high protection of journalism, no misuse of defamation charges, independent regulatory authority, and high access to information standards. Since 2020, the MPM has introduced digital indicators to consider the increasing influence of digital transformations on media pluralism. The result is most evident in the Market Plurality area, the highest risk domain in the most recent MPM implementation (CMPF, 2022). It focuses on the economic risks to media pluralism, which derive from a lack of transparency and the concentration of ownership, news media concentration, online platforms concentration and competition enforcement, the sustainability of the media industry and the exposure of journalism to commercial interests. In Croatia, market plurality scored 65% (Bilić et al., 2022), close to 66% risk for all countries (CMPF, 2022).

Transparency of Media Ownership scores a medium risk of 50% in Croatia (see Figure 7.1), compared to 54% in the European Union (see Figure 7.2). One of the critical problems in Croatia is a complicated mechanism for tracking cross-ownership structures since the print media report ownership changes to the Croatian Chamber of Commerce and all electronic media to the Council for Electronic Media. Due to convergence and digital transformations, it is common for traditional media and telecommunications companies to set up online outlets that expand their audience reach and revenue models. A cumbersome mechanism for monitoring capital shares and print circulation does not allow efficient monitoring of these changes. In addition, benchmarks for electronic publications are not set in the EMA, making the digital market poorly regulated. Comparatively, the EU score is similar, mainly because of the Anti-Money Laundering Directive introduced in 2018, which indirectly influenced ownership transparency EU-wide and harmonised the area. Still, some countries impose 'significant restrictions' for access, requiring payments (CMPF, 2022).

The News Media Concentration indicator scores a medium risk of 60% in Croatia. Article 64 of the EMA states that all the regulations apply adequately to providers of media services via satellite, internet, cable and other permitted forms of transmission. This implicitly includes electronic publications, although they are

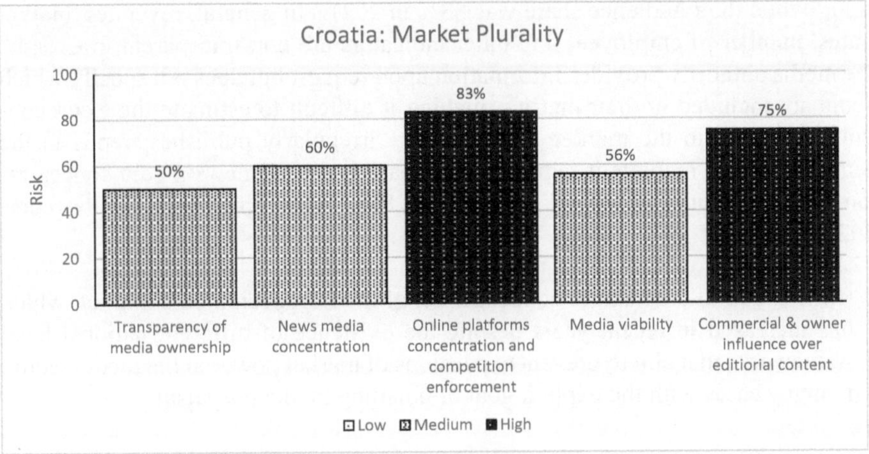

Figure 7.1 Media market plurality in Croatia in 2022.

Source: Bilić et al. (2022).

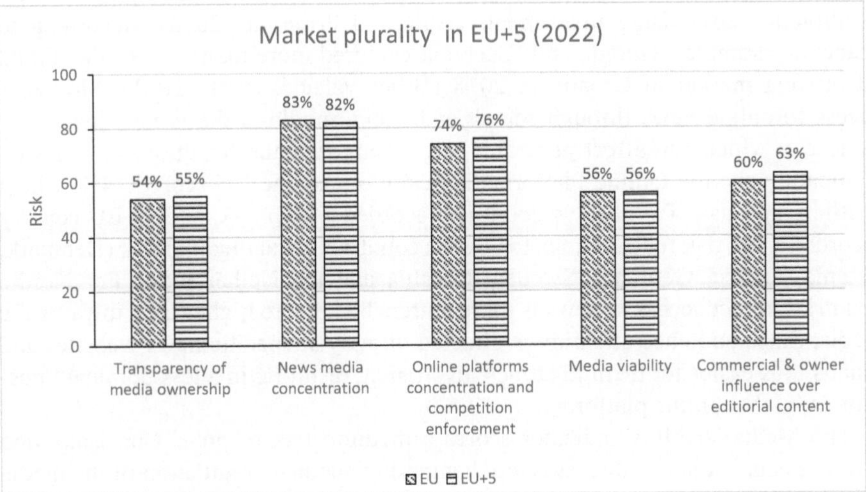

Figure 7.2 Market plurality in EU+5 (2022).

Source: CMPF (2022).

not mentioned as such in this article. None of the media reaches impermissible concentration based on the law (capital shares and print circulation). However, some markets are highly concentrated, especially if we consider audience concentration, which is not calculated for impermissible concentration in Croatia. For example, the market share of the country's top four online news media was 50% in 2020,[7] while their audience share was 83% in 2021.[8] In general, revenues, market shares, number of employees and other indicators are non-transparent in Croatia. The media authority provides information upon request but does not specify which media are included in their metrics, making it difficult to estimate the exact concentration level in the market. The authority irregularly publishes trends in the electronic media markets it regulates. Comparatively, the news media concentration indicator scores a high risk in the EU at 83%. According to the CMPF report (2022, p. 49):

> [t]his is due to the historic concentration of the European media market, which has increased in recent years despite the existence of different national legal frameworks that aim to prevent expansions of market power in the media sector, in many cases with the explicit goal of pursuing media pluralism.

Declining revenues from advertising and sales and competition with digital platforms move EU markets towards increasing concentration (Bilić, Prug, et al., 2021).

The Online Platforms Concentration and Competition Enforcement indicator scores a high risk of 83% for Croatia. There is no regulatory body monitoring concentration in advertising where digital platforms dominate the news industry in attracting advertising investments (Bilić and Primorac, 2018). According to academic estimates, Google and Facebook captured more than 75% of the digital advertising market in Croatia in 2018 (Bilić, Valečić, et al., 2021). Side-door access to online news through search and social media is the predominant way of access, which can affect generated advertising revenue for the news industry. Comparatively, the Online Platforms indicator across the EU scored 74%, which is still a high risk. Twenty-five countries recorded a high risk, and no EU country recorded a low risk for this indicator. Seven countries are at medium risk (Denmark, Estonia, France, Germany, Sweden, Czechia and the Netherlands). For Nordic countries, direct access to news is more entrenched due to higher trust towards the media. Since audience attention is directed directly at specific news websites and brands, it is easier for them to attract advertising, resulting in a less dominant position by global online platforms.

The Media Viability indicator scores a medium risk of 56%. Consistent and relevant data is unavailable, severely hampering adequate regulation of the media sector. For example, the exact number of employed journalists is unknown, making it challenging to estimate trends during economic downturns such as the one caused by the pandemic. The trade union only records the number of union members, while the journalists' association only records membership numbers. The advertising industry monitors overall investments in the media without differentiating between news media and other media. The EU measurement records the same risk level of 56%. There is a similar trend of poor data availability in other EU countries. In 2020, the risk level was at 69%, mainly because of the impact of the pandemic. The economic recovery characterised 2021, and it also impacted the media industry. However, the increase in media industry revenues was lower than the GDP increase in most countries, and it 'did not benefit all the media sectors, with newspaper and local media still suffering most, and it impacted very differently across the different countries' (CMPF, 2022, p. 58).

The Commercial and Owner Influence on Editorial Content indicator scores a high risk of 75%. The MA in Article 26 introduces the 'Media Statute' self-regulatory measure, which is intended to regulate the participation of journalists in cases of appointing editors, managing working conditions, determining journalistic responsibility, resignation procedures due to ownership or management changes that alter program schemes and content (so-called consciousness clause). Self-regulation proved to be highly inefficient in limiting commercial interests. The influence is usually visible in favourable reports and avoidance of negative views about significant advertisers. When asked about the main external effects on their profession, Croatian journalists mention advertisers first, followed by competing media companies and national and local politicians (Ivanuš, 2021, p. 84). In the EU27, the score for this indicator is 60%. Regulations do not always address advertorials, and many newsrooms remain financially vulnerable. Political and economic interests in many countries are intertwined, disincentivising owners from granting absolute freedom to editors and journalists (CMPF, 2022, p. 68). Only five countries recorded a low risk for this indicator: France, Germany, Luxembourg, the Netherlands and Portugal. Fifteen eastern and southern European countries recorded a high risk: Albania, Bulgaria, Croatia, Greece, Hungary, Latvia, Lithuania, Montenegro, Poland, Romania, Serbia, Slovenia, Sweden, the Czech Republic and Turkey.

7.4 Conclusion

Competition rules are insufficient to secure a plural environment, as the MPM data for Croatia and the EU demonstrate. Despite countering recent trends, a liberal and market-favouring approach towards the media still dominates European Commission media policy-making and, by extension, the Croatian post-accession period. The rationality behind this type of governmentality is evident in the expectations that competition leads to efficiency and general interest. The multiplicity of channels and outlets operating in the Croatian media industry cannot be denied. External pluralism is secured, even though print, television and digital markets are concentrated. However, none pass the (imprecise and weak) legally defined concentration thresholds.

In some cases, such as investigative journalism, private television stations expose political corruption and act as critical voices in the public sphere. However, the fact that they sometimes act in the public interest does not necessarily entail that they are, or will always be, fulfilling that role. The primary consideration for producing specific programmes by private companies is profitability. Due to the lack of investigative journalism by the PSM and the low visibility of community media in the general public, critical journalism programme is easily monetised by mainstream media. However, the fact that private actors coordinate their activity based on profitability considerations is not novel and requires further clarification. It has nothing to do with a moral condemnation of profit-seeking behaviour. Competitive behaviour entails something different, which, in the context of the media industry, boils down to constant pressure to be the first to publish something new and the pressure to immediately report on something that the competing companies are reporting on. Nevertheless, new topics and breaking news topics are not always the topics that deserve the general public's attention.

The implicit media policy of leaving the media space predominantly to market actors while ignoring internal pluralism, especially in the form of public service remit and the role of community media, allowed specific negative trends such as sensationalism and scandal-chasing to grow. Coupled with political interference and lawsuits directed at journalists, this creates a highly volatile public space with low respect for the rule of law and high risks for media pluralism, especially visible in the market plurality domain (Bilić et al., 2022; CMPF, 2022; European Commission, 2022a). The Croatian political leaders hold the blame for the inefficiency in managing public resources in the last 30 years, primarily because of corruption and politicised appointments to public offices. However, the fact that there is political interference does not mean that state subsidies, public service media and community media should not be essential mechanisms for securing internal plurality in the public sphere.

The European Parliament (European Parliament, 2008), the European Commission (2022b) (European Media Freedom Act) and the Council of Europe (Council of Europe, 2018) recognise public and community media as vital cornerstones for securing internal media pluralism. The political will to strengthen these media entities and, within them, foster appointments based on expertise, not political preferences, should be the starting point for securing internal media pluralism. Only then can the balance between external and internal pluralism be established, with journalism moving beyond the market as the primary mechanism for allocating public communication. Media pluralism is a matter of political will, media regulation and democratic standards, not a side effect of market competition. Even after ten years of EU membership, Croatia still has a long way to go to recognise and act upon this issue.

Notes

1 Relevant EU actors include the Council of the European Union, which adopts directives; the European Commission, which executes laws and policies; and the European Parliament as a co-legislator (with the EC). The judicial powers are with the Court of Justice of the EU and the General Court. Regulatory instruments include primary legislation such as treaties on which the EU is founded. Secondary legislation includes regulations, directives, decisions, recommendations, and opinions. Member states must transpose directives into national regulation, with minor deviations being allowed. There are also soft law instruments, such as communications by the EC. Finally, the European media policy is shaped by numerous interests, such as divergences between the EC and member states or interests representing different visions of what media mean for society and how their potential is best realised (Donders et al., 2014, pp. 6–10).

2

> The provisions of the Treaty establishing the European Community shall be without prejudice to the competence of Member States to provide for the funding of public service broadcasting insofar as such funding is granted to broadcasting organisations for the fulfilment of the public service remit as conferred, defined and organised by each Member State, and insofar as such funding does not affect trading conditions and competition in the Community to an extent which would be contrary to the common interest, while the realisation of the remit of that public service shall be taken into account.
>
> (Treaty of Amsterdam, 1997)

3 It was rebranded to Telemach in 2020. The United Group owns the company, which also owns Nova TV.

4 The former Yugoslavia had signed the International Covenant on Civil and Political Rights (ICCPR) in 1967 and ratified it in 1971. Croatia declared succession in 1992. The European Convention on Human Rights (ECHR) was ratified in 1997. Croatia holds freedom of expression as one of the highest constitutionally guaranteed rights. Article 38 of the Constitution of the Republic of Croatia (OG 56/90, 135/97, 08/98, 113/00, 124/00, 28/01, 41/01, 55/01, 76/10, 85/10, 05/14) guarantees freedom of thought and expression. Roles and responsibilities for the media are further defined in the Media Act (MA) (OG 59/04, 84/11, 81/13, 114/22), Electronic Media Act (EMA) (OG 111/21, 114/22), and the Croatian Radio-television Act (CRTA) (OG 137/10, 76/12, 46/17, 73/17, 94/18, 114/22). Article 3 of the MA guarantees freedom of expression and the media. Article 4 of the EMA guarantees freedom of expression and electronic media. The CRTA in Article 6 guarantees the promotion of human rights and liberties in the HRT programs. The media market is also regulated through market competition, electronic communications legislation (e.g. broadcasting licenses), conflict of interest prevention and other laws with direct and indirect effects on media freedom. The media are within the purview of the Ministry of Culture and Media. The leading media authority is the Council for Electronic Media (VEM), which regulates radio, television, digital news websites, and other electronic media services. There is no regulatory body responsible for the print media. Telecommunications are regulated by the Croatian Regulatory Authority for Network Industries (HAKOM).

5 Croatia has participated in the implementation since 2015.

6 The media pluralism risk levels are calculated as low (0–33%), medium (34–66%), and high risk (67–99%).

7 Data provided by the Agency for Electronic Media.

8 Data provided by Ipsos based on the average monthly share of unique visitors (January–November 2021).

References

AEM (2023) *AdScanner: Gledanost televizijskog programa SIJEČANJ 2023*. Available at: www.aem.hr/istrazivanje-gledanosti-televizije/ (17.10.2023).

AZTN (2022) *Istraživanje tržišta tiska za 2021*. Available at: www.aztn.hr/ea/wp-content/uploads/2016/10/Istra%C5%BEivanje-tr%C5%BEi%C5%A1ta-tiska-za-2021.-2.pdf (17.10.2023).

Batorfy, A., Bleyer-Simon, K., Szabo, K., and Galambosi (2022) *Monitoring Media Pluralism in the Digital Era: Application of the Media Pluralism Monitor in the European Union, Albania, Montenegro, the Republic of North Macedonia, Serbia and Turkey in 2021. Country Report: Hungary* (Centre for Media Pluralism and Media Freedom (CMPF); Media Pluralism Monitor (MPM); 2022; Country Reports) [Technical Report]. Available at: https://cadmus.eui.eu/handle/1814/74692 (17.10.2023).

Becker, J., Weissenbacher, R., and Jäger, J. (2021) 'Uneven Development in the EU: Processes of Core-Periphery Relations', in D. Bigo, T. Diez, E. Fanoulis, B. Rosamond, and Y. A. Stivachtis (eds.) *The Routledge Handbook of Critical European Studies*. Routledge, pp. 224–238.

Bilić, P. (2020) *Monitoring Media Pluralism in the Digital Era: Application of the Media Pluralism Monitor in the European Union, Albania and Turkey in the Years 2018-2019* (Centre for Media Pluralism and Media Freedom (CMPF); Media Pluralism Monitor (MPM); 2020; Country Reports) [Technical Report]. Available at: https://cmpf.eui.eu/mpm2020-results/ (17.10.2023).

Bilić, P., Petričušić, A., and Balabanić, I. (2015) *Media Pluralism in Croatia. A Test Implementation of the Media Pluralism Monitor 2015* (Centre for Media Pluralism and Media Freedom (CMPF); Media Pluralism Monitor (MPM); 2015; Country Reports) [Technical Report]. European University Institute.

Bilić, P., Petričušić, A., Balabanić, I., and Vučković, V. (2016) *Media Pluralism Monitor 2016. Monitoring Risks for Media Pluralism in the EU and Beyond. Country Report: Croatia* (Centre for Media Pluralism and Media Freedom (CMPF); Media Pluralism Monitor (MPM); 2016; Country Reports) [Technical Report]. European University Institute. Available at: https://cadmus.eui.eu/bitstream/handle/1814/46790/Croatia_EN.pdf?sequence=1&isAllowed=y (19.10.2023).

Bilić, P., Petričušić, A., and Eterović, R. (2017) *Monitoring Media Pluralism in Europe: Application of the Media Pluralism Monitor 2017 in the European Union, FYROM, Serbia & Turkey Country Report: Croatia* (Centre for Media Pluralism and Media Freedom (CMPF); Media Pluralism Monitor (MPM); 2017; Country Reports) [Technical Report]. European University Institute. Available at: https://cadmus.eui.eu/bitstream/handle/1814/61133/2018_Croatia_EN.pdf?sequence=1&isAllowed=y (19.10.2023).

Bilić, P., and Primorac, J. (2018) 'The Digital Advertising Gap and the Online News Industry in Croatia', *Medijske Studije*, *9*(18), pp. 62–80. Available at: https://doi.org/10.20901/ms.9.18.4 (17.10.2023).

Bilić, P., Prug, T., and Žitko, M. (2021) *The Political Economy of Digital Monopolies: Contradictions and Alternatives to Data Commodification* (1st edition). Bristol University Press.

Bilić, P., and Švob-Đokić, N. (2016) 'The Pendulum Model of Croatian Media Policy: Digitalisation between Public Interests and Market Competition', *European Journal of Communication*, *31*(5), pp. 503–518. Available at: https://doi.org/10.1177/0267323116659976 (17.10.2023).

Bilić, P., Valečić, M., and Prug, T. (2021) *Monitoring Media Pluralism in the Digital Era: Application of the Media Pluralism Monitor in the European Union, Albania, Montenegro, the Republic of North Macedonia, Serbia and Turkey in the Year 2020. Country Report: Croatia* (Centre for Media Pluralism and Media Freedom (CMPF); Media Pluralism Monitor (MPM); 2021; Country Reports) [Technical Report]. European University Institute. Available at: https://cadmus.eui.eu/bitstream/handle/1814/71940/croatia_results_mpm_2021_cmpf.pdf?sequence=1&isAllowed=y (17.10.202).

Bilić, P., Valečić, M., and Prug, T. (2022) *Monitoring Media Pluralism in the Digital Era: Application of the Media Pluralism Monitor in the European Union, Albania, Montenegro, the Republic of North Macedonia, Serbia and Turkey in the Year 2021. Country Report: Croatia* (Centre for Media Pluralism and Media Freedom (CMPF); Media Pluralism Monitor (MPM); 2022; Country Reports) [Technical Report]. European University Institute. Available at: https://cadmus.eui.eu/handle/1814/74684 (17.10.2023).

Brogi, E., Carlini, R., Nenadić, I., Parcu, P. L., and Viola de Azevedo Cunha, M. (2021) 'EU and Media Policy: Conceptualising Media Pluralism in the Era of Online Platforms. The Experience of the Media Pluralism Monitor', in P. L. Parcu and E. Brogi (eds.) *Research Handbook on EU Media Law and Policy*. Edward Elgar, pp. 16–31.

Car, V., and Bilić, P. (2023) *Critical Junctures in the Croatian Media System Privatisation, Liberalisation and Commercialisation between 1990 and 2020*. South Eastern Europe, Accepted for publication.

CMPF (2022) *Monitoring Media Pluralism in the Digital Era: Application of the Media Pluralism Monitor in the European Union, Albania, Montenegro, the Republic of North Macedonia, Serbia and Turkey in the Year 2021* (Centre for Media Pluralism and Media Freedom (CMPF); Media Pluralism Monitor (MPM); 2022) [Technical Report]. European University Institute. Available at: http://hdl.handle.net/1814/74712 (17.10.2023).

Council of Europe (2018) *Recommendation CM/Rec(2018)1[1] of the Committee of Ministers to Member States on Media Pluralism and Transparency of Media Ownership*. Available at: https://search.coe.int/cm/Pages/result_details.aspx?ObjectId=090000168 0790e13 (17.10.2023).

De facto (2022) *Slušanost radiopostaja*. Available at: www.de-facto.hr/ (17.10.2023).

Donders, K. (2012) *Public Service Media and Policy in Europe*. Palgrave Macmillan UK. Available at: https://doi.org/10.1057/9780230349650 (17.10.2023).

Donders, K., Loisen, J., and Pauwels, C. (2014) 'Introduction: European Media Policy as a Complex Maze of Actors, Regulatory Instruments and Interests', in K. Donders, C. Pauwels, and J. Loisen (eds.) *The Palgrave Handbook of European Media Policy*. Palgrave Macmillan, pp. 1–18.

Donders, K., and Moe, H. (2014) 'European State-Aid Control and PSB: Competition Policy Clashing or Matching with Public Interest Objectives?', in K. Donders, C. Pauwels, and J. Loisen (eds.) *The Palgrave Handbook of European Media Policy*. Palgrave Macmillan, pp. 426–441.

Donders, K., and Pauwels, C. (2008) 'Does EU Policy Challenge the Digital Future of Public Service Broadcasting?', *Convergence: The International Journal of Research into New Media Technologies*, *14*(3), pp. 295–311.

DZNAP (2023) *Čitatelji su spremni platiti – istraživačko novinarstvo, a Hrvatska je zadnja u EU po udjelu sadržaja za koji se plaća*. Available at: https://dznap.hr/citatelji-su-spremni-platiti-istrazivacko-novinarstvo-a-hrvatska-je-zadnja-u-eu-po-udjelu-sadrzaja-za-koji-se-placa/ (19.10.2023).

European Commission (2020) *European Democracy Action Plan*. Available at: https://eur-lex.europa.eu/legal-content/EN/TXT/?uri=COM%3A2020%3A790%3AFIN&qid=1607079662423 (19.10.2023).

European Commission (2022a) *2022 Rule of Law Report Country Chapter on the Rule of Law Situation in Croatia* [2022 Rule of Law Report]. Available at: https://commission.europa.eu/system/files/2022-07/27_1_194032_coun_chap_croatia_en.pdf (19.10.2023).

European Commission (2022b) *Proposal for a Establishing a Common Framework for Media Services in the Internal Market (European Media Freedom Act) and Amending*

Directive 2010/13/EU. Available at: https://eur-lex.europa.eu/legal-content/EN/TXT/?uri=CELEX:52022PC0457 (19.10.2023).

European Parliament (2008) *European Parliament Resolution of 25 September 2008 on Community Media in Europe (2008/2011(INI))*. Available at: https://eur-lex.europa.eu/LexUriServ/LexUriServ.do?uri=OJ:C:2010:008E:0075:0079:en:PDF (19.10.2023).

European Parliament (2024) *European Parliament Legislative Resolution of 13 March 2024 on the Proposal for a Regulation of the European Parliament and of the Council Establishing a Common Framework for Media Services in the Internal Market (European Media Freedom Act) and amending Directive 2010/13/EU (COM(2022)0457 – C9-0309/2022 – 2022/0277(COD))*. Available at: www.europarl.europa.eu/doceo/document/TA-9-2024-0137_EN.html (2.4.2024).

Flew, T., Iosifidis, P., and Steemers, J. (2016) 'Global Media and National Policies: The Return of the State', in T. Flew, P. Iosifidis, and J. Steemers (eds.) *Global Media and National Policies: The Return of the State*. Palgrave Macmillan, pp. 1–15.

Grbeša, M., and Volarević, M. (2021) 'Media in Croatia: From Freedom Fighters to Tabloid Avengers', *Publizistik*, *66*(3), pp. 621–636. Available at: https://doi.org/10.1007/s11616-021-00683-y (19.10.2023).

Habermas, J. (1996) *Between Facts and Norms: Contributions to a Discourse Theory of Law and Democracy*. The MIT Press.

HURA (2023) *HURA Media AdEx medijska potrošnja*. Available at: https://hura.hr/istrazivanja/medijska-potrosnja-u-hr/ (19.10.2023).

Ivanuš, Ž. (2021) 'Novinarska etičnost pod pritiskom interesnih skupina—Iskustva hrvatskih novinara', *Media, Culture and Public Relations*, *12*(1), pp. 73–90.

Jakubowicz, K. (2008) 'Finding the Right Place on the Map: Prospects for Public Service Broadcasting in Post-Communist Countries', in M. Sükösd and K. Jakubowicz (eds.) *Finding the Right Place on the Map: Central and Eastern European Media Change in a Global Perspective*. Intellect Ltd, pp. 101–124.

Karppinen, K. (2013) *Rethinking Media Pluralism*. Fordham University Press. Available at: www.jstor.org/stable/j.ctt13wzz1r (19.10.2023).

Katsirea, I. (2014) 'The Television without Frontiers Directive', in K. Donders, C. Pauwels, and J. Loisen (eds.) *The Palgrave Handbook of European Media Policy*. Palgrave Macmillan, pp. 297–311.

KU Leuven (2009) *Independent Study on Indicators for Media Pluralism in the Member States – Towards a Risk-Based Approach* (p. 167) [Prepared for the European Commission Directorate-General Information Society and Media, SMART 007A 2007-0002]. Available at: https://ec.europa.eu/information_society/media_taskforce/doc/pluralism/pfr_report.pdf (19.10.2023).

Lider (2019) *TOP 15: Koji su oglašivači, mediji i sektori potrošili najviše novca na oglase u 2018*. Available at: https://lidermedia.hr/aktualno/top-15-koji-su-oglasivaci-mediji-i-sektori-potrosili-najvise-novca-na-oglase-u-2018-37615 (19.10.2023).

McChesney, R. W. (2008) *Communication Revolution: Critical Junctures and the Future of Media*. The New Press.

Michalis, M. (2014) 'Focal Points of European Media Policy from Inception till Present: Plus ça change?', in K. Donders, C. Pauwels, and J. Loisen (eds.) *The Palgrave Handbook of European Media Policy*. Palgrave Macmillan, pp. 128–141.

Micova, S. B. (2021) 'The Audio-Visual Media Services Directive', in P. L. Parcu and E. Brogi (eds.) *Research Handbook on EU Media Law and Policy*. Edward Elgar, pp. 264–281.

Mučalo, M. (2020) 'Komercijalni FM radio u kontekstu hrvatske medijske politike', *Medijske Studije*, *11*(21), pp. 87–103.
Nölke, A. (2021) 'Capitalist Diversity in Europe', in D. Bigo, T. Diez, E. Fanoulis, B. Rosamond, and Y. A. Stivachtis (eds.) *The Routledge Handbook of Critical European Studies*. Routledge, pp. 161–172.
Nowak, E. (2014) 'Between Economic Objectives and Public remit: Positive and Negative Integration in European Media Policy', in K. Donders, C. Pauwels, and J. Loisen (eds.) *The Palgrave Handbook of European Media Policy*. Palgrave Macmillan, pp. 96–109.
Nyberg, L. (2021) 'The Market as Norm: The Governmentality of State Aid Regulation', in D. Bigo, T. Diez, E. Fanoulis, B. Rosamond, and Y. A. Stivachtis (eds.) *The Routledge Handbook of Critical European Studies*. Routledge, pp. 188–200.
Official Journal of the European Union (1989) *Council Directive 89/552/EEC, CONSIL, 298*. Available at: http://data.europa.eu/eli/dir/1989/552/oj/eng (17.10.2023).
Official Journal of the European Union (1997) *Treaty of Amsterdam, EUMS15, 340 OJ C*. Available at: http://data.europa.eu/eli/treaty/ams/pro_9/sign/eng (19.10.2023).
Official Journal of the European Union (2012) *Treaty of the Functioning of the European Union, 326 OJ C*. Available at: http://data.europa.eu/eli/treaty/tfeu_2012/oj/eng (19.10.2023).
Official Journal of the European Union (2018) *Directive (EU) 2018/1808, L 303/69*. Available at: https://eur-lex.europa.eu/eli/dir/2018/1808/oj (17.10.2023).
Official Journal of the European Union (2022a) *Regulation 2022/1925, 265 OJ L*. Available at: http://data.europa.eu/eli/reg/2022/1925/oj/eng (19.10.2023).
Official Journal of the European Union (2022b) *Regulation (EU) 2022/2065, 277 OJ L*. Available at: http://data.europa.eu/eli/reg/2022/2065/oj/eng (19.10.2023).
Perišin, T. (2008) 'Televizijske vijesti: U potrazi za vrijednostima', *Medijska istraživanja: znanstveno-stručni časopis za novinarstvo i medije*, *14*(2), pp. 63–86.
Peruško, Z. (2022) 'Digital News Report 2022: Croatia', *Reuters Institute or the Study of Journalism*. Available at: https://reutersinstitute.politics.ox.ac.uk/digital-news-report/2022/croatia (19.10.2023).
Splichal, S. (2000) 'Reproducing Political Capitalism in the Media of East-Central Europe', *Medijska Istraživanja: Znanstveno-Stručni Časopis Za Novinarstvo i Medije*, *6*(1), pp. 5–17.
Tambini, D. (2021) *Media Freedom* (1st edition). Polity.
Ungerer, H. (2014) 'The Reasons for Intervention through Competition Policy', in K. Donders, C. Pauwels, and J. Loisen (eds.) *The Palgrave Handbook of European Media Policy*. Palgrave Macmillan, pp. 405–425.
van Cuilenburg, J., and McQuail, D. (2003) 'Media Policy Paradigm Shifts: Towards a New Communications Policy Paradigm', *European Journal of Communication*, *18*(2), pp. 181–207. Available at: https://doi.org/10.1177/0267323103018002002 (19.10.2023).
Vozab, D., and Peruško, Z. (2021) *Digitalne publike vijesti u Hrvatskoj 2017–2021. [Digital News Audiences in Croatia 2017-2021]*. Zagreb: CIM – Centar za istraživanje medija i komunikacije i Fakultet političkih znanosti, Sveučilište u Zagrebu. Available at: https://cimfpzg.files.wordpress.com/2021/06/digital-news-izvjestajhrvatska-2017-2021-za-web-1.pdf (19.10.2023).

8 Competitiveness, Convergence, and Innovation

Assessment of Impacts of the First EU Membership Decade

Nevenka Čučković, Valentina Vučković and Krešimir Jurlin

8.1 Introduction

The main aim of this chapter is to analyse how the Croatian economy has transformed and adjusted to the EU single market in the last ten years since its accession to the EU and to assess what impact this transformation had on the competitiveness and development of the Croatian economy. Since July 2013, Croatia has fully integrated into the EU economy, removing barriers to the flow of goods, services, and capital. That fact immensely affected the performance at the firm level and business environment quality, which is crucial for the economy's competitiveness as a whole. Consequently, the EU membership directly affected many other aspects of social and economic life, including Croatian citizens' standard of living. The topics that we, in particular, would focus on are how macroeconomic competitiveness has changed and transformed since accession in 2013 and its effects on microeconomic competitiveness, i.e. the business sector, entrepreneurship development, and innovation. In short, we will examine the main advantages and challenges that EU membership has brought to the Croatian economy in the last decade and identify the main policy challenges that remain for the future.

First, a positive impact of becoming a full-fledged member of the EU is stronger export growth to the EU market, which has been one of the main driving forces of economic growth after the accession. At the same time, the Croatian economy found itself constrained by many EU rules and norms that needed to be respected and required sometimes painful transformations at the level of the business sector. Conversely, the generous EU funds have contributed significantly to the progress of institutional convergence and development of the overall business environment, R&D, innovation, and consequently, the competitiveness of the corporate sector in Croatia, especially small and medium enterprises (SMEs). Empirical data suggest their positive contribution to business performance indicators at the firm level; however, many problems still need to be resolved to increase their efficiency and competitiveness, including low productivity issues to achieve greater economic convergence and a broader societal impact.

DOI: 10.4324/9781003394013-8

This text explores the following questions: Has the accession of Croatia to the EU in 2013, despite the negative impact of the global financial crisis and other crises that followed after that one (COVID-19, earthquakes, energy crisis caused by the war in Ukraine), had generally favourable effects on the levels of economic competitiveness, convergence, and innovation development? In short, after ten years, were the benefits of EU membership higher than the costs? Did the Croatian economy increase its competitiveness and successfully converge to the average EU development level? What are the factors contributing to and, on the other side, hindering the catching-up process? How did the business sector, especially SMEs, adjust to the EU single market and narrow the efficiency and innovation performance gap? Finally, what are the policy priorities for the future to reap more benefits from the EU membership?

We will use various qualitative and quantitative research methods and techniques to answer these questions. They include desk research, a review of the previous in-depth research studies, and published work, including those in which the authors have participated, as well as our own econometric and impact assessment analyses based on Eurostat, Community Innovation Survey (CIS), Horizon 2020 Dashboard, World Bank, World Economic Forum (WEF), and Institute for Management Development (IMD) and other collected statistical data.

The text is structured as follows. After the Introduction, in Section 8.2, we provide a brief theoretical and empirical background and review the related literature to provide the conceptual framework for our analyses. Then, we continue with empirical studies in Section 8.3. Regarding the comparison of achieved progress at the national economic level, we focus in this section on the economic and institutional convergence process. In Section 8.4, we continue presenting the empirical evidence on the micro-level, i.e. at the level of the enterprise sector, with a particular focus on reviewing the progress of the SMEs regarding innovation activities as the driving force of increased competitiveness. In concluding Section 8.5, we sum up the presented empirical evidence for the first decade of the EU membership and identify the main challenges that remain to be addressed.

8.2 Brief Theoretical and Empirical Background

The reviewed theoretical and empirical literature mostly supports the rationale for the European integration process and joining the EU single market, especially if the accession countries' previous trade, investments, and other economic relations were intensive. Many authors examined the potential impact and effects of the process of EU integration and accompanying Europeanisation of economic policies in terms of their benefits and costs for national economies, both before and after the actual accession of the new member states to the EU (Radaelli, 2003; Taylor et al., 2013; Börzel and Risse, 2003; Mrak et al., 2004, Grabbe, H. 2006 and many more). The rationale for the achieving benefits of European integration and Europeanisation of economic policies for the accessing national economy proved to be accurate and is empirically evidenced for many new member states from Central and Eastern Europe (CEE) that joined in 2004 and 2007 (see Lavrač and Majcan, 2006; Stulec et al., 2014; Hunya, 2017; Samardžija, 2018; Stojčić et al., 2018). Due to the removal of all tariffs and customs and reduction of transaction costs, domestic production could generally benefit from cheaper production inputs and an increase in productivity, resulting in increased competitiveness of the economy and, consequently, larger shares of exports in the EU market. In general, the trade creation effects are therefore prevailing outcomes beneficial for entrepreneurship development and competitiveness of the accession economy. All these positive expectations drove Croatian adjustment to the EU single market in the last decade. This chapter will precisely focus on summing up the effects of Europeanisation on competitiveness, convergence, and innovation development in Croatia in its ten years of full EU membership.

As for Croatia is concerned, the trade liberalisation with the EU started much before the actual accession in 2013, as this market was a prime market for Croatia's exports and imports for many decades. However, it is essential to consider that Croatia, due to its political situation and war on its territory, was a latecomer to the EU compared to the other post-socialist CEE countries. After fulfilling all the EU conditionality, which was a relatively slow and tiring process because of mentioned political circumstances and constraints, Croatia finally joined the EU on 1 July 2013.

Several research studies have attempted to assess the foreseeable impact of joining the EU single market on the Croatian economy before and at the time of the accession, either as part of a larger sample of CEE new member states (NMS) or separately. For example, one of the earliest and most extensive studies analysed the potential economic benefits and costs of Croatia's entry into the EU, covering 15 broad areas ranging from foreseeable macroeconomic effects of accession on capital flows, trade, investment, prices, and fiscal developments to tourism, agriculture, health, science, research, environmental protection, etc. (Ekonomski institut Zagreb [EIZ], 2007). According to the study, the net financial effects of the accession for Croatia in the first three years of membership were estimated to be positive and at the average level of 0.2% of the annual GDP. The average expected short-term rise of prices due to the accession was estimated at a maximum of 1.4%. Based on the analyses carried out in this study, the authors concluded that the estimated long-term benefits of membership outweigh the short-term costs.

Lejour et al. (2009) examined the economic implications of EU membership of Croatia, focusing on the accession to the internal market and institutional reforms that the EU membership would trigger. Their findings suggested that consumption per capita in Croatia could rise by about 2.5% as a result of accession to the internal market, while if succeeding in reforming its domestic institutions in response to the EU membership, GDP per capita in Croatia could increase even more by an additional 8%. Also, Holzner (2013) econometrically assessed the potential accession impact of Croatia joining the EU in terms of the significant macroeconomic effects. Holzner distinguished the possible short-term and long-term effects based on the model's results. The main positive short-term contribution was seen in the potential growth of exports to the EU by 2.2 percentage points in the first year of the membership, while the exports to the Central European Free Trade Agreement (CEFTA) members[1] would decrease by 0.7%. The benefits are also foreseen on the side of Croatian consumers as consumer prices in Croatia could fall by around 0.39%. However, due to the lower efficiency and competitiveness of its economy, the real economic output would initially fall by 0.41% (in the short term).

Furthermore, Stojčić et al. (2021) analysed whether the intra-EU trade flows and the integration of CEE industries in the forward and backward EU value chains increase the share of entrants and high-growth firms in a sample of manufacturing firms from 11 CEE countries (Bulgaria, Croatia, Czech Republic, Estonia, Hungary, Latvia, Lithuania, Poland, Romania, Slovakia, and Slovenia). The authors showed that the gains from EU integration occur across low- and high-technology-intensive sectors through easier access to more sophisticated and advanced markets. However, these gains also seem stronger among early entrants to the EU.

Rukavina (2022) shows that Croatia as a part of the EU when compared to the hypothetical situation of remaining outside of the EU has achieved increases in exports and savings and a decline in government expenditures, household consumption, and agricultural productivity. In addition, her analysis showed that after 2013 and 2014, there was an upward trend of the observed indicators. Still, it did not lead to more profound shifts and dynamic expectations, except in the example of exports in 2019, which recorded above-average growth.

The process of Europeanisation and convergence to the EU institutions, policies, rules, and norms constituted an important integration pillar that supports the efficient functioning of the economy and society as a whole of a new EU member state. Bartlett et al. (2017) explored in a comparative perspective the patterns of change in the quality of institutions of six countries at different stages of European integration over the seven years from 2004 to 2011. Among them, the two countries were from the European Neighbourhood Policy (ENP) region, two were from the Western Balkans in the process of membership negotiation (Croatia was included in the analyses), and two were EU Member States from South East Europe. The study reveals significant differences between the country groups in the extent of institutional convergence, perceptions of corruption, and the pace of democratic consolidation. The authors conclude that in contrast to the Western Balkan countries negotiating accession, in the examined period, the EU did not play an essential role as a "transformative power" in the two ENP countries over the period up to 2012 and that the process of institutional reform was incomplete due to the absence of a clear European perspective. Furthermore, Bartlett et al. (2017) stress that the aim of EU assistance has primarily been to support the Europeanisation process by institution-building and promoting economic reforms in line with the EU acquis and EU norms. The "external incentives" model, as Schimmelfennig and Sedelmeier (2004) define it, considers the full membership of the EU as the successful result and ultimate benefit of the accession process, while the costs are the losses that key actors might incur by opening up their economies to competition and losing privileged positions in the market and political system. Bartlett et al. (2017) argue that the carrot of eventual EU membership acts as an incentive to elites to take difficult decisions and move along the path of the accession process. On the other side, rent-seeking elites in the accession and neighbourhood countries have much to lose from genuine reforms of their economies, legal systems, and societies.

Jurlin and Čučković (2010) measured the level of institutional convergence of CEE economies that joined the EU in 2004 and 2007 before and after accession. They compared it to accession countries such as Croatia at that time. They argue that the pressure to converge to the EU institutional environment was much higher before accession. At the same time, most of the new members of the CEE lost momentum in institutional reform after the accession. It is interesting to see that some authors (Petak and Kotarski, 2019) show that a similar process also happened in Croatia after accession to the EU, especially when implementing anti-corruption measures.

Also, Vučković et al. (2021), using the Worldwide Governance Indicators (WGI) of the World Bank (2022b) and varieties of capitalism approaches, explored the institutional convergence of CEE countries. At the average level of institutional quality, their results showed convergence at the level of CEECs with the coordinated market system (Hungary, Poland, Croatia, Czech Republic, and Slovenia) and the level of EU25, while in the Mediterranean group of countries, divergence was observed.

Jurlin et.al. (2018) examined Croatia's competitiveness, smart specialisation, and investment in the first five years since it joined the EU, which coincided with the post-financial crisis period. They compared four selected CEE peer countries: Hungary, Slovakia, the Czech Republic, and Slovenia. The analyses focused on the impact of the central EU policies and financial instruments, strategic approaches, policies, and mechanisms that aimed to enhance the competitiveness of EU member states. The authors showed the potential of the available financial and other instruments and their effects on CEE countries as a path for Croatia to achieve their more substantial impacts on competitiveness and the smart specialisation of its economy.

Bartlett (2018) stresses that the first couple of years of Croatia's EU membership was marked by a relatively deep recession caused by the global financial crisis, which persisted even after Croatia joined the EU. This sharply contrasted with the other NMS from CEE, whose economies recovered much faster. Bartlett argues that some Croatian macroeconomic policies, such as austerity measures and exchange rate policy, also contributed to an extraordinarily long recession, which resulted in severe macroeconomic imbalances, among which high levels of foreign and public debt were most severe. Namely, foreign and public debt financed most of the pre-accession economic development. They led to the Excessive Deficit Procedure formally introduced by the EU almost immediately after Croatia joined the EU. He argues that the cause of the prolonged recession was also partly related to Croatia's mode of "political capitalism", which was characterised by the close connections of political and business elites, which were draining the available public sources and thus affecting competitiveness, efficiency, and productivity of the economy. Such a situation hindered competitive entrepreneurship development capable of responding adequately to the recessionary shocks and overcoming crises sooner.

When looking into the economic convergence process at the local and county levels in Croatia, Puljiz and Rukavina (2022) demonstrate that although the overall catching-up process is much stronger after 2014, i.e. after joining the EU, the convergence at the local and county levels is somewhat uneven and divergent. Namely, the poorer communities and counties did not benefit much from the change in the general position of the national economy after accession. Furthermore, based on the analysis of personal income data, the research indicates that although income inequality generally reduces, the core of the change happens in middle-income counties. At the same time, the poorest administrative units are left behind in the convergence process.

8.3 Catching-Up and Convergence Processes with the EU Internal Market: Some Empirical Evidence

A challenging global context and multiple crises throughout the decade of Croatia's EU membership had a determining impact on Croatia's overall catching-up and convergence processes towards the average EU development level.

Economic and social convergence, as defined by Eurofound (2021), is a balanced economic prosperity and social progress across the EU countries. Upward convergence as a concept is at the core of the EU policy, especially after the global financial crisis, aiming to provide stability and sustainability for the Union in the long run. This concept is implemented by supporting less developed NMS, particularly from CEE, to catch up with average high-income levels of the EU, thus avoiding dangerous downward divergence in capacity for coping with economic crises. The lessons learned from the Greek crisis in 2008–2013 were incorporated into the EU policy of mitigating the effects of the global financial crisis.

Although economic and social convergence goes hand in hand, in this section, we will focus on Croatia's economic and institutional convergence as a tool for catching up with more developed EU member states.

World Bank's (2022a) study argues that a six-year-long recession in Croatia, caused by the global financial crisis, was a major setback regarding the economic convergence progress with the EU. Such an extraordinarily long recovery from the hardships that the Croatian economy experienced in 2009–2014 had offset, to a large degree, the potential initial benefits because of joining the EU. Looking back to the past decade, benefits and costs of EU membership should not overlook this fact. This means that the Croatian economy was much weaker when joining the club, and it took her years to recover to pre-financial crisis levels.

In addition, the external shocks that followed after the start of the 2020 COVID-19 pandemic were even more profound regarding the disastrous consequences on the economic growth in Croatia. The two devastating earthquakes with magnitudes of 5.5 (Zagreb) and 6.2 (Petrinja) (on a Richter scale), respectively, caused severe damages and costs to both the public and private sectors' infrastructure. According to the World Bank (2023), the total damage and costs of both earthquakes related only to the health and education sectors are estimated at 2.35 billion euro. Furthermore, the latest negative impacts of energy crises caused by the Russian invasion of

Ukraine in 2022 only aggravated the whole economic situation. To illustrate, the real GDP in 2020 plunged by –8.4%, while the impact of global energy crises decreased by almost 40% economic recovery rate from 13.1% achieved in 2021 to 6.5% in 2022. All these exogenous shocks resulted in a relatively incremental and fragmental catching-up process with the average EU level of development. As a reminder, Croatia started the EU membership with 61% of the average EU income level, and in 2022 it reached only 73% (Figure 8.1). However, it is also worth noting that one of the reasons for the apparent rise in GDP per capita adjusted for purchasing power parity (PPP) is the fall in the number of inhabitants, as Croatia is faced with strong depopulation trends.

World Bank report (2022a) further stresses that only with the implementation of ambitious economic reforms could Croatia reach the EU average income in 15 years and with moderate reforms only in 2050. Moreover, according to the report (World Bank, 2022a), the significant lag in total factor productivity (TPF) is

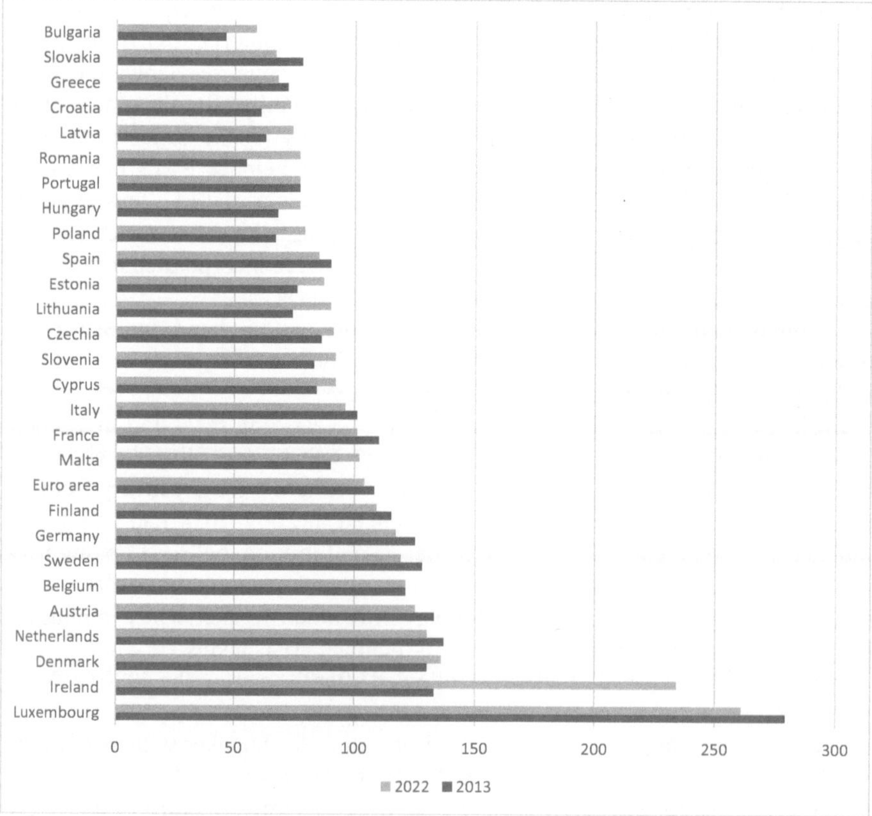

Figure 8.1 Index of GDP per capita in purchasing power parity (PPP), EU27=100.

Source: Eurostat (2023).

the leading cause of why Croatia is converging slower than most of the EU NMS from CEE.

The earlier comprehensive World Bank study (2009) also singled out the problem of low TPF at the firm level as an important limitation to the faster growth and competitiveness of the Croatian economy. The study points towards the need to improve the allocative efficiency of factors through advancing the structural reforms as this is the main source of the problem and is causing the inadequate efficiency and low TPF of the enterprise sector compared to the peer CEE countries. That means that more productive firms do not prevail in a larger share of output in Croatia and that inefficient firms linger for a very long time and do not exit the market fast enough to make space for more productive and efficient firms to make a stronger impact on growth. A similar conclusion could be found in the later study performed by the Institute of Economics Zagreb (EIZ, 2014). Authors Iootty et al. (2014) presented some powerful micro-evidence on productivity growth based on the representative sample of Croatian enterprises since the beginning of the recession in 2008–2012. Based on these results, they argue that economic dynamism (e.g. new products, new markets, production technologies, and new forms of business process organisation) which generally positively contributes to productivity is low in Croatia compared to that in CEE. It is evident when looking at the existing firm entry and exit processes in that period. The striking result from their study is that in this period of deep recession in 2008–2012, the market was eliminating even the potentially productive firms, suggesting also an inefficient market selection process. Apart from more efficient bankruptcy procedures that enable a faster creative destruction process, the authors suggest adopting policies that enhance market contestability and better regulation of the product market as well as measures to help finance the market entry in promising new sectors such as services in particularly retail and infrastructure.

Although the low level of productivity has many causes that could be found at the firm level and also in the general level of quality of the business environment, the World Bank 2022 report, which captures the developments after Croatia joined the EU, singles out that it is primarily due to inefficient market allocative mechanisms and institutions, which significantly affect the competitiveness and productivity of the economy. Therefore, to contribute to faster productivity growth, Croatia especially needs to speed up through reforms, which should incentivise research and development and continuously invest in managerial and employee skills at firm and country levels. We will shed more light on these areas in Section 8.4.

However, as opposed to coping with the initial consequences of the financial crisis on her own, Croatia had a rather beneficial impact on the speed of 2021 recovery following the COVID-19-caused recession, i.e. full V shape recovery in only one year (European Commission [EC], 2022a,b). The same is valid for coping with recessionary pressures caused by the latest energy and food crises caused by the Russian invasion of Ukraine in 2022. The recovery was largely driven by the strong performance in the tourism sector and resilient consumer spending, surpassing initial expectations.

Table 8.1 Market integration of Croatia

	2016	*2017*	*2018*	*2019*	*2020*	*2021*
Trade openness (%)	50.3	53.3	54.3	54.9	51.0	58.0
Trade with EA in goods and services (%)	28.6	29.6	30.4	30.7	28.1	31.7
World Bank's Ease of Doing Business Index Rankings	43	51	58	51	51	51
IMD World Competitiveness Ranking	58	59	61	60	60	59
Internal Market Transposition Deficit (%)	2.2	1.3	0.3	0.2	1.2	-
Real house price index	102.0	105.0	109.8	118.4	127.0	132.8

Source: European Commission (2022a, p. 100).

It is also important to stress that despite the multiple crises, there has been some progress made in the internal EU market integration, especially after recovery from the global financial crisis, as the European Commission (EC) Convergence Report shows (2022a, p. 100) (see Table 8.1).

Precisely, it is argued that the Croatian economy is well integrated with the EU internal market and Eurozone through trade, financial, and investment linkages. The level of integration into the internal market was particularly important when the EC assessed Croatia's readiness for joining the Eurozone in the summer of 2022. In 2016–2021 the trade openness increased significantly from 50.3% to 58%, respectively. As outlined, the degree of openness rose significantly in 2021 after declining to as low as 51% in 2020 as international trade and Croatia's tourism and travel services exports were particularly hit by the pandemic. The trade with the Euro Area (EA) also improved steadily from 28.6% to 31.7% in 2021, with Germany, Italy, Slovenia, and Austria being the main partners.

Regarding the degree of transposition of the internal market norms, Figure 8.2 shows the OECD Indicators of Product Market Regulation (PMR), which are a comprehensive and internationally comparable set of indicators that measure the degree to which policies promote or inhibit competition in areas of the product market, i.e. the economy-wide regulatory and market environments. We can see that Croatia, in the first five years of the EU membership, recorded an improvement in this indicator relative to the accession year, however, with worse results in the area of *Distortions Induced by State*, which is one of the high-level indicators, along with the dimension *Barriers to Domestic and Foreign Entry.*

Another set of data that can illustrate these aspects is the Fraser Institute's Economic Freedom of the World index, which measures the degree to which the policies and institutions of countries are supportive of economic freedom (Gwartney et al., 2022) and is often used in the literature as a proxy for business environment quality and structural reforms. Precisely, these data show that, although recording an increase in the economic freedom summary index after the year 2013, Croatia is lagging behind the EU27 and NMS average (left side of Figure 8.3) as well as that the best score is continuously recorded in the areas of *Sound Money* and *Freedom to trade internationally* (right side of Figure 8.3), which is not a surprise

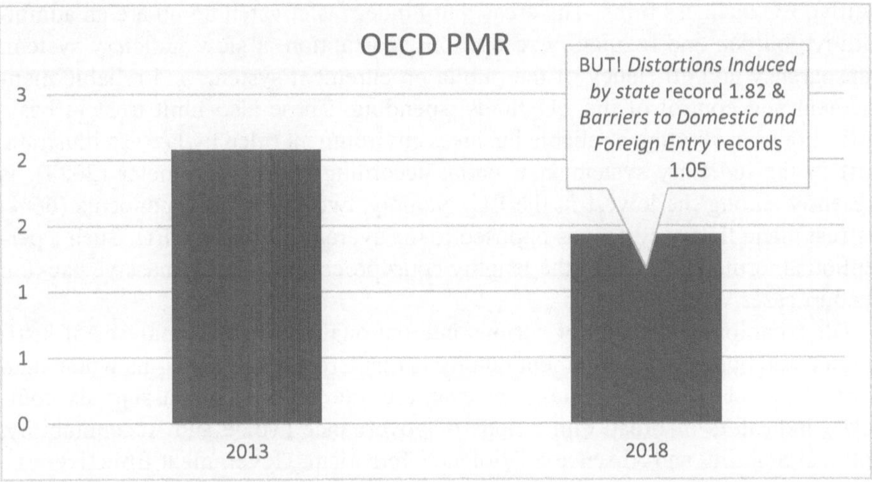

Figure 8.2 Product Market Regulation, 2013–2018.

Source: OECD 2018 and 2013 PMR database.

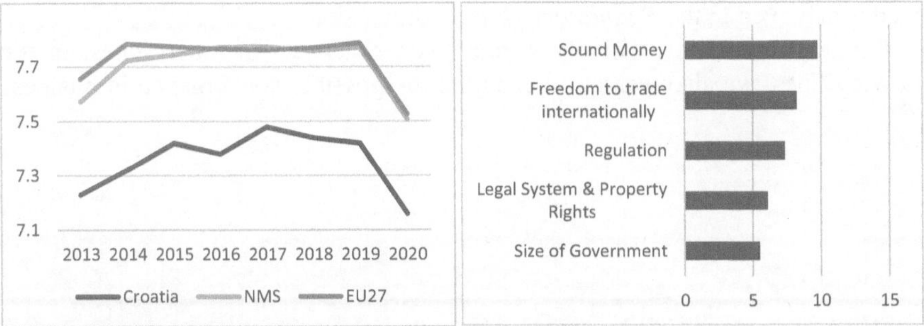

Figure 8.3 Economic Freedom of the World, 2013–2020.

Note: The right-side figure shows Croatia's average score values in 2013–2020 for a specific sub-pillar of the Economic Freedom of the World index.

Source: Fraser Institute and authors' calculation.

since Croatia has achieved the most progress within the so-called first generation of structural reforms, especially in financial and trade liberalisation.

Faster convergence in Croatia's business sector's performance efficiency is mainly constrained by the quality of the business environment, which is, according to most of the international indices (such as World Bank, IMD, and WEF), below both the EU and NMS average. Although specific progress in this area is evident, positive change is still too weak to provide adequate incentives for scaling-up competitive and innovative business development to catch up with highly competitive EU business firms. The areas that hinder faster catching up are an administrative burden and regulatory restrictions, corruption, a slow judiciary system, transparency and efficiency of the public procurement system, and reliable management and control of the EU funds' spending. These also limit trust in basic institutions constituting a reliable business environment ruled by law. To illustrate, trust in the judiciary system in Croatia, according to Eurobarometer (2023), is presently among the lowest in the EU. Namely, two-thirds of respondents (66%) distrust the judiciary system as opposed to the average 42% in the EU. Such a perception is formed because of the lengthy court proceedings and a massive backlog of court cases.

The common conclusion of various international reports and analyses of institutional and business environment quality is that Croatia still performs worse than most of the EU Member States. For example, the WGI encompassing six composite indicators of broad dimensions of governance (Voice and Accountability, Political Stability and Absence of Violence/Terrorism, Government Effectiveness, Regulatory Quality, Rule of Law, and Control of Corruption),[2] presented in Figure 8.4, show that Croatia ranks low in control of corruption, regulatory quality, and the rule of law. These are all dimensions that reveal the (in)ability of the government to enable the development of the private sector (Kaufmann et al., 2010). However, it is worth noticing that the most significant progress in the pre-accession period is achieved in the *Regulatory Quality* dimension.

Although Croatia is relatively weaker than other EU member states, in the following lines, we also wanted to examine the possible convergence in business

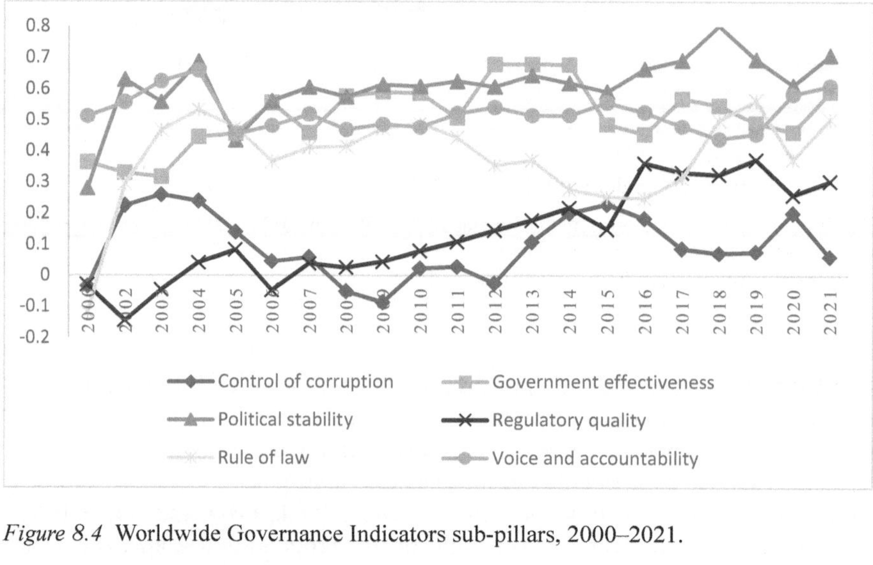

Figure 8.4 Worldwide Governance Indicators sub-pillars, 2000–2021.

Source: World Bank (2022b).

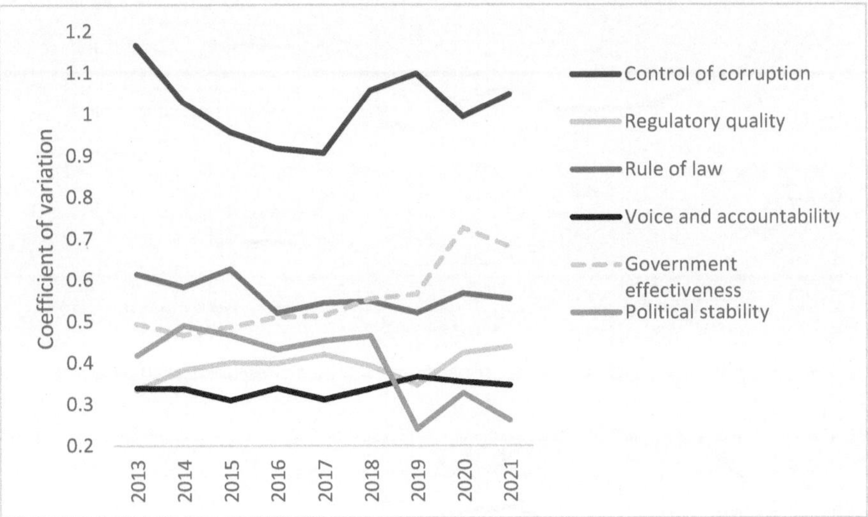

Figure 8.5 Sigma convergence for NMS group of countries, 2013–2021.

Source: Authors' calculation based on World Bank data.

environment quality presented by the above data within two country groups, i.e. NMS (Figure 8.5) and the entire EU27 (Figure 8.6). We first do this exercise by the commonly used measure of convergence – sigma convergence calculated as the coefficient of variation (i.e. a measure of dispersion for each group of countries) for the period from 2013 to 2021. It is assumed that σ-convergence is present when the coefficient of variation declines between the examined periods. The results are pretty mixed, with repeated periods of convergence and divergence in both groups of countries. Overall, regarding the sub-pillar of *Political Stability and Absence of Violence* (i.e. the possibility of the government being destabilised or overthrown through unconstitutional or violent actions), in both groups of countries, we can say that there is a general trend of convergence in the observed period. Regarding the variable *Government Effectiveness* (i.e. the quality of public services provided, the degree of civil service independence, the effectiveness of policies implemented, and the government credibility), there is evident divergence in both groups of countries. Regarding the *Control of Corruption* (including petty and grand corruption, and state capture), there was a convergence episode between 2013 and 2017, followed by a period of divergence, which lasted longer in the NMS group of countries. Regarding *Regulatory Quality* (i.e. implementation of policies and regulations that encourage the private sector development), it can be concluded that the divergence episodes prevail in both countries. However, in the EU27 group, the episode of convergence was more prolonged than in NMS. The variable of *Voice and Accountability* (participation in elections, freedom of

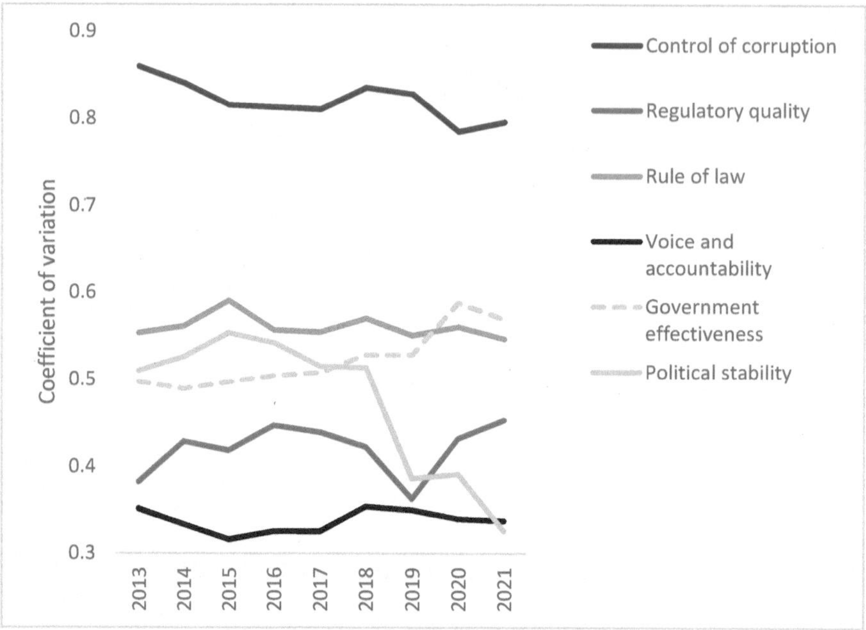

Figure 8.6 Sigma convergence for EU27 group of countries, 2013–2021.

Source: Authors' calculation based on World Bank data.

expression and association, and free media) is relatively stable throughout the observed period in both groups. The *Rule of Law* variable (capturing effective law enforcement, strong property rights, the likelihood of crime and violence) for the entire EU remains relatively stable, while we observe more considerable variations with prevailing divergence episodes for the NMS.

Next, we also performed an analysis of beta unconditional convergence in order to examine whether countries with initially lower quality of institutions achieve more significant improvement in institutional quality as a proxy for the business environment. We performed a simple cross-section regression analysis in which the change of institutional quality g is regressed on its initial level $I_{0,i}$, and a significant and negative β coefficient implies convergence:

$$g_i = \alpha + \beta I_{0,i} + \varepsilon_i$$

A positive and significant value of β implies the presence of divergence. Finally, if the parameter β is not statistically significant, we conclude there is neither convergence nor divergence. Along with the membership period, from 2013 to 2021, we analysed the possible convergence for the entire period for which data are available (i.e. 1996–2021). We have included this period to highlight

Table 8.2 Beta convergence

Indicator		*EU27 (n=27)*	
		1996–2021	*2013–2021*
Voice and Accountability	**β-coefficient**	−0.335***	−0.135*
	St. Error	0.106	0.078
	R^2	0.28	0.11
Political Stability and Absence of Violence	**β-coefficient**	−0.677***	−0.537***
	St. Error	0.077	0.074
	R^2	0.76	0.68
Government Effectiveness	**β-coefficient**	−0.267**	−0.046
	St. Error	0.103	0.082
	R^2	0.21	0.02
Regulatory Quality	**β-coefficient**	−0.231**	1.067***
	St. Error	0.107	0.083
	R^2	0.16	0.86
Rule of Law	**β-coefficient**	−0.351***	−0.091
	St. Error	0.107	0.063
	R^2	0.30	0.08
Control of Corruption	**β-coefficient**	−0.228**	−0.139**
	St. Error	0.093	0.068
	R^2	0.19	0.14
Average institutional quality[a]	**β-coefficient**	−0.228**	−0.102*
	St. Error	0.074	0.059
	R^2	0.28	0.11

Source: Authors' calculation.

Note: * $p < 0.1$, ** $p < 0.05$, *** $p < 0.01$.

[a] Calculated as the average of the above six governance indicators.

that the EU integration is a process that starts even before the actual membership and, as such, is reflected in institutional quality through the adoption of *acquis communautaire*.

The obtained results show that there is beta convergence in a group of EU27, in all institutional indicators in the 1996–2021 period. In the 2013–2021 period, it is interesting to see that in the area of *Regulatory Quality*, the divergence is confirmed. This could be explained by the fact that, once countries have become EU members, their institutional development loses momentum (see, e.g., Schönfelder and Wagner, 2016), a scenario usually described by the reform fatigue term, which could also be the case for Croatia (see Table 8.2).

These mixed results could have implications for NMS and Croatia as the latecomer because the gap in institutional quality is still significant, which slows down further institutional convergence as an important pillar of economic convergence. In addition, this could imply the existence of so-called club convergence, i.e. a situation when groups of countries converge to different steady-states, and additional analyses would be required to show which club Croatia belongs.

8.4 Impact of the EU Membership on the Competitiveness and Innovation of the Business Sector

When countries become members of the EU, they no longer take advantage of traditional economic policy instruments (such as quotas, customs, and exchange rates), but what remains are fiscal policy instruments and structural reforms (Vučković, 2018). Furthermore, as it is often emphasised, in countries with fiscal leeway, targeted fiscal policy towards productivity-enhancing investments in infrastructure and education and innovation could revive productivity growth, support employment, and broaden aggregate demand (WEF, 2019).

The Global Competitiveness Index, an annual yardstick for policy-makers to assess their progress against the complete set of factors that determine productivity, is organised into 12 pillars covering broad socioeconomic elements within which Innovation capability is one of them (WEF, 2019). Let us look at the longer-term trends (2007–2017) in the GCI of Croatia, compared, e.g. with Romania and Bulgaria, which entered the EU in 2007. We can see that contrary to them, after the accession year, Croatia recorded a fall in GCI score after 2013, which started to increase after 2015, i.e. in the post-global financial crisis recovery period.

Moreover, the last Global Competitiveness Report 2019 (WEF, 2019, p. 174) that included Croatia reveals the performance rank regarding all 12 pillars encompassed by the index and points out that Croatia records the lowest score (38) in the *Innovation capability* pillar (73rd among a total of 141 countries). In addition to the *Innovation capability* pillar, we should consider the performance within the *Business dynamism* pillar, which encompasses elements crucial to the innovation processes, such as the growth of innovative companies, companies embracing disruptive ideas, and attitudes towards entrepreneurial risk. In this pillar, Croatia has the weakest rank among the 141 countries in the research (101st).

The innovation process is widely considered a primary driver of increases in productivity and competitiveness both at the firm and the national economic levels. The importance of innovation (especially R&D) for competitiveness is also highlighted within the European Innovation Scoreboard, which provides a comparative analysis of innovation performance in EU countries, other European countries, and regional neighbours. Thus, in Figure 8.8, we show Croatia's summary innovation index (SII) relative to the EU average. The data show that innovation performance has been increasing over time, at more moderate rates until 2019 and higher rates in 2020–2022. Based on this, we cannot say that after the accession Croatia experienced a significant push for innovation performance measured by SII.

However, when looking at the latest 2022 European Innovation Scoreboard (EC, 2022a,b), the data show that Croatia is an Emerging Innovator with a performance of 66.5% of the EU average (i.e. now above the EU average) and with the country's performance gap to the EU becoming smaller. More precisely, in 2022, Croatia was ahead of Bulgaria, Romania, Poland, Latvia, and Slovakia but behind Hungary (in the group of Emerging Innovators). It is essential to mention that Croatia was beyond the EU average in innovation performance for many years, especially for SMEs. However, the innovation gap is getting smaller as the

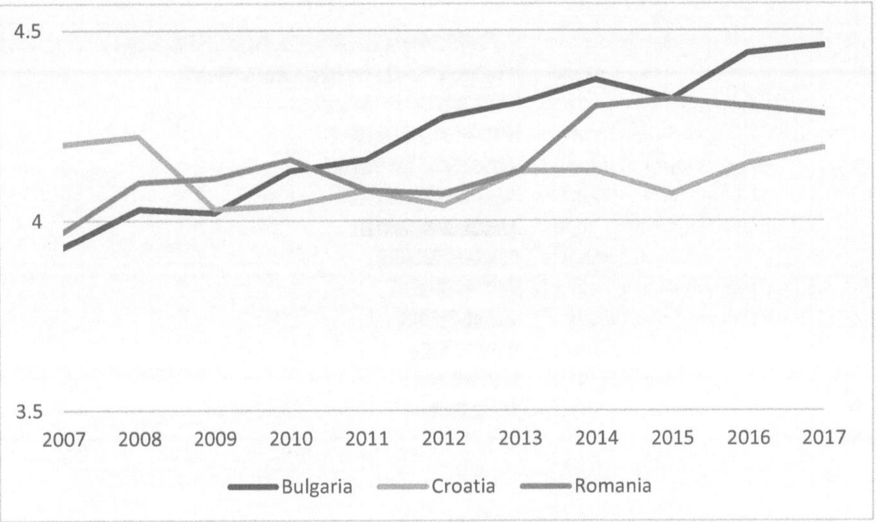

Figure 8.7 Global Competitiveness Index scores, 2007–2017.

Source: World Bank TCdata360.

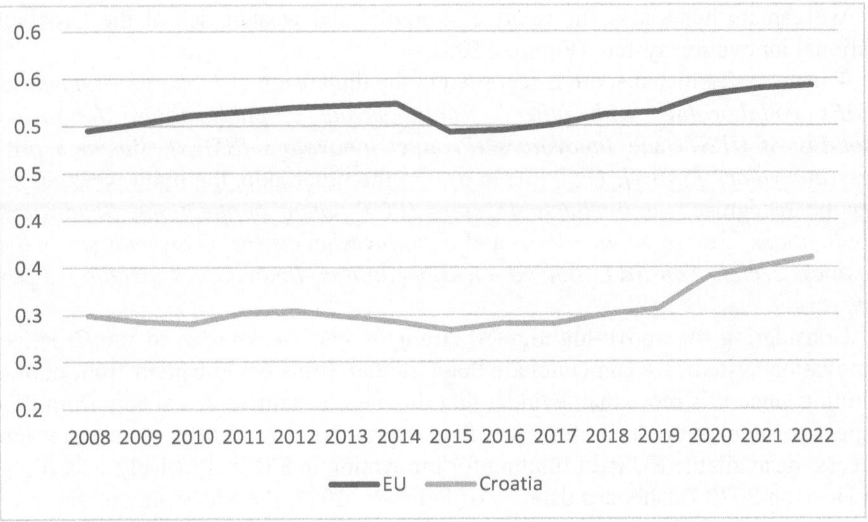

Figure 8.8 Summary Innovation Index, 2008–2022.

Source: European Innovation Scoreboard data (various years).

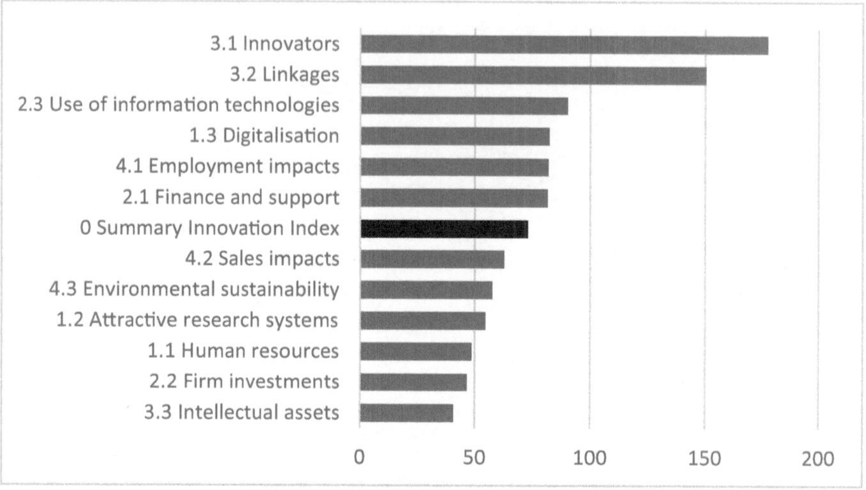

Figure 8.9 Innovation performance by sub-pillars of SII, 2022.

Source: European Commission (2022b).

performance increased by 15.5% in 2022 relative to 2015, which is higher than the average EU rate (9.9%) for the same period.

We can further assess the relative strengths and weaknesses of the Croatian national innovation system (Figure 8.9).

The most significant score is recorded in the dimension of *Linkages (Innovative SMEs collaborating with others, Public-private co-publications, Job-to-job mobility of HRST)* and *Innovators (Product innovators [SMEs], Business process innovators [SMEs])* (EC, 2022a,b). On the other side, the main weaknesses can be recognised in *Intellectual assets (PCT patent applications, Trademark applications, Design applications)* and *Firm investments (R&D expenditure in the business sector, Non-R&D Innovation expenditures, Innovation expenditures per employee)*.

Considering the above-highlighted strengths and weaknesses in the Croatian innovation system, we can conclude that Croatian firms could benefit from public funding since it is more than evident that there are considerable barriers from this aspect to innovation. Therefore, we find it promising for SMEs to acquire and access the available EU R&I funding for innovation in SMEs. Precisely, according to Horizon 2020 Dashboard data, as of February 2023, the SMEs in Croatia have got in a total of 25.28m EUR from Horizon 2020 funding programmes, which represent 18.3% of the country's total.[3] Furthermore, the positive effects of the availability of funds for innovation are also reflected in the data on firms with innovation activities (Figure 8.10), which show that in the period 2018–2020 (Eurostat, Community Innovation Survey [CIS], 2020), the share of all firms with

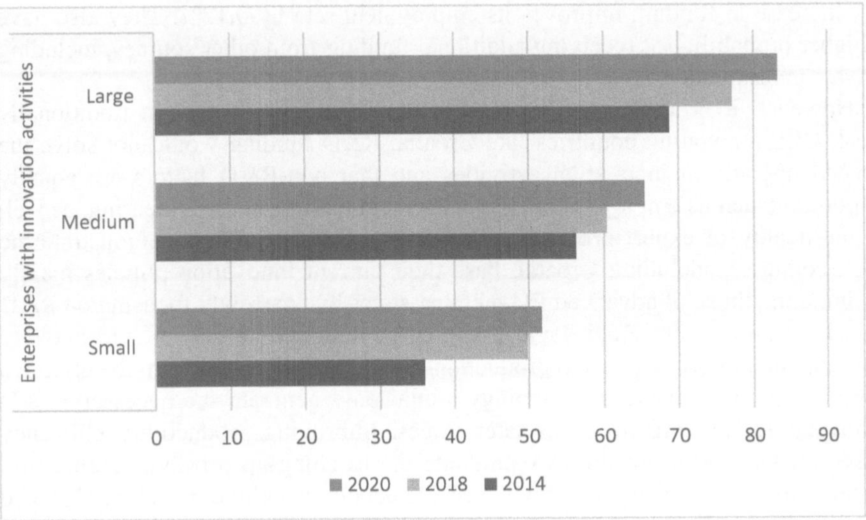

Figure 8.10 Enterprises with innovation activities (%), 2014–2020.

Source: Eurostat.

innovation activities increased relative to 2016–2018 (Eurostat, CIS, 2018) and 2012–2014 (Eurostat, CIS, 2014).

In the following lines, we briefly assess the available research evidence and insights on the impact of Croatia's EU membership on enhancing and upgrading this process in SMEs. Namely, Croatian SMEs represent above 99% of all enterprises, participate with 55% in total exports, 66% in total profits of the enterprise sector, and employ 72% of workers in the enterprise sector (FINA, 2021). Their importance for the economic growth of Croatia has significantly grown in the post-recession recovery period (2015–2019).

The existing research shows that joining the EU increased financing potentials and access to finance for small and medium firms in Croatia. Čučković and Vučković (2018), in their work, review and assess the impact of the EU R&D funding as a way of incentivising innovation activities of SMEs and found that the increased availability of such funding was very beneficial for the catching-up process of the new EU member states, including Croatia.

The increased availability of EU funding was particularly beneficial for further entrepreneurial development and the SMEs' business performance, which were relatively financially constrained due to their size and modest capital, especially before accession to the EU. Čučković and Vučković (2021), based on their econometric analyses of the selected innovation and economic performance indicators, show that SMEs from the EU NMS that received EU funds perform better than they would have without such funding. The results show that an increase in Horizon

2020 funds by EUR 1 increases the recipient SME's turnover by EUR 1.33, and a 1% increase in funding improves its employment rate by 0.12%. They also have a higher probability of receiving additional funding from other sources, including private investment.

However, it is also essential to take into consideration that in traditionally weak CEE innovating countries like Croatia, R&D funding would not solve the needed upgrade in innovation activities and that non-R&D factors are equally important (such as employee skills, management quality, and engineering, as well as the quality of export products). Radošević's (2017) findings demonstrate the CEE countries, including Croatia, base their current innovation policies mainly on imitating those of advanced EU member states by "narrowly focusing on R&D drivers of innovation" (Radošević, 2017, p. 2). Radošević argues that technology upgrades and improvements to production capabilities that stem from the effective use of imported advanced technology would only generate the necessary R&D innovation-driven growth at its later stages. Improving productivity efficiency based on innovation would also stimulate the catching-up process, leading to a faster convergence with more developed EU economies. Stojčić et al. (2020) also accented strengthening indigenous innovation and production capabilities as crucial to the innovation process and output, which has a potentially larger impact on the growth of CEE countries including Croatia and on catching up with advanced EU members.

Although Croatian SMEs have profited a lot from opportunities offered by the enlarged market after Croatia joined the EU in 2013, it is evident from the above overview that in terms of innovation in SMEs, Croatia still needs much to catch up with a more developed part of the EU. Nevertheless, even in the first five years of its membership, the Croatian SME sector expanded considerably. As a result, it improved its general business performance in terms of turnover, value-added, profitability, productivity, innovation output, and employment, as well as its general market position compared to large enterprises (IRMO, 2017).

At the same time, joining the EU aggravated pressure in terms of increased competitiveness and innovation, especially during the years of the protracted economic crisis that was intense in Croatia until 2015, but also in 2020 during the most severe blows of COVID and in 2022 during the energy crisis and inflation. However, the flexible and opportunity-seeking nature of the SMEs proved to be the main drivers of resilience and recovery in the post-crisis recovery periods in Croatia. In addition, in 2021–2022, this sector benefited more effectively from the available EU funding by implementing the National Plan for Recovery and Resilience (Government of the Republic of Croatia, 2021a,b).

It is also encouraging to see that considerable progress in enterprise sector innovation was achieved in post-COVID economic recovery in 2021 and 2022, according to European Innovation Scoreboard (European Commission, 2022b). The SMEs have achieved significant progress in innovation activities in the post-COVID-19 recovery period. Their product innovators are around 134% of the average EU level, while the SME's business process innovators are at 121%. In

2022 the SMEs' business process innovators increased by 10.7%, while the product innovators decreased by 17.8% compared to 2021.

The descriptive analysis of trends in all of the above data during Croatia's membership period could only indicate that observed changes coincided and were incentivised with the EU accession. But without more sophisticated econometric estimation, which is beyond the scope of this chapter, we cannot conclude that there is a causal relation to the accession since it is crucial to include in such analyses a larger set of economic, social, political, and institutional control variables.

As for the future, joining Eurozone and Schengen area as of January 2023, besides macroeconomic effects, could also have beneficial implications on the efficiency and competitiveness of the business sector, especially SMEs. It is expected that the immediate impact would be lowering transaction costs and the consequent rise in investors' interest. For some sectors, such as tourism and transport, the significant benefits might show already in the short run, according to some calculations of the Croatian Chamber of Commerce. Furthermore, Deskar Škrbić and Kunovac (2020) argue that eliminating volatility related to the exchange rate due to the introduction of the Euro could contribute to additional trade and financial convergence and additional stabilisation of the business cycles of the Croatian business sector, given the high similarity of business cycles between Croatia and Eurozone members. All these would also reduce the sector's vulnerability to damaging blows of external shocks in the future.

8.5 Concluding Remarks and Implications for the Future Policy

Summing up the main conclusions of this chapter, several key points deserve a particular accent. First, the whole decade of Croatia's EU membership (2013–2023) was overshadowed by coping with crises' impacts of various sorts and lengths. It is safe to say that, for Croatia and the EU, it was a decade of crisis. First, the membership started with a deep and prolonged recession caused by the global financial crisis; then there was a COVID-19 pandemic in 2020 plus two devastating earthquakes on top of it; and most recently, in 2022, global energy and food crises after the Russian invasion of Ukraine that fuelled high inflation and disrupted global supply and value chains. Because of all of these, the first decade of the membership was highly challenging for the competitiveness of the Croatian economy and its convergence process to the average EU levels of development.

Moreover, the mentioned blows of exogenous shocks had a substantial negative impact on the overall economic position of Croatia as the new EU member state. Under such circumstances, the Croatian economy could not reap the full benefits of EU membership. Nevertheless, it would not be fair to blame only exogenous reasons for all the negative impacts, as some also attributed to the unfinished agenda of structural reforms, as pointed out by the recent convergence study of the World Bank (2022a).

Nevertheless, from the convergence process perspective, the decade was not wasted as the position of the Croatian economy has track of improvement.

However, due to the reasons previously mentioned, this change did not match the progress achieved in the first decade by the EU NMS from the 2004 and 2007 enlargement rounds. Namely, in the first membership decade, the GDP levels in Croatia, measured by PPP, increased only by 12% or 1.2% per annum (Eurostat, 2023). For illustration, in the first decade of Romanian EU membership (2007–2017), that increase was from 34% to 57% of the average GDP per capita in PPP, which made Romania the third best performer straight after Poland and Slovakia who were the frontrunners (Hunya, 2017).

Based on the empirical data, the Croatian economy's macroeconomic competitiveness and performance substantially improved in the last decade. As a result, its position increased in the most global competitiveness ranks, such as WGI, WEF, and IMD. However, many concerted policy efforts should be directed further to enhance micro-competitiveness and the general efficiency of the business sector. In this respect, further improvement of business environment quality, which could provide incentives for boosting it, remains one of the main policy challenges. The other essential policy challenges are improving employee and management skills and R&D business linkages, which could scale up the overall innovation capabilities and activities of the sector.

Regarding enhancing the innovation process in the last decade, tangible, although non-linear, progress has been achieved mainly with the help of generous EU funding, especially since 2020. Interestingly, quite an upsurge in SME product innovation was achieved in the COVID-19 crisis of 2020 and 2021, while a significant surge of business process innovations was achieved in 2022, according to European Innovation Scoreboard (2022). However, such progress is still relatively modest to achieve more substantial breakthroughs, which could affect their international competitiveness at the EU and global levels. In this respect, SMEs, as influential innovation creators and conduits in Croatia, require concerted policy efforts at multiple levels to develop their innovation and catching-up capabilities further and to increase their potential to absorb available R&I funds from the EU and other sources, which will help them scale up this process.

Addressing productivity issues, rightly accented by the World Bank (2022a) study, is one of the main policy priorities for the future as the overall competitiveness of the Croatian economy depends on it. Unfortunately, inadequate convergence of TPF in the enterprise sector limits the faster catching-up process. Therefore, changing the position of Croatia, which is presently at the bottom of the economic development rank in the EU, depends very much on making progress in this area.

In short, being part of a larger EU market has shielded the Croatian economy in turbulent times brought about by multiple crises in the first decade of its membership. It made mitigating and combating the blows of external shocks much easier than being on its own as a small and open economy. However, at the same time, a lot of thorough transformation and structural economic reforms have been postponed for better times as most of the significant resources; skills and strength in the last decade were absorbed by interventionistic economic crisis management.

Notes

1 Prior to accession to the EU Croatia was a part of Central European Free Trade Agreement (CEFTA).
2 For a detailed definition of each of the indicators, see Kaufmann et al. (2010). The indicators are expressed in the standard normal units, ranging from –2.5 to 2.5.
3 https://webgate.ec.europa.eu/dashboard/sense/app/a976d168-2023-41d8-acec-e77640154726/sheet/0c8af38b-b73c-4da2-ba41-73ea34ab7ac4/state/analysis

References

Bartlett, W. (2018) 'The New Kid on the Block: Croatia's EU Membership in the Shadow of the Eurozone Crisis', in C. Schweiger and A. Visvizi (eds.) *Central and Eastern Europe in the EU Challenges and Perspectives under Crisis Conditions.* London: Routledge.

Bartlett, W., Čučković, N. and Jurlin, K. (2017) 'A Comparative Perspective on Institutional Quality in Countries at Different Stages of European Integration', *Tijdschrift voor Economische en Sociale Geografie*, 108(1), pp. 92–108. Available at: https://doi.org/10.1111/tesg.12196 (06.10.2023).

Börzel, T. and Risse, T. (2003) 'Conceptualizing the Domestic Impact of Europe', in K. Featherstone and C. Radaelli (eds.) *The Politics of Europeanization.* Oxford: Oxford University Press.

Čučković, N. and Vučković, V. (2018) 'EU R&D Funding as a Way of Incentivizing Innovation of SMEs: A Review of Impacts', *Croatian Economic Survey*, 20(2), pp. 97–127. Available at: https://doi.org/10.15179/ces.20.2.4 (06.10.2023).

Čučković, N. and Vučković, V. (2021) 'The Effects of EU R&I Funding on SME Innovation and Business Performance in New EU Member States: Firm-Level Evidence', *Economic Annals*, 66(228), pp. 7–41. Available at: https://doi.org/10.2298/EKA2128007C (06.10.2023).

Deskar-Škrbić, M. and Kunovac, D. (2020) 'Twentieth Anniversary of the Euro: Why are Some Countries Still Not Willing to Join?', *Economists' view*. Available at: www.hnb.hr/-/s-039 (26.03.2023).

Ekonomski institut Zagreb (2007) 'Pristupanje Europskoj uniji: očekivani Ekonomski učinci'. Available at: www.eizg.hr/publikacije/knjige/pristupanje-europskoj-uniji-ocekivani-ekonomski-ucinci/632 (09.10.2023).

Ekonomski institut Zagreb (2014) 'Productivity Analysis in Croatia: An Assessment Using Firm Level Data'. Available upon request at: www.eizg.hr/projects/past-projects/productivity-analysis-in-croatia-an-assessment-using-firm-level-data-pacr/1747 (09.10.2023).

Eurobarometer (2023) Standard Eurobarometer 98 – Winter 2022–23. Available at: https://europa.eu/eurobarometer/surveys/detail/2872 (31.03.2023).

Eurofound (2021) 'Monitoring convergence in the European Union: Looking backward to move forward – Upward convergence through crises, Challenges and prospects in the EU series', Publications Office of the European Union. Available at: www.eurofound.europa.eu/publications/flagship-report/2021/monitoring-convergence-in-the-european-union-looking-backwards-to-move-forward-upward-convergence (06.10.2023).

European Commission (2022a) 'Convergence Report', *European Economy Institutional Papers*, 179. Available at: https://economy-finance.ec.europa.eu/publications/convergence-report-2022_en (09.10.2023).

European Commission (2022b) European Innovation Scoreboard. Available at: https://research-and-innovation.ec.europa.eu/statistics/performance-indicators/european-innovation-scoreboard_en (11.10.2023).

Eurostat (2023) Purchasing Power Parities and GDP Per Capita – Flash Estimate. Available at: https://ec.europa.eu/eurostat/statistics-explained/index.php?title=Purchasing_power_parities_and_GDP_per_capita_-_flash_estimate (09.10.2023).

Eurostat, Community Innovation Survey (CIS) (2014). Available at: https://ec.europa.eu/eurostat/databrowser/view/inn_cis9_type/default/table?lang=en&category=scitech.inn.inn_cis9

Eurostat, Community Innovation Survey (CIS) (2018). Available at: https://ec.europa.eu/eurostat/databrowser/view/inn_cis11_inact/default/table?lang=en&category=scitech.inn.inn_cis11.inn_cis11_inno

Eurostat, Community Innovation Survey (CIS) (2020). Available at: https://ec.europa.eu/eurostat/databrowser/view/inn_cis12_inact/default/table?lang=en&category=scitech.inn.inn_cis12.inn_cis12_inno

Financijska agencija (FINA) (2021) Rezultati poslovanja poduzetnika u 2021 - razvrstani po veličini. Available at: www.fina.hr/novosti/rezultati-poslovanja-poduzetnika-u-2021.-godini-razvrstani-po-velicini (09.10.2023).

Government of the Republic of Croatia (2021a) National Plan of Recovery and Resilience. Available at: https://planoporavka.gov.hr/UserDocsImages/dokumenti/Plan%20oporavka%20i%20otpornosti%2C%20srpanj%202021..pdf?vel=13435491 (09.10.2023).

Government of the Republic of Croatia (2021b) National Development Strategy Croatia 2030 (in Croatian). Available at: https://hrvatska2030.hr/

Grabbe, H. (2006) *The EU's Transformative Power: Europeanization through Conditionality in Central and Eastern Europe*. Basingstoke: Palgrave Macmillan.

Gwartney, J., Lawson, R., Hall, J. and Murphy, R. (2022) 'Economic Freedom of the World: 2022 Annual Report', Fraser Institute. Available at: www.fraserinstitute.org/sites/default/files/economic-freedom-of-the-world-2022.pdf (09.10.2023).

Holzner, M. (2013). Impact of Croatian EU Accession on Regional Trade Patterns, wiiw Policy Notes and Reports, No.10, The Vienna Institute for International Economic Studies. Available at: https://wiiw.ac.at/impact-of-croatian-eu-accession-on-regional-trade-patterns-dlp-2982.pdf (09.10.2023).

Hunya, G. (2017) 'Romania: Ten Years of EU Membership', *Romanian Journal of European Affairs*, 17(1), pp. 5–15.

Iootty, M., Correa, P., Radas, S. and Škrinjarić, B. (2014) 'Stylized Facts on Productivity Growth: Evidence from Firm-Level Data in Croatia', *World Bank Policy Research Working Paper*, No. 6990. Available at: https://papers.ssrn.com/sol3/papers.cfm?abstract_id=2475077 (09.10.2023).

IRMO (2017) 'Analitička podloga za izvješće o napretku provedbe sporazuma o partnerstvu između Republike Hrvatske i Europske komisije', Available at: https://strukturnifondovi.hr/wp-content/uploads/2018/01/Izvje%C5%A1%C4%87e_IRMO_final.pdf (9.10.2023).

Jurlin, K. and Čučković, N. (2010) 'Comparative Analysis of the Quality of European Institutions 2003–2009: Convergence or Divergence?', *Financial Theory and Practice*, 34(1), pp. 71–98.

Jurlin, K., Samardžija V. and Basarac Sertić, M. (2018) 'Competitiveness, Smart Specialisation and Investment in New EU Member States and Croatia', in Samardžija. V. (ed.), *The Challenges of the European Policies Implementation in Croatia*. Zagreb: Institute for Development and International Relations.

Kaufmann, D., Kraay, A. and Mastruzzi, M. (2010) 'The Worldwide Governance Indicators: Methodology and Analytical Issues', World Bank Policy Research Working Paper. Available at: https://openknowledge.worldbank.org/handle/10986/3913 (09.10.2023).

Lavrač, V. and Majcan, B. (2006) 'Economic Issues of Slovenian Accession to the EU', Working Paper No.31. Ljubljana: Institute of Economic Research. Available at: https://esiweb.org/pdf/slovenia_Lavrac-Majcen_econ%20issues%20of%20SLO%20EU%20accession-2006.pdf (09.10.2023).

Lejour, A., Andrea M. and Verweij, G. (2009). 'The Economic Effects of Croatia's Accession to the EU', *Eastern European Economics*, 47(6), pp. 60–83.

Mrak, M., Rojec, M. and Silva-Jauregui, C. (eds.) (2004) *Slovenia: From Yugoslavia to European Union*. Washington, DC: World Bank.

Petak, Z. and Kotarski, K. (eds.) (2019) *Policy-Making at the European Periphery: The Case of Croatia.* Cham: Palgrave Macmillan.

Puljiz, J. and Rukavina, I. (2022) 'Analiza konvergencijskog procesa na lokalnoj i regionalnoj razini u Hrvatskoj/Convergence Process Analysis at Local and Regional Levels in Croatia', *Ekonomski pregled*, 73(5), pp. 698–715.

Radaelli, C. (2003) 'The Europeanization of Public Policy', in K. Featherstone and C. Radaelli (eds.) *The Politics of Europeanization.* Oxford: Oxford University Press.

Radošević, S. (2017) 'Upgrading Technology in Central and Eastern European Economies', *IZA World of Labour*, 2017(338), pp. 1–11.

Rukavina, I. (2022) 'Evaluation of Macroeconomic Outcomes and the Seven-Year Membership of Croatia in the European Union', *Public Sector Economics*, 46(1), pp. 1–42.

Samardžija, V. (ed.) (2018) *The Challenges of the European Policies Implementation in Croatia.* Zagreb: Institute for Development and International Relations.

Schimmelfennig, F. and Sedelmeier, U. (2004) 'Governance by Conditionality: EU Rule Transfer to the Candidate Countries of Central and Eastern Europe', *Journal of European Public Policy*, 11(4), pp. 661–679.

Schönfelder, N. and Wagner, H. (2016) 'Impact of European Integration on Institutional Development', *Journal of Economic Integration*, 31(3), pp. 472–530.

Stojčić, N., Anić, I.-D. and Svilokos, T. (2021) 'The Entrepreneurial Gains from Market Integration in the New EU Member States', *Small Business Economics*, 57, pp. 1–20.

Stojčić, N., Srhoj, S. and Coad, A. (2020) 'Innovation Procurement as Capability Building: Evaluating Innovation Policies in Eight Central and Eastern European Countries', *European Economic Review*, 121(2020), pp. 103330.

Stojčić, N., Vojinić, P. and Aralica, Z. (2018) 'Trade Liberalization and Export Transformation in New EU Member States', *Structural Change and Economic Dynamics*, 47, pp. 114–126.

Štulec, I., Vučković, V. and Baković, T. (2014) 'Impact of Croatian EU Accession on Its Foreign Trade and Customs System', *Ekonomski vjesnik/Econviews*, 27(2), pp. 381–392.

Taylor, A., Geddens, A. and Lees, C. (2013) *The European Union and South East Europe: The Dynamics of Europeanization and Multilevel Governance*. New York: Routledge.

Vučković, V. (2018) 'Competitiveness of Croatia: The Role of Business Environment', *InterEULawEast*, 5(1), pp. 73–90.

Vučković, V., Šimić Banović, R. and Basarac Sertić, M. (2021) 'Governance Trends among New EU Member States: Is There Institutional Convergence?', *Sustainability*, 13(24), pp. 1–16.

World Bank (2009) *Croatia's EU Convergence Report: Reaching and Sustaining Higher Rates of Economic Growth.* Washington, DC: World Bank.

World Bank (2022a) *Croatia Country Economic Memorandum – Laying the Foundations: Boosting the Productivity to Ensure Future Prosperity in Croatia*. Available at: https://documents1.worldbank.org/curated/en/099094501312328131/pdf/P1752220c6def203a0b7f00017cc624fc24.pdf (09.10.2023).

World Bank (2022b) Worldwide Governance Indicators. Available at: www.govindicators.org (09.10.2023).

World Bank (2023) Greening Public Human Development Buildings in Croatia: Support for the Implementation of the European Green Deal in the Croatian Health and Education Sectors. Available at: https://openknowledge.worldbank.org/server/api/core/bitstreams/a79b02be-9ad8-458d-b18a-b9304cc775f5/content (09.10.2023).

World Economic Forum (WEF) (2019) Global Competitiveness Report 2019. Available at: www3.weforum.org/docs/WEF_TheGlobalCompetitivenessReport2019.pdf (09.10.2023).

9 Free Movement of People

Implications for Croatian Labour Market

Predrag Bejaković and Željko Mrnjavac

9.1 Introduction

Labour mobility refers to the movement of people between different regions or countries primarily seeking work or better employment opportunities. Croatia became a member state (MS) of the European Union (EU) on 1 July 2013 and was granted access to the EU single market. Thus, the nation gains access to "the basic four EU freedoms" – free movement of trade in goods, services, capital and labour. These freedoms allow for the more effective reallocation of domestic factors of production, opening up new business and trade opportunities and ultimately improving the prospects for MS economic growth and social development. Meanwhile, due to Croatia's EU membership transitory, transitional restrictions on free labour mobility from Croatia to other MS labour markets went into effect. Consequently, Croatia's labour market has become increasingly integrated with other EU MSs, providing new opportunities for labour mobility.

As a result of labour mobility, Croatia has experienced both benefits and challenges. On the one hand, Croatian workers have gained access to job opportunities in other EU MSs, which has helped to reduce registered unemployment. On the other hand, labour mobility has also resulted in a severe brain drain, as many highly skilled workers have left the country searching for better opportunities abroad.

In order to address these challenges, the Croatian government has implemented a number of policies aimed at improving the country's labour market and encouraging labour mobility but also to support staying in Croatia and/or returning from abroad. These policies include investing in education and training programmes to develop the skills of the country's workforce, promoting entrepreneurship climate and innovation support. Such measures also comprise various activities in reducing red tape and lowering tax and fiscal burden, which are needed to attract foreign investment and to create new job opportunities. The country's government is committed to a more sustainable and inclusive labour market that benefits all workers and supports economic growth. However, such measures until now have not achieved the full expected results.

This chapter explores the factors and consequences of the free movement of people and its implications for the Croatian labour market. The main aim and focus

DOI: 10.4324/9781003394013-9

of the chapter is to explain that in the circumstances of severe labour shortage, immigrants are essential for the normal functioning of the Croatian economy. At the same time, emigration from Croatia lessened the severe problems of open unemployment. After this section notes, Section 9.2 gives the theoretical framework and the literature review on labour mobility in the EU context, with the basic facts about labour mobility, its characteristics, causes and consequences. Section 9.3 deals with motivations for possibilities and limitations of internal migrations, while Section 9.4 examines the importance of international emigration from Croatia. Section 9.5 is dedicated to the reasons, scope and consequences of international immigration into Croatia. Section 9.6 contains the final discussion and conclusion.

9.2 The Theoretical Framework and the Literature Review on Labour Mobility in the EU Context

As mentioned, migrants leave areas of high unemployment and/or low incomes for more prosperous parts of the same country or some other countries, attracted by higher wages and/or better employment prospects. In this way, migration helps reduce regional disparities and mitigate the impact of shocks on economic activity. While economic growth and job creation are strongly linked to the willingness to move to another area or country, the supply of jobs also determines the arrival of job seekers.

Zimmermann (2004) accentuates that migration is a controversial and challenging phenomenon in today's globalised world. Labour migration occurs only when significant economic growth has been achieved and numerous new jobs have been created, so there is a relatively high demand for labour, encouraging citizens of other regions or countries to emigrate. In imaginary economies with perfect mobility of production factors, certain regions will immediately adapt to asymmetric shocks. When factors of spatial labour mobility are limited and prices and wages are inflexible, the effects of asymmetric shocks persist. Then, the differences in the economic development of individual regions or countries must be solved by other mechanisms, such as interregional fiscal transfers in the case of a nation-state (Fidrmuc, 2001). However, this is not the case in the real world, most often due to bureaucratic reasons as well as poor or inadequate qualifications and educational attainments of workers, so the possibilities of moving from poor to rich countries are very limited (World Bank, 2005). High emigration rates perpetually have significant effects on the sender-country labour market. In addition to the direct loss of the labour force, remittances have a robust negative impact on the labour market participation of sender households (Mansoor and Quillin, 2006; Chami et al., 2018). When migrants return to their home country, they bring new working knowledge and experience (Fengler et al., 2021), enriching the human capital (Bahar and Rapoport, 2018), increasing the value of foreign direct investment (Kugler and Rapoport, 2005) and trade (Orefice et al., 2022).

Recent labour migrations in Southeast Europe are primarily a response to poor performance and unfavourable conditions on the labour market, insufficient productivity of capital or lack of investment, poor quality of life in emigrating countries and increased demand for unskilled labour in immigration EU MSs (Regional Cooperation Council and International Organization for Migration, 2015). People migrate not only due to the difference in wages and salaries and economic reasons but also to avoid war, civil conflicts and insecurity in the country of origin due to their national affiliation, gender or other characteristics, like religious beliefs or sexual orientation. Therefore, one could deem that the quality of life, in a broader sense, encourages or limits migration. Differences in political stability, respect for human rights and the general rule of law also affect migration, as these factors serve as proxies for the level of personal sense of security.

Many people voluntarily decided or were forced to leave their home countries when these societies did not provide sufficient guarantees for the necessary physical, mental or material protection. Very often, there was a poor quality of public goods and government, an unsatisfactory, unsafe and unpredictable business climate, widespread and deeply rooted corruption and high unemployment. The costs of moving include financial costs like travel fees, lost wages during the move and psychological costs brought on by being apart from family and friends, which also impact the decision to relocate. According to the human capital model, the likelihood of migrating decreases with age, reflecting the reduced predicted lifetime advantage from moving for older people (Zimmermann, 2004). Motivations for migration can be grouped according to political, economic, demographic, social and cultural factors on the one hand and push and pull factors on the other (Table 9.1).

Regarding the connection between education and migration, Borjas (1987) points out that migration is influenced by the average salary level and the dispersion of salaries, which shows interregional differences in rewarding competencies and educational levels. This means that regions (countries) with a relatively egalitarian distribution of wages will primarily attract unskilled and low-qualified workers. At the same time, highly qualified people will try to migrate to areas with greater inequality in the distribution of wages, where there is also a greater return to education.

Zimmermann (2004) states that the challenges of the connection between migration and education can be outlined in several waves. *The first wave* of unskilled and low-qualified workers migration mainly consisted of the poor and desperate who came to developed countries looking for a way out of an unenviable and unpromising position. *The second wave* of migration includes the most skilled persons in the workforce because, in the 21st century, human capital is the most important source of economic growth. Most developed economies are characterised by a strong and growing unsatisfied demand for a qualified labour force, driven by technological changes, the ageing of the resident population and the decrease in the working-age domicile population. Current and future needs for skilled workers can hardly be met by the domestic workforce and/or the existing education systems. All developed countries, especially Europe, are increasingly competing to attract foreign qualified labour to fill the resulting gaps. *The third wave* in the global

Table 9.1 Motivation for migration

Type of factors	*Push factors*	*Pull factors*
Political	Conflicts, war, violence, insecurity Bad and crooked government Disrespect of human and political rights Corruption and disrespect of the rule of law	Security Political freedom
Economic and demographic	Poverty Unemployment Low salaries and wages Adverse dispersion of wages Absence of essential or poor-quality health and education services Unfavourable entrepreneurial and investment climate Impossibility to apply entrepreneurial skills	Possibility of getting higher salaries and wages The likelihood of improving the standard of living The possibility of personal and professional development and training Possibility to apply and improve entrepreneurial skills
Social and cultural	Disrespect and discrimination based on ethnic, gender, religious or other affiliation Lack of possibilities to apply acquired knowledge and skills Limited possibilities or impossibility for professional promotion Absence of probability to improve quality of life and lack of perspective	Family reunification The return of the diaspora to the mother country Freedom from discrimination Possibility to apply acquired knowledge and skills Possibilities for professional promotion Existence of probability for improvement and a tangible perspective of well-being

Sources: Harris and Todaro (1970); Fidrmuc (2001); World Bank (2006); Adamović and Mežnarić (2006); Regional Cooperation Council and International Organization for Migration (2015).

impact of migration on the economy is the necessary productive mix of skilled and unskilled workers at the workplace. It is increasingly evident that the need for more qualified workers reduces the incentives to employ people with lower educational and qualification levels. *The fourth wave* is the mobility of production factors due to the competition in the labour market. If people do not move or are not allowed to go freely to work in other areas or abroad, they will be replaced by the mobility of goods and capital. For example, cheap labour is embedded in imported goods, especially threatening domestic production, in which low-skilled workers primarily participate.

Lessons from previous labour migrations to developed countries are primarily related to the fact that the integration of immigrants into the labour market was relatively slow but constant. At the same time, the influence of the local population and employees was not particularly strong, but mostly, the citizens accepted the newcomers positively. The first generations of immigrants mostly had a lower level of education and a worse quality of life than the native population. However, in the second generation, these differences decreased and disappeared. Therefore, the children of immigrants were quite similar to those of the native population and were equally educated, employed, worked and professionally advanced. However, the situation has changed with globalisation and the unique pressure on unqualified and unskilled people, i.e., the increased demand for highly skilled people.

The flows of goods and capital in today's world are fundamentally different from those during the early period of globalisation. During the early period of globalisation, mostly unqualified and unskilled people emigrated, while the most critical feature of contemporary international migration is a substantial brain drain and often the movement of the most active and courageous part of the population. At the same time, increased international free flows of goods also reduce the scope of international labour mobility as labour-intensive products can be made in post-transition and developing countries.

An essential characteristic of migration is its capacity to facilitate the adjustment of regions to idiosyncratic (specific or distinctive) shocks, which are often related to tradition, habits and broader social conditions. When factors of production are adequately mobile, labour and capital move in response to output shocks until marginal returns are equalised across regions. If, on the other hand, factor mobility is inadequate, asymmetric shocks lead to tenacious interregional differentials in unemployment and wages. For the US state-level data, Blanchard and Katz (1992) measure regional adjustment and conclude that most adjustment happens via labour mobility after an initial growth in unemployment rather than capital mobility or price and wage adjustment. Of course, one should remember that labour in the US is very mobile and responds quickly to idiosyncratic economic shocks and conditions.

In contrast, the EU, Decressin and Fatás (1995), analysing the situation in the EU, find that the effects of such shocks are absorbed chiefly by changes in labour-force participation rather than migration. Therefore, wage and unemployment differentials are more significant and persistent in the EU than in the US. However, in the EU expansion after 2000, countries significantly lagging in wages and employment opportunities are included. Their access to freedom of movement has much stronger consequences in the internal market.

In analysing the causes and consequences of migration, particularly a brain drain of the highly educated population, Le Bras (2003) deems that there are many uncertainness and disparities in the predictions of migration flows and effects against simple, intuitive expectations. He stipulates numerous possible sources of such situation, like *political premises* of migration statistics, when data is intentionally overstated or diminished to avoid the immigration push; desire to realise ideological *wishful thinking*, when some data are intentionally included, while others were left out with the desire to confirm presupposed believes; and *ethnocentrism* in manipulating with statistical data which often leads to biased pictures or twisted conclusions, like the idea that the new generations of immigrants mostly follow parent trajectories and are not moving on the social structure hierarchy. Such factors influence the analysis of external emigrations, which are also under the impact of internal migration in Croatia, explained in the following text.

9.3 Possibilities and Limitations of Internal Migrations

In the period after the Second World War, migration trends mainly were linked with increasing "deagrarisation" – where agriculture no longer constitutes an exclusive source of living as many rural families have been able to find work in secondary and tertiary activities in cities, but still living in rural areas. Croatia is relatively small, so they were daily commuters – so-called workers-peasants. They also supplemented their family income from various resources related to agriculture, production from arable land, livestock, vineyards etc. Later, mainly during the 1960s and 1970s, people were permanently leaving rural areas and settling in cities, achieving urbanisation in a relatively short period of 10–15 years. Also, many returnees from working abroad (who often left rural areas for temporary work abroad, primarily from Germany and Austria) were resettled with their families, most often in large cities, rarely returning to the villages where they had lived before. The returnees from abroad have mostly inhabited large cities or their immediate environment. However, instead of industrialisation and urbanisation, from the economic and demographic point of view of the optimal system of regional centres, supplementing it with administrative and social functions, the concentration of economic and other functions and population continued until the 1960s in several Croatian cities, and after that until 1990s dominantly in three (Zagreb, Split, Rijeka) (Akrap, 2014).

In approximately the last 30 years, Croatian citizens have had a low space mobility within the country. For example, in 2021, 71,864 persons changed their residence within Croatia, 1.8% of the total population. The most significant number of persons who migrated within the country was younger persons aged 20–39 (45.9%), while the share of females in the total number of persons who migrated was 54.6%. Within the total number of persons who migrated to Croatia in 2021, 40.5% migrated between counties, 38.5% between towns/municipalities of the same county and 21.0% between settlements of the same town/municipality. Most migrations between towns/municipalities within the same county were recorded in the County of Split-Dalmatia.[1] Furthermore, in the County of Primorje-Gorski Kotar, most migrations between counties were recorded in the City of Zagreb and the County of Zagreb (Croatian Bureau of Statistics, 2022).

The share of 2% of the total population who changed their residence within Croatia has been mostly the same for extended periods. As there is no international comparative data for the last census 2021, according to census data 2011, the share of people who lived in another place the previous year (2010) within the country in Croatia was also 2% of the total population. The data shows that internal migration in Croatia is very low compared to other EU MSs – like Finland. Denmark and Sweden – where it is above 12%. Croatia's situation is slightly better than in Poland, Bulgaria and Romania, where around 1% of the population has changed residence (Hakansson and Bejakovic, 2020).

The possible reasons for the low internal geographic mobility of the population in Croatia are manifold. Many jobless persons in Croatia are unwilling to accept work in other countries despite comparatively generous one-off financial assistance and travel and relocation expenses reimbursement. For example, according to ~~the data from~~ the Croatian Employment Service (various years), seasonal jobs in tourism are active mostly workers from the coastal areas (around two-thirds of all workers), while around one-fifth are those for those from Slavonian counties. The workers from Croatia's north-western and central regions participate with a relatively small share (around 15%) (Hrvatski zavod za zapošljavanje, various years).

Moreover, family links are also much more robust in Croatia than in the West European states, partially due to the tradition, multigenerational family households and legal obligation of the children to take care of their elderly, but also partially due to the comparatively weak coverage of preschool institutions (crèches and kindergartens) in small towns and rural areas (Dobrotić and Matković, 2023). Such institutions are insufficient in a significant part of Croatia, so grandmothers and grandfathers often take care of their grandchildren. A possible movement to another city or county almost always means losing essential family members' support. The situation is probably even worse regarding the affordability of and accessibility to old-age and infirm persons' accommodation institutions. Thus, in the conditions of non-existence or adequate accessibility to institutional accommodation, it is pretty standard for younger family members to take care of and support elderly parents or relatives, which hinders or prevents their spatial mobility.

A further reason for the low residential mobility in Croatia is the high transaction cost of moving.[2] The costs to buy a dwelling are higher, and the time it takes to register it in Croatia is longer than in Sweden (Palm, Jingryd and Kordić, 2019). According to Caldera Sanchez and Andrews (2011), the population has higher geographical mobility in countries with lower transaction costs. Furthermore, there are vast differences in the quality of life and employment possibilities in the bigger cities, particularly the capital of Zagreb, on the one hand, and smaller cities and rural areas on the other. Croatia has a considerable concentration of healthcare capacities in the bigger cities, particularly the capital of Zagreb. In contrast, accessibility to healthcare services is terrible in rural areas, particularly on islands and mountainous regions. A very similar situation is with educational institutions, particularly quality tertiary education.

As mentioned, the main direction of internal migration in Croatia has been to Zagreb. At the same time, many middle-sized towns in the continental part of the country, like Slavonski Brod, Karlovac, Vinkovci and Sisak, are burdened with the remnants of old state companies and severe lag in economic development and employment possibilities. Therefore, if there is no employment possibility in a person's native town, while in bigger cities and/or Zagreb where there are available vacant working places, the dwellings are hardly affordable, it should not be a surprise that many persons, mainly young, decide to emigrate abroad.

9.4 Importance of International Emigration from Croatia

When looking for employment in another MS, EU citizens can look for a job, accept employment and get support from the host country's public employment service. They are entitled to equal treatment concerning job terms, social and tax obligations, and benefits. Furthermore, EU employees can live anywhere they want with their families. In 2013, about 7 million EU citizens – or 3.3% of the EU's total labour force – were working and living in a member country other than their country of citizenship. Furthermore, there were just over 1.1 million cross-border or frontier workers and around 1.2 million posted workers. These are workers seconded to another in the EU MS to carry out short-term assignments (Andor, 2014).

Until 2022, according to the European Commission, the Directorate-General for Employment, Social Affairs & Inclusion (2022) mentioned that the number of EU citizens currently living or working abroad increased to 9.9 million or 3.8% of the EU total working-age population. The mentioned increase has been primarily caused by workers from the countries who joined the EU more recently. Over the last 20 years, the two most significant developments have prompted new labour mobility patterns within the EU. First, the accession of new Central and Eastern European countries in 2004, 2007 and 2013 led to significant east–west flows on top of the traditional south–north flows. Second, the Eurozone crisis has increased imbalances in EU labour markets and led to pronounced labour outflows from the countries on the euro area's periphery. As a result, although east–west labour mobility is more pronounced, south–north mobility is again increasing.

Croatia has traditionally been a country of immigration from the surrounding area, which has succeeded in compensating for emigration that primarily has gone to European countries. According to the official data by the Croatian Bureau of Statistics (2022), in the period 2012–2021, Croatia immigrated 204,300 persons, while 316,569 individuals emigrated abroad, which means a negative net migration balance of 112,269 persons or 2.6% of the population in 2021 (Table 9.2).

Draženović, Kunovac and Pripužić (2018) indicate that the official statistics from recipient EU MSs show that the number of emigrants is up to 2.6 times higher than the official Croatian records show. The official Croatian statistics are significantly lower because they include only officially reported emigration. However, they show that the number of emigrants has tripled since 2013 (from 15,262 emigrants

Table 9.2 International migration of population of the Republic of Croatia

Year	*Immigrants*	*Emigrants*	*Net migration*
2012	8959	12,877	–3918
2013	10,378	15,262	–4884
2014	10,638	20,858	–10,220
2015	11,706	29,651	–17,945
2016	13,985	36,436	–22,451
2017	15,553	47,352	–31,799
2018	26,029	39,515	–13,486
2019	37,726	40,148	–2422
2020	33,414	34,046	–632
2021	35,912	40,424	–4512
TOTAL	204,300	316,569	–112,269

Source: The Croatian Bureau of Statistics (2022).

in 2013 to 47,352 emigrants in 2017, the year that recorded the highest number of emigrants). Similar conditions were recorded in countries that became new EU members before Croatia, like Latvia (Hazans, 2003) and Slovakia (Bajzíková and Bajzik, 2020). Almost in all new MSs, people willing to emigrate reveal behaviour consistent with the well-known classical human capital model: young and more educated individuals were more likely to move.

Of 40,424 persons who emigrated from Croatia in 2021, 37,623 (93.1%) went to European countries, of which 20,884 decided to move to EU MSs. By far, the most popular destination of emigration from Croatia is Germany, where only in 2021, emigrated from Croatia 13,077 persons of which 12,906 (or 98.7%) were Croatian citizens. Germany is followed by Austria (3425 total emigrants from Croatia) and Ireland (866 total emigrants from Croatia). Jurun, Curic and Bekavac (2021), on the sample of 661 persons, examine the main reasons for emigration from Croatia to Germany (and probably to all other countries). In the opinion of the interviewed persons, central emigration "push" factors are high unemployment, relatively low wages, limited possibilities of permanent employment or professional advancement, debts, legal insecurity and a general feeling of distrust and hopelessness. The interviewees would return from emigration in the case of a better economic situation, reforms in healthcare, education and judiciary system, as well as lessening of corruption. These are severe adverse characteristics of Croatian society, but such changes and improvements cannot be realised quickly.

According to the latest report for 2021 by the European Commission, Directorate-General for Employment, Social Affairs and Inclusion (2022), in general, the number of EU working-age people living in an EU or EFTA country other than their home country – so-called *EU movers* – had increased to some extent at the beginning of 2020 compared to 2019. There were 9.9 million EU movers, up around 100,000 or 1.6% from the previous year. This is slightly less than the 2.5% increase that was recorded in 2019 in comparison with 2018 and a 3.2% increase in 2018 compared to 2017. EU movers represented 3.8% of the population at the beginning of 2020. Germany hosts 3.3 million movers, around one-third of their total number, while Spain, Italy and France host approximately 1 million each, so they host another one-third together. The composition of EU movers by citizenship has not changed significantly since 2015, with the most prominent part (around 20%) of emigrants from Romanian, followed by emigrants from Italy and Poland (11% each), Portugal (7%), Croatia and Bulgaria (5% each).

On the EU level, in 2020, the number of Croatian working-age movers grew by 9% and mainly occurred in Germany and Austria, which hosted the most extensive parts of emigrants from Croatia. In Germany, their number in recent years has stagnated. At the same time, there was a pronounced increase between 2019 and 2020 in Austria because Croatians gained full access to the Austrian labour market in July 2020. Austria was the last EU MS to end the transitional period for Croatian citizens following Croatia's entry into the EU. Therefore, while Germany is still the primary destination of migration trends from Croatia with around 204,000 Croatian citizens, more and more Croatians live now in Austria, so their number is above 83,000. The development pattern of emigration from Croatia is very similar to the population from Romania, Italy and Poland, net outflows of nationals increased until 2016 and then decreased. Thus, net outflows from Croatia decreased by almost 50% between 2017 and 2019.

However, there is also a pronounced trend of return mobility, particularly from Ireland, which was previously very popular for Croats. Based on the data by the Irish Central Statistics Office obtained on demands, it can be assessed that, before the COVID-19 pandemic, 22,000 Croats lived on the territory of the Republic of Ireland. The exact number is difficult to determine due to the dynamic migration process in both directions. According to Patković (2023), currently, in Ireland, there are between 17,000 and 19,000 Croats, which is significantly less than the number who left in the last 20 years. The number of arrivals is decreasing, and the return to Croatia is continuously present, hardly talked about or written about. People are reluctant to talk about it because the community sees them as failures, although that is not the case. A smaller number of them go to third countries. Currently, the main problem in Ireland is accommodation, because there are not enough apartments and houses. Because of this, the price of accommodation has significantly increased, so in Dublin, a bed in a room with more people costs from EUR 700 to 800. In Germany, Croats and the population from Bulgaria, Italy, Poland and Romania recorded negative net mobility in 2018 and 2019 (European Commission, Directorate-General for Employment, Social Affairs and Inclusion, 2022).

The mentioned trend of return mobility can be at least partially related to the economic improvement in Croatia. Between 2012 and 2019, GDP in Croatia grew by 20.9%, above the EU average of 11.5% for the same period. The global financial crisis that engulfed Europe had the most profound and most protracted lasting consequences in Croatia. After a significant drop after the end of the crisis, a recovery followed, which was slowed down again by the COVID-19 pandemic. The total unemployment rate in Croatia between 2012 and 2019 decreased significantly and, at 6.6% in 2019, remains slightly lower than the EU average of 6.7% for that year. Youth unemployment decreased by 25.5 percentage points in the seven observed years, and employment figures for this category increased by 3.1 percentage points. Women's employment rates also improved and reached 61.6% in 2019. In 2020, due to the COVID-19 pandemic, unemployment rates increased, most significantly for youth – by 4.5 percentage points, reaching 21.1% (Eurostat, 2023). However, the situation improved in 2021 and 2022, so at the end of January 2023, the Croatian Employment Service (CES) registered 122,369 unemployed persons, which decreased by 6.6% compared to the same month of 2022. If compared to the same month in 2022, there was a negligible increase in unemployment in the age group from 15 to 19 (by 0.1%) and a decrease in all other age groups. In January 2023, the employers reported 27,792 job vacancies with the CES, which is 5.3% more than in January 2022 (Croatian Employment Service, 2023).

Furthermore, in all sectors, nominal wages in Croatia increased between 2013 and 2021. The average monthly paid-off net earnings per person in paid employment in legal entities for 2021 amounted to €946, which is €226 or 30.9% higher than the net wage in 2013, which was €735 (Croatian Bureau of Statistics, 2013–2022). The difference in educational attainment is a critical determinant of the differences in average wages per sector, so the return on higher education attainment is somewhat higher in the private sector.

Skills are the passport to employment; the better skilled an individual, the more employable they are. Good skills also tend to secure better-quality jobs and better earnings. On 1 April 2022, the measure *Adult educational vouchers* were launched, and both employed and unemployed persons can apply for vouchers. Up to €1333, the voucher can be used for adult education and lifelong learning in private and public education institutions exclusively for obtaining digital and green skills (Eurydice – European Commission, 2023). A total of 30,000 vouchers will be offered over the next four years. To qualify for a voucher, a person must be at least 15 years old and have a primary school education. The same conditions apply regardless of whether applicants are employed in the private, public or state sector. Education programmes last up to six or ten months, depending on whether the applicant is unemployed or employed. This measure is not intended to motivate people to stay or return to Croatia. However, in any case, the measure shows the importance that the government is giving to education and, therefore, could motivate some citizens to return to Croatia or stay in its labour market. The problems of labour force shortages are more and more noticeable in almost all economic sectors in Croatia, and they can be only partially lessened by increased international immigration into Croatia.

9.5 Reasons, Scope and Consequences of International Immigration into Croatia

Croatia joined the EU in 2013 and opened the labour market to the foreign labour force. However, even before 2013, there were workers, mainly from Bosnia and Herzegovina, Romania and Bulgaria, searching for jobs in shipyards, the construction industry, the tourist sector and/or as providers of personal services. Their number was not significant, around a few thousand per year.

In 2018, there was a significant increase in shortage vacancies compared to 2012 and 2016 (Croatian Employment Service, 2013, 2017, 2019). However, almost the same occupations suffered from shortages of vacancies in 2012, 2016 and 2019, although the total number has increased over the last ten years. For construction, particular shortages are masons, bricklayers, roof-makers and carpenters. Accommodation and food service activities are experiencing growing recruitment problems for waiters, chefs, cleaners and helpers in hotels and camps. In the healthcare sector, it relates mainly to the shortages of medical doctors and nurses, and such vacancies affect both urban and rural areas. However, there are more significant problems with filling vacancies in rural and mountain areas and on islands. The shortage problems in the healthcare sector are additionally caused by inadequate regional adjustment and concentration of health capacities in the big cities. Wholesale and retail trade faces problems with shortages in the whole country, particularly on the Adriatic coast (especially during summer) and in the Cities of Zagreb and Split.

The most critical driver of labour shortages is the following: (a) low job attractiveness (for the health sector, particularly for medical doctors and nurses, work is strenuous, in shifts and during the night, very often during the weekends and holidays, with many overtime hours; furthermore, there is the considerable number of overtime worked by all medical staff); (b) unfavourable working conditions (for occupations in construction there are health and safety concerns, work related to the noise, dust, work on altitude and/or on open space, heat during the summer, cold during the early spring and late fall); (c) a lack of qualified workforce within high-skilled occupations (Like specialist doctors, nurses, and graduated civil engineers, , education lasts for an extended period; possibilities for professional promotion are relatively limited; and young people are not willing to enrol in educational programmes for these occupations.); (d) low wages and salaries (offered remuneration is mainly below the industry standard and/or is considered too low; moreover, there are many possibilities for work abroad, mainly in other EU MSs, with better conditions and significantly higher wages and salaries); (e) type of labour (for many workers in tourism and catering – chefs, waiters, maids and the like – it is a seasonal and very intensive work during the tourist season, whereas the prospects for professional promotion are limited, while there are limited employment possibilities out of season); (f) adverse public image of a particular occupation (occupations in various sectors like construction – bricklayers, carpenters and others – and tourism – waiters, cooks, cleaners and helpers in hotels and restaurants – generally have a poor social image, relatively low salaries, and limited possibilities for professional promotion).

Unfortunately, no easy remedies can significantly improve the working conditions and salaries in construction, but even small steps in improving security and health could be praiseworthy. The tourist sector is experiencing growing recruitment problems. Waiters, chefs, cleaners and helpers in hotels, restaurants, camps and other establishments are needed. However, due to the work's seasonal nature and limited employment possibilities out of season, young people are not willing to enrol in educational programmes for these occupations. The same explanation can be used for a widespread lack of bakers, pastry cooks and confectionery makers. Non-high-skilled jobs are also classified as bottlenecks, notably within the metal processing industry (such as blacksmiths, hammersmiths, and metal working machine tool setters and operators), primarily due to relatively unfavourable working conditions, low salaries and limited possibilities for professional promotion.

The Croatian Employers' Association has been the main initiator of discussions on labour shortages, demanding for a more extended period the increase in the number of quotas for foreign workers. Therefore, it should not be surprising that the number of immigrants in Croatia has constantly increased since 2012 (except in 2020, as presented in Table 9.2). While before such bottleneck jobs in construction and tourism, as well as in other sectors in Croatia, had been chiefly fulfilled from the states of the former Yugoslavia, primarily Bosnia and Herzegovina, Serbia and North Macedonia, these reservoirs of the labour force are very often empty or are rapidly discharging, because local population left for the jobs in West

Europe. Therefore, more and more immigrants into Croatia in various sectors of the economy are from faraway countries, like India, Bangladesh, Nepal and similar. Therefore, there are a lot more workers from Asia and Africa doing the jobs that Croats no longer want to do, but often Croatia, for them, is a springboard for the work and the higher salaries in other parts of the EU. Therefore, Paul Bradbury (2023), an Irishman naturalised in Croatia, asks, in conditions of many Croats leaving while foreigners arriving in increasing numbers, how to preserve Croatia?

Considering that Croatia still does not have an immigration policy that could, based on the demographic and social conditions, the new Aliens Act[3] (*Zakon o strancima*, OG 133/20, on force from the beginning of 2021), create normative preconditions to establish the principles for implementing a comprehensive immigration policy for at least five years. The government can decide on the number, criteria and conditions for the immigration of third-country nationals for each calendar year. According to the mentioned Act, the CES, since the beginning of 2021, has been responsible for implementing two new business processes: *The labour market test* and *issuing the opinion on the request for residence and work of foreign workers*. Article 98 stipulates that prior to applying for the issuance of a stay and work permit, the employer is obliged to require a labour market test from the CES, except when the stay and work permit is extended for the same employer and the exact third-country national. The labour market test consists of checking the unemployment records and the job placement services for recruiting workers from the national labour market. The CES carries out job placement services if the unemployment records show that there are persons who meet the employer's recruitment requirements and inform the employer about the labour market test results. If the labour market test shows that there are no available persons in the unemployment records who meet the employer's recruitment requirements or if the requirements cannot be met by the unemployed persons migrating within the country, the employer may apply for a stay and work permit within 90 days from the day of receipt of a notification on the labour market test results. Article 101 of the Act specifies when the Management Board of the CES can issue a decision on professions for which the employer is not required to request the labour market test. The word is primarily for the professions with shortages in the national, regional and local labour market, which cannot be solved by domestic migration, but also for implementation of strategic and investment projects and other circumstances relevant to economic growth and sustainable development.

Article 99 of the Act explains that a favourable opinion of the CES can be obtained if the employer: (a) performs economic activities in a sector registered in Croatia; (b) has paid all due public contributions (income tax payments and mandatory insurance contributions); (c) has employed at least one citizen of the Republic of Croatia, or EEA national, or citizen of the Swiss Confederation to a permanent and full-time position in the Croatian territory in the last six months; and (d) has not been convicted of criminal offences by a final ruling in the area of labour relations and social insurance. The CES will not issue a favourable opinion if the number of citizens of Croatia, EEA nationals or citizens of the Swiss Confederation employed by the employer is less than 1/4 of the total number of employed workers.

Thus, in 2021, 2518 employers requested implementing a labour market test for 28,838 workers for 488 different occupations. After the test, employers received a positive notification for the possibility of employing 22,872 foreign workers, but employers submitted a request for a residence and work permit for only 8754 workers. In 2021, 66,917 requests for opinions on the request for residence and work of foreign workers were received and processed, of which 8754 were workers based on a previously conducted labour market test, and the rest of the requests referred to occupations for which the Administrative Council of the Institute decided that it is not necessary to carry out labour market test, as these are occupations that are permanently lacking in the Croatian labour market. As mentioned earlier, the requests were submitted by 9055 employers for 408 different occupations.

According to Butković, Samardžija and Rukavina (2020), the number of foreign workers, particularly immigrants from third countries, has constantly increased. While number of persons included in new employee quotas in 2016 was almost negligible (2300), it grew up to 2020 to significantly 64,604. A majority of these workers began to work in the construction sector. There is no publicly available comprehensive data on the educational attainment of foreign workers in Croatia. However, it can be supposed that most are low to low-skilled workers (except for the healthcare sector). However, it is pretty apparent that foreign workers are not taking employment possibilities from the Croatian population but are working on jobs or in places which are not attractive to the domestic population. Therefore, they have an essential role in preserving Croatia's economy, which will be otherwise in an impasse, with grave consequences for the whole economy and the society.

According to the official data by the Ministry of Interior, there are about 22,400 registered Ukrainian refugees in Croatia. More than 95% of them are women and children. According to the information, only 968 persons have been employed through the mediation of the CES (Hrvatska za Ukrajinu, 2023).

9.6 Discussion and Conclusion

The examples of several countries (especially Ireland and Portugal in the past and new EU MSs today) show that integration into the EU, due to the achievement of faster economic growth and development and a more significant inflow of foreign direct investments, can be a significant stimulus in reducing unemployment. Accelerated economic development is decisive in alleviating poverty and limiting the desire to migrate. This is still not a *sufficient* prerequisite for success. However, without a doubt, it is of central importance to increase employment opportunities because work is the most crucial capital of Croatia's inhabitants. At the same time, while Poles and Romanians only got a real opportunity to go to work in the West in more significant numbers after joining the EU, Croatian temporary workers have been an integral part of the workforce there for decades. At the same time, the importance of foreign currency remittances that they sent home to Croatia should not be ignored, while this was not the case with Poland, Romania and other countries that experienced hard communism. On the other hand, due to the significant differences in the income level between EU members and Croatia, one cannot expect a more significant influx of foreign workers to Croatia from the EU, except perhaps a slightly larger number from Romania and Bulgaria. However, even that number has been relatively limited due to their possibilities to search for jobs in the old MSs with significantly higher wages and better working conditions.

While in previous generations, emigration to some other European country, mainly leaving for North or South America, was a lifetime decision, the European Commission, Directorate-General for Employment, Social Affairs & Inclusion (2022) states that this is not the case anymore with current emigrations. Thus, more than half of the movers in the EU are 20–49 years old and many of them return after having gained some years of professional experience abroad. Therefore, one should not be too afraid of brain drain because, due to modern technology and appropriate, efficient policy, Croatian experts in the world can be almost in daily contact with domestic scientific, educational and innovative institutions and represent a bridge that connects Croatian economy and society with the most developed in the world.

Finally, it can be assessed that young persons in Croatia are fully aware of the importance of the rule of law, full active citizenship and the need to be self-reliant. Furthermore, they are probably not well educated and skilled in entrepreneurship attitudes and behaviour as well as risk-taking, which hinder their willingness and decisions for business activities in the private sector. If they can, through emigration to foreign countries, gain and/or improve these skills (including digital literacy), enhance their knowledge and practice of foreign language and return in a relatively short period to Croatia, this could be a win–win situation for former migrants as well as for the Croatian society as a whole. It should be noted that the characteristics of migration from Croatia since joining the EU are different from the large labour migrations in which primarily male industrial and construction workers migrated, a large part of whom left their children in their homeland and only a part of them stayed permanently and subsequently moved their families abroad (Čapo, 2019). Now, more and more young and educated people of both sexes and entire families are migrating, increasing the danger that the departure is permanent (Balija, 2020).

Bearing in mind the significant increase of residence and work permits for citizens of third countries in Croatia in recent years, it is crucial to harmonise the Croatian labour market with immigration policy in order to ensure the immigration of foreign labour force for deficient occupations, but also to a certain extent to protect the Croatian labour market. Until now, there have been no severe cases of tensions, stigmatisation and fake news, mainly related to the refugees from Ukraine. However, bearing in mind that the so-called waves of solidarity, as well as the interest of the general public and the media in a particular topic, do have a lifespan that is not endless. For example, there are increasingly loud comments on social networks from individuals who believe that because of the support given to immigrants in general, and particularly to Ukrainian refugees, the local population in need is suffering. Although there is a long tradition of labour immigration to Croatia, it came from neighbouring countries. Croatians are now unprepared and unaccustomed to meeting migrants of other races and cultures for the first time.

This is a complex and sensitive process that Western countries went through several decades ago.

When thinking about sustainable strategies, it would be highly desirable and necessary for them to extend solidarity and inclusive and supportive public policies and local practices to foreign workers who are already here and will most certainly continue to come from other regions. Croatia is a small country, which is not the most desired destination for migrants. Nevertheless, some people will stay in Croatia, as they have stayed until now. If the domicile population and its government welcome people with long-term and well-thought-out plans, which will also include part of the solution for demographic, economic and even infrastructural renewal, then the current fear and discomfort in front of others will be reduced. If Croatia will be successful in achieving long-term sustainable economic development and growth, it can become an attractive future destination for foreign workers but also for its population that left Croatia in the previous migration waves.

Notes

1 This is mainly due to the costly dwellings in the City of Split, where there is a strong trend towards letting tourists instead of using apartments for permanent living. Therefore, young persons are almost forced to move to a narrow regional ring with significantly lower dwelling prices. For example, between 2001 and 2021, the number of inhabitants in Split decreased by 28,117 persons (14.9%). During these years, the number of inhabitants of two of many other neighbouring suburbs, Solin and Podstrana, increased by 8913 persons (5851 and 3062, respectively).

2 Expenditures above and beyond payment for the apartment or house, including time and money for identifying potential sellers, negotiating contracts, monitoring compliance, controlling documentation. The main problem with the housing market lies in the administrative procedure of obtaining the ownership certificate at land registries and cadastres. It is estimated that almost 50% of all real estate in Zagreb needs to be correctly registered in official registries, which prevents the development of the mortgage market and induces uncertainties for potential buyers. Thus, the potential buyers face severe problems because of unclear legal property relations or disordered property records.

3 English version of the Act is available at https://mup.gov.hr/UserDocsImages/zakoni/ALIENS%20ACT%20(Official%20Gazette%20No%20133_2020).pdf

References

Adamović, M., and Mežnarić, S. (2006) 'Migration of Croatian scientists', *AEMI Journal*, 4–5(1), pp. 81–92.

Akrap, A. (2014) 'Promjene broja i prostornog razmještaja stanovništva Hrvatske i županija 1961-2011', (Changes in the number and spatial distribution of the population of Croatia and counties 1961-2011) in V. Puljiz, J. Tica, D. Vidović (eds.) *Migracije i razvoj Hrvatske* (Migration and Development of Croatia). Zagreb: Hrvatska gospodarska komora, pp. 25–69.

Andor, L. (2014) *Labour mobility in the EU*. Brussels: European Commission.

Bahar, D., and Rapoport, H. (2018) 'Migration, knowledge diffusion and the comparative advantage of nations', *The Economic Journal,* 128(612), pp. F273–F305. Available at: https://onlinelibrary.wiley.com/doi/full/10.1111/ecoj.12450 (21.3.2024).

Bajzíková, Ľ., and Bajzik, P. (2020) 'Mobility and working opportunities in the EU and Slovakia', *Management*, 25(1), pp. 103–115. Available at: https://hrcak.srce.hr/file/347 143 (10.03.2023).

Balija, M. (2020) 'Razmjeri recentnog egzodusa iz Hrvatske – analiza podataka službenih statistika RH i zemalja useljavanja hrvatskog stanovništva' (Scales of the recent exodus from Croatia - analysis of data from the official statistics of the Republic of Croatia and the countries of immigration of the Croatian population), *Podravina: časopis za geografska i povijesna multidisciplinarna istraživanja*, 19(37), pp. 5–25.

Blanchard, O.J., and Katz, L.F. (1992) 'Regional evolutions', *Brookings Papers on Economic Activity*, 1(1), pp. 1–75. Available at: www.jstor.org/stable/2534556?origin=crossref&seq=1 (10.03.2023).

Borjas, G.J. (1987) 'Self-selection and the earnings of immigrants', *American Economic Review*, 77(4), pp. 531–553.

Bradbury, P. (2023) 'Croats leaving, foreigners arriving, how to preserve Hrvatska', *Total Croatian News*, 6 February 2023. Available at: www.total-croatia-news.com/editorial/66472-croats-leaving (15.03.2023).

Butković, H., Samardžija, V., and Rukavina, R. (2020) *National Report Croatia Foreign Workers in Croatia: Challenges and Opportunities for Economic and Social Development.* Zagreb: Institute for Development and International Relations.

Caldera Sanchez, A., and Andrews, D. (2011) 'To move or not to move: What drives residential mobility rates in the OECD?', OECD Economics Department Working Papers No. 846, Paris: OECD. Available at: www.oecd-ilibrary.org/docserver/5kghtc7kzx21-en.pdf?expires=1711657275&id=id&accname=guest&checksum=696426CF3644F225EAB5F62B0DA39AB1 (10.03.2023).

Čapo, J. (2019) *Dva doma: hrvatska radna migracija u Njemačku kao transnacionalni fenomen* (*Two homes_ Croatian labor migration to Germany as a transnational phenomenon*). Zagreb: Durieux

Chami, R., Ernst, E., Fullenkamp, C., and Oeking, A. (2018) 'Is there a remittance trap?'. Washington: The International Monetary Fund. Available at: www.imf.org/en/Publications/fandd/issues/2018/09/is-there-a-remittance-trap-chami (10.03.2023).

Croatian Bureau of Statistics (2013–2022) *Statistics in Line*. Available at: https://podaci.dzs.hr/hr/statistika-u-nizu/ (10.03.2023).

Croatian Bureau of Statistics (2022) *Migration of population of the Republic of Croatia, 2021*. Available at: https://podaci.dzs.hr/2022/en/29029 (10.03.2023).

Croatian Employment Service (2013, 2017, 2019) *Yearly report*. Zagreb: Croatian Employment Service.

Croatian Employment Service (2023) 'Monthly statistics bulletin', *Croatian Employment Service*, 36(1). Available at: www.hzz.hr/app/uploads/2022/09/HZZ-bilten-01_2023-2.pdf (10.03.2023).

Decressin, J., and Fatás, A. (1995) 'Regional labor market dynamics in Europe', *European Economic Review*, 39(9), pp. 1627–1655.

Dobrotić, I., and Matković, T. (2023) 'Understanding territorial inequalities in decentralised welfare systems: early childhood education and care system expansion in Croatia', *Public Sector Economics*, 47(1), pp. 89–110.

Draženović, I., Kunovac, M., and Pripužić, D. (2018) 'Dynamics and determinants of emigration: the case of Croatia and the experience of new EU member states', *Public Sector Economics*, 42(4), pp. 415–447.

European Commission, Directorate-General for Employment, Social Affairs & Inclusion (2022) *Annual Report on Intra-EU Labour Mobility 2021*. Brussels: European Commission.

Eurostat (2023) 'September 2023 Euro area unemployment at 6.5%'. *Euroindicators*. Available at: ec.europa.eu/eurostat/documents/2995521/17791746/3-03112023-AP-EN.pdf/7de0add9-2fd1-b656-b90d-63aaa97f72ff (21.03. 2024).

Eurydice – European Commission (2023) 'Croatia –Funding in Education'. Brussels: Eurydice – European Commission. Available at eurydice.eacea.ec.europa.eu/national-education-systems/croatia/funding-education

Fengler, S., Lengauer, M., and Zappe, A.-C. (eds.). (2021) *Reporting on Migrants and Refugees. Handbook for Journalism Educators*. Paris: UNESCO.

Fidrmuc, J. (2001) 'Migration and Adjustment to Shocks in Transition Economies, Working Paper Department of Economics', *ZEI Working Paper, No. B 23-2001*. Available at: www.econstor.eu/bitstream/10419/39504/1/338027955.pdf (10.03.2023).

Hakansson, P.G., and Bejakovic, P. (2020) 'Labour market resilience, bottlenecks and spatial mobility in Croatia', *Eastern Journal of European Studies*, 11(2), pp. 5–25.

Harris, J. R., and Todaro, M. (1970) 'Migration, unemployment and development: A two-sector analysis', *The American Economic Review*, 60(1), pp. 126–142.

Hazans, M. (2003) 'Potential emigration of Latvian labour force after joining the EU and its impact on Latvian labour market', *SSRN Electronic Journal*. Available at: https://papers.ssrn.com/sol3/papers.cfm?abstract_id=73930 (10.03.2023).

Hrvatska za Ukrajinu (2023) *Aktualne informacije*. Available at https://hrvatskazaukrajinu.gov.hr/

Hrvatski zavod za zapošljavanje (various years) *Godišnje izvješće (Yearly Report)*. Zagreb: *Hrvatski zavod za zapošljavanje (various years)*.

Jurun, E., Curic, M., and Bekavac, L. (2021) 'A Research on Emigration as the Fundamental Obstacle to Croatian Economic and Social Development', in P. Misevic, Lj. Kontic, T. Galovic (eds.) *Economic and Social Development: Book of Proceedings*. Zagreb: Varazdin Development and Entrepreneurship Agency and University North, pp. 37–46.

Kugler, M., and Rapoport, H. (2005) 'Skilled Emigration, Business Networks and Foreign Direct Investment', *Discussion Papers in Economics and Econometrics*, No. 0503, Available at: www.researchgate.net/publication/5001950_Skilled_Emigration_Business_Networks_and_Foreign_Direct_Investment (24.10.2023).

Le Bras, H. (2003) *L'adieu aux masses. Démographie et politique*. La Tour-d'Aigues: Editions de l'Aube.

Mansoor, A., and Quillin, B. (2006) *Migration and Remittances: Eastern Europe and the Former Soviet Union*. Washington: The World Bank. Available at: https://documents1.worldbank.org/curated/en/183131468024337798/pdf/384260Migratio101OFFICIAL0USE0ONLY1.pdf (24.10.2023).

Orefice, G., Rapoport, H. and Santoni, G. (2022) 'How Do Immigrants Promote Exports? Networks, Knowledge, Diversity.' *IZA Discussion Paper No. 15722*. Available at: http://dx.doi.org/10.2139/ssrn.4281277 (24.10.2023).

Palm, P., Jingryd, O., and Kordic, L. (2019) 'Housing and Transaction Costs', in P. Håkansson and H. Bohman (eds.) *Investigating Spatial Inequalities: Mobility, Housing and Employment in Scandinavia and South East Europe (SEE)*. Bingley: Emerald, pp. 123–138.

Patković, N. (2023) 'Jasno je zašto sve više Hrvata odlazi iz ove zemlje. A znam i zašto se o tome baš i ne priča...' (It is clear why more and more Croats are leaving this country. And I also know why it's not really talked about...'), *Jutarnji list*, 12 March. Available at: www.jutarnji.hr/vijesti/svijet/jasno-je-zasto-sve-vise-hrvata-odlazi-iz-ove-zemlje-a-znam-i-zasto-se-o-tome-bas-i-ne-prica-15314825 (13.03.2023).

Regional Cooperation Council and International Organization for Migration (2015) *Labour Mobility as a Factor of Development in Southeast Europe Regional Overview*. Vienna and Sarajevo: Regional Cooperation Council and International Organization for Migration. Available at: https://publications.iom.int/books/labour-mobility-factor-development-south-east-europe (10.03.2023).

World Bank (2005) *World Development Report: Equity and Development*. Washington: The International Bank for Reconstruction and Development and World Bank.

World Bank (2006) *Global Economic Prospects Economic Implications of Remittances and Migration*. Washington: The International Bank for Reconstruction and Development and World Bank.

Zimmermann, K.F. (2004) 'European Labour Mobility: Challenges and Potentials', Discussion Paper No. 1410. Available at: https://docs.iza.org/dp1410.pdf (10.03.2023).

10 From "Troubled" Newcomer to Euro Area Member

Croatian Integration Success under Brussels Surveillance

Maroje Lang[1]

10.1 Introduction

The coordination of economic policies is a cornerstone of the single currency, as emphasised in its name – the Economic and Monetary Union (EMU). The Treaty of Maastricht, which instituted the euro as a shared currency, implemented a mechanism to limit government deficits and public debt as protective measures against possible monetary financing of individual Member States (MSs) (Eichengreen, 2008). This notion was further enhanced in 1997 via the Stability and Growth Pact (SGP), assigning the European Commission a distinctive role in overseeing the fiscal and economic policies of MSs (Heipertz and Verdun, 2010). However, the framework in place at that time was not designed to prevent the accumulation of macroeconomic imbalances in the period prior to the Global Financial Crisis (GFC). This financial turmoil triggered economic governance reform that introduced the European Semester, a more encompassing surveillance and policy coordination system.[2]

This chapter investigates the impact of EU economic governance procedures and Brussels surveillance on Croatia's macroeconomic policies and structural reforms. Spanning over the last three decades, it offers a new perspective on how the EU has influenced economic policies in Croatia. It complements the existing literature, such as Samardžija et al. (2018), Maletić et al. (2019) and Munta (2021), that has investigated certain aspects of this process, mainly focusing on the impact of the recent European Semester on Croatia. Also, recent research, such as Šimović and Deskar-Škrbić (2019) and Rebić and Arčabić (2023), primarily inspired by experience since the entry into the EU and launch of corrective procedures, has provided new insights about the impact of the EU on the cyclicality and nature of fiscal policy in Croatia.

This chapter argues that as a small country with strong public support for EU integration, Croatia was eager to conduct the necessary reforms and measures as an applicant, a candidate and a new MS. It transposed EU rules, established the required institutions before the accession and managed fiscal consolidation and structural reforms as a new MS. The reputation gained in this process was essential in finalising the EU integration and entry into the Euro Area (EA).[3] Similarly,

DOI: 10.4324/9781003394013-10

the effort to create a framework for the European Structural and Investment Funds (ESIF) resulted in large transfers from the EU that supported growth and convergence.

However, this process was not without a cost, as embracing EU objectives could not replace the national development agenda. Prolonged recession and high unemployment fuelled emigration to richer MSs. Demographic problems require reforms that would encourage the return of its population and the immigration of educated workers. Whereas Croatia successfully consolidated its public finances, implementing structural reforms has been more difficult.

The chapter is organised into five sections. After the introduction, Section 10.2 examines the period before Croatia acceded to the EU, focusing on candidacy years and the accession period preceding the entry into the EU. Section 10.3 discusses the challenging early years of EU membership when Croatia entered corrective procedures. Section 10.4 analyses the road to euro adoption that coincided with the COVID-19 crisis. Sections 10.5 and 10.6 concludes.

10.2 Seeking an Anchor – Economic Policies before EU Membership

10.2.1 Precandidate Years

The first decade of Croatia's independence was marked by political and economic instability. It was also a period of significant change as Croatia transitioned from a sub-sovereign socialist economy to a fully independent, market-based country. The delay in Western integration strengthened Croatia's aspiration for EU membership and commitment to common rules. Croatia reformed its legal and institutional structures and economic policies as a candidate country. However, the pre-accession economic dialogue could not prevent the emergence of macroeconomic imbalances in the mid-2000s, leading to a prolonged recession that lasted almost a decade. As a result, further preparations for coordinating economic policies were needed before accession.

The dissolution of the former Yugoslav Federation was preceded by a decade-long recession and economic instability, which spiralled into hyperinflation in the early 1990s. The Homeland War of 1991, coupled with the loss of traditional markets, further weakened the economy. Under those circumstances, Croatia had to stabilise its economy and set it on a new market-based path.[4] The 1990s were a period of significant change, as Croatia transitioned from a sub-sovereign socialist economy to a fully independent market-based country. The former planning institutions were dissolved, but a new and effective system was not established.

In 1993, Croatia successfully implemented the Stabilisation Economic Programme, which ended the hyperinflation and marked the beginning of exchange rate-based economic stability for the next 30 years. A group of Croatian economists designed it based on similar programmes (including the 1987 IMF programme for former Yugoslavia).[5] However, as a small and increasingly open economy, Croatia was continuously exposed to capital flows, and safeguarding against them required external support.

During this period, Croatia established strong relations with international financial institutions and received help in designing economic policies and structural reforms related to the transition to a market economy. Between 1994 and 2006, Croatia signed five IMF Stand-by programmes to preserve macroeconomic stability.[6] These precautionary programmes included policy guidance, helping to maintain fiscal discipline, restructuring public enterprises and reforming the financial sector. Croatia also cooperated closely with the World Bank (WB) and European Bank for Reconstruction and Development in various investments and reforms, including business environment, financial sector and public sector.

Engaging with external expertise was beneficial in safeguarding macroeconomic stabilisation and implementing reforms. Nevertheless, Croatia's internal efforts, complemented by support from international financial institutions, enabled the country to overcome the challenges of war and economic turmoil and progress towards EU candidacy (Figure 10.1).

Fiscal policy in the 1990s, however, contributed to the problems that Croatia is still facing. After a tumultuous period in the early 1990s, temporary fiscal consolidation was achieved as a precursor to the 1993 Stabilisation Programme. However, current expenditures and transfers grew rapidly due to expanding the public sector and providing benefits (early retirement and benefits to war veterans). The Ministry of Finance also did not effectively control defence and reconstruction expenditures. Fiscal statistics were calculated on a cash basis, with privatisation receipts considered as revenue, thus reducing the cash deficits. Despite limited access to markets and financing primarily conducted through accruing arrears, public spending growth had no practical constraints. In 1998, the introduction of the value-added tax (VAT) generated strong but temporary revenue growth, which was used to increase spending further. However, as the economy weakened

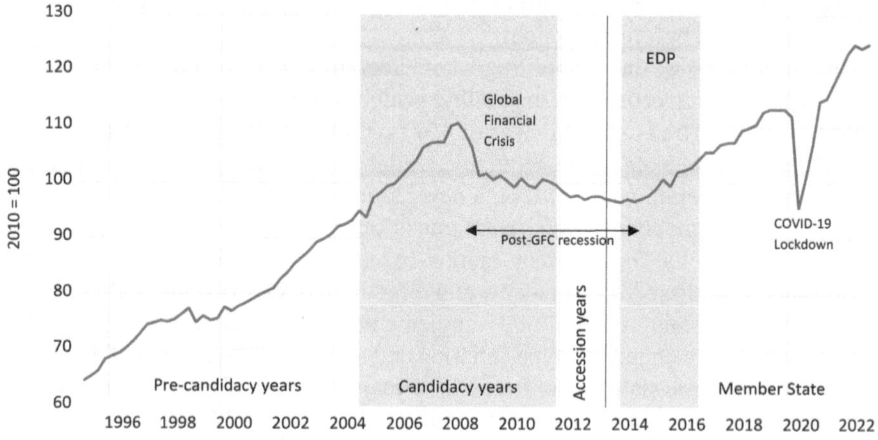

Figure 10.1 GDP and EU integration process.

Source: Eurostat.

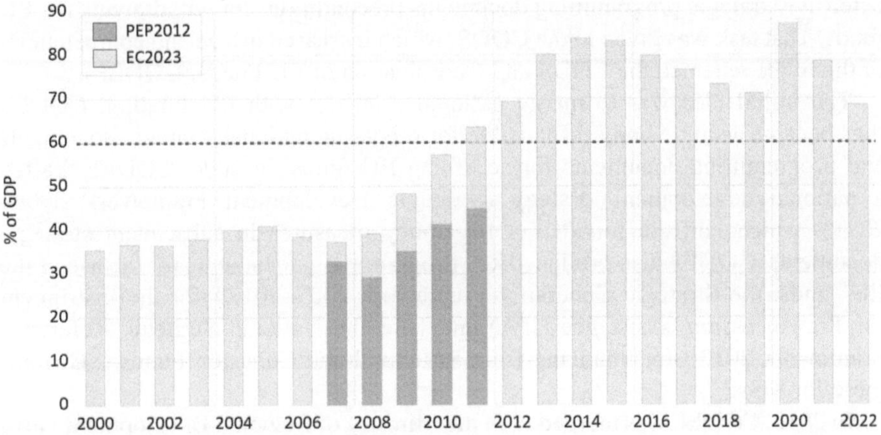

Figure 10.2 Net lending and structural deficit.

Notes: Lines represent EDP deficit criterion = −3% and MTO = −1%; shipyard guarantees were included as expenditures of 0.9% of GDP in 2009, 0.8% in 2010 and 2.7% in 2011.

Source: Ameco May 2023.

and faced adverse external shocks, public finances soon turned into deficits (see Jurković, 2002 and Figure 10.2).

10.2.2 Candidacy Years and Pre-accession Economic Programmes

The EU-required reforms and policy dialogue influenced the effort to recreate a strategic and policy planning system during the candidacy years from 2004 to 2011. However, this surveillance did not prevent the build-up of macroeconomic imbalances that led to a prolonged recession after the GFC. Moreover, the attempts to increase the use and access to EU pre-accession assistance (and later ESIF directed resources and focus towards the EU objectives.

The Stabilization and Association Agreement (SAA), signed in 2001 and entering into force in 2005, marked the beginning of Croatia's journey towards EU membership. In order to meet the accession criteria, Croatia had to transpose the *acquis communautaire*, implement market reforms and develop the institutions necessary for the EU membership. Policy dialogue with the EU began through Pre-Accession Economic Programmes (PEP).

PEPs were incorporated into the emerging framework for strategic planning that Croatia was trying to establish after former planning institutions were dissolved in the early 1990s.[7] In 2000, a newly elected government established the Central Office for Development Strategy (CODS) to create a national development strategy and streamline reforms.

The EU accession path made Croatia eligible for financial assistance through EU funds, creating a unique opportunity to accelerate socioeconomic development.[8]

However, this also required a significant strengthening of capacities to prepare extensive strategic programming documents preconditions for withdrawing the EU funds. That task was given to the CODS, which increased in size and competencies of the office renamed the CODS and Coordination of EU Funds (CODEF).

The initial idea was to merge national priorities with EU funding. CODEF thus became a single body responsible for preparing national strategic documents and programming documents for accessing EU funds. In 2006, CODEF drafted a national development strategy (Strategic Development Framework 2006–2013)[9] which laid the foundation for policy measures in subsequent strategic documents. CODEF also produced key programming documents for the use of the EU funds: the Strategic Coherence Framework 2007–2013[10] for the Instrument for Pre-Accession Assistance (IPA) and later the National Strategic Reference Framework 2013[11] for financing from Structural and Cohesion Funds (SCF) eligible for MSs.[12]

In 2012, CODEF was merged with the Ministry of Regional Development into a new Ministry of Regional Development and EU Funds (MRDFEU) to increase further the resources necessary for more substantial utilisation of EU funds. CODEF (and later MRDFEU) thus became the main counterpart on the national level in policy dialogue with the EU regarding structural reforms. At the same time, the Ministry of Finance continued to be responsible for fiscal policy.

However, despite numerous strategic documents, implementing the development strategy was challenging, and government priorities were only gradually incorporated into the budgetary process. In 2005, the Standard Methodology for the Assessment of Financial Impact[13] was introduced, which required all programmes issued at the national level to include their financial assessment. Additionally, the 2008 Budget Act[14] introduced three-year strategic planning into the budget (Mirošević, 2012). However, it was only with the adoption of the Law on Systems of Strategic Planning and Development Management of the Republic of Croatia[15] in 2017, that fully connected budget and strategic planning and introduced monitoring of the implementation of strategic documents based on indicators.

Croatia submitted its first Pre-PEP in October 2004 and continued to submit them annually until it acceded to the EU.[16] The PEPs outlined medium-term macroeconomic, fiscal and structural reform policies to strengthen economic and institutional convergence with the EU. However, PEPs were primarily designed to foster policy dialogue on economic and structural policies and reflected policies designed within other frameworks. Despite this, the PEP's structure, which required a specific approach for assessing fiscal policies (cyclical adjustment, ageing costs, debt sustainability etc.) and the need to communicate structural reforms, helped develop strategic planning in Croatia.

While PEPs contributed to Croatia's economic policy, they did not prevent the emergence of macroeconomic imbalances in the mid-2000s, as the previous growth model relied on infrastructure and real estate investment financed by foreign borrowing. Furthermore, the procyclical expansive fiscal policies overstretched public finances, while several government entities operated outside fiscal statistics and were less financially constrained. The 2008 crisis ended such a growth model, triggering a prolonged recession until 2015 when real GDP contracted by more than 10%. Sustainability concerns arose due to large and growing foreign and public debt while increasing interest payments exerted additional pressure on public finances.

To address rising deficits, the government introduced a series of measures. In 2009, a temporary "crisis" income tax surcharge was introduced, and the general VAT rate was raised from 22% to 23%. On the expenditure side, public investments, material expenditures and subsidies experienced significant cuts, while the agreed wage increase was postponed, and new hiring was restricted. Following the 2011 election, the new government implemented a substantial fiscal consolidation package in 2012 aimed at fiscal devaluation. The general VAT rate was raised to 25%, excise taxes were also increased and contributions on wages were reduced. Reforms in collecting social contributions and VAT ("fiscalisation") in 2013 further boosted revenues. On the expenditure side, measures were implemented to control and reduce public wages through a centralised payroll system and reductions in salary supplements, along with adjustments to larger pensions, while public investment remained low. However, these measures' highly procyclical and contractionary nature adversely affected the economy.[17]

As Croatia became a candidate country and experienced economic recovery in the 2000s, the need for IMF support declined, and no new programmes were signed after the expiration of the 2004 Stand-by Arrangement in 2006. This significantly decreased the IMF's influence on economic policies, although Article IV consultations remained a vital signal to financial markets and credit agencies. In 2012, when the finance minister expressed concerns about market access and argued for possible IMF assistance, the EC emphasised that, as an acceding country, Croatia should rely primarily on EU support.

The WB has remained an essential partner for Croatia, involved in development and structural reforms while providing valuable technical expertise. With its regional office in Zagreb, the WB has maintained continuous cooperation with Croatia.[18]

10.2.3 Phasing-In: Voluntary Participation in the 2013 European Semester

After signing the Accession Treaty in December 2011, Croatia became an active observer in the European Institutions. This allowed Croatia to become familiar with the working methods of EU institutions and observe the decision-making processes. It also involved the application of a reformed EU economic governance framework.[19]

With the new status, Croatia was increasingly treated as an MS, and preparations were made to apply EU economic governance procedures. The Croatian desk within the Directorate-General for Economic and Financial Affairs (DG ECFIN) was moved from the directorate responsible for enlargement to the directorate responsible for monitoring economic policies in MS.[20] This transition shifted the EC's focus towards addressing Croatia's macroeconomic imbalances and fiscal challenges.

Before EU accession, Croatia used a less strict approach in compiling fiscal statistics based on a modified accrual basis following the IMF's GFS 1986 standards, with a narrow definition of the government sector. As a result, some government policies were carried out through state-owned enterprises (SOEs) and guarantees, which were not accounted for in fiscal statistics. With the accession, the responsibility for compiling fiscal statistics shifted from the Ministry of Finance to the Croatian Bureau of Statistics (CBS). Eurostat collaborated closely with CBS in 2012–2013 to improve data quality and align Croatia's reporting with the European System of National and Regional Accounts (ESA). Expanding the sectoral classification of the government and including SOEs and guarantees (shipyards) led to a significant upward revision of deficits and debt. The planned transition from ESA 95 to ESA 2010 raised further concerns. These concerns proved valid as the current estimate of government debt in 2010 is now nearly 20 percentage points of GDP higher than reported initially under the old methodology (Figure 10.3).[21]

Croatia's prolonged recession and escalating public debt raised concerns exacerbated by the consecutive upward revisions of the debt stock. There were fears that the worsening fiscal situation might jeopardise market access and necessitate financial assistance, similar to other heavily affected MSs. The Ministry of Finance shared those concerns, which could explain the implementation of significant consolidation measures undertaken after the GFC, particularly in 2012 and 2013.

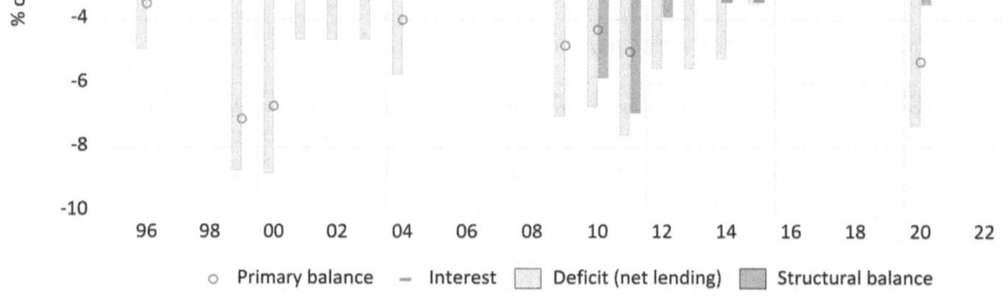

Figure 10.3 Public debt as a share of GDP.

Notes:

1. Shaded bars represent debt data as initially reported in the 2012 PEP; 2. PEP2012 corresponds with data under the old methodology reported in 2012 PEP. EC2023 corresponds to the latest Eurostat data (May 2023).

Source: Eurostat and 2012 Pre-Accession Economic Programme.

Policy dialogue intensified, and after several high-level meetings between Croatian and EC officials, Croatia was invited to participate in the 2013 European Semester voluntarily. This approach aimed to integrate Croatia into the EU economic governance cycle gradually. In April 2013, the Croatian government adopted the 2013 Economic Programme.

In May 2013, the EC published its assessment of Croatia's 2013 Economic Programme, identifying significant imbalances. Unlike MS participating in the European Semester, the EC's assessment was limited to the Services Working Document (SWD) and omitted Country-Specific Recommendations (CSRs).[22] Instead, in June 2013, the Council adopted conclusions that acknowledged Croatia's voluntary participation in the European Semester. The Council emphasised the expectation for Croatia to meet the SGP requirements while also emphasising the need for a credible consolidation path that balances growth-enhancing expenditure and allows for the co-financing of EU funds. This signalled the forthcoming implementation of corrective procedures.

Voluntary participation in the European Semester highlighted misalignments with Croatia's budgetary and strategic planning (Ott, 2013). The existing budgetary planning did not conform to the European Semester cycle, although it contained all the necessary elements. The budgetary planning commenced from a three-year Strategy of Government Programmes, serving as the foundation for budgetary allocations published in the Economic and Fiscal Policy Guidelines by the end of June. However, EU regulations mandated the simultaneous submission of the annual National Reform Programme (NRP) and Convergence Programme (CP) by the end of April. Based on this experience, the 2015 Budget Act[23] have revised the budgetary preparation process. The NRP replaced the Strategy of Government Programmes as the underlying strategic document. Furthermore, the CP, published in April 2014 along with the NRP, included macroeconomic and fiscal forecasts. These forecasts served as the basis for the Fiscal Guidelines in the summer, which remained relevant for budgetary planning at the functional and regional levels. The Guidelines also encompassed elements under national competencies not included in the NRP.

10.3 "Troubled" Newcomer

10.3.1 Excessive Deficit Procedure

Although macroeconomic and fiscal imbalances recognised in the Council Conclusion in June 2013 warranted immediate action, the EC followed the established European Semester cycle, so corrective Excessive Deficit Procedure (EDP) and close monitoring of excessive macroeconomic imbalances were launched after several months.[24] These procedures were implemented in line with the strict approach practised then. At the same time, some flexibility was applied to avoid imposing harsh sanctions on a new member and setting precedents at the EU level. Croatia successfully implemented the requested consolidation and addressed the imbalances on time, earning a reputation crucial in garnering support for its later entry into the EA.

Croatia's accession to the EU in mid-2013 occurred in the late stage of the European Sovereign Debt Crisis. This led to the creation of the European Semester and a stricter approach to addressing macroeconomic and fiscal imbalances.

Before accession, Croatia had implemented fiscal consolidation measures, but fiscal deficits remained above the 3% limit, and public debt rose rapidly. The EC advised additional savings in the 2014 Budget to avoid activating EDP. In October 2013, the Croatian government formed a Coordinating Body to monitor and implement fiscal consolidation measures, but the required adjustments to meet necessary targets were deemed unacceptable.

In October 2013, Eurostat's EDP notification[25] included Croatia for the first time, confirming a significant deficit of 5% in 2012 and quickly rising public debt (55.5% in 2012). Furthermore, estimates indicated a breach of the deficit limit in 2013. The 2013 Economic and Fiscal Policy Guidelines, published in September, projected a further increase in the planned general government deficit to 5.5% in 2014. The projected general government gross debt ratio in 2014 and 2015 exceeded the 60% limit.

In November 2013, the EC prepared a report on the breach of fiscal targets under Article 126(3) of the Treaty on the Functioning of the European Union (TFEU). The Economic and Fiscal Committee (EFC) discussed the report, directed the EC to proceed and asked Croatia to "bring its house in order". In December, the EC issued its proposals to the Council. In January 2014, the Council adopted a Decision on the Existence of an Excessive Deficit, effectively launching the corrective EDP.

In its EDP recommendations, the EC adhered to strict principles practised then. The consolidation requested was substantial, and mitigating factors proposed by Croatian authorities could not be considered.[26] The EC concluded that Croatia did not meet the criteria for both the deficit and debt.[27] The newly introduced debt reduction benchmark was applied for the first time, necessitating measures beyond the deficit adjustment alone. The strongest action was required in the first year, with consolidation measures amounting to 2.3% of GDP in 2014 and a further 1% in 2015 and 2016. Moreover, the recommended measures had to be implemented within three months.

Croatian authorities were required to act swiftly and implement additional measures to achieve the requested consolidation. Having already implemented a series of budgetary savings in previous years, the proposed consolidation included revenue and expenditure measures in similar amounts. The initial package enacted through the March Budget Amendment, however, was deemed insufficient, as some measures were considered one-offs and lacked a permanent impact. Therefore, additional measures had to be introduced through a separate government decision in April.

The EC demonstrated flexibility in encouraging Croatian authorities to take necessary measures and sought to avoid imposing financial sanctions on the country, thus potentially setting precedents at the EU level. An open and intensive dialogue between the EC and Croatian authorities played an important role. EC officials urged Croatia to implement the required measures before initiating the

Table 10.1 EDP consolidation measures (in % of GDP)

		2014	2015	2016
REVENUE MEASURES				
1	Tax on winnings from games of chance	0.03	0.05	
2	Changes in the system of contributions for pension insurance based on hazardous work	0.12	0.04	
3	Withdrawal of the SOE profits	0.02		0.17
4	Increase in health insurance contributions from 13% to 15%	0.49	0.24	
5	Reinvested earnings			0.29
6	Introduction of tax on interest on savings		0.07	
7	Fees for telecommunication services	0.05		
8	Increase in excise duties on energy products	0.11	0.13	0.04
9	Increase in excise duties on tobacco.		0.03	0.02
10	Reduction of income tax		–0.37	
TOTAL REVENUE MEASURES		**0.8**	**0.2**	**0.5**
EXPENDITURE MEASURES				
1	Wages		0.05	
2	Intermediary consumption	0.33	0.1	0.05
3	Subsidies	0.37	0.03	0.13
4	Social benefits and social transfers	0.29	0.03	0.12
5	Other current transfers and capital transfers	0.11	0.1	0.21
6	Investments	0.17	0.1	0.08
TOTAL EXPENDITURE MEASURES		**1.3**	**0.4**	**0.6**
	Extrabudgetary users, agencies, funds and SOE's	0.4	0.9	
TOTAL FISCAL ADJUSTMENT		**2.5**	**1.6**	**1.1**

Source: Croatian Convergence Programme 2017–2020.

EDP and provided an ex-ante estimate of the proposed measures. Acknowledging the challenging macroeconomic situation, the EC postponed the activation of the EDP until January, granting an additional year beyond the two-year fiscal consolidation limit. The EC also used a bottom-up approach to assess the effective actions taken by Croatia, as the Spring Forecast did not include the complete set of consolidation measures, and forecasted numbers exceeded reference values.

In June, the EC assessed the actions taken and put the EDP in abeyance, halting the potential imposition of financial sanctions. Despite elections in 2015 and a brief technocratic coalition government in 2016, Croatian authorities remained committed to the requested fiscal consolidation, albeit possibly prolonging the recession and causing adverse long-term effects on growth due to the emigration of unemployed workers.

According to Deskar-Škrbić and Milutinović (2021), Croatia's fiscal consolidation strategy, primarily based on expenditure measures with high multipliers, was growth-detrimental and partially self-defeating. A different set of measures might have shortened the recession in Croatia and improved overall fiscal outcomes. The study contended that procyclical consolidation during a recession was detrimental to potential growth and fiscal sustainability. As shown in Figure 10.4,

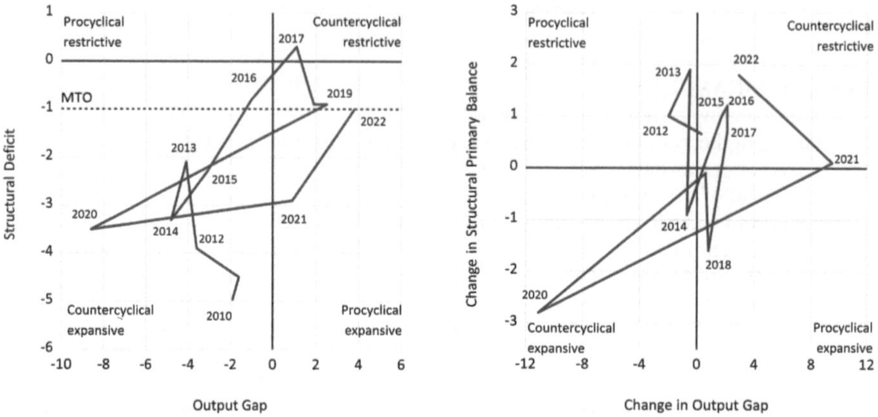

Figure 10.4 Fiscal stance (a) and fiscal impulse (b).

Notes: All values are in % of GDP; shipyard guarantees were included as expenditures of 0.9% of GDP in 2009, 0.8% in 2010 and 2.7% in 2011.

Source: Ameco May 2023.

Croatia conducted its fiscal consolidation during a recession. While fiscal consolidation from 2011 to 2013 was a deepening recession (movement to NW), the EDP coincided and helped with broader economic recovery.

After achieving the necessary consolidation and reducing the deficit below 3% along with a declining debt trajectory, Croatia successfully concluded the EDP in June 2017. This was a significant accomplishment, considering many other MSs required extensions. The commitment to fiscal consolidation and prudent fiscal policies generated trust and reputation, which played a crucial role in Croatia's eventual entry into the EA.

The EDP included additional structural recommendations to support fiscal consolidation, including expenditure review for wage rationalisation, social security and subsidies to create fiscal space for growth-enhancing spending. Recommendations also emphasised enhancing tax compliance and administration efficiency, strengthening budgetary programming and strengthening the Fiscal Policy Committee. Structural reforms were emphasised to address labour market rigidities, improve the business environment and enhance the quality of public administration to promote growth. These measures were reiterated in the CSRs and EDP monitoring, although they did not influence the decision to close the EDP after the fiscal situation improved.[28]

10.3.2 Macroeconomic Imbalances and Structural Reforms

An important lesson from the recent crisis was that macroeconomic imbalances must be addressed before causing problems. With that aim, the EU created a new macroeconomic imbalance procedure (MIP) along with CRS requesting necessary reforms.

In November 2013, Croatia was included for the first time in the Alert Mechanism Report (AMR), which highlighted problems in MSs.[29] The MIP scoreboard pointed out several problematic areas in the Croatian economy, including high unemployment, a negative net international investment position and declining export market shares. The scoreboard called for an in-depth review (IDR) to understand better the nature and potential risks for the new Member State.

The EC increased pressure on Croatia to implement reforms. In February 2014, an IDR diagnosed excessive imbalances, leading to the launch of a macroeconomic imbalance procedure (MIP) with specific monitoring. Policy action was requested in previously identified areas, including sizeable external liabilities, declining export performance, highly leveraged firms and fast-increasing general government debt, all within a context of low growth and poor adjustment capacity. In April 2014, Croatia's first NRP focused on the issues raised by the IDR. In June 2014, the first CSRs for Croatia were issued, with the highest number (eight) of recommendations among all MSs and specific and short deadlines for their implementation.[30]

The first monitoring report in November 2014 called for increased reform momentum. By February 2015, the Country Report (IDR) threatened to initiate the Excessive Imbalances Procedure (EIP), noting that actions taken in response to one recommendation resulted in significant progress, two resulted in some progress, while the other five recommendations showed limited or no progress. In June 2015, Croatia received six recommendations that essentially repeated previous CSRs despite efforts to streamline the European Semester by reducing the number of CSRs.

Political instability complicated the situation, and the third monitoring report in December 2015 noted a delay in implementing reforms due to elections. The March 2016 Country Report was softer due to the economic recovery and a new government, reflecting the further decrease in 2016 CSRs. However, the October 2016 NRP Implementation Report was delayed as only a few reforms were implemented due to another election round.

Economic recovery started in 2015, primarily supported by the positive effects of the EU membership.[31] Exports and inflow of EU funds (net positive financial flows) gradually improved both fiscal and macroeconomic situations, which was also reflected in the decreasing number of recommendations despite limited progress in their implementation. In February 2019, two years after the EDP ended, the EC concluded that Croatia no longer had *excessive* imbalances and emphasised recent policy actions and commitments (due to efforts to meet criteria for entry into the eurozone, as explained in the next section). May 2022 Spring Package concluded that macroeconomic imbalances were no longer present in Croatia due to strong economic recovery despite the COVID-19 crisis and reform efforts in the context of the euro adoption strategy and Recovery and Resilience Plan (RRP).

However, the implementation of structural reforms after the accession to the EU was difficult. The February 2020 Country Report concluded that Croatia made progress in implementing 57% of the CSRs since 2014. Fiscal policy and the labour market stood out with notable advancements: Croatia pursued responsible fiscal policies, corrected its excessive deficit and implemented labour market reforms to enhance flexibility. Nevertheless, gaps in the fiscal framework and pending reforms, such as the full operationalisation of the Fiscal Policy Commission, remain. Efforts have shown positive results in the business environment, justice system and financial sector. Challenges persist in reducing court backlogs and resolving older cases, but banking sector weaknesses have been addressed. Public administration, social benefits and healthcare have seen slower progress. While some steps have been taken to harmonise state agencies and implement active labour market policies, more is needed for modern public administration. Limited improvements have been observed in social benefits and tackling healthcare payment arrears. Lastly, the pension system faced setbacks, especially with trade union demands causing reversals in reforms.[32]

In conclusion, the implementation of structural reforms and MIP and CSRs was not successful, unlike the fiscal consolidation, which is in line with general findings by Efstathiou and Wolff (2019), who show that the implementation of CSRs is more vital in periods of fiscal and economic weaknesses. One of the lessons is that structural reforms are more difficult to implement. Also, fiscal consolidation has a more assertive national counterpart (Ministry of Finances), which shares the same concern about fiscal sustainability. Third, financial sanctions linked to EDP are much stronger than those of the MIP (the excessive imbalance procedure was never triggered at the EU level). These lessons, shared with the overall low implementation of the CSR, contributed to the EU's new approach in the context of the New Generation EU and Recovery and Resilience Facility (RRF), where payments are directly connected with the implementation of agreed reform measures. In other words, MSs are rewarded for successfully implementing structural reforms instead of being penalised for non-implementation. However, it needs to be emphasised

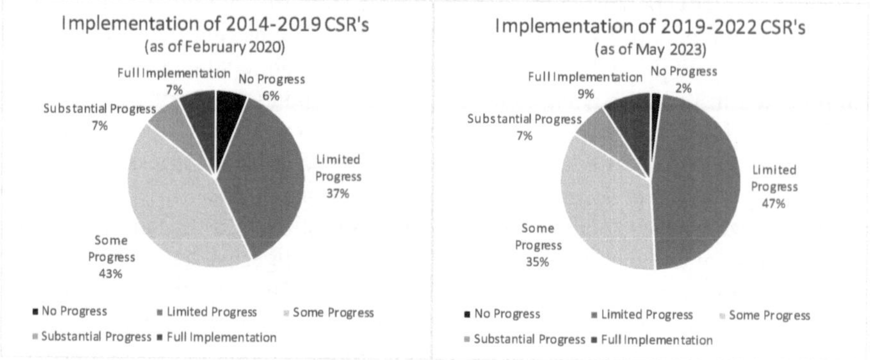

Figure 10.5 Implementation of country-specific recommendations.

Source: European Commission.

that the significant structural reform involved joining the EU and entering the single market, and no further reform could have a similar importance or effect.

10.3.3 Coordination of National Semester

To actively participate in the European Semester and fulfil its obligations, Croatia established the Coordination for the European Semester based on a similar structure introduced in October 2013 to ensure the implementation of fiscal consolidation measures. The Coordinating Body, which comprised the majority of ministers, was created to ensure the successful implementation of necessary reforms and consolidation measures. Operating through two operative teams led by the Ministry of Finance for the CP and the MRDFEU for the NRP, the coordination mechanism facilitated the timely preparation of policy documents and effective coordination among stakeholders. By aligning Croatia's macroeconomic and fiscal policies with EU objectives outlined in the Annual Growth Survey (AGS), the coordination aimed to achieve a coherent and coordinated approach to policy implementation.[33]

Over the years, the coordination system for Croatia's participation in the European Semester underwent several changes. In 2014, the operative team was replaced with seven expert teams to cover CSRs and later the NRP priority areas. Since 2020, the coordination of the European Semester has been centralised in the Office of the Prime Minister, under the direct responsibility of the Prime Minister.[34] This coordination structure has also been utilised for other economic governance issues, such as adopting the euro and the National RRP (NRRP).

10.4 Honour Prize – Euro Area Membership

10.4.1 Euro Strategy and Fulfilling of Convergence Criteria

With the restoration of economic growth and fiscal consolidation, Croatia continued its path towards deeper EU integration. Adherence to fiscal rules and improving macroeconomic imbalances generated a positive reputation and subsequent support for entry into the EA. However, Croatia's determination and ownership of the process were key factors, as specific EU procedures had to be adjusted to include recent changes in the EU. Croatia entered the European Exchange Rate Mechanism II (ERM2) in 2020 after a decade-long pause in the ERM2 enlargement process. Entry into ERM2 included new requirements, such as joining the Single Supervisory Mechanism (SSM) and close cooperation with the ECB. The economy recovered quickly from the COVID-19 shock and benefited from the new Recovery and Resolution Facility. Croatia fulfilled the Maastricht convergence criteria in 2022 and became the 20th EA member in 2023. Determination for the entire EU integration and adherence to common rules were thus rewarded.

After completing the corrective procedures and with the positive impact of EU membership on growth, the Croatian pro-European government turned its attention towards the next phase of European integration: joining the monetary area. This decision established an anchor for prudent fiscal policy years after the EDP.

Based on its experience with EU accession, Croatia was prepared for a lengthy and challenging process of euro adoption. The first step was to thoroughly evaluate the costs and benefits of euro adoption and gain public support. The second step was to secure support from the EU institutions and MS for entry into the ERM2 through strict adherence to the SGP rules and resolving macroeconomic imbalances.[35] Interestingly, the final step of fulfilling the prescribed convergence criteria was the easiest part of the process.

In 2017, the Croatian government and central bank conducted a thorough analysis of the costs and benefits of adopting the euro and studied the details of the entry procedure. Croatia has had a history of euroisation, and its monetary policy has been based on a stable exchange rate, with the euro serving as an anchor.

After a public consultation that confirmed the support for the common currency, the government adopted the Euro strategy as the central pillar of economic policy in the upcoming period. To push for the necessary policy measures, the government created the National Council for the Introduction of the Euro as the Official Currency in the Republic of Croatia, which the Prime Minister himself chaired.

Prudent fiscal policy was essential to Croatia's journey towards the euro. By adhering to the preventive rules, Croatia could implement countercyclical fiscal policies, resulting in savings during the economic expansion and a significant reduction in public debt. Croatia gradually tightened its medium-term objective and signed the Treaty on Stability, Coordination, and Governance (TSCG) in the EMU in 2018,[36] which imposed stricter rules and policy coordination. Despite facing a significant fiscal deficit and an increase in debt in 2020 (the first year of the COVID-19 crisis), when the General Escape Clause was activated, Croatia quickly reduced its deficit to under 3% in 2021. It achieved a nominal surplus in 2022 despite the adverse external shocks. This success was primarily due to a quick recovery[37] and fiscal prudence. However, progress in the area of structural reforms continued to be limited. In addition, due to the COVID-19 crisis, the EU's policy priorities shifted towards resilience and recovery, resulting in lighter recommendations, as explained in section 4.2, which did not change the focus on fiscal consolidation.

The main technical challenge in meeting the convergence criteria was participation in the ERM2. While other convergence criteria can be achieved automatically through economic convergence, the exchange rate criterion requires participation in the ERM2, which is subject to a political decision. As a result, the EU institutions and MSs can delay the entry for an aspiring country to join the ERM2, effectively blocking its path to the euro.

Entering the ERM2 presented a challenge for Croatia as the process was outdated when it began its journey towards adopting the euro. The last expansion of the ERM2 had taken place in 2005, well before the GFC and subsequent EU economic governance reforms, which included the establishment of the Banking Union. However, the Bulgarian and later Croatian aspirations to join the ERM2 contributed to an update in the procedure. The updated process introduced ex-ante and ex-post requirements, including close cooperation with the ECB in bank supervision. Since joining the SSM was a prerequisite for EA membership, new entrants had to be ready to join the SSM before adopting the euro.[38] In July 2019, Croatia's government and central bank agreed to join the ERM2 and pledged to cooperate closely with the ECB.[39] They outlined various measures to develop the macroprudential framework, strengthen anti-money laundering efforts, improve statistics, enhance governance of state-owned property and reduce administrative and financial burdens. Despite the challenges posed by the COVID-19 crisis, Croatia remained committed to the process and successfully entered the ERM2 in July 2020.

Croatia proceeded with its preparation for Euro membership in two main areas. The first one involved the implementation of post-ERM2 commitments. The second came with adopting the Euro Changeover Plan in December 2020. In order to effectively implement the plan, the government established an operative steering committee and six coordination committees. These committees were charged with various responsibilities, including the coordination of communication activities, the preparation of technical measures, the development of legislative proposals and the monitoring of the implementation process. They aimed to ensure a smooth and successful transition to the euro by addressing all aspects of the changeover, including practical, legal and communication-related issues.

Fulfilling the convergence criteria was mainly due to solid fundamentals, as Croatia had met all the criteria except ERM2 membership for several years. Additionally, the EU suspended fiscal rules during the pandemic, effectively pausing the fiscal criteria.[40] Although the economic and fiscal situation deteriorated sharply in 2020, Croatia consolidated its deficit in 2021 and 2022, alleviating concerns regarding the fiscal situation. The most challenging criterion was price stability, based on minimum inflation in the EU, which became problematic due to uneven price increases across the EU following the post-COVID-19 recovery and the Russian aggression on Ukraine, with Eastern MSs being particularly affected. Croatia narrowly met this target during the regular biannual convergence assessment in May 2022, and the European Commission concluded that the current price shock was temporary.[41] After receiving positive assessments from the European Commission and the European Central Bank, the Council decided in July 2022 that Croatia fulfilled the necessary conditions for adopting the euro. Croatia's entry into the EA was scheduled for 2023. The euro changeover proceeded smoothly, with the main issue being a slight price increase, in line with the experiences of other countries that joined the EA.

10.4.2 COVID-19 – Recovery and Resilience Plan

The EU promptly responded to the COVID-19 crisis by shifting its policy priorities and mobilising significant funds. The General Escape Clause was invoked in March 2020, suspending fiscal rules to allow for more substantial national fiscal support. The European Council introduced the NextGenerationEU (NGEU) in July 2020, including the RRF aimed at a sustainable and resilient recovery focused on green and digital transition. To access funding from the RRF, MSs had to submit

NRRPs outlining proposed reforms and investments, with payments connected to implementing those measures.[42]

The suspension of fiscal rules enabled Croatia to maintain public spending and support vulnerable households and businesses impacted by the pandemic despite a significant decline in revenues in 2020. Croatia closely followed the fiscal guidance provided by the European Commission, implementing targeted and temporary measures that did not jeopardise long-term fiscal sustainability. The 2020–2022 CSRs focused on transitory fiscal support and investment, mainly through the use of the RRF, while also emphasising the effectiveness of public spending. Despite experiencing a severe recession due to lockdown measures in 2020, the Croatian economy rebounded quickly and returned to its pre-crisis growth trajectory, improving fiscal indicators. The increase in energy prices resulting from the Russian aggression on Ukraine, coupled with the global impact of the pandemic, created an additional external shock that required additional fiscal support. However, owing to revenue growth and controlled expenditures, the budget achieved a surplus in 2022, and forecasts indicate that government debt will fall below the 60% threshold by 2024.[43]

In May 2021, Croatia adopted the NRRP as a prerequisite for accessing funds from the RRF. The NRRP serves as a framework for implementing structural reforms and investments that will be financed through the RRF. It encompasses two main stages: the first focuses on immediate pandemic response and economic recovery, and the second emphasises a transition towards a sustainable and digital future. This transition includes investments in renewable energy, digital infrastructure and support for small- and medium-sized enterprises. The plan comprises 146 investment projects and 76 reforms, backed by 6.3 billion euros in grants. Approximately 40.3% of the plan's resources are allocated to climate-related objectives, while 20.4% are targeted to fostering the digital transition.[44]

Unlike previous EU funds, the RRF introduces a new financial incentive for MSs to implement reforms. The payment system of the RRF is based on the progress and implementation of the proposed measures, which can help MSs achieve their targets for structural reforms. In July 2021, the Council approved Croatia's NRRP, allowing for payments linked to the proposed measures' successful implementation. This payment mechanism aims to enhance the effectiveness and efficiency of the funding process and ensure that funds are used to support meaningful reforms and investments.[45]

10.5 Conclusion

Croatia has successfully integrated the EU economic governance framework into its policy and planning process over the last two decades. This was primarily driven by its determination to become part of the EU and practical reasons. The absence of a functioning policy planning system before EU accession meant that the new system was quickly directed towards meeting the requirements and linking the EU funds with national priorities, thus offering a significant potential for a new and less-developed Member State like Croatia.

Croatia's positive experience with externally driven reforms in the 1990s and 2000s, prior to EU accession, also contributed to a quick fiscal consolidation and prudent fiscal policy after joining the EU, which led to macroeconomic improvements and growth. An open approach, along with rapid fiscal consolidation and improvement of macroeconomic imbalances, was recognised by EU institutions and MSs, generating the necessary support for full EU integration. Strong political support and fiscal consolidation were vital for this integration. Without the determination of Croatian authorities, the preventive arm would not achieve similar fiscal results.

The upcoming EU economic governance framework reform, which proposes more substantial national ownership, will challenge Croatia. External pressure for prudent policies and reforms has been integral to policy formulation during the last three decades, including recent successes with fiscal consolidation. Plans to reduce public debt under the 60% limit will result in weaker Brussels fiscal surveillance. However, the NRRF's implementation requirement could support structural reforms. Croatia has never developed strong strategic planning or capacities for integral policy proposals and reforms. Instead, the country relies on external support, mainly from the WB, for developing policies. Accession to the OECD will be significant in that process, as it will impose additional reform requirements and standards and provide technical expertise. Nevertheless, Croatia needs to develop its capacity for policy planning and analysis by enhancing the existing coordination framework and establishing a specialised planning institution.

Notes

1 The author is an advisor at the Croatian National Bank, deputy president of the Croatian Fiscal Policy Commission and former Assistant Minister of Finance. The article draws on his experience. Views in the article do not necessarily represent the views of those institutions (https://orcid.org/0000-0003-4366-511X).

2 The Six Pack Reform 2011 strengthened fiscal and macroeconomic surveillance in the EU by incorporating policies into the European Semester, implementing expenditure benchmarks, initiating excessive deficit procedures based on debt levels, introducing a macroeconomic imbalance procedure with preventive recommendations, and imposing financial sanctions. The subsequent Two Pack reforms in 2013 enhanced budgetary coordination by establishing a common timeline and rules and introduced heightened surveillance for Member States encountering financial stability challenges, receiving financial assistance or emerging from adjustment programmes.

3 In 2023, Croatia entered both the and Schengen Area. Although there were some connections between Euro Area those two integrations, the prescribed rules and conditions that had to be met were different. This chapter focuses on the Euro Area, and Schengen is not directly addressed.

4 For more on long-term economic problems, see Odak (2022).

5 For further details, see Anušić et al. (1995).

6 Details on the IMF's relations with Croatia are available at www.imf.org/en/Countries/HRV.

7 In 1996, as part of the transition from a planned to a market economy, the government dissolved the *former* Institute for Social Planning (which was renamed into the State Institute for Macroeconomic Analysis and Forecasting in 1992) responsible for

macroeconomic policies during the socialist system, resulting in the loss of Croatia's central capacity for macroeconomic policy. As central government bodies, Ministries failed to build policy formulation and development capacities, including utilising external expertise. The initial enthusiasm in the 1990s that attracted experts to the government administration waned, hindering the administration's capability development. A dual system of government wages was implemented to enhance EU funds usage, leading to the departure of public servants from ministries and policy formulation activities. Once pivotal in policy design, the remaining public institutes experienced reduced demand for their analyses and shifted focus to scientific research and profit-oriented activities.

8 Pre-accession assistance was small compared to later ESIF, but it facilitated the development of necessary infrastructure for their later use.

9 Available at https://razvoj.gov.hr/istaknute-teme/publikacije/strateski-okvir-za-razvoj-2006-2013/1262.

10 Available at: www.esiweb.org/pdf/croatia_Croatia-Strategic%20coherence%20framework-2007-2013_final.pdf.

11 Available at https://strukturnifondovi.hr/wp-content/uploads/2017/03/nsrf_en.pdf.

12 For the discussion of how EU priorities entered national strategic documents, see Bajo and Ljepović (2014).

13 Official Gazette 70/2005.

14 Official Gazette 87/2008.

15 Official Gazette 123/2017.

16 PEPs are available at https://mfin.gov.hr/glavni-izbornik-2725/highlights-2848/croatia-and-the-eu/economic-programs-within-the-eu/pre-accession-economic-program-pep/2921

17 For consolidation measures, see Deskar-Škrbić and Raos (2018).

18 For more on the WB activities in Croatia, see www.worldbank.org/en/country/croatia

19 During the aftermath of the Global Financial Crisis, the European Sovereign Debt Crisis emerged due to the global economic slowdown and capital outflows from certain MS. In response, the EU undertook a comprehensive reform of its economic governance system, introducing new institutions, procedures and enhanced coordination. The reform addressed fiscal and macroeconomic imbalances more rigorously to prevent future crises. More on EU economic and fiscal governance is available at https://economy-finance.ec.europa.eu/economic-and-fiscal-governance_en

20 Setting up the Croatian desk within the EC took some time as new people had to be hired and transferred to this desk. Initially, the Croatian desk was placed in a unit responsible for monitoring Czechia, Slovakia and the Netherlands. In mid-2014, it was transferred to another unit monitoring Spain, which had experience in dealing with fiscal and macroeconomic imbalances.

21 October 2014 EDP notification reported data under ESA2010 for the first time. The definition of the government sector was extended to transport infrastructure (highways, railroads, ports), HRT, and numerous communal utilities owned by local government. Dunn et al.(2014) estimate that the impact of the switch to ESA2010 led to an increase of the public debt share in GDP by 7.8 percentage points at the end of 2013. For more about the reform in fiscal statistics, see Galinec and Kandžija (2018).

22 The Council endorsed Country Specific Recommendations for the 2013 European Semester on July 7, 2013, a week after Croatian membership. However, no recommendations for Croatia were issued as Croatia was not yet a member of the EU when this year's European Semester started.

23 Official gazette 15/2015.

24 The European Commission postponed launching the corrective procedures until the formal October 2013 Fiscal Notification and the Autumn 2013 Economic Forecast.
25 Available at ec.europa.eu/eurostat/web/government-finance-statistics/excessive-deficit-procedure/edp-notification-tables.
26 Croatia argued that prolonged recession, the negative short-term fiscal impact of EU membership and transitory costs of pension reform contributed to fiscal imbalances. However, those factors could not be considered as planned deficits significantly exceeded the reference value.
27 Interestingly, the debt was below the 60% limit then but on an increasing path, forecasted to breach the limit. However, later statistical revisions showed that the debt was already above the limit.
28 Croatia was much more successful in fiscal consolidation than in implementing structural reforms recommended in the EDP and reiterated in many succeeding documents through time.
29 November 2012 Ageing Report also, for the first time, included Croatia. However, it concluded that Croatia's ageing costs were contained due to previous pension reform and the introduction of capitalised pillars despite the negative demographic outlook.
30 These recommendations advised Croatia to implement budgetary measures, strengthen fiscal planning, and consider additional growth-friendly measures. The retirement system was also highlighted, with suggestions to harmonise retirement ages, integrate pensions, and enhance the cost-effectiveness of the healthcare sector. Labour market reforms were also recommended, including the second phase of labour law reform, wage-setting system review and improved education outcomes. The tax and benefits systems were urged to be reviewed and improved, along with measures to enhance the business environment and administrative processes. Public property management, anti-corruption measures and transparency in public procurement were emphasised. The recommendations also included the judicial system's quality and efficiency and the comprehensive screening exercise for the financial sector.
31 This positive effect aligns with the experience of other new Member States (see Rapacki and Prochniak, 2009).
32 European Commission (2020). Country Report Croatia, SWD/2020/510.
33 See Maletić et al. (2019) for discussing Croatian first five years in the European Semester.
34 Official Gazette 89/2020.
35 It was necessary as specific changes in the EU procedure for the EA enlargement were needed due to institutional changes introduced since the last entry into the ERM2.
36 Croatia did not ratify chapters 3 and 4 of the TSCG enforcing stricter rules until they automatically applied for entry into the EA in 2023. However, Croatia continuously supported closer coordination – Croatia wanted to co-sign the TSCG in January 2012 with other MS during its first participation as an observer at the European Council. However, it was denied as it was not yet a full member.
37 The incidence of COVID-19 weakened during the summer months, so Croatia profited from increased (post-pandemic) demand for tourist services.
38 Entry into the SSM had its requirements, including an Asset Quality Review of the national banking system.
39 CNB sent the letter of request to establish close cooperation with the ECB on May 27, 2019, and proceeded with activities in that direction. The Croatian banking system has been stable during the entire period due to macroprudential policies implemented before the GFC. As a result, the comprehensive assessment of five big Croatia banks went

smoothly, and the ECB concluded that there were no challenges to entry into the close cooperation and, later, EA.

40 Fiscal convergence criteria are determined through the open EDP, and due to the EC's decision not to initiate any new EDPs during the pandemic, the fiscal criteria were automatically met.

41 European Commission Convergence Report 2022 available at https://economy-finance.ec.europa.eu/euro/enlargement-euro-area/convergence-reports_en and ECB Convergence Report 2022 available at www.ecb.europa.eu/pub/convergence/html/ecb.cr202206~e0fe4e1874.en.html.

42 The RRF represents a significant shift in the EU's crisis response, adopting a comprehensive package to address the COVID-19 pandemic's economic impact. It conditions funds for reform implementation and the strengthening of competitiveness. The NRRPs now play a central role in the adapted European Semester, creating a framework for new economic governance in the EU.

43 Inflation had a significant role in reducing debt to GDP ratio.

44 More on Croatian NRRP is available at https://planoporavka.gov.hr/.

45 The EC stated that Croatia had addressed all 2019 and 2020 CRSs, although limited progress was achieved in most areas (see Figure 10.5).

References

Anušić, Z., Rohatinski, Ž., and Šonje, V. (1995) *A Road to Low Inflation: Croatia 1993/1994*. Zagreb: Government of the Republic of Croatia.

Bajo, A. and Ljepović, Saša. (2014) 'Formulation of strategic development priorities of the Republic of Croatia', *Newsletter - an occasional publication of the Institute of Public Finance*, 16(89), pp. 1–14. https://doi.org/10.3326/nle.2014.89

Deskar-Škrbić, M. and Milutinović, D. (2021) 'Design of fiscal consolidation packages and model-based fiscal multipliers in Croatia', *Public Sector Economics*, 45(1), pp. 1–61.

Deskar-Škrbić, M. and Raos, V. (2018) 'Karakter fiskalne politike i politička ekonomija fiskalne konsolidacije u Hrvatskoj u poslijekriznom razdoblju', in H. Blažić and M. Grdinić (eds.) *Tax Policy and Fiscal Consolidation in Croatia*. Rijeka: Ekonomski fakultet Sveučilišta u Rijeci, pp. 153–179.

Dunn, M., Akritidis, L., and Biedma, L. (2014) 'The impact of ESA 2010 on key indicators of the national accounts in Europe', *EURONA—Eurostat Review on National Accounts and Macroeconomic Indicators, Eurostat*. Available at: https://cros-legacy.ec.europa.eu/system/files/EURONA%202%20%20art1.pdf (23.10.2023).

Efstathiou, K. and Wolff, G. (2019) 'What Drives National Implementation of EU Policy Recommendations?', *Bruegel,* 30346(4), pp. 1–28. Available at: www.bruegel.org/working-paper/what-drives-national-implementation-eu-policy-recommendations (23.10.2023).

Eichengreen, B. (2008) *The European Economy since 1945: Coordinated Capitalism and Beyond*. Princeton, NJ: Princeton University Press.

European Commission (2020). Country Report Croatia, SWD/2020/510.

Galinec, D. and Kandžija, T. (2018) 'The Impact of Stock-Flow Adjustments on Changes in Croatian General Government Debt Level', *Zbornik radova Ekonomskog fakulteta Sveučilišta u Mostaru* (Special Issue 2018.), pp. 214–227. Available at: https://doi.org/10.46458/27121097.2018.SI.214 (24.10.2023).

Heipertz, M. and Verdun, A. (2010) *Ruling Europe: The Politics of the Stability and Growth Pact*. Cambridge: Cambridge University Press.

Jurković, P. (2002) 'Fiskalna politika u Hrvatskoj u razdoblju 1994. – 2000. g.', *Ekonomija/Economics*, 9(2), pp. 269–291.

Maletić, I., Galinec, D., Japunčić, T., and Župan, S. (2019) *Pet godina Republike Hrvatske u Europskom semestru*. Zagreb: Ured zastupnice u Europskom parlamentu Ivane Maletić.

Mirošević, H. (2012) 'Analiza razvojnih dokumenata Republike Hrvatske', *Radni materijali EIZ-a*, 5, pp. 5–35. Available at: https://hrcak.srce.hr/93373 (23.10.2023).

Munta, M. (2021) *EU Socioeconomic Governance in Central and Eastern Europe: The European Semester and National Employment Policies*. Abingdon, NY: Routledge.

Odak, D. (2022) *40 izgubljenih godina hrvatskog gospodarstva*. Zagreb: Školska knjiga.

Ott, K. (2013) 'Utjecaj Europskog semestra na proračunski proces u Hrvatskoj', *Newsletter: povremeno glasilo Instituta za javne finacije*, 15(77), pp. 1–4. doi:10.3326/nlh.2013.77.

Rapacki R. and Prochniak M. (2009) 'The EU Enlargement and Economic Growth in the CEE New Member Countries', *European Economy. Economic Papers*, 367.

Rebić, P. and Arčabić, V. (2023) 'Održivost i karakter fiskalne politike u Republici Hrvatskoj', *Ekonomska misao i praksa*. Available at: https://hrcak.srce.hr/300381 (23.10.2023).

Samardžija, V., Jurlin, K., and Skazlić I. (2018) 'Značaj Europskog semestra za reforme u Hrvatskoj i odabranim novim članicama EU-a', in V. Samardžija (ed.) *Izazovi provedbe europskih politika u Hrvatskoj / The challenges of implementing European policies in Croatia*. Zagreb: IRMO, str. 21–68.

Šimović, H. and Deskar-Škrbić, M. (2019) 'Fiscal Policy and European Semester in Croatia: Why Should We Focus on Public Debt?', in Z. Petak and K. Kotarski (eds.) *Policy-Making at the European Periphery. New Perspectives on South-East Europe*. Cham: Palgrave Macmillan, pp. 169–186.

11 The Transformative Impact of EU Cohesion Policy in Croatia

Jakša Puljiz, Sanja Maleković and Ivana Biondić

11.1 Introduction

This chapter deals with the impact of the EU Cohesion policy on public investments and the policy environment in Croatia. Given its level of economic development, accession to the EU provided vast possibilities for Croatia to use Cohesion policy funds. These funds have been pivotal for building up public investment budgets in Central and Eastern European countries after they acceded to the EU. Strengthening public investments has been particularly important for Croatia, given their substantial fall after the economic crisis in 2009 broke out. However, new and significant funding possibilities which are "transposed" to concrete projects are only the first, although most visible, manifestation of the benefits and effects that Cohesion policy brings to member states, especially those significantly lagging.

The complexity of Cohesion policy generates many different patterns of influence on domestic actors. Along with thousands of implemented projects in multiple thematic areas, including some landmark projects such as the construction of the Pelješac bridge, significant policy changes were (and still are) taking place in Croatia. Changes range from normative and institutional adaptions, multiannual planning, policy evaluations, multilevel governance and partnership to the targeting of specific thematic areas and the use of special instruments for particular territories within the country. Given the wide-ranging impact of Cohesion policy on domestic policymaking, our text seeks to examine the entire added value of Cohesion policy for Croatia. We aim to identify the main patterns of changes and to connect them with policy results, which is very difficult given the scarce evidence base. We discuss Cohesion policy influence on the central as well as on the subnational level in Croatia since both levels are exposed to intensive adaptation pressures in order to manage (central level) and use (both central and subnational) new funding instruments.

We start by providing an overview of Cohesion policy-induced changes covering two significant aspects: effects on regional disparities and policymaking, emphasising the situation in Central and Eastern Europe. Next, we examine the Croatian case, first by discussing the central strategic planning and institutional adaptations taking place after the accession. Afterwards, we turn the attention to the importance of Cohesion policy for Croatia's public finances and investments.

DOI: 10.4324/9781003394013-11

A close examination of the main changes on the subnational level confirms the exceptional importance of this policy for the local and regional authorities, both in financial and non-financial terms. Finally, we present the main conclusions on the collected evidence on the Cohesion policy's impact on Croatia and provide some questions related to the forthcoming period.

11.2 Cohesion Policy, Regional Development and the Europeanisation Process

Cohesion policy as we know it today has been part of the EU policy framework since the 1988 reform. During this period, it has become one of the most well-known EU policies. Its importance stems primarily from its relevance in budgetary terms, its multilevel nature and its link to EU enlargement (Dabrowski and Graziano, 2016). Cohesion policy is perceived as the key EU policy to spur economic convergence and reduce territorial disparities across the EU. Studies by the European Commission demonstrate broad economic, social and environmental benefits for the targeted regions. According to the study of the EC (2017), by 2023, the EU gross domestic product (GDP) is expected to be more than 1% higher due to investments from Cohesion policy funds in the 2014–2020 period. More importantly, long-term benefits from the policy are substantial. The EC estimated that 15 years after the end of the 2014–2020 period, each 1 euro spent on the policy will generate 2.7 euro of additional GDP (European Commission [EC], 2022). Positive effects differ significantly among the member states and regions depending on their GDP level, available funding, investment policy mix and specific structural features.

In contrast to EC estimates, academic literature does not provide conclusive answers about its effectiveness. Very extensive literature surveys by Hagen and Mohl (2009), Marzinotto (2012), Pienkowski and Berkowitz (2015) and Dall'erba and Fang (2017) show a general lack of consensus over the contribution of Cohesion policy to regional convergence. Darvas et al. (2019) point to numerous difficulties in assessing the effects of Cohesion policy on convergence as it operates in very different local economic and social contexts and produces effects that have significant spatial spillovers across regions. They also remind us of various drawbacks of the applied methodologies, including the macro-economic modelling, counterfactual evaluations and various issues with econometric specifications.

In trying to explain the problems with the convergence of less developed regions, several studies pointed to the low administrative capabilities of the regional and local authorities (Milio, 2007; Zaman and Georgescu, 2009; Aiello et al., 2019). Rodriguez and Ketterer (2020), based on the econometric study involving 256 Nomenclature of Territorial Units for Statistics (NUTS) 2 regions in the period 1999–2013, emphasise the importance of improvement in the quality of government for the regional growth of low-income regions. According to the authors: "… low-growth regions that have failed to improve government quality or reduce corruption have been incapable of making the most of Cohesion Policy interventions". Bachtler et al. (2017) apply a qualitative approach when examining factors affecting the effectiveness of Cohesion policy and conclude that policy still suffers from a lack of conceptual thinking, lack of clarity and specificities of the Cohesion policy-funded programmes that reduce their positive impact on the development of less-developed regions. The policy mix of Cohesion policy interventions also seems to be an essential factor. Cristofoletti et al. (2023) argue that change in the policy mix with more emphasis on the *soft* instead of complex infrastructure investments from Cohesion policy funds positively impacted the GDP growth rate for more developed regions in the EU. Scotti et al. (2022) investigate the sectoral importance of Cohesion policy investments on the growth of EU NUTS 2 regions in the 2007–2014 period and estimate that expenditures in energy, research and development (R&D) and transportation sectors stimulate higher GDP per capita growth but also that growth effects are enhanced when expenditures are more diversified across sectors. The study by Crescenzi and Giua (2020) on the impact of Cohesion policy on GDP and employment growth in the 2000–2014 period on a sample of NUTS 3 regions shows that the results of the policy are connected to the heterogeneous national macro-institutional and policy implementation conditions in different regions, thus advocating the vital role of macro-factors. Some studies have connected the effectiveness of Cohesion policy with a different level of development of targeted regions. Mohl (2008) and Fiaschi et al. (2018) found a positive impact of Cohesion policy in the case of the least developed NUTS 2 regions with GDP per capita less than 75% of the EU average, while positive results are insignificant or missing for regions with GDP per capita between 75 and 100% of the EU average.

Besides its impact on economic growth, the Cohesion policy benefits EU member states' policy design and governance (Tömmel, 2016), especially for Central and Eastern Europe (CEE) countries (Scherpereel, 2010). The European Commission (2016) has identified seven areas of added value of the Cohesion policy for policymaking in member states: (i) financial investment for smart, sustainable and inclusive growth; (ii) concentration of resources on regions that are most in need; (iii) generation of innovative solutions to regional and local development; (iv) mobilisation of actors from all levels of governance towards the achievement of common goals; (v) support to structural reform processes; (vi) increased efficiency and quality of public expenditure; and, (vii) enhancement of institutional and administrative capacity. Given the wide range of policy areas affected by Cohesion policy, it is hardly a surprise to see strong interest of scholars in the transformational impact of Cohesion policy, especially in the field of Europeanisation. The concept of Europeanisation has often been used as a toolkit for examining the impact of Cohesion policy on the process of decentralisation and regionalisation in the member states (Hooghe and Keating, 1994; Nanetti, 1994; Hughes et al., 2004; Bruszt, 2008; Bachtler and McMaster, 2008; Bache et al., 2011), and the way how domestic regional policies were shaped in the member states (Scherpereel, 2010). However, as Dabrowski and Graziano (2016) warn, applying clear-cut methodology to measuring Europeanisation outcomes of Cohesion policy across the EU member states is difficult due to various factors such as differences in the degree of decentralisation, the size of the financial and administrative capacity of the municipalities (being one of the primary beneficiaries) but also due to differences in the attitudes of the local leaders.

In the case of CEE countries, institutional adaptations in order to satisfy the formal requirements as set by respective EU regulations on Cohesion policy funds took place in all CEE countries. Still, the change in policy mentality and real policy transformation was a slow process, particularly in the first phase. Despite the pre-accession instruments that should have prepared the countries for effective participation in Cohesion policy, most new member states had serious weaknesses in their legal frameworks, administrative structures and management systems upon accession (Bachtler et al., 2014). The work of national institutions has been affected by the high turnover of staff, the lack of skills, weak coordination and frequent institutional change (McMaster, 2006; Bachtler and McMaster, 2008). In short, the first years following the accession (programme period 2000–2006) were marked by the necessary institutional adjustment to satisfy the requirements but without the actual changes in the institutional behaviour (Bruszt, 2008). However, some studies indicate that CEE countries have been generally successful in building up their administrative capacity in the following years and doing so much faster and better than policymakers and academic commentators expected (Bachtler et al., 2014). This success can be partly explained by the fact that Cohesion policy is a policy domain with more present EU influence due to a coercive regulatory framework. One of the additional explanations lies in the political priority given to building up the administrative capacity in those countries to demonstrate the absorption capacity to the net paying member states and thus "defend" a substantial level of cohesion funding for CEE countries (ibid.). Despite the general improvement of the administrative capacity, countries like Bulgaria and especially Romania had severe difficulties absorbing EU funds years after their accession (Surubaru, 2017; Incaltarau et al., 2020).

An additional aspect of the Europeanisation process refers to the multilevel nature of Cohesion policy and implementation of the partnership principle across the member states. Cohesion policy is one of the prominent examples of multilevel governance that assembles different levels of governance and different types of actors in shaping and making the policy (Hooghe, 1998; Mairate, 2006; Piattoni and Polverari, 2016). As such, it enables subnational actors to have their say in the design of the Cohesion policy itself. As Piattoni and Polverari (2016: 74–75) note:

> Most ideas that later shape Cohesion policy are generated through informal contacts at events such as conferences, dialogues between specialised European Parliament and Committee of the Regions committee members and institutional trialogues. This complex web of consultations shapes the needs, demands and expectations of the constituencies variously represented by these bodies.

However, to which extent the multilevel nature and emphasis on the partnership principle have strengthened the position of regional and local authorities in the overall domestic policy context is still a matter of discussion, in particular for CEE countries. Some studies suggest that the empowerment of regional and local actors through Cohesion policy in CEE countries has been limited. It is explained by the change in the position of the EC that, at the time of accession, favoured a more centralised approach in order to ensure better management of available funds (Leonardi, 2005) as well as the goal of the national governments to remain firmly in control concerning their relationship to subnational authorities (Bailey and De Propris, 2002). Bachtler and McMaster (2008) tested the idea that implementing EU Structural funds necessarily leads to a more substantial overall role of regions. Their study suggests that the role of regions has increased in terms of their legitimacy, institutional capacity and stability. However, the authors also conclude that the limitations and barriers to regional participation in implementing EU Structural funds currently outweigh the opportunities. Nevertheless, we should be aware that most of these studies were prepared at a rather early stage of participation of CEE in Cohesion policy and that some new developments might have occurred since. In any case, central governments remain the key players in Cohesion policy, corresponding with the lack of progress in decentralisation in CEE countries (Scherpereel, 2010; Pálné Kovács, 2016). One notable exception is Poland, where authorities have decided to decentralise a part of the EU funds management to the regional level. Therefore, their regions were positioned to lead their specific investment policies with budgets surpassing domestic sources. Even though there were limits in the design and implementation of the regional strategic programmes due to the strong involvement of national authorities, the impact on capacity building at the regional level has been considerable (Scherpereel, 2010).

Given its compound institutional architecture and cross-sectoral approach, administrations participating in the Cohesion policy had to develop specific coordination mechanisms and skills to ensure efficient work. For many state administrations in Central and Eastern Europe lacking experience in coordinating large multi-sectoral programmes, the Cohesion policy provided new tools and incentives to foster cross-sectoral cooperation. A similar development occurred in one of the essential principles of Cohesion policy – the partnership principle. The partnership principle is based on grassroots involvement (Piattoni and Polverari, 2016). It is considered vital in bringing EU policymaking closer to the realities of the Member States, thus allowing greater bottom-up involvement. One of the most known structures reflecting the partnership principle is the so-called Monitoring committees that represent an obligatory part of the institutional framework for managing Cohesion policy in member states. Monitoring committees consist of representatives of public administration, socio-economic partners like trade unions, employers' associations, local and regional authorities, NGOs and the European Commission in an advisory capacity. For CEE countries, such institutional arrangements which promoted institutional openness, dialogue and inclusion were a significant novelty and, as such, had made a positive contribution to the development of the overall institutional capacity. However, in some CEE countries, the initial enthusiasm for new opportunities was replaced with disappointment as established committee routines diminished the bodies' potential, leading to disengagement (Batory and Cartwright, 2011).

Strong policy learning effects are an additional set of benefits associated with Cohesion policy. They typically involve improvement in strategic planning and design of policy instruments (Mairate, 2006; Perkmann, 2007). As Mairate (2006: 171) points out: “Multi-annual programming is an essential element for maintaining long-term added value. It has facilitated greater strategic planning, especially at the regional level, which in many countries was a neglected aspect of regional development”. Furthermore, due to its intense monitoring and evaluation system, policy learning in the case of Cohesion policy is firmly embedded into the policy cycle, thus directly stimulating the capacity of involved actors for policy design (Leonardi, 2005; Batterbury, 2006; Fratesi, 2016). The existence of the evaluation practice has resulted in continuous questioning of the design of various policy elements and their subsequent adaptations. Such an approach has benefitted policy learning, especially for CEE countries where evaluation capacity was almost non-existent before accession. However, improvements in the overall evaluation culture in those countries tend to go much slower than the mere production of evaluation reports (Bachtler et al., 2014), thereby slowing down the positive learning effects.

11.3 Accession to the EU and the New Institutional and Strategic Setting

In this and the following two chapters, we analyse the impact of the Cohesion policy on Croatia, focusing on the following main dimensions: institutional and strategic-planning framework, public finances and investments at the subnational level. The impact on economic growth and regional disparities is only briefly touched upon since the evidence base for a proper assessment is still very scarce. The approach is mainly based on the previously emphasised set of added values of the Cohesion policy according to the European Commission, but with a somewhat different structure, more adapted to the Croatian context.

Preparations for the use of EU funds in the post-accession period involved the setting up of the new legal, institutional and strategic planning framework. The passing of the Law on the Institutional Framework for the Implementation of ESI funds in the period 2014–2020 (OJ 92/2014) provided a legal basis for further by-laws and other related documents, such as the Common National Rules that have finally shaped the domestic management and control framework. Croatia’s approach to shaping the “rules of the game” for using EU funds has been highly prescriptive in normative terms. This is highly visible when looking at the content of the Common National Rules. They contain detailed instructions on the management and control processes for relevant state bodies. While such an approach ensures a highly standardised workflow across the system, it is also partially responsible for the low efficiency of critical elements such as the selection and contracting procedures (Puljiz et al., 2021).

The number of involved institutions in the management and control of Cohesion policy programmes grew significantly compared to Instrument for Pre-accession Assistance (IPA) programmes. For illustration, the management and control system for the Operational Programme Competitiveness and Cohesion (OPCC)

2014–2020 included 24 different central-level institutions, composed mainly of line ministries with a few additional state agencies.[1] The central coordination and management role for Cohesion policy funds was taken over by the newly created Ministry of Regional Development and EU funds, and it has continued with its coordination role for the period 2021–2027 as well, thus confirming its pivotal role in the Croatian EU funds management system. The number of employees dealing with management and control also increased drastically compared to the pre-accession period, from 816 in May 2012 to 2,145 in June 2022 (Government of the Republic of Croatia [GRC], 2016, 2022). The increase in the number of institutions and employees has further enhanced the spreading of knowledge on the Cohesion policy-related topics across the central administration. However, it also contributed to the complexity of the overall system. EU rules also led to the establishment of two Monitoring committees for the Cohesion policy programme, one for OPCC covering the European Regional Development Fund (ERDF) and Cohesion Fund (CF) and another for Operational Programme Efficient Human Resources 2014–2020 covering European Social Fund+ (ESF+). Such working bodies, consisting of many actors from the national and regional levels and discussing the implementation of the most critical national investment programmes, have been a novelty in Croatian policy practice.

The complex institutional setting has been closely connected to the content of the Cohesion policy programmes. The strategic planning framework for the use of European Structural and Investment (ESI) funds in the 2014–2020 period envisaged 11 thematic areas, covering many different topics like R&D, small and medium enterprises (SME) development, information and communication technology (ICT), energy efficiency, environmental protection, transport, education and employment, social inclusion and strengthening of public administration. Such a broad thematic coverage was conducive to the involvement of a higher number of sectoral bodies in the management of the policy. The apparent reason is their sectoral relevance for specific thematic areas, but bodies also perceived EU funds as the opportunity to increase their policy power in the overall governance system. Another issue related to such comprehensive thematic coverage is that Cohesion policy in Croatia could quickly become a “policy for everything and everyone”, generating policy risks similar to the ones previously noted by Bachtler et al. (2017) on the lack of strategic focus of Cohesion policy.

Once the strategic framework for the seven-year perspective on the EU level is clear, member states can concentrate on the preparation of their national programmes describing in detail the planned interventions. This is a critical point in the overall policy cycle, designed to ensure that interventions are planned strategically and with a decisive intervention logic that will provide significant long-term benefits to the country/region in question. In the case of Croatia, this strategic planning process (referred to as *programming* in Cohesion policy terminology) had several significant benefits for its policymaking capacity. First, it was the first time that the Croatian administration dealt with a long-term strategic planning process, which involved a clear and secured financial framework, elaboration of the performance framework and detailed information about the implementation process.[2]

The latter has been in contrast with long-standing policy practice in Croatia, within which the elaboration of the strategic documents was not followed by the implementation details and guidelines (Sumpor and Đokić, 2012).

Furthermore, the elaboration of national (operational) programmes for Cohesion policy implementation took place under the guidance and as part of the negotiation process between national authorities and the EC on the content of the programmes. Given the vital experience of EC services in the programming process, this had valuable policy-learning effects for the Croatian administration, especially in the case of the first programming cycle for the 2014–2020 period. Additionally, the organisation of the programming process required strong horizontal coordination, bringing further benefits for the performance of the coordination function, an area in which the Croatian administration demonstrates long-standing deficiencies (Maleković et al., 2011; Musa and Petak, 2015). Finally, due to the adherence to the partnership principle, various partners from the regional and local levels, as well as socio-economic partners, had to be involved in programming, which consequently raised their capacity to understand the policy logic and contribute to its content.

One of the critical shortcomings of Croatia's programming process for the 2014–2020 period was the lack of a previously elaborated national strategic document to ensure coherence and a framework for elaborating programming documents (Bajo and Puljiz, 2017). Having in mind this experience, Croatian authorities decided in 2017 to start with the elaboration of the overall national strategic planning framework that included the adoption of the Law on Strategic Planning and Development Management System in 2017, while the National Development Strategy for the period until 2030 has been adopted by the Croatian Parliament in 2021. Many examples of good practices from the Cohesion policy can be found in the new national strategic planning framework, such as a robust monitoring and reporting framework, obligatory evaluation and a clear link of policy interventions with the budgetary planning process. The fact that the same institution, Ministry of Regional Development and EU Funds (MRDEUF), has the role of coordinator for the use of ESI funds and that it led the process of creating a national framework for strategic planning points to the transfer of good practices from Cohesion policy to domestic public policies, including areas outside the direct responsibility of Cohesion policy itself.

Besides the elaboration of the primary programming documents, preparation for the use of EU funds also required the elaboration of additional strategic planning documents, such as the Smart Specialisation Strategy (S3). The elaboration of S3 was guided and monitored by the EC, as has been the case with all other member states. The importance of S3 was exceptional in policy terms as it represented the first national strategic document providing both a thematic and financial framework for investments in research and innovation activities. In addition, the financial framework was substantial compared to previous public investments in research and innovation activities. The thematic areas for investments were identified through the so-called entrepreneurial discovery process (EDP), an approach promoted by the EC based on previous academic work (Foray et al., 2009; McCann and Ortega-Argilés, 2015). EDP rests on a solid participatory approach and bottom-up logic that should, among other benefits, reduce the risk associated with the top-down "picking the winner" approach (McCann and Ortega-Argilés, 2015). The approach was a novelty for the period 2014–2020, and as such, it represented a challenge both for EC and member states. In the case of Croatia, the final document was not without shortcomings, such as insufficient intervention logic and deficiencies in the policy mix and definition of instruments (World Bank Group, 2021a). An additional important novelty associated with S3 has been the new national innovation policy governance system built around S3 and included new working bodies such as the Competitiveness Clusters, the Thematic Innovation Councils, the S3 Interministerial Working Group and the National Innovation Council. However, as the analysis from the World Bank Group (2021b) shows, the new governance system still has many shortcomings that affect its effectiveness.

Elaboration of S3 has been part of the additional adaptations the EC requires for payments to start flowing to Croatia. In the 2014–2020 financial perspective, they are referred to as the "ex-ante conditionalities", while in the 2021–2027 period, they are called "enabling conditions". Behind both terms is a list of necessary actions that member states must fulfil to improve the institutional, strategic and legal environment for investments supported by EU funds. The fulfilment of those requirements was a condition for EC to start with payments for projects on the ground. Namely, experience from the past has shown that many investments from EU funds have proven to be less effective due to various shortcomings within the domestic investment policy (Barca, 2009). Scholars have welcomed the idea of such conditionality as contributing to the more efficient absorption of EU funds (Bachtler et al., 2017) and policy design and implementation (McCann and Ortega-Argilés, 2015). Typically, ex-ante conditions included activities necessary to ensure the existence of a relevant framework for sectoral strategic planning and monitoring, sufficient administrative capacity including areas such as state aid rules, alignment with specific EU policies such as SMEs, energy, environment and climate, social issues, politics and education and progress in public administration reform.

For 2014–2020, each member state had to fulfil 7 general and 29 thematic ex-ante conditions, further separated at the level of several evaluation criteria for each condition. In the case of Croatia, data from the Partnership Agreement shows that out of the 117 evaluation criteria required to fulfil the ex-ante conditions at the time the Partnership Agreement was drawn (October 2014), only 30 were fully or partially fulfilled (26%), while 87 or 74% unfulfilled (GRC, 2014). According to EU rules, all ex-ante conditions had to be fulfilled by the end of 2016. This put the Croatian administration under tremendous pressure and required extensive administrative efforts in the months and years after formally adopting the programme framework for using Cohesion policy funds. Ultimately, all requirements were successfully met, and the first proceeds for implementing the projects began to flow from the EU budget to the national budget. The ex-ante conditionality approach continued in 2021–2027 under a new name – "*enabling conditions*". The main difference compared to the previous period is a shorter list of conditions, a more concise set of objective criteria for their application and their use in the entire perspective.

11.4 Impact on Public Finances and Investments

Presence of the strong effect of Cohesion policy on policymaking in less developed member states is partially based on its regulatory framework, but one of the most important factor are certainly additional funding opportunities that come with the policy. In case of Croatia Cohesion policy funds very quickly became one of the critical components of the national investment policy. During the 2014–2020 financial perspective, Croatia had access to approximately 9 billion euros in current prices from three Cohesion policy funds: ERDF, CF and ESF+ . Combined with the funds of the Common Agricultural Policy and Common Fisheries Policy – European Agricultural Fund for Rural Development (EAFRD) and European Maritime and Fisheries Fund (EMFF), the total financial envelope amounted to around 12.2 billion euros. This amount, on an annual level, represents about 3.4% of Croatia's GDP, while Cohesion policy funds alone amount to about 2.6% of GDP. Comparing these shares with the share of public investment to GDP in 2014–2020 of 3.8% it becomes obvious that EU funding is the primary source of public investments in Croatia.[3] According to the EC, Croatia has the highest share of EU funding compared to the GDP of all EU member states(EC, 2022: 294). In the period 2021–2027, the total value of Cohesion policy funding is 8.7 billion euros,[4] which is less than in the previous period but still highly significant, meaning the policy will preserve its importance for public investment spending.

Access to Cohesion policy and other EU funds significantly strengthened Croatian public finances, as inflows from the EU budget are far more significant than outflows, making Croatia one of the largest net recipients of the EU budget. According to EC data in 2019–2021, for 1 euro transferred to the EU budget, Croatia received an average of 4.9 euros. In other words, Croatia benefited from almost five times more financial support from the EU budget compared to its contribution to the budget. Such favourable financing is primarily the result of funding through Cohesion policy funds, as seen in the following table.

As indicated in Table 11.1, the Cohesion policy was responsible for 45% of total receipts from the EU budget in 2015–2021 and, therefore, represented the single

Table 11.1 Croatia's receipts from the EU budget for different EU policies 2015–2021, mil. euro

	2015	*2016*	*2017*	*2018*	*2019*	*2020*	*2021*
Cohesion policy	222.6	497.3	272.4	552.4	1,346	1,115.9	1,125.3
Common agricultural policy	251.9	293.1	306.6	456.9	590.3	692.4	721.4
Aid for natural disasters						692.2	319.2
Next Generation EU							881.9
Other EU policies	130.1	131	84.1	111	137.4	187.9	186.1
Total	604.6	921.4	663.1	1,120.3	2,073.7	2,688.4	3,233.9

Source: Authors' calculation based on EC data.[11]

most important source of EU funding. Together with the Common Agricultural Policy, it accounts for around 75% of the total inflow for the observed period. The importance of those two policies would be even higher were there no receipts from the EU Solidarity Fund and the first payments from the Next Generation EU instrument in 2020 and 2021. According to the Ministry of Finance data, revenues from the EU budget represented 13.9% of the total budget's revenues in 2021, out of which Cohesion policy funds accounted for 9.0%. The budgetary importance of EU funds increased sharply compared to 2014 and 2015 when they amounted to 1.9 and 4.2%. Cohesion policy funds participated in the total budget revenues with only 0.7 and 1.6%, respectively.[5] However, the actual financial impact of Cohesion policy funding exceeds the above figures due to national co-financing requirements, which is nominally 15%. However, the actual co-financing is always higher than the nominal one due to various specific rules such as rules on eligibility of expenditure and rules on state aid (ÖIR, 2007).

Given its substantial financial leverage and the focus on capital expenditures, it is clear that Cohesion policy funding plays a crucial role in public investments in Croatia. In 2020, public investment exceeded the share of 5% of GDP for the first time since 2009. Although this achievement is partly related to the substantial decline in GDP in 2020 due to the crisis caused by COVID-19 and the decrease in personal consumption, the trend is clear. After an extended period, the share of public investments in GDP is approaching record levels from the end of the first decade of the 2000s. The recovery of public investments has been strongly supported by Cohesion policy funds, as shown in Table 11.2.

It took several years for the Cohesion policy to have a more substantial impact on public investment. As shown in Table 11.2, in the 2014–2017 period, the increase in Cohesion Policy funds was insufficient to prevent a decline in the share of public investment in GDP. However, since 2018, the trend has reversed, mainly due to a substantial increase in EU funding but also due to the recovery of domestic

Table 11.2 Investments and Cohesion policy funding in Croatia, 2014–2021

	Share of budget inflows from Cohesion policy in GDP	*Share of public investments in GDP*	*Share of private sector investments in GDP*	*GDP growth*
2014	0.2%	3.8%	12.2%	–0.4%
2015	0.5%	3.5%	12.6%	2.5%
2016	1.0%	3.2%	13.4%	3.6%
2017	1.0%	2.7%	13.8%	3.4%
2018	1.4%	3.5%	13.2%	2.8%
2019	2.1%	4.3%	12.9%	3.4%
2020	3.0%	5.6%	12.3%	–8.6%
2021	3.2%	4.7%	11.8%	13.8%

Source: Eurostat for the share of investments in GDP and authors' calculation for the share of budget inflows from Cohesion policy in GDP based on data from the Ministry of Finance and the Croatian Bureau of Statistics.

public investments (except for 2021). On the other hand, the importance of private sector investment has been declining since 2017, with the lowest share in GDP recorded in 2021, indicating the limited potential of EU funding to boost private sector investment. The dominant impact of EU funding on domestic public investment will be further accentuated in the coming years due to the high level of support from the EU Recovery and Resilience Fund (RRF).

Besides the apparent size of the additional funding for investments, another important dimension of Cohesion policy impact is the thematic structure of investments. For the periods 2014–2020 and 2021–2027, Cohesion policy rules required that all investments should correspond to specific EU thematic objectives that were agreed at the beginning of each period. The so-called thematic concentration rules have additionally guided the national distribution of funds across the thematic objectives. These specific rules require that a certain minimal percentage of the total allocation needs to be spent for a limited number of thematic objectives. The rationale is to reach a critical mass of support for critical policy areas like R&D or energy efficiency. The level of thematic concentration differs for different categories of NUTS 2 regions, and more developed regions have to satisfy stricter thematic concentration conditions. For example, in the 2014–2020 period, in NUTS 2 regions with GDP per capita less than 75% of the EU average, a minimum of 50% of total ERDF support had to be invested into the following 4 out of 11 thematic objectives: research and innovation, ICT, competitiveness of SMEs and energy efficiency. In the case of regions with GDP per capita over 90% of the EU average, this minimum share was set at 80%, meaning that domestic policymakers can spend only 20% of ERDF funds outside of those four objectives. Similar conditions are set for ESF+, while CF allocations are from the time the establishment of this fund intended for large infrastructure projects, mainly in transport and environmental protection.

Despite the thematic concentration rules, less developed member countries still have considerable room for manoeuvre in negotiations with the EC on allocating funds for different thematic areas. Therefore, the thematic distribution of allocations provides a valuable indication of the member states' investment priorities and makes member states' spending strategies an essential factor for the overall impact of Cohesion policy funding on growth (Medve-Balint, 2018; Scotti et al., 2022). Table 11.3 shows the distribution of Cohesion policy allocations by different spending categories for Croatia, comparable countries and the EU as a whole for the 2014–2020 perspective.

Croatia has allocated most of the funding for environmental and other infrastructure (37.6%), followed by investments into human capital (18.1), development of private sector (16.0) and transport infrastructure (15.1). The most minor funds were planned for R&D (9.1) and technical assistance. Compared to peer countries, Croatia stands out for high support to the private sector, mainly SMEs (similar to Hungary) and a lower level of support for transport infrastructure (similar to Hungary and Slovenia). In addition, Croatia has the second-lowest share of allocation in R&D, surpassing only Romania and far below the most successful peer countries (Slovenia and the Czech Republic).[6]

Table 11.3 Cohesion policy allocations by main spending categories, 2014–2020

	RTD	*AIS*	*TRNSP*	*INFR*	*HC*	*TA*	*TOTAL*
Croatia	**9.1**	**16.0**	**15.1**	**37.6**	**18.1**	**4.0**	**100**
Romania	4.8	8.7	29.6	32.7	20.9	3.3	100
Bulgaria	11.3	7.0	24.9	33.6	19.5	3.7	100
Hungary	10.4	15.0	17.6	33.4	22.2	1.6	100
Slovakia	9.8	7.8	27.2	32.4	18.8	4.1	100
Latvia	14.7	6.5	27.8	33.1	15.5	2.4	100
Slovenia	23.7	4.3	12.2	32.5	23.3	4.0	100
Czechia	16.6	3.3	27.9	31.4	16.8	3.9	100
EU-27	14.7	8.9	19.8	28.3	25.1	3.2	100

Source: EC (2022: 297).

Notes: RTD – Research, technology and development; AIS – aid to the private sector, mainly SMEs; TRNSP – transport; INFR – other infrastructure (environmental, health, social, ICT); HC – human capital; TA – technical assistance.

As for the allocation into human capital development (employment, education, inclusion), Croatia fares similar to most peer countries. Comparing allocations between the 2014–2020 and the 2021–2027 period is difficult since the structure of thematic objectives is different. However, for some areas, the comparison reveals exciting findings. According to EC data, Croatia planned a slightly larger share of total allocations for research and innovation (11.5 versus 9.1%) but still significantly below the share in the case of the majority of the more developed member states. On the other hand, support for small and medium enterprises was significantly reduced (6.2 versus 12.2%). The reduction of support for SMEs is in line with the general trend at the EU level, but in the case of Croatia, it has been at a more significant rate.[7] Another change is a higher share of investment in human capital compared to the previous period (29.7 versus 18.1%) and a smaller share of investment in transport infrastructure (11.6 versus 15.1%). These developments confirm that, due to the impact of the Cohesion policy, Croatia continues to make further adjustments to its investment strategy providing more significant support to critical areas of competitiveness such as R&D and human capital. Cohesion policy has also changed the focus of Croatian public investments compared to the pre-accession period. It has enabled strong support for areas of high importance for long-term sustainable growth that were neglected before the accession, such as research and innovation, SMEs, energy efficiency, railways, ICT infrastructure, water and waste infrastructure and others (Puljiz et al., 2019).

Besides the investment strategy, another critical factor determining policy impact is spending effectiveness. The latest available data on implementation shows that Croatia's results are mixed, depending on the thematic area (see Table 11.4).

The most successful thematic area of actual spending at the end of 2021 was the Competitiveness of SMEs, where the spending almost equals the planned amounts, indicating a full absorption. Excellent results are also recorded in the case of the Low-carbon economy, which mainly covers investments in energy efficiency in the

Table 11.4 Contracting and payment rates per thematic objective for Croatia and EU-27 in the period 2014–2020, situation on December 31, 2021*

Thematic objective	*Planned amount – HR (mil. EUR)*	*Contracting rate – HR*	*Absorption rate – HR*	*Contracting rate – EU-27*	*Absorption rate – EU-27*
Research and Innovation	689	130.8%	48.2%	126.0%	65.0%
Competitiveness of SME	1.293	124.8%	97.8%	131.9%	83.6%
Environmental protection	1.566	213.2%	42.1%	128.3%	52.3%
Transport infrastructure	1.280	131.1%	47.1%	120.0%	70.9%
Social inclusion	835	134.9%	74.7%	113.2%	67.0%
Low-carbon Economy	530	141.7%	87.6%	115.7%	58.5%
Information and communication technologies	226	146.6%	12.9%	113.2%	59.4%
Climate change adaptation and risk prevention	209	139.1%	40.3%	133.3%	57.6%
Educational and vocational training	755	112.0%	51.6%	118.0%	70.9%
Sustainable and quality employment	366	133.7%	65.9%	110.8%	70.8%
Efficient public administration	179	92.1%	33.4%	112.7%	56.1%
Fostering crisis repair and resilience**	562	52.9%	0.3%	47.6%	9.1%
Total (ERDF, CF, ESF+)	**8.490**	**153.6%**	**56.0%**	**114.6%**	**60.6%**

Source: Authors' calculations based on EC data.[12]

Notes: *Data in the table refer to values for ERDF, CF and ESF+ only; **This thematic objective has been added in 2020 due to COVID-19 crises and earthquakes in Croatia.

public and private sectors. Investments in Social inclusion also show substantial progress in absorption and, to a lesser extent, employment-related activities. All other areas show relatively slow progress, with 50 and more per cent of allocations that remain unspent two years before the final deadline for implementation. Slow absorption in many areas indicates the presence of systemic weaknesses that affect the success of the investment. The situation in the area of environmental protection is of particular concern, with the so-called overcontracting approach, that is, the size of the contracted amount by far exceeding the planned funds. Over-contracting is a policy practice often used to improve absorption, particularly in the case of large infrastructure projects with plodding progress in implementation (cf. Centre for the Study in Democracy, 2017 for a similar situation in Bulgaria). However, such an approach entails a high risk of additional expenditures falling on the domestic budget due to a high level of contractual obligations that EU funds cannot cover within a given time limit. A comparison with contracting values for the EU level confirms that Croatia practices a much higher value of over-contracting across a whole range of sectors and in total than the EU average. This indicates potential difficulties regarding the need for additional financing from the domestic budget finances.[8]

Compared to the EU average, Croatia needs to catch up in implementing projects in ICT infrastructure, transport, public administration, education and training and R&D. On the other hand, it fares much better in terms of projects in energy efficiency and competitiveness of SMEs. The general situation with absorption will indeed be further improved by the end of 2023. However, a certain level of difference in terms of absorption across the thematic areas will remain.

How to explain the significant thematic differences in the absorption of funds? Varying size of available funding certainly plays a role, but there are also sector-specific reasons. Absorption in areas where the primary users are from the private sector (small and medium-sized enterprises and energy efficiency) is much better than in areas where local utility companies or large public companies such as Croatian Railways manage projects. Various shortcomings affect the ability of public actors to prepare high-quality project proposals and ensure their timely implementation. Part of the problem concerns the lack of relevant prior experience with similar investments. According to Puljiz et al. (2019), the weak investment track record in certain areas meant a lack of technical and other expertise to prepare and manage investments, consequently affecting absorption. They also emphasise the slow organisational transformation of significant beneficiaries such as Croatian railways and water management companies to a new, stricter regime for the preparation and management of infrastructure projects, as well as institutional fragmentation in sectors such as water management. According to the World Bank Group (2019), the implementation of EU projects in Croatia is hindered by limited administrative capacities, excessive regulation of national rules, insufficient strategic planning and weak inter-ministerial and inter-agency coordination. Highly complex project-selection rules, while bringing the benefits of standardising day-to-day operations, are slowing the absorption (Puljiz et al., 2021). Furthermore, national rules and procedures in some instances go beyond the standards required by EU regulation, thus indicating the ill practice of gold-plating (ibid.).

11.5 Cohesion Policy and Challenges at the Subnational Level

Croatia's system of regional (county) and local self-government has often been characterised as fragmented and with a weak financial and administrative capacity of the units (Krtalić et al., 2020; Đulabić and Čepo, 2017; Koprić, 2015; Jurlina

Alibegović, 2010). The accession process, as such, did not have any impact on the territorial organisation of subnational units, and the system has remained the same as prior to the accession. In such circumstances, decentralisation of management of EU funds was not a realistic option. Croatian authorities have decided that all Cohesion policy programmes would be managed exclusively at the central level, both in 2014–2020 and 2021–2027. However, counties play a role in the design and implementation of Cohesion policy programmes as consulting partners of particular (political) importance, mainly related to the political weight of the county prefects. The importance of the county level is further emphasised by the prominent role played by the county development agencies (CDAs). CDAs were established in the pre-accession period and were the first institutions at the subnational level to specialise in topics related to EU funds. They played a significant role in the networking of local stakeholders and strengthening the absorption capacity of EU funds already in the pre-accession period (Bache and Tomšić, 2013; Puljiz, 2011; Đulabić and Manojlović, 2011). Most of their initial efforts focused on preparing applications for EU funding, mainly for the cross-border cooperation programmes with the EU member states, one of the few programmes in which local and regional authorities could participate. The CDAs also played an essential role in preparing the first multi-sectoral strategic documents at the county level. Their role and importance were further expanded upon accession, as the new development (2014) introduced the role of regional coordinators for each county unit, and this role is in the vast majority of cases assigned to CDA. The new status additionally emphasised their prominent role in strategic planning processes at the county level but also led to closer cooperation with the MRDEUF in matters of planning and management of EU funds and other related topics. An increase has followed the increase in the activity level in the number of staff employed by regional coordinators. According to MRDEUF data, 21 regional coordinators had 550 employees in September 2023, or, on average, 26.2.[9] For comparison, in 2010, CDA employed 153 employees, or only 7.3 on average (Puljiz, 2011).

While the counties were already quite active in the pre-accession period in seeking funding opportunities from the EU, the picture at the local level is more diverse. According to Ott et al. (2016), 90% of counties, 47% of cities and 15% of municipalities received EU grants from 2011 to 2014. However, the situation changed in the following years with the increasing role of EU funds. According to budget data collected from the Ministry of Finance, all counties, 82% of cities and 65% of all municipalities received grants from EU funds in 2022.[10] The role of European funds was vital for capital expenditures. In 2022, capital transfers from EU funds to local and regional budgets amounted to 36% of their total capital expenditures. This is only a partial picture, as some significant EU-funded investments at the local level have been led by off-budget beneficiaries such as water utilities that are not included in these statistics. Therefore, the actual share of EU funding in the total capital expenditure at the local and regional level is much higher, most probably over 50%.

Besides the institutional adaptations that were mainly visible in the proliferation of various agency-type institutions, a further type of adaptation refers to the designation of new policy concepts and instruments. New approaches were mainly present in the area of urban development. The Law on Regional Development (2014) introduced the classification of urban areas for regional policy purposes, paving the way for the use of Integrated Territorial Investments (ITI), a Cohesion policy mechanism designed for the first time for 2014–2020. ITI enables the combining of funding from several priority axes of one or more operational programmes financed from the ESF and EDRF in order to design and implement multi-sectoral activities in a limited geographical area, usually an urban area. In financial terms, it foresees a special financial envelope for each ITI area, whereby the subnational actors propose the boundaries of ITI areas. ITI areas must prepare a territorial development strategy that serves as a strategic framework for identifying project proposals. Also important, ITI areas need to be involved to some extent in managing EU funds, at least in the project selection process. All these features make ITI a potentially excellent policy tool for the promotion of strategic thinking at the local level as well as for the strengthening of vertical and territorial coordination and cooperation (Tosics, 2017).

In the case of Croatia, seven and later eight ITI areas were established in the 2014–2020 period, with the total funding from ERDF, ESF+ and CF amounting to 345 million euros. Investments targeted several areas: brownfield redevelopment, urban transport, entrepreneurship, district heating, cultural heritage, employment, education and social services. Furthermore, since ITI areas cover significant cities and the surrounding smaller municipalities, this new instrument has stimulated territorial cooperation. Such an approach has starkly contrasted with the usual practice of weak planning and project-implementation cooperation between urban centres and their neighbouring units. Despite intense efforts, the results regarding achieving cross-sectoral and territorial integration were mixed. As Puljiz (2022) notes, the integrated approach was successful in the planning phase regarding the networking of targeted units and improving communication and coordination within the ITI area. Being the instrument that promotes networking and cooperation both within the targeted ITI area and vertically between the central and the local levels, its learning and capacity-building effects were significant. In particular, the fact that cities were actively involved in the project selection process meant that the ITI mechanism represented a first example of the subsidiarity practice, where specific responsibilities for managing EU funds were delegated to the subnational level. On the other hand, achieving integration at the project level proved to be a very demanding process, which is why the success of the integrated approach in the case of urban areas has remained somewhat limited (ibid.).

A similar instrument was applied to five smaller cities in the less developed areas of Croatia. It also included a locally based strategic planning framework (so-called Intervention plans) with individual financial allocation and a wide range of potential intervention areas to be supported. According to MRDEUF data, their level of financing in per capita terms was significantly higher in comparison to the ITI areas, indicating a much greater potential for achieving changes in their growth pattern. The interim evaluation indicated that the planning framework has been of high quality and that all cities respected the participatory approach in planning and implementation. On the other hand, the evaluation emphasised that their absorption capacity for implementation of such complex programmes has been minimal and required more attention from the part of the national policymakers than was provided (PJR, 2020).

Another new and potentially valuable policy instrument for the subnational level is the so-called Industrial transition plans. This instrument represented one of the activities required to fulfil one of the enabling conditions for the 2021–2027 period set by the EU regulation called "Activities for industrial transition management" (MRDEUF, 2021). Industrial transition plans were devised during 2020–2022 as special plans for all NUTS 2 units except the City of Zagreb (Pannonian Croatia, Northern Croatia and Adriatic Croatia). Based on the analysis of global trends and regional capacity, a limited number of priority niches for industrial development have been identified. Priority niches are later grouped into regional value chains (RVC), which represent the thematic backbone for further policy actions with the end objective of improving the position of RVCs vis-à-vis relevant global value chains. Regional industrial transition plans constitute an integral part of the new S3 till 2029. Being part of S3 meant that the elaboration of plans had to follow the methodology of the EDP, requiring a substantial effort to be invested in different discussions with the business sector and a thorough understanding of their needs and potentials. Funding for the implementation of industrial transition plans has been provided by the Integrated Territorial Programme 2021–2027, thus confirming the critical role of Cohesion policy in the design and implementation of this instrument. A distinct feature of elaborating the industrial transition plan is the very high national ownership of the process. Even though the first impulse for the introduction of the industrial transition plan came from the EU regulation, the majority of subsequent actions were the "product" of Croatian authorities coordinating the process. Since the implementation of transition plans takes place during the 2021–2027 period, it is still premature to assess its impact on the region's innovation performance.

Along with the new instruments, the Cohesion policy established various networks involving regional and local actors. Besides the obligatory Monitoring committee overseeing the implementation of Operational programmes, a range of additional working bodies has been created to support the implementation of operational programmes. For example, there is a working body involving representatives of all ITI areas and MRDEUF that serves for the coordination and monitoring of progress. A similar body has been created for the interventions targeting five small cities in deprived areas. Furthermore, for each of the three Industrial transition plans, there are several coordination and working bodies operating at the NUTS 2 level. While the effectiveness of the new bodies remains an open question, they can be considered as additional opportunities for policy discussion at the central level.

11.6 Conclusion

In this chapter, we have examined how the Cohesion policy has influenced the public investment practice in Croatia. Similar to the cases of other CEE countries, the EU Cohesion policy has had numerous and varied influences on the member states, some tangible and some non-tangible. The increase in public investments is just one, although the most visible, manifestation of the changes occurring in the post-accession period. In the case of Croatia, Cohesion policy funds have strongly supported the recovery of public investments and contributed to Croatia's economic growth dynamics, especially from 2018 onwards. Given the significant level of available financial resources, a continuation of the positive impact on the growth in 2021–2027 is expected. Besides the size of additional funding for investments *per se*, highly important were also various less-visible policy adaptations aiming to improve the effectiveness of investments, i.e., the contribution to long-term growth and the fulfilment of crucial national strategic objectives.

More strategic and coherent reasoning on investments is one example of such a contribution. Due to a range of requirements stemming from the EU regulation, Croatia had to establish a wide-reaching and budgetary backed-up national planning framework for using EU funds. One of the most important results of the new planning framework was the improved investment targeting of areas critical for Croatia's sustainable long-term growth, some of which were neglected prior to accession. Research and innovation, SME development, energy efficiency and railway infrastructure are only some of the most prominent areas that reaped benefits from the new funding opportunities. Ex-ante conditionalities set by Cohesion policy rules triggered further activities to improve the overall political environment for investments through an improved sectoral planning framework and various administrative capacity-building exercises. The new policy regime also included a series of institutional adjustments necessary to respond to the multi-sectoral nature of the Cohesion policy but also to reflect the great importance of the partnership principle. The establishment of cross-sectoral and partnership-type bodies like Monitoring committees, as well as many other working bodies, was a noticeable departure from the pre-accession policy practice of working in a "silo mentality".

The significant differences in the rate of absorption among different thematic areas are an indicator and reminder that the availability of EU funding, as well as the induced policy adjustments, did not by themselves solve problems of sectoral gaps in the investment capacity. Large infrastructure projects in railways, water supply and waste infrastructure continue to represent the most challenging areas in terms of project implementation, resulting in plodding progress in meeting strategic goals. On the other hand, areas with greater involvement of the private sector fare much better, both in terms of the direct results of Cohesion policy funding and the overall effectiveness of the policy. Croatia's innovation performance, as well as the competitiveness of the SME sector, has improved since accession, and this improvement can be partly attributed to Cohesion policy funding, as indicated by Čučković et al. in this book.

The subnational level has been one of the major winners of the first post-accession period, which is expected considering that a large portion of the funding was directed towards projects managed by local and regional authorities. The post-accession period was particularly productive for urban areas that were mostly passive during the pre-accession period. Through participation in new policy instruments such as ITIs and interventions for small towns in deprived areas, a number of urban areas have been involved in intensive policy learning and capacity-building activities. At the regional level, CDA further strengthened their capacities for strategic planning and project preparation, as evidenced by a significant employee increase. Many more and less formal networks involving various actors at the national, regional and local levels have been created since the accession, thus improving communication and collaboration on various issues related to Cohesion policy. However, these new governance methods are still relatively fresh and require much more attention from the part of policymakers in order to keep them "alive" in the future.

The identified policy changes show that the Cohesion policy has become the primary architect of the public investment policy in Croatia. Moreover, it will continue with this role until the end of the current financial period 2021–2027. Despite various evidence collected so far, some critical questions remain open about the effects of the observed changes. On the policy design level, it is still difficult to assess whether policy changes induced by the Cohesion policy have irreversibly improved public investment policy in Croatia. The issue of the Cohesion policy-induced policy practice spillovers to areas where EU funding in Croatia is absent or insignificant is still open. On the level of policy impact, the contribution of investments from Cohesion policy funds to the fulfilment of crucial national development goals remains another open issue to be further explored once more data are available. For example, whether investments from EU funds contributed to the reduction of regional disparities would be interesting to examine in a more detailed manner.

At the moment, Croatia is reaping benefits from the highest level of EU funding ever, thanks to the combined effect of ESI funds, the EU RRF, as well as receipts from the EU Solidarity Fund for reconstruction efforts following the devastating earthquakes in 2020. In such circumstances, Croatian policymakers tend to concentrate the entire policy focus on the issue of absorption while putting aside further policy adaptations to enhance the management of public investment policy in general and regardless of the funding source. The exception, of course, remains the situation when the EU mandates such adaptations.

Notes

1 Visual representation of the management and control system for the period 2014–2020 is available at https://strukturnifondovi.hr/eu-fondovi/esi-fondovi-2014-2020/

2 The level of detail was such that many important elements of the future public calls for financing were already specified in the programmes. Such an approach was critical for the EC to ensure maximum control of other programmes' implementation already in the planning phase (personal view from the authors).

3 Data on public investments are taken from the Eurostat database (https://ec.europa.eu/eurostat/databrowser/view/sdg_08_11/default/table?lang=en). However, it should be taken into account that not all spending of Cohesion Policy funds represents a public investment in the sense of Eurostat's definition, which is based on the gross fixed capital formation concept. For example, a significant part of EU spending goes to employment,

education and training, which are not considered investments according to Eurostat's definition of public investment.

4 It also includes allocations for the EU Just Transition Fund, created for the 2021–2027.

5 Data on the national budget was received from the various tables and reports on the execution of the state budget available at the website of the Ministry of Finance https://mfin.gov.hr/proracun-86/86

6 While a comparison of allocation shares for R&D indicates a certain lack of ambition in the case of Croatia, the picture is somewhat different if we consider the size of the economy. In comparison of the share of allocation for R&D in the national GDP, Croatia fares better than Slovenia (1.57 % of GDP versus 1.34% of GDP in the case of Slovenia, based on GDP data for 2014).

7 According to data from the Cohesion open data platform (https://cohesiondata.ec.europa.eu/), the share of support for SMEs between the 2014–2020 and 2021–2027 period has been reduced from 7.6 to 6.4% in total ESI funding in the EU-27 level.

8 This risk has been partially mitigated by transferring part of expensive infrastructure projects in water management from Cohesion policy programmes to the National Resilience and Recovery Plan that the EU Recovery and Resilience Facility.

9 Data was retrieved from https://razvoj.gov.hr/upisnik-regionalnih-koordinatora-i-lokalnih-razvojnih-agencija/4007

10 Data was collected directly from the Ministry of Finance.

11 Data are available at: https://commission.europa.eu/strategy-and-policy/eu-budget/long-term-eu-budget/2014-2020/spending-and-revenue_en

12 Data are available at: https://cohesiondata.ec.europa.eu/cohesion_overview/14-20

References

Aiello, V., Reverberi, P. M., and Brasili, C. (2019) 'Regional diversity in experiences of cohesion policy: The cases of Emilia-Romagna and Calabria', *Papers in Regional Science*, 98(6), pp. 2275–2293.

Bache, I., Andreou, G., Atanasova, G., and Tomsic, D. (2011) 'Europeanization and multi-level governance in Southeast Europe: The domestic impact of EU Cohesion policy and pre-accession aid', *Journal of European Public Policy*, 18(1), pp. 122–141.

Bache, I., and Tomšić, D. (2013) 'Europeanization and nascent multilevel governance in Croatia', in I. Bache, and G. Andreou (eds.) *Cohesion Policy and Multilevel Governance in South East Europe*. London: Routledge, pp. 68–80.

Bachtler, J., Begg, I., Charles, D., and Polverari, L. (2017) 'The long-term effectiveness of EU Cohesion policy. Assessing the achievements of the ERDF, 1989–2012', in J. Bachtler, P. Berkowitz, S. Hardy, and T. Muravska (eds.) *EU Cohesion Policy. Reassessing Performance and Direction*, London: Routledge, pp. 11–20.

Bachtler, J., and McMaster, I. (2008) 'EU Cohesion policy and the role of the regions: Investigating the influence of Structural Funds in the new member states', *Environment and Planning C: Government and Policy*, 26(2), pp. 398–427.

Bachtler, J., Mendez, C., and Oraže, H. (2014) 'From conditionality to Europeanization in Central and Eastern Europe: Administrative performance and capacity in cohesion policy', *European Planning Studies*, 22(4), pp. 735–757.

Bailey, D., and De Propris, L. (2002) 'EU structural funds, regional capabilities and enlargement: Towards multilevel governance?', *Journal of European Integration*, 24(4), pp. 303–324.

Bajo, A., and Puljiz, J. (2017) 'Institucionalna potpora za strateško planiranje i gospodarski razvoj Republike Hrvatske', *Aktualni osvrti*, 93, pp. 1–4.

Barca, F. (2009) 'An agenda for a reformed Cohesion Policy. A place-based approach to meeting European Union challenges and expectations', Independent Report prepared at the request of Danuta Hübner, Commissioner for Regional Policy, Brussels.

Batory, A., and Cartwright, A. (2011) 'Re-visiting the partnership principle in Cohesion policy: The role of civil society organizations in Structural funds monitoring', *JCMS: Journal of Common Market Studies*, 49(4), pp. 697–717.

Batterbury, S. C. (2006) 'Principles and purposes of European Union Cohesion policy evaluation', *Regional Studies*, 40(2), pp. 179–188.

Bruszt, L. (2008) 'Multilevel governance—The Eastern versions: Emerging patterns of regional developmental governance in the new member states', *Regional & Federal Studies*, 18(5), pp. 607–627.

Crescenzi, R., and Giua, M. (2020) 'One or many Cohesion policies of the European Union? On the differential economic impacts of Cohesion policy across member states', *Regional Studies*, 54(1), pp. 10–20. https://doi.org/10.1080/00343404.2019.1665174

Cristofoletti, E., Gabriele, R., and Giua, M. (2023) 'Gaining in impacts by leveraging the policy mix: Evidence from the European Cohesion policy in more developed regions', *Journal of Regional Science*, pp. 1–20. Available at: https://doi.org/10.1111/jors.12666 (09.11.2023).

Dabrowski, M., and Graziano, P. R. (2016) 'Cohesion policy and Europeanisation', in S. Pitattoni, and P. Polverari (eds.) *Handbook on Cohesion Policy in the EU*. Edward Elgar Publishing, pp. 107–120. ISBN: 978 1 78471 566 3

Dall'erba, S., and Fang, F. (2017) 'A meta-analysis of the estimated impact of Structural funds on regional growth', *Regional Studies*, 51, pp. 822–832.

Darvas, Z., Mazza, J., and Midoes, C. (2019) 'How to improve European Union Cohesion policy for the next decade', CORE, UK, Issue No. 8, Bruegel, p. 21.

Đulabić, V., and Čepo, D. (2017) 'Regionalism and sub-regional representation: A guide to the county transformation of Croatia', *Hrvatska i komparativna javna uprava*, 17(4), pp. 539–568. https://doi.org/10.31297/HKJU.17.4.2

Đulabić, V., and Manojlović, R. (2011) 'Administrative aspects of regional and Cohesion policy in Croatia: In search of a better coordination of parallel processes', *Croatian and Comparative Public Administration*, 11(4), pp. 1041–1074.

European Commission (EC) (2016) 'Strategic plan 2016–2020', DG regional and urban policy. Available at: https://commission.europa.eu/publications/strategic-plan-2016-2020-regional-and-urban-policy_en (12.11.2023).

European Commission (EC) (2017) Staff working document: The value added of ex ante conditionalities in the European Structural and Investment funds, SWD (2017) 127 final, parts C and D.

European Commission (EC) (2022) Cohesion in Europe towards 2050. Eighth report on economic, social and territorial cohesion. Available at https://ec.europa.eu/regional_policy/information-sources/cohesion-report_en (12.11.2023).

Fiaschi, D., Lavezzi, A., and Parenti, A. (2018) 'Does EU Cohesion policy work? Theory and evidence', *Journal of Regional Science*, 58(2), pp. 386–423.

Foray, D., David, P. A., and Hall, B. (2009) 'Smart specialisation – The concept', *Knowledge Economists Policy Brief No. 9*. Available at: https://ec.europa.eu/invest-in-research/pdf/download_en/kfg_policy_brief_no9.pdf (12.11.2023).

Fratesi U. (2016) 'Impact assessment of EU Cohesion policy: Theoretical and empirical issues', in S. Pitattoni, and P. Polverari (eds.) *Handbook on Cohesion Policy in the EU (79–91).* Edward Elgar Publishing, pp. 443–461. ISBN: 978 1 78471 566 3

GRC – Government of the Republic of Croatia (2014) Partnership agreement between the Republic of Croatia and the European Commission for the use of EU Structural and Investment Funds for growth and jobs in the period 2014–2020 (in Croatian). Available at: https://razvoj.gov.hr/o-ministarstvu/djelokrug-1939/eu-fondovi/financijsko-razdoblje-eu-2014-2020/sporazum-o-partnerstvu/323 (12.11.2023).

GRC – Government of the Republic of Croatia (2016) Report on the implementation of the decision on employment in central state administration bodies, offices of the Government of the Republic of Croatia, legal entities with public powers and foundations included in the management and control systems of the use of European structural and investment funds in the Republic of Croatia for the period from November 26, 2014 to December 31, 2015 (in Croatian). Available at: https://vlada.gov.hr/sjednice/5-sjednica-vlade-republike-hrvatske-18468/18468 (12.11.2023).

GRC – Government of the Republic of Croatia (2022) Report on the use of European Structural and Investment funds and pre-accession aid programs of the European Union for the period from January 1 to June 30, 2022 (in Croatian). Available at: www.sabor.hr/hr/izvjesce-o-koristenju-europskih-strukturnih-i-investicijskih-fondova-i-pretpristupnih-programa-4 (12.11.2023).

Hagen, T., and Mohl, P. (2009) 'Econometric evaluation of EU Cohesion policy – A survey', Discussion Paper No. 09-052, *Zentrum für Europäische Wirtschaftsforschung (ZEW).* Available at: http://ftp.zew.de/pub/zew-docs/dp/dp09052.pdf (12.11.2023).

Hooghe, L. (1998) 'EU Cohesion policy and competing models of European capitalism', *Journal of Common Market Studies*, 36(4), pp. 457–477.

Hooghe, L., and Keating, M. (1994) 'The politics of European Union regional policy', *Journal of European Public Policy*, 1(3), pp. 367–393.

Hughes, J., Sasse, G., and Gordon, C. (2004) 'Conditionality and compliance in the EU's eastward enlargement: Regional policy and the reform of sub-national government', *Journal of Common Market Studies*, 42(3), pp. 523–551.

Incaltarau, C., Pascariu, G. C., and Surubaru, N. C. (2020) 'Evaluating the determinants of EU funds absorption across old and new member states – The role of administrative capacity and political governance', *Journal of Common Market Studies*, 58(4), pp. 941–961.

Jurlina Alibegović, Dubravka (2010) 'Innovative municipal development financing. The case of three Croatian cities', in L. Ramirez, and K. Gulelat (eds.) *Strategic Planning for Local Development: Case Studies from Small and Mid-Sized European Cities*. Belgrade and Budapest: UN-HABITAT SIRP and Local Government and Public Service Reform Initiative, Open Society Institute, pp. 167–188.

Koprić, I. (2015) 'Teritorijalna organizacija Hrvatske: prema novom uređenju', in Hrvatska akademija znanosti i umjetnosti (ed.) *Nova upravno-teritorijalna organizacija Hrvatske*. Zagreb: Hrvatska akademija znanosti i umjetnosti (HAZU), pp. 21–44. ISBN 978-953-347-035-1

Krtalić, S., Šuman-Tolić, M., and Primorac, M. (2020) 'Ovlasti i odgovornosti lokalnih jedinica', in A. Bajo, and M. Primorac (eds.) *Financije županija, gradova i općina.* Zagreb: Ekonomski fakultet Sveučilišta u Zagrebu, pp. 127–171.

Leonardi, R. (2005) *Cohesion Policy in the European Union. The Building of Europe*. Basingstoke: Palgrave Macmillan.

Mairate, A. (2006) 'The "Added Value" of European Cohesion policy', *Regional Studies*, 40(2), pp. 167–177.

Maleković, S., Puljiz, J., and Tišma, S. (2011) 'New opportunities for regional and local actors in Croatia in supporting socio-economic development', *Southeastern Europe*, 35, pp. 168–190.

Marzinotto, B. (2012) 'The growth effects of EU Cohesion policy: A meta-analysis', working paper 2012/14, Bruegel. Available at: http://bruegel.org/2012/10/the-growth-effects-of-eu-cohesion-policy-a-meta-analysis/ (12.11.2023).

McCann, P., and Ortega-Argilés, R. (2015) 'Smart specialization, regional growth and applications to European Union Cohesion policy', *Regional Studies*, 49(8), pp. 1291–1302. DOI:10.1080/00343404.2013.799769

McMaster, I. (2006). 'Czech regional development agencies in a shifting institutional landscape'. *Europe-Asia Studies*, 58(3), pp. 347–370.

Medve-Bálint, G. (2018) 'The Cohesion policy on the EU's Eastern and Southern Periphery: Misallocated funds', *Studies in Comparative International Development*, 53(2), pp. 218–238. Available at: https://link.springer.com/article/10.1007/s12116-018-9265-2 (12.11.2023).

Milio, S. (2007) 'Can administrative capacity explain differences in regional performances? Evidence from Structural funds implementation in Southern Italy', *Regional Studies*, 41(4), pp. 429–442.

Ministry of Regional Development and EU Funds (2021) Plan for industrial transition of Pannonian Croatia. Available at: https://razvoj.gov.hr/industrijska-tranzicija-panonske-sjeverne-i-jadranske-hrvatske/4830 (12.11.2023).

Mohl, P., and Hagen, T. (2008) 'Does EU Cohesion policy promote growth? Evidence from regional data and alternative econometric approaches', Centre for European Economic Research Discussion Paper No. 08–086. Available at: https://papers.ssrn.com/sol3/papers.cfm?abstract_id=1298935 (12.11.2023).

Musa, A., and Petak, Z. (2015) 'Coordination for policy in transition countries: Case of Croatia', *International Public Administration Review*, 13(3–4), pp. 117–159.

Nanetti, R. (1994) 'Cohesion policy and territorial restructuring in the member states', *Anuari (Barcelona: Societat Catalana d'Economi)*, 11, pp. 101–113.

ÖIR (2007) 'The leverage effect of the European Cohesion policy under the SF', Final Report for the Committee of the Regions.

Ott, K., Bronić, M., and Stanić, B. (2016) 'EU grants to counties, cities and municipalities 2011–2014', Institute for Public Finance. Available in Croatian at: https://repozitorij.ijf.hr/islandora/object/ijf:440 (12.11.2023).

Pálné Kovács, I. (2016) 'Cohesion policy in Central and Eastern Europe: The challenge of learning', in S. Piattoni, and L. Polverari (eds.) *Handbook on Cohesion Policy in the EU*. Cheltenham, Gloucestershire: Edward Elgar Publishing, pp. 302–323.

Perkmann, M. (2007) 'Policy entrepreneurship and multilevel governance: A comparative study of European cross-border regions', *Environment and Planning C: Government and Policy*, 25(6), pp. 861–879.

Piattoni, S., and Polverari, L. (2016) *Handbook on Cohesion Policy in the EU*. Edward Elgar Publishing, pp. 566–576. ISBN: 978 1 78471 566 3

Pienkowski, J., and Berkowitz, P. (2015) 'Econometric assessments of Cohesion policy growth effects: How to make them more relevant for policy makers?', Regional working paper 02/2015, European Commission, Directorate-General for Regional and Urban Policy.

PJR (2020) Consolidated report on the evaluation of Intervention plans and programs for physical, economic and social regeneration of small towns on war-affected areas (in

Croatian). Available at: https://strukturnifondovi.hr/wp-content/uploads/2021/11/OBJEDINJENO-IZVJESCE-O-VREDNOVANJU-TIJEKOM-PROVEDBE-IP-A-I-PROGRAMA.pdf (12.11.2023).

Puljiz, J. (2011) *Analiza regionalnih kapaciteta za korištenje EU fondova na županijskoj razini.* Zagreb: Institut za razvoj i međunarodne odnose.

Puljiz, J. (2022) 'Integrirani pristup urbanom razvoju – hrvatska iskustva', in D. Jurlina-Alibegović, A. Markić Boban, and K. Fiesinger (eds.) *Prilika ili prijetnja? Reforma lokalne i regionalne samouprave u Hrvatskoj.* Zagreb: Ekonomski institut, pp. 157–180.

Puljiz, J., Maleković, S., and Keser, I. (2019) 'Cohesion policy in Croatia: What have we accomplished so far?', in Z. Petak, and K. Kotarski (eds.) *Policy-Making at the European Periphery: The Case of Croatia.* London: Palgrave Macmillan, pp. 285–302.

Puljiz, J., Maleković, S., and Tišma, S. (2021) 'The efficiency of public administration in Croatia in the selection of projects co-financed through European Union funds (in Croatian)', *Croatian and Comparative Public Administration,* 21(2), pp. 325–353.

Rodríguez-Pose, A., and Ketterer, T. (2020) 'Institutional change and the development of lagging regions in Europe', *Regional Studies,* 54(7), pp. 974–986.

Scherpereel, J. A. (2010) 'EU cohesion policy and the Europeanization of Central and East European regions', *Regional & Federal Studies,* 20(1), pp. 45–62.

Scotti, F., Flori, A., and Pammolli, F. (2022) 'The economic impact of structural and Cohesion funds across sectors: Immediate, medium-to-long term effects and spillovers', *Economic Modelling,* 111, pp. 105833.

Sumpor, M., and Đokić, I. (2012) 'Strategic planning as a tool for better public policy governance – The case of Croatia', in L. Galetić et al. (eds.) *An Enterprise Odyssey: Corporate Governance and Public Policy – Path to Sustainable Future.* Zagreb: Sveučilišna tiskara, pp. 1027–1038.

Surubaru, N. C. (2017) 'Administrative capacity or quality of political governance? EU Cohesion policy in the new Europe, 2007–13', *Regional Studies,* 51(6), pp. 844–856.

Tömmel, I. (2016) 'The commission and Cohesion policy', in S. Pitattoni, and P. Polverari (eds.) *Handbook on Cohesion Policy in the EU.* Edward Elgar Publishing, pp. 107–120. ISBN: 978 1 78471 566 3

Tosics, I. (2017) 'Integrated territorial investment—A missed opportunity', in J. Bachtler, P. Berkowitz, S. Hardy, and T. Muravska (eds.) *EU Cohesion Policy. Reassessing Performance and Direction.* London/New York: Routledge, pp. 284–296.

World Bank Group (2019) Country partnership framework for the Republic of Croatia for the period FY 2019-2024. Available at: https://documents1.worldbank.org/curated/en/501721557239562800/pdf/Croatia-Country-Partnership-Framework-for-the-Period-of-FY19-FY24.pdf (12.11.2023).

World Bank Group (2021a) Analysis of the Croatia smart specialization strategy: Logical framework, instruments, and indicator results. Available at: https://mzo.gov.hr/UserDocsImages//dokumenti/EUfondovi/OPKK_2014-2020/Pregled-javnih//Analiticki%20izvjestaj%204.%20komponente.pdf (12.11.2023).

World Bank Group (2021b) Analysis of design and implementation of croatian S3 governance. Available at: https://mzo.gov.hr/UserDocsImages//dokumenti/EUfondovi/OPKK_2014-2020/Pregled-javnih//Analiticki%20izvjestaj%204.2.%20komponente.pdf (12.11.2023).

Zaman, G., and Georgescu, G. (2009) 'Structural fund absorption: A new challenge for Romania', *Journal for Economic Forecasting,* 6(1), pp. 136–154.

12 Croatia and the EU Green Agenda

Ana-Maria Boromisa, Marina Funduk and Sanja Tišma

12.1 Introduction

This chapter deals with the Europeanisation of the EU green agenda in Croatia. The EU green agenda aims to transform the EU's economy and society in a more sustainable, resilient and fair way that supports achieving the global climate goals in the Paris Agreement. Achieving climate goals is essential, as climate change and environmental degradation represent an existential threat (IPCC, 2021, 2022; World Economic Forum, 2021). The EU will address these threats by becoming the first climate-neutral continent by 2050. The EU Green Deal is a blueprint for transformation. It includes a wide range of measures, legislation and policies to reduce greenhouse gas emissions, increase the use of renewable energy, improve energy efficiency, promote circular economy (CE), protect biodiversity and ensure a fair and just transition to a sustainable economy.

In Croatia, the aim of climate neutrality has yet to be formally adopted. According to the Standard Eurobarometer survey (summer 2022), only 12% of Croatian citizens think climate change is an essential European issue, while 5% think it is an important national issue. At the EU level, these shares are 20% and 15% (Standard Eurobarometer 97, 2022). Citizens and decision-makers do not recognise climate change and environmental degradation as a severe threat; thus, implementing the EU green agenda in Croatia is challenging. Innovative solutions are necessary to raise awareness of the relevance of the green agenda to create political will for policy creation and capacity for implementation.

First, we identify the main features of the European Green Agenda and examine to which extent these are Europeanised in Croatia on policy, legislative and normative levels. The European Green Deal (EGD) is outlined together with the main policy areas necessary for implementation. These EU policies are paired with relevant Croatian policies. The policy analysis includes EU and national strategic documents.

Next, the level to which the policies and the processes are Europeanised in Croatia is examined. The transposition and implementation of relevant policies are considered a criterion for evaluating Europeanisation at the level of legislation. For monitoring the alignment of the Croatian green agenda with the EU, we use formal monitoring mechanisms (European Semester reports and infringement procedures).

DOI: 10.4324/9781003394013-12

Legislative alignment is monitored through official reports and infringement procedures. The normative Europeanisation is evaluated by analysing the institutional capacity to adhere to EU policies, media coverage and public opinion. The conclusions are formulated based on the analysis of the EU green agenda and its implementation in Croatia.

12.2 Theoretical Background

As a member state of the EU, Croatia is subject to the rules and regulations of the EU, including those related to the EU green agenda. EGD set a European green agenda; the focus is on policies for its implementation. Through the process of Europeanisation, Croatia is expected to actively participate in creating European policies, adopt national policies coherent with the EU policies and standards and implement these policies.

Europeanisation is a term that first appeared in the 1990s (Ladrech, 1994; Saurugger, 2013:169) and most frequently indicates the impact of the EU on the national system of formulating and implementing public policies (Petak, 2012:17).

The interpretation of Claudio M. Radaelli is used to analyse the Europeanisation process in environmental and climate policies. Radaelli defines Europeanisation as

> processes of construction, diffusion and institutionalisation of formal and informal rules, procedures, policy paradigms, styles, 'ways of doing things' and shared beliefs and norms which are first defined and consolidated in the EU policy process and then incorporated in the logic of domestic (national and subnational) discourse, political structures and public policies.
>
> (2002:108)

His definition highlights three particular features of Europeanisation. The first one is that Europeanisation can derive from different stages and forms of the policy process: policy formulation (construction), putting policy into practice (institutionalisation), and in a much less structured manner (diffusion), where the EU's role may be pretty limited (Radaelli, 2004:3). Another vital feature is that Europeanisation is not simply about formal policy rules but about fewer tangible aspects, such as beliefs and values (ibid.). The third feature is that the concept of Europeanisation is about the impact of European policy within member states. It thus entails two steps: adoption at the EU level and then incorporation at the domestic level (ibid.:4). Radaelli states that his definition is grounded in an understanding of Europeanisation as an interactive process. His definition indicates that Europeanisation is not a linear but a circular process which includes both European construction and integration (uploading) and the impact of that process on the national level (downloading), which in turn affects European integration (uploading) (Saurugger, 2013:171).

The process of Europeanisation can occur through various channels, including legal, policy and normative mechanisms. In the case of the EGD, Europeanisation is occurring through the adoption of EU strategies (policies), directives, regulations, decisions (legally binding mechanisms), as well as recommendations and opinions (normative mechanisms). Implementing the policy goals requires internalisation and the Europeanisation of national policies.

Normative mechanisms refer to the influence that social norms, values and beliefs have on behaviour. They can be vital in the process of Europeanisation, as they can help shape the behaviour of member states in ways consistent with EU policies and norms. For example, the normative framework promoted by the EGD encourages member states to adopt more ambitious targets for reducing greenhouse gas emissions or to promote the use of renewable energy sources (RES). Also, normative mechanisms are essential for encouraging member states to adopt more sustainable and environmentally friendly policies.

The process of Europeanisation is not a one-way process, however. Member states can also influence EU policies and norms through their actions and policies. In the case of Croatia, the country has the opportunity to shape EU green policies through its involvement in providing input and feedback within the EU institutions. Through this process, Croatia can contribute to achieving the goals of the EGD while also benefiting from the economic and environmental benefits of a more sustainable and resilient economy. Thus, Europeanisation emphasises the importance of EU policies, regulations and norms in shaping the behaviour of member states while also recognising the role that member states play in shaping EU policies and norms.

Regarding the development of green policies or environmental protection policies in the EU, it can be stated that these are strongly regulated and highly harmonised sectoral policies (McCormick, 2010; Jordan and Liefferink, 2004; Jordan et al., 2012) which are a result of many years of upgrading in terms of institutionalisation and expansion in terms of significance, visibility and authority. There are approximately three phases in developing European environmental protection policies (Jordan and Liefferink, 2004). The first period of environmental policy development began in 1972 with the creation of institutional foundations and the determination of basic principles. With the adoption of the European Single Act in 1987, the second phase of the development of environmental protection policies began. A European Single Act introduced a new chapter called 'Environment', which strengthens the legal basis of environmental protection policy intending to preserve the quality of the environment, protecting human health and ensuring the rational use of natural resources. The third phase of developing environmental protection policies, which continues today, began in 1992 with the Maastricht Treaty (Treaty on European Union). With the adoption of the Maastricht Treaty, the environment officially became a policy area of the EU. In 1997, the Treaty of Maastricht was supplemented by the Treaty of Amsterdam, which introduced an obligation according to which environmental policy must become an integral part of all sectoral policies of the EU.

Environmental protection, environmental regulations and awareness of preserving the environment and nature in the Republic of Croatia gained importance in the context of accession to the EU. Croatia started the accession process in 2003 and became a member state in 2013. The screening process showed that environmental legislation in Croatia was incompatible with the *aquis*, which made negotiations on the environmental chapter (chapter 27) particularly challenging. Transition periods defined in the Treaty of Accession of the Republic of Croatia to the European Union relate to the most demanding water and waste directives. The most prolonged transition period for complete alignment with the Municipal Wastewater Treatment Directive (Council Directive 91/271/EEC, OJ L 135, 30.5.1991, p. 40) expires by the end of 2023. Croatia still struggles to meet some obligations and faces increasing infringement procedures related to 'green' topics. Environment (with eight cases) and energy (with five cases) are the most challenging sectors and make up 50% of all pending cases (European Commission, 2020a).

12.3 Central Policies for the EU Green Agenda

12.3.1 The European Green Deal

The EGD (European Commission, 2019), adopted in 2019, is the framework for the EU's development until 2050. It sets a comprehensive plan to achieve carbon neutrality by 2050 and ensure sustainable growth. The EGD addresses the threats of climate change (by mitigation and adaptation measures), environmental degradation (focusing on preserving and restoring biodiversity, improving air and water quality) and social inequality. EGD recognises the need for a just transition to a sustainable economy, which is circular and resource-efficient.

Based on the EGD, major EU and Croatian green policies are identified (Table 12.1).

The general development framework of Croatia provides the National Development Strategy (NDS) of the Republic of Croatia until 2030 (Official Gazette of the Republic of Croatia (2021b). NDS outlines four strategic priority clusters which are coherent with the EGD: (i) sustainable economy and society, (ii) strengthening resilience to crises, (iii) green and digital transition and (iv) balanced regional development. Adopting the NDS strengthened 'European' themes in the public debate (Mus, 2021).

12.3.2 Climate

The EGD aims to achieve climate neutrality by 2050. Croatian policies (defined by the NDS and the Low-Carbon Development Strategy) do not include climate neutrality goals. The NDS states that 'Croatia supported raising the EU's common goal of reducing greenhouse gas emissions by at least 55% by 2030 compared to 1990 levels and the 2050 climate neutrality target'. However, the NDS sets a lower goal – a 35% reduction of greenhouse gas (GHG) emissions compared to 1990 by 2030 – and does not set the time frame for achieving climate neutrality. Instead, it states that Croatia will analyse the feasibility of increasing targets and revise NDS and other strategic planning documents once these goals are legislatively adopted at the EU level and integrated into sectoral regulations. According to the Low-Carbon

Table 12.1 Overview of EU and Croatian policies relevant to the EU Green Deal

Policies for the EU green agenda and implementation in Croatia		
Area	*EU*	*Croatia*
General development document	European Green Deal	National Development Strategy of the Republic of Croatia until 2030 National Recovery and Resilience Plan 2021–2026
Climate policy	European Climate Law (Regulation [EU] 2021/1119) EU Strategy on Adaptation to Climate Change 2030 Climate Target Plan European Climate Pact	Low-Carbon Development Strategy of the Republic of Croatia Strategy for Adaptation to Climate Change in the Republic of Croatia for the period to 2040 with a view to 2070 Integrated Energy and Climate Plan for the Republic of Croatia for the period 2021–2030
Energy policy	Energy Union Framework Strategy Clean energy for all Europeans Fit for 55* RePowerEU	Energy Development Strategy of the Republic of Croatia for the period until 2030, with a view to 2050 Integrated Energy and Climate Plan for the Republic of Croatia for the period 2021–2030
Buildings	Renovation Wave New European Bauhaus	Long-Term Building Renovation Strategy until 2050 Program for Energy Refurbishment of Public Buildings 2021–2030 Program for Energy Refurbishment of Cultural Heritage Buildings Program for the Development of Green Urban Infrastructure Program for Circular Management of Space and Buildings
Industrial policy and circular economy	New Industrial Strategy Circular Economy Action Plan	Smart Specialisation Strategy Waste Management Strategy Waste Management Plan Decision on Implementation of the Waste Management Plan
Environmental protection and biodiversity	8th Environment Action Programme EU Action Plan: Towards Zero Pollution for Air, Water and Soil Chemicals Strategy for Sustainability Towards a Toxic-Free Environment Biodiversity Strategy New EU Forest Strategy for 2030 Soil Strategy	Nature Protection Strategy and Action Plan for of the Republic of Croatia for the period from 2017 to 2025

(*Continued*)

Table 12.1 (Continued)

Policies for the EU green agenda and implementation in Croatia		
Area	*EU*	*Croatia*
Mobility	Sustainable and Smart Mobility Strategy	Transport Development Strategy 2017–2030
Agriculture	Common Agricultural Policy (CAP) From Farm to Fork Strategy	Agriculture Strategy 2020 National Farm-to-Fork Strategy Croatia CAP Strategic Plan

Source: Authors, based on Boromisa (2020).

Note: *Fit for 55 package includes various sectors of the economy. For more, see European Commission (2023b).

Development Strategy (Section 12.3.1), achieving 55% GHG emissions reductions is highly unlikely due to financial constraints.[1] Strategies in Croatia are not legally binding. Thus, the lack of climate neutrality targets indicates a need for more political will to address the climate crisis. Public awareness about the climate crisis is relatively low, and there is no public pressure for climate action.

The Climate Law defines EU-binding climate change mitigation requirements (Official Journal of the European Union (2021). It sets a 2050 climate neutrality target and an intermediate target of 55% reduction of greenhouse gases by 2030 compared with 1990 levels. The *2030 Climate Target Plan* elaborates on how these goals can be achieved (European Commission, 2019). It includes revising key climate regulations: EU Emission Trading System (EU ETS), regulation on Land Use, Land Use Change and Forestry (LULUCF), Effort Sharing Regulation and national targets for RES.

EU ETS is a carbon market based on a system of cap-and-trade of emissions allowances for energy-intensive industries, the power generation sector and the aviation sector. The EU ETS reform increased the overall ambition of emissions reductions by 2030 in the sectors covered by the EU ETS to 62% compared to 2005 levels. Also, additional sectors are included in ETS: maritime transport, a separate ETS is set for buildings, road transport and fuels. The reform includes faster reduction of emissions allowances in the system, gradual phasing-out of free allowances for some sectors, implementation of the global carbon offsetting through a carbon border adjustment mechanism and reduction scheme for international aviation. Temporarily established, the Social Climate Fund will finance measures and investments to support vulnerable households, micro-enterprises and transport users and help them cope with the price impacts of the extension of the EU ETS to buildings, road transport and additional sectors over the period 2026–2032.

The 2018 LULUCF regulation (Official Journal of the European Union, 2018) set a binding commitment for the EU to reduce emissions and increase removals in the land use and forestry sectors. Revised LULUCF regulation (Official Journal of the European Union, 2023) sets an increased EU-level target of at least 310 million tonnes of CO_2 equivalent net greenhouse gas removals by 2030. Binding national targets are defined for each member state: for Croatia, the 2030 net removals target is –5527 ktCO_2 eq. In 2016–2018 average was 4933 kt of CO_2 eq, which shows that Croatia should increase net removals by 11% (–593 kt of CO_2 eq, Regulation EU 2023/839, Annex III).

The Effort Sharing Regulation sets binding annual greenhouse gas emissions targets for member states in sectors not covered by the EU ETS or the LULUCF regulation. The new overall EU-level greenhouse gas emissions reduction target for effort-sharing sectors for 2030 is 40% (previously, it was 29%). For Croatia, the target to decrease GHG emissions in 2030 compared to 2005 is now set at 16.7% (compared to 7% before the revision) (European Commission, 2020d). The 7% target is included as the primary goal of the Low-Carbon Development Strategy of the Republic of Croatia until 2030, with a view to 2050.

Croatian policies and laws are yet to be aligned with revised European targets. The Law on Climate Activities and Protection of the Ozone Layer (Official Gazette of the Republic of Croatia, 2019) , as the key Croatian climate policy document, defines (i) Low-Carbon Development Strategy of the Republic of Croatia, (ii) Strategy for Adaptation to Climate Change in the Republic of Croatia, (iii) Action Plan for the Implementation of the Low-Carbon Development Strategy of the Republic of Croatia, (iv) Action Plan for the Implementation of the Climate Change Adaptation Strategy in the Republic of Croatia, (v) Integrated Energy and Climate Plan of the Republic of Croatia and (vi) Program to Mitigate Climate Change, Adapt to Climate Change and Protect the Ozone Layer.

The Low-Carbon Development Strategy of the Republic of Croatia until 2030, with a view to 2050 (Ministry of Economy and Sustainable Development of the Republic of Croatia, 2021) , the Strategy for Adaptation to Climate Change in the Republic of Croatia for the period to 2040 with a view to 2070 (Official Gazette of the Republic of Croatia, 2020) and the Integrated Energy and Climate Plan for the period 2021–2030 (National Energy and Climate Plan – NECP) have been adopted since 2019. However, they have to be revised to be aligned with EGD. The revision of the NECP is launched, as required by Regulation (EU) 2018/1999. The government had to adopt an Action Plan for the Implementation of the Low-Carbon Development Strategy of the Republic of Croatia and an Action Plan for the Implementation of the Climate Change Adaptation Strategy in the Republic of Croatia by July 2021 (Article 127, the Law on Climate Activities and Protection of the Ozone Layer). These programs have yet to be adopted. Binding targets are becoming more ambitious (e.g., from 7 to 16.7%, emission reductions, Council of the EU, 2022), and the gap between Croatian and EU climate policies is increasing, slowing Europeanisation in this policy area.

The governance issues further complicate implementation. At a national level, adaptation should be guided by the five-year action plan. At the county and city levels, climate change mitigation and adaptation and ozone layer protection plans should be part of the environmental program of each county and each large city. The counties must submit data on activities related to low-carbon development and adaptation to climate change every two years. Large cities do not have reporting obligations.[2] As a result, data on the implementation of the programs is partial. The need for better data and the need to make adaptation more systemic are well recognised and included among the goals of the EU Climate Adaptation Strategy (European Commission (2021g). More systemic adaptation includes mainstreaming climate-resilience considerations in all relevant policy fields and at all levels of governance. In Croatia, national-level action plans are missing. Implementation of the city-level plans needs to be systematically monitored. Thus, systemic adaptation, necessary for alignment with the EU policy goals, is yet to be launched.

Croatia is highly exposed and vulnerable to extreme weather conditions. Croatia ranked 31st among 182 countries according to the Global Climate Risk Index 1999–2018 (Germanwatch, 2020). Economic damages per capita from 1980 to 2021 caused by weather- and climate-related extreme events were among the highest in the EU (European Environment Agency [EEA], 2022b).[3] Sectors that are expected to be most exposed to the impact of climate change are water resources, agriculture, forestry, fisheries and aquaculture, biodiversity, energy, tourism and health (Strategy for Adaptation to Climate Change in the Republic of Croatia, OG 47/2020). Due to the importance of tourism for Croatia's economy,[4] climate action is necessary for its economic sustainability. Some local communities recognise this need and implement comprehensive activities in various policy fields, such as settlement and housing arrangements, utility management, spatial and urban planning, protection and improvement of the natural environment, fire protection and civil protection. Also, they participate in initiatives towards climate neutrality (carbon-neutral islands, 'smart cities') and innovative platforms.[5] Generally, Croatia is slow to adopt and implement European climate policy, but some progressive local communities show initiative and ambition.

12.3.3 Energy

A secure, sustainable and competitive energy system is the goal of the EU energy policy. Progress in five dimensions of the Energy Union – energy security, solidarity and trust; a fully integrated internal energy market; energy efficiency; decarbonisation; research, innovation and competitiveness – is necessary to achieve goals. Decarbonisation of the energy system reduces import dependency and contributes to the security of supply. It also makes energy systems more environmentally/climate sustainable. The Clean Energy package[6] was adopted in 2019 to accelerate the EU's transition to a clean energy system. It provides instruments to promote energy-efficient technologies and reduce energy consumption. Defined targets include the share of RES (32% RES in the overall energy mix by 2030), energy efficiency (at least 32.5% to 2030 compared to projections of the expected energy use in 2030) and savings (new energy savings of 0.8% each year).

The EGD increased ambition (40% share of RES). In 2022, because of the Russian invasion of Ukraine and the need to step up European energy independence from fossil fuels as part of the RePowerEU initiative, the Commission proposed further increasing this target to 45% by 2030. In March 2023, a provisional agreement for a binding target for 2030 of at least 42.5%, aiming for 45%, was reached. The 32.5% energy efficiency target (defined by the Energy Efficiency Directive – EED II, EU 2018/2002) translates into the final energy consumption of 956 Mtoe and/or primary energy consumption of 1273 Mtoe in the EU by 2030. Within the Fit for 55 packages, the Commission proposed a 9% increased energy efficiency target of (787 Mtoe in final and 1023 Mtoe in primary energy consumption), while in the context of the REPowerEU plan, this target was further increased to 13% (750 Mtoe in final and 980 Mtoe in primary energy consumption). The negotiations are ongoing. The current energy savings obligation (for 2021–2030) is to achieve new energy savings of 0.8% each year of final energy consumption for 2021–2030. Within the REPowerEU plan, the Commission proposed to nearly double the annual energy savings obligation (in Article 8) by 1.5% of final energy consumption from 2024 to 2030.

In Croatia, key energy policy objectives are secure, affordable and quality energy supply with a gradual reduction of GHG emissions, in line with EU goals (Energy strategy of the Republic of Croatia for the period until 2030, with a view till 2050, Ministry of Economy, Labour and Entrepreneurship of the Republic of Croatia, 2020) . The Energy Strategy considers three energy transition scenarios: business as usual, moderate and accelerated transition. Depending on the scenario, emission reductions by 2030 range from 32.8 to 37.5% and the target was 36.4%. This target was sufficiently ambitious at the time of adoption (as the EU-wide target was 32%) but is significantly below the Fit for 55 target. The Croatian national energy efficiency target is not very ambitious but planned policies and measures for achieving this target are insufficient (European Commission, 2020f).

The Croatian Energy Strategy is technology-neutral and relies on the market for implementation (i.e. private sector investments). There is interest in investments,[7] but lack of implementing regulations, the delayed and partial transposition of EU policies and (perception of) corruption are among the barriers to market development. Implementing regulations of the 2021 Electricity Market Law (Official Gazette of the Republic of Croatia, 2021c) and the Law of Renewable Energy and High-Efficiency Cogeneration (Official Gazette of the Republic of Croatia, 2021a) are still not adopted (as of June 2023).[8] Regarding the transposition of the EU law, in 2021, Croatia's conformity deficit reached 1.9% (compared to the EU average of 1.2%), and Croatia had the second highest conformity deficit in the EU. Overall, 10% of all infringement cases against Croatia (36 out of 361 cases) and 25% of active cases (18 of 74 active cases) in 2021 were related to energy (European Commission, 2021a).

Corruption Perception is high: Croatia was ranked 63rd out of 179 economies in Transparency International's Corruption Perception Index in 2020. The corruption cases in the energy sector, including high officials (such as the privatisation of national oil and gas company INA and 142 MW Krš-Pađene wind park), show that it is more than perception. In 2009, INA's strategic partner, MOL, gained management rights while still having minority ownership. Former Croatian Prime Minister Ivo Sanader was sentenced to six years in jail for accepting a bribe of €10m from MOL (Hopkins, 2019). In 2022, after almost two years of investigations, the indictment was launched against former Secretary of State in the Ministry of Administration

Josipa Rimac for the criminal offences of trading in influence, abuse of position and bribery related to procedure and amount of support granted to biggest wind park in Croatia, Krš-Pađene (USKOK, 2022). In short, the Europeanisation of the energy sector is slow and partial, as there is no sufficient political will and/or capacity to formulate policies aligned with the EU.

12.3.4 Buildings

Buildings are responsible for about 40% of the EU's energy consumption and 36% of greenhouse gas emissions.[9] EU flagship initiative Renovation Wave (European Commission, 2020e) and temporary Recovery and Resilience Facility (RRF) recognise the potential role of buildings in achieving climate neutrality and economic recovery. Achieving an overall 55% GHG reduction target requires a reduction of buildings' GHG emissions by 60%, their final energy consumption by 14% and energy consumption for heating and cooling by 18% compared to 2015 levels (European Commission, 2020g).

Buildings are being renovated at a 0.4 to 1.2% rate in the member states (European Commission, 2020j). In Croatia, the rate is 0.7% (LTRS, 2020). To achieve EGD targets, it is necessary to increase the rate and depth of building renovation significantly. Thus, Renovation Wave aims to at least double the annual energy renovation rate of buildings by 2030 (i.e. to renovate 35 million buildings, which requires 275 billion EUR of additional investment every year compared to the level of investment between 2012 and 2016) and to foster deep renovation.[10] Renovation Wave proposes enabling regulatory (revision of Energy Performance of Buildings Directive [EPBD] and the EED), financing, and other measures to achieve 2030 climate targets.

The proposed revision of EPBD gradually increases minimum energy performance standards from Nearly Zero Energy Building (nZEB) to ZEB. EED identifies the exemplary role of buildings used by public bodies and requires that 3% of the total floor area of central government-owned and occupied be renovated yearly. Revision proposes to expand the scope of the renovation requirement to all buildings owned (and not necessarily occupied) by public bodies and requires that all renovations achieve nearly zero energy levels.

Many policies regulate greening building stock in Croatia: Low-Carbon Development Strategy (prepared by the Ministry of Economy and Sustainable Development), Long-Term Buildings Renovation Strategy (LTRS), Program of Energy Renovation of Public Buildings until 2030, Program for the Development of Green Urban Infrastructure and Program for Circular Management of Space and Buildings (all prepared by the Ministry of Construction, Physical Planning and State Assets), Program for Renovating Buildings that are cultural heritage (prepared by Ministry of Culture and Media). The LTRS until 2050 includes the identification of constraints (legal and financial, as well as lack of knowledge and awareness) and suggests solutions. The lack of legal requirements for reconstruction or energy renovation of the buildings has led to poor maintenance. The potential of multi-apartment buildings to reduce energy consumption and drive sustainable self-generation is not being sufficiently used. The lack of knowledge and awareness can be illustrated by the fact that Croatia still needs to identify cost-optimal minimum requirements for the energy performance of buildings, which resulted in formal proceedings against Croatia for non-alignment with EPBD.

Croatia is aiming for an annual average renovation rate of 1.6%, with specific annual rates gradually increasing from 0.7% in 2021 to 3% in 2030. Estimated investment needs by 2050 to achieve an overall reduction in CO_2 emissions by 81.1% are 1.47 billion EUR per year; cumulative by 2050, almost 105 billion EUR (21.78 billion EUR 2030). National Recovery and Resilience Programme allocates 767 million EUR for investments in decarbonising buildings for 2021–2026. The total six-year allocation of this significant investment program corresponds to half of the annual investment needs, clearly showing that implementation cannot rely only on grants. New financial mechanisms are needed. In addition, it is necessary to raise awareness of the benefits of building renewal and the cost of non-action. Progress in the Europeanisation of this sector, including full implementation of the EU requirements, could support this process.

12.3.5 Circular Economy and New Industrial Policy

CE is an economic model aimed at reducing waste to a minimum by reusing, repairing, refurbishing and recycling existing materials and products. It involves sharing, leasing, reusing and extending the life cycle of products. In practice, it implies reducing waste to a minimum, thus requiring changes in production and consumption. According to the latest Circularity Gap Report 2021, the global economy is only 8.6% circular, i.e. 91.4% of all we use is wasted (World Bank, 2021).

The EU Action Plan for the CE, adopted in 2015, set a comprehensive strategy to promote the CE in the EU. It included measures in key sectors. In 2020, a new CE Action Plan (CEAP) was adopted (European Commission, 2020i) and updated in 2021 (European Commission, 2021e). It outlines the EU's vision for a CE and planned actions to achieve it. CEAP includes measures to promote sustainable production and consumption patterns, reduce waste and pollution and promote resource efficiency and circularity. Relevant sectors include food, construction, electronics, textiles, plastics and waste management. Sustainability and circularity issues are gaining importance in other sectors as well.

The relevant legislation relates to production and waste (e.g., Waste Framework Directive [WFD], Packaging and Packaging Waste Directive [PPWD], Ecodesign Directive) and horizontal principles (Taxonomy Regulation). The Commission also develops technical screening criteria for evaluating contributions to the transition to a CE (European Commission, 2023a).

The EU's Industrial Strategy (European Commission, 2020a, 2021e) aims to promote a competitive, innovative and sustainable European industry capable of addressing global challenges, including climate change. It set actions to support vital industrial ecosystems, such as the automotive, aerospace and energy sectors, and to promote the development of new technologies and business models that support sustainability and resilience (European Commission, 2021d).

Croatia has recognised the importance of managing resources more efficiently to benefit long-term economic and environmental sustainability. For instance, the Partnership Agreement between Croatia and the EU during the period until 2020 identified that 'moving towards a resource-managing economy in an efficient and climate-resilient way can give the possibility of increasing employment, creating new jobs and strengthening social inclusion'. It was recognised that waste management in Croatia has great potential because preventing waste generation, increasing recovery and recycling improve resource management efficiency and increase business opportunities (the Partnership Agreement). Operative Programme Competitiveness and Cohesion 2014–2020 allocated 1.98 billion euros for environmental protection and sustainability of resources, out of which 475 million for waste management, i.e. enabling implementation of the Sustainable Waste Management Strategy and Waste Management Plan. In 2020–2022, the World Bank provided technical support to Croatia to speed progress towards CE targets and incorporate CE approaches into waste management practices. National Recovery and Resilience Plan 2021–2026 provides for the establishment of efficient waste management. Among the Operative Programme Competitiveness and Cohesion priorities, 2021–2027 is fostering a transition to a circular and resource-efficient economy. For this priority, 167 million euros is allocated. Planned activities mainly relate to waste management.

The measures for circularity of the industry are considered within the national Smart Specialisation Strategy (S3). The S3 for the period until 2020 included various aspects of sustainability but did not deal with circularity. The new S3 until 2029 can help implement the EU's Industrial Strategy and CEAP. The draft of the Croatian S3 strategy for the period until 2029 identifies that the CE approach has significant room for improvement in waste management (e.g., increasing the rate of recovery of packaging waste) as well as in production practices and design (for more, see Government of the Republic of Croatia [GRC], 2022). The identified priority areas include smart and clean energy, smart and green mobility, sustainable and circular food and adapted and integrated wood products, which clearly emphasises circularity more than the previous S3.

The importance of circularity has been recognised in Croatia and articulated in national documents, but the circular development model has yet to take off in Croatia (Akbar and Pleština, 2022). Implementation efforts are focused on waste management. Significant EU funding was available in the 2014–2020 financial period, but implementing reforms is not systematic (Boromisa et al., 2022).

12.3.6 Mobility

Transport emissions represent around one-quarter of the EU's total GHG emissions. Thus, the modernisation and greening of the fleets and infrastructure provide an opportunity to make transport more sustainable and competitive. Cities have only partially followed EU guidelines developed within the Urban Mobility Package in

2013, so investments into more sustainable urban mobility remained limited. Some cities have increased the quality and quantity of public transport. However, there is no clear trend of switching to more sustainable modes of transport, nor has there been a significant reduction in the use of passenger cars.

The Sustainable and Smart Mobility Strategy (European Commission, 2021c) seeks to reduce the carbon footprint of the EU's transport sector by 90% until 2050. It includes measures for more sustainability (uptake of zero-emission vehicles, greening freight transport, creating zero-emission airports and ports), smart (improving multimodal mobility) and resilient transport (affordable and accessible transport, improved safety) (European Commission, 2020b). The 2030 milestones include

- At least 30 million zero-emission cars on European roads;
- 100 European climate-neutral cities;
- Doubling high-speed rail traffic across Europe;
- Carbon-neutral scheduled collective travel for journeys under 500 km;
- Large-scale deployment of automated mobility;
- Market-ready zero-emission marine vessels.

A transport component of the RePower package focuses on promoting more economical driving and shifting to more public transport and active mobility.

Croatia's Transport Development Strategy (2017–2030) is generally coherent with the EU goals. Its objectives relate to public transport and zero-emission modes, road transport, railway transport, air transport, maritime transport, inland waterways and cross-sectoral considerations. Principal investments are related to road infrastructure, and implementing decarbonisation efforts is slower than planned. With a 6.6% share of renewables (including liquid biofuels, biomethane and 'green' electricity) in transport, Croatia has yet to reach its 2020 target (10%).

In Croatia's Recovery Plan, 728 million euros is allocated for sustainable mobility. This includes upgrading railway lines, autonomous electric taxis with supporting infrastructure adapted for people with disabilities, installing 1,300 charging stations for electric vehicles and introducing zero-emission vehicles and vessels. However, the policies on increasing sustainability and decreasing transport emissions must be clarified, e.g., the Croatian Hydrogen Strategy for the period until 2050 (Official Gazette 40/2022) outlines the use of hydrogen in transport but does not include an investment or financial plan.

12.3.7 Agriculture

The EGD increases green ambitions for the 2023–2027 Common Agricultural Policy (CAP). The new CAP and the Farm to Fork Strategy (F2F) aim to address challenges relating to environmental sustainability, socio-economic equity, health and nutrition, trade and globalisation. F2F's Strategy aims to create a more sustainable and healthy food policy by promoting sustainable farming practices, reducing food waste and improving the quality of food (European Commission, 2019). The

Strategy includes a social aspect, through its aim to secure access to sufficient, nutritious and affordable food, as well as an environmental aspect, through its aim to ensure that the food production and supply chain has a neutral or positive environmental impact. Specifically, the environmental aims are 'that the freshwater and sea-based resources on which the food system depends are preserved and restored. That land, soil, water, air, plant and animal health and welfare are protected. That biodiversity loss is reversed' (European Commission, 2020b). The greening of agriculture includes a revision of the Sustainable Use of Pesticides Directive[11] and reinforcement of environmental risk assessment for pesticides, enhanced provision for and promotion of alternative control techniques, such as crop rotation, mechanical weeding, use of biological pesticides, recycling organic waste into renewable fertilisers, a reduction of nutrient losses by at least 50%, development of sustainable fertilisation techniques (European Commission, 2020b). Reducing food waste, pollution and damage to biodiversity throughout the whole value chain is necessary to increase the sustainability and efficiency of agriculture.

The Croatian agricultural sector lags behind the EU average in competitiveness and productivity. It contributes to 3.3% GDP (1.7% within the EU) and 6.2% employment (4.5 within the EU). Significant social challenges exist as rural areas suffer from negative demographic trends, depopulation and lack of basic infrastructure. Small family agricultural holdings characterise Croatian agriculture. Croatia has more than 134,000 farms; almost 70% cover less than 5 hectares, while the average farm manages about 11 hectares of land. The production structure is dominated by low-value crops (grains are produced on about 60% of arable land), which limits higher land productivity. R&D investments are low (about 0.81% GDP compared to 2% in the EU, data for 2008–2017).

The Agricultural Strategy of the Republic of Croatia (OG 26/2022) defines four strategic goals: (i) increasing the productivity and competitiveness of the agri-food sector; (ii) strengthening the sustainability and resilience of agricultural production to climate change; (iii) restoring the rural economy and improving living conditions in rural areas; and (iv) fostering innovation in the agri-food sector.

Achieving these goals requires addressing structural constraints (low productivity, competitiveness and investment levels) and risks (climate change) while protecting the good state of the soil and climate. Increasing competitiveness and addressing social issues are key challenges. In this respect, greening agriculture in Croatia means primarily greening the jobs, i.e. making them decent and sustainable.

12.3.8 Zero Pollution Action Plan

The EU Action Plan Towards Zero Pollution of Air, Water and Soil sets goals to reduce pollution to levels that are not harmful to health and natural ecosystems, respecting planetary boundaries and creating a toxic-free environment (European Commission, 2021f). It defines the following 2030 targets:

- Improving air quality to reduce the number of premature deaths caused by air pollution by 55%;

- Improving water quality by reducing waste, plastic marine litter (by 50%) and microplastics released into the environment (by 30%);
- Improving soil quality by reducing nutrient losses and chemical pesticide use by 50%;
- Reducing by 25% the EU ecosystems where air pollution threatens biodiversity;
- Reducing the share of people chronically disturbed by transport noise by 30%; and
- Significantly reducing waste generation and by 50% residual municipal waste.

Here, we present the main issues related to air, water and soil. Biodiversity is addressed in a dedicated subsection, and waste is in the CE and new industrial policy section.

Air pollution is recognised as the most significant risk to human health in the EU. It causes serious illnesses such as asthma, cardiovascular problems and lung cancer, and vulnerable groups are affected the most. In 2020, 96% of the EU urban population was exposed to levels of fine particulate matter above the health-based guideline set by the World Health Organization (EEA, 2022a). Air pollution damages the environment and ecosystems through excess nitrogen pollution and acid rain. It creates economic costs, as it leads to lost working days and high healthcare costs.

The clean air policy is based on ambient air quality standards, reducing air pollution emissions and emissions standards for key sources of pollution. The zero-pollution action plan sets the target to reduce the number of premature deaths due to exposure to fine particulate matter by 55% by 2030, compared to the 2005 level. In 2020, exposure to concentrations of fine particulate matter above the 2021 World Health Organization guideline level resulted in 238,000 premature deaths in the EU-27 (4,128 in Croatia). This is a 45% decrease compared to 2005. Therefore, a revision of the ambient air quality directives plans to align the air quality standards more closely with WHO recommendations and to tackle air pollution at source (e.g., pollution from agriculture, industry, transport, buildings and energy supply). Croatia complies with current non methane volatile organic compounds (NMVOC), NO_x and SO_2 targets but has difficulties meeting targets regarding NH_3 emissions (EEA, 2023).

EU water policy aims to protect water resources and fresh and saltwater ecosystems and ensure clean drinking and bathing water. Generally, water quality throughout the EU is highly standard and continuously monitored and improved. Most EU countries' population is mainly connected to the water supply network (93% in Croatia). At the EU level, over 90% of urban wastewater is dealt with in line with EU standards. In Croatia, the challenge is an underdeveloped and non-functional public drainage system, so several built treatment plants (28) could not operate.[12]

Croatia is generally aligned with the requirements of the EU water directives (primarily the Water Framework Directive), the exception being a register of impoundments. Small abstractions and small wastewater discharges are exempt from controls. Rules for controlling diffuse pollution from agriculture are implemented only in Nitrate Vulnerable Zones. Financing is identified as a crucial barrier to the implementation of planned measures.

In the EU, 95% of food comes from soil. Europe's land and soils are dramatically degrading, and 60–70% of soils are unhealthy. Soil degradation leads to yearly losses of 50 billion EUR. The EU Soil Strategy for 2030 aims to improve soil health and sets the vision to have all soils in healthy condition by 2050 and to make protecting, restoring and sustainably using soils the norm. Planned Soil Health Law will provide a comprehensive legal framework for soil protection. Until 2050 following goals are set (see European Commission, 2021a):

- All EU soil ecosystems are healthy and more resilient;
- There is no net land take, and soil pollution is reduced to levels that are not harmful to people's health or ecosystems; and
- Protecting soils, managing them sustainably and restoring degraded soils is a common standard.

Planned actions include

- Tabling a legislative proposal and legally binding targets on soil health by 2023 and providing additional guidance on best practices in promoting its agenda;
- Making sustainable soil management the new normal by proposing a scheme for land owners to get their soils tested for free, promoting sustainable soil management through the CAP and sharing best practices;
- Considering proposing legally binding objectives to limit drainage of wetlands and organic soils and to restore managed and drained peatlands to mitigate and adapt to climate change;
- Investigating streams of excavated soils and assessing the need and potential for a legally binding soil passport' to boost the CE and enhance the reuse of clean soil;
- Restoring degraded soils and remediating contaminated sites;
- Preventing desertification by developing a standard methodology to assess desertification and land degradation;
- Increasing research, data and monitoring of soil; and
- Mobilising the necessary societal engagement and financial resources.

In Croatia, the most widespread degradation problems are soil erosion by water and soil compaction. Together with soil salinity and soil contamination, these processes decrease the soil's ability to provide ecosystem services in quantity and quality. Croatia still needs to establish comprehensive monitoring of its soils. Thus, currently, the less visible degradation processes in Croatia (microplastics, metal contamination) are not recognised as an important threat to soil quality and productivity (Bogunović et al., 2022). Croatia plans greater investments to reduce the population's exposure to environmental pollution: water, air and soil (EEA, 2020).

12.3.9 Biodiversity

The EU Biodiversity Strategy for 2030 outlines a plan to protect nature and reverse the degradation of ecosystems (European Commission, 2020c). Forests are identified as particularly important for biodiversity, and hence, the Biodiversity Strategy for 2030 is accompanied by the New EU Forest Strategy for 2030 (European Commission, 2021b). The 2030 Biodiversity strategy identifies the main drivers of biodiversity loss (land and sea use change, overexploitation of natural resources, climate change, pollution and invasive alien species) and benefits of protecting and restoring biodiversity (for the agriculture and food production sector, potential economic benefits for businesses, increased resilience to environmental changes).

The commitments for the period until 2030 relate to

- Share of legally protected land and sea areas (30% of the EU's land area and 30% of the EU's sea area) and integrate ecological corridors as part of a true Trans-European Nature Network;
- Strict protection of at least a third of the EU's protected areas, including all remaining EU primary and old-growth forests;
- Effective management of protected areas requires clear conservation objectives and measures and appropriate monitoring;
- Propose legally binding EU nature-restoration targets in 2021, subject to an impact assessment;
- Restore significant areas of degraded and carbon-rich ecosystems;
- Ensure that habitats and species show no deterioration and that at least 30% of those in unfavourable conservation status reach favourable status, or at least show a positive trend;
- Reverse the decline in pollinators;
- Reduce the risk and use of chemical pesticides by 50% and reduce the use of more hazardous pesticides by 50%;
- Manage at least 25% of agricultural land under organic farming and significantly increase the uptake of agro-ecological practices;
- Remediate significant areas of contaminated soil sites;
- Plant 3 billion trees for biodiversity, according to ecological principles;
- Restore at least 25,000 km of free-flowing rivers;
- Reduce by 50% the number of 'red list' species threatened by invasive alien species;
- Reduce losses of nutrients from fertilisers by 50%, resulting in a reduction in the use of fertilisers of at least 20%;
- Support cities with more than 20,000 inhabitants to put in place ambitious urban greening plans by the end of 2021;
- Eliminate or minimise the harmful effects of fishing and extraction activities on sensitive species and habitats; and
- Eliminate or reduce the by-catch of marine species to a level that allows their recovery and conservation.

In addition, the New EU Forest Strategy aims to ensure that the amount of used wood remains within the sustainability limits and is optimally utilised in line with the cascading principle and the CE approach. Priorities for wood use in line with the cascading principle, which was already enshrined in the EU Forest Strategy 2014–2020, are as follows: (i) use for wood-based products, (ii) extending their service life, (iii) reuse, (iv) recycling, (v) bio-energy and (vi) disposal. The Strategy is accompanied by a roadmap for planting at least 3 billion additional trees in the EU by 2030, which is required for sustainable re- and afforestation. The roadmap defines seven milestones that enable progress monitoring. Implementation is supported by the 8th Environment Action Programme (Official Journal of the European Union, 2022), whose priority objectives include preserving and restoring ecosystems and biodiversity.

The primary strategic document for nature protection in Croatia is the Nature Protection Strategy and Action Plan of Croatia from 2017 to 2025 (Official Gazette of the Republic of Croatia, 2017). The Strategy brings five strategic goals, developed in line with the Strategic Plan for Biodiversity 2011–2020 and the EU Biodiversity Strategy until 2020. Thus, the new policies (after 2025) should consider evolving the EU framework and strengthen implementing instruments. The Natura 2000 covers 36.73% of the land territory in Croatia and 15.42% of the coastal sea. It consists of 743 conservation areas important for species and habitat types (Sites of Community Importance – SCI) and 38 conservation areas important for birds (Special Protection Areas - SPA). Around 26% of the ecological network in Croatia is protected in one of the nine national categories of protected areas (87% of protected areas are included in the Natura 2000 ecological network). Croatia is developing almost 200 local management plans for the protected and/or ecological network areas.

12.3.10 Financing

Implementing the EGD requires reforms and significant public and private investments. The scale of the investment challenge is beyond the capacity of the public sector alone. To attract private investment, developing an enabling investment environment is necessary. It requires stable, predictable and coherent rules. Capacities for project preparation and implementation should be systematically strengthened. Banks (including central, development and commercial banks) and the financial sector are crucial. They can re-orient investments towards more sustainable technologies and businesses, sustainably finance growth over the long term and contribute to creating a low-carbon, climate-resilient and CE (see, for instance, Mack, 2023).

In 2020, the Commission presented the EGD I Investment Plan, which should mobilise at least 1 trillion euros of sustainable investments by 2030, of which 503 billion from the EU budget and about 114 billion euros of national co-financing. The rest should be provided from other private and public sources.[13] The Investment Plan will create an enabling framework to facilitate and stimulate the public and private investments needed for the transition to a climate-neutral, green, competitive and inclusive economy.

According to the Low-Carbon Development, necessary investments for 55% emissions reduction by 2030 are estimated at 33.8 billion euros. EU funding is identified as the primary source of funding. The total funding available for Croatia under the current Multi-year Financial Framework and RRF is about 21 billion euros (Kotarski, 2022).[14] Roughly 40% of RRF is dedicated to the green agenda and about 30% of the Cohesion Policy Funds, indicating a huge financial gap. This is further complicated because the absorption of funds is slower than planned. Thus, it is necessary to improve the absorption capacity and provide additional sources of financing. Improving absorption capacity requires prioritising and allocating resources (human and financial) in line with priorities, as well as thorough and timely preparation of projects and institutional structures for implementation and monitoring. Additional sources of financing might include new financing mechanisms and instruments of sustainable finance (e.g., green bonds).

12.3.11 Fair Transition

The EGD promotes fair transition for people and regions. In 2021, the Commission proposed a Council Recommendation on a fair transition towards climate neutrality as part of the Fit for 55 package (European Commission, 2021d). It guides member states in addressing the social and labour aspects of the green transition. The green agenda is the most challenging for people and households dependent on fossil fuels and most affected by the green transition, notably those already in vulnerable situations. This includes low- and lower-middle-income households, who spend a high share of their income on essential services such as energy, transport and housing, as well as micro, small and medium-sized enterprises.

The potential for job creation is estimated at 1 million additional quality jobs in the EU by 2030 and 2 million by 2050. New job opportunities are expected in the key sectors addressed in EGD: construction, sustainable transport, renewable energy production or the CE (including repair and reuse business models). The proposed Council Recommendation encourages member states to support people who will transition into new jobs and must adapt their skill set through training.

The Just Transition Mechanism (JTM) is a pivotal tool to support the most affected regions and alleviate the transition's socio-economic impact. Just Transition Fund provides dedicated funding for the most affected regions, defined by territorial just transition plans. Based on the specific challenges and development needs relevant to each territory, these plans define objectives to be met by 2030, the types of operations envisaged and specify governance mechanisms.

Croatia's Just Transition Fund with approved 179 million euros will support transition in Sisak-Moslavina and Istria counties. Sisak-Moslavina County is among one of the most deprived regions. It hosts, among others, a chemical company and a refinery. It is estimated that the transition of the refinery will affect around 7% of the total population employed in the county with the highest unemployment rate registered in Croatia. On the other hand, Istria is one of the most prosperous regions in Croatia but is also facing challenges related to green transition. Its coal power plant produces 6% of the energy output for the whole country and the cement industry (European Commission, 2020h). The EU-supported investments in Istria are estimated to create 300 direct and 300 indirect jobs and to reskill 200 people, adapting the local workforce to new green jobs and providing local firms with the skills they need for economic transformation (European Commission, 2022).

Existing estimates of implementation reforms' social (and employment) impacts are not comprehensive. The updated Croatian Energy and Climate Plan estimates that 105,000 additional jobs could be created due to the implementation of the EU green agenda in 2024–2030, along with investments of 5.2 billion euros. For every million euros invested in energy renovations for the construction sector, on average, 18 new jobs are created in the EU. In the Republic of Croatia, this number is 29, 11.5 direct, 9.5 indirect and 8 induced (BPIE, 2020). Thus, coherent implementation of green strategies and policies could lead to a fair transition, provided that implementing capacities are systematically developed (cf. Dozol et al., 2023).

12.4 Conclusion

The EU Green Deal defines the EU green agenda. It includes long-term policies, legislation and targets dealing with the economy, society and environment, i.e. sustainability. Generally, adopting and implementing key policies in Croatia is slower than planned. The main challenges are a lack of sense of urgency, lack of political will, weaknesses in the strategic planning process, insufficient institutional capacities for preparing and implementing policies and investment projects, and inadequate financing. Delays in preparing and implementing strategic documents, laws and action plans and implementing projects directly decrease absorption capacity for the EU funding. Lack of financing further slows down reforms and increases risks of infringement procedures. Thus, it is necessary to ensure the enforcement of regulations by aligning them with the current needs and capacities. Also, more active participation in community-level policy-making would contribute to the self-understanding of citizens as European. The success of Europeanisation in areas of green agenda might be evaluated not merely as adherence to EU norms and reducing the differences between old and new countries, but also as active participation in policy-making.

The problems related to Croatia's weak capacity for policy-making and implementation have long been known but only partially addressed. For instance, within the EU European Semester, the Council of the EU recommended that Croatia strengthen monitoring of potential commitments at central and local levels, to reduce the territorial fragmentation of public administration and simplify the functional distribution of competencies. Also, the Council recommended increasing the capacity of competent authorities to develop and implement public projects and policies. However, the policy response to these recommendations has been slow and inadequate.

Europeanisation of EU green policies in Croatia requires political will. EU policies certainly stimulate domestic policy actions, but more is needed to achieve the domestic goals of the EU green agenda. Political self-interest is an essential source of political will. Therefore, it is necessary to underline the political benefits that politicians and bureaucrats can derive from supporting the green agenda. This includes using the allocated funds to expose political opponents and addressing the fear of losing power. Under such circumstances, it is necessary to advocate for greening reforms and show politicians that a green agenda can enhance their popularity and power. Generating demand for green reforms among citizens, civil society and the private sector can also contribute to the Europeanisation of the EU green agenda. Active and engaged citizens are crucial elements for promoting the green agenda. Providing information, education and training for citizens is essential to boost the interest and confidence of key policy stakeholders in the success of these reforms.

Notes

1 Achieving a 35% reduction of GHG by 2030 compared to 1990 (in all sectors) requires investments of 13.8 billion euros. Achieving a 55% GHG reduction requires an additional 20 billion euros (i.e. 33.8 billion). According to the Low-Carbon Development Strategy, achieving up to 44.8% GHG reductions by 2030 is feasible.

2 There are 21 counties and 17 large cities in Croatia. The large city is defined as an economic, financial, cultural, health, transport and scientific centre of development of the broader environment with more than 35,000 inhabitants. The capital, the City of Zagreb, is also a county with reporting obligations.

3 The share of damages exceeds 0.25 % of GDP annually. Only 3% of damages is ensured. For comparison, more than 50% of damages are ensured in Denmark and Norway, 56 and 55 %, respectively (EEA, 2022b).

4 In 2019 (i.e. just before the pandemic), the share of tourism in GDP was 25%. It fell to 9% in 2020 and reached 15% in 2022 (Statista, 2023).

5 The Island of Krk adopted a goal to become a climate-neutral island by 2030; the city of Split participates in the Smart city initiative, and Zagreb is part of the programme "100 climate-neutral cities by 2030".

6 The Package included eight legislative acts covering a range of issues, including energy efficiency (Energy Efficiency Directive [EU] 2018/2002), renewable energy (Renewable Energy Directive [EU] 2018/2001), electricity market design (Internal electricity market – Regulation [EU] 2019/943, standard rules for the internal electricity market – Directive [EU] 2019/944) and governance of the Energy Union (Governance of the Energy Union and Climate Action [EU] Regulation 2018/1999).

7 In the period 2021–2022, the Ministry of Economy and Sustainable Development received 216 expressions of interest for implementation of tenders for issuing energy approvals with a total planned installed capacity of 5953,506 MW (MINGOR, 2022)

8 For example, public consultations on Decree on criteria for public tenders for energy approval and issuing energy approval were launched in June 2023. According to the Electricity market law, the government was supposed to adopt this regulation in January 2022 (three months after entry into force of the Law).

9 These figures refer to the use and operation of buildings, including indirect emissions in the power and heat sector, not their complete life cycle. The embodied carbon in

construction is estimated to account for about 10% of total yearly greenhouse gas emissions (European Commission, 2020e).

10 Deep renovation includes energy efficiency measures for the envelope and technical systems and reducing the annual heating and primary energy consumption by at least 50% compared to pre-renovation energy consumption.

11 Sustainable Use of Pesticides Directive: https://eur-lex.europa.eu/legal-content/EN/TXT/PDF/?uri=CELEX:02009L0128-20091125&from=EN

12 River Basin Management Plan 2016–2021 (Hrvatske vode, 2015).

13 These assessments are indicative because they did not consider, for example, investment needs in climate change adaptation or other environmental issues, such as biodiversity. Also, not included are the public investments needed to meet the social costs of transition and the costs of inaction. The Covid-19 pandemic and the halt of the economy have increased investment needs.

14 Within the 2021–2027 financial period, EU funds allocated to the Republic of Croatia amount to almost 14 billion euros from the Multi-year Financial Framework and a little over 11 billion euros from the Next Generation EU. Within the Recovery and Resilience Facility, 9.9 billion euros is available for Croatia: 6.4 billion euros in grants and 3.6 billion in loans until 2026. However, the Croatian Recovery and Resilience Plan relies solely on grants. The Partnership Agreement allows Croatia to use 9 billion euros in grants from EU funds until 2027.

References

Akbar, S. and Pleština, S. (2022) Rethinking Waste: How a Circular Economy Can Help Croatia Achieve a More Sustainable Future. World Bank.

Bogunovic, I., Filipovic, L., Filipovic, V. and Kisic, I. (2022) 'Agricultural Soil Degradation in Croatia', in P. Pereira, M. Muñoz-Rojas, I. Bogunovic and W. Zhao (eds.) *Impact of Agriculture on Soil Degradation II. A European Perspective*. Cham: Springer, pp. 1–34. DOI:10.1007/698_2022_919

Boromisa, A. (2020) *Tko će i kako provoditi Europski zeleni plan?* Fes: Zagreb.

Boromisa, A., Golubovac, N. and Vetma, N. (2022) 'Governance of the waste management in Croatia', *Journal of Legal, Ethical and Regulatory Issues*, 25, pp. 1–18.

BPIE (2020) Building Renovation – A Kick-Starter for the EU Recovery. Available at: www.renovate-europe.eu/wp-content/uploads/2020/06/BPIE-Research-Layout_FINALPDF_08.06.pdf (15.11.2023).

Council of the EU (2022) Paquet "Ajustement à l'objectif 55". Proposition de RÈGLEMENT DU PARLEMENT EUROPÉEN ET DU CONSEIL modifiant le règlement (UE) 2018/842 relatif aux reductions annuelles contraignantes des émissions de gaz à effet de serre par les États membres de 2021 à 2030 contribuant à l'action pour le climat afin de respecter les engagements pris dans le cadre de l'accord de Paris. – Orientation Générale. Available at: https://eur-lex.europa.eu/legal-content/EN/TXT/?uri=CELLAR:1ca552fd-f79f-11ec-b94a-01aa75ed71a1 (15.11.2023).

Dozol, A., Ambasz, D., Shmis, T., Boromisa, A.-M., Brajkovic, L., Kotnik, J., Marasović, D., Ramljak, D. and Ustinova., M. (2023) *Greening Public Human Development Buildings in Croatia: Support for the Implementation of the European Green Deal in the Croatian Health and Education Sectors.* Washington, DC: World Bank Group.

Eptisa Adria (2017) Draft Action Plan (2017) for the implementation of the Low Carbon Development Strategy. Available at: http://prilagodba-klimi.hr/wp-content/uploads/docs/Akcijski%20plan%202019-2023.pdf (01.04.2023).

European Commission (2019) *The European Green Deal*. COM (2019) 640 final. Brussels.
European Commission (2020a) A European industrial strategy: A new industrial strategy for a globally competitive, green and digital Europe. Available at: https://ec.europa.eu/commission/presscorner/detail/en/fs_20_425 (15.11.2023).
European Commission (2020b) Commission Staff Working Document, Commission Recommendations for Croatia's CAP Strategic Plan accompanying the document Communication from the Commission to the European Parliament, the Council, the European Economic and Social Committee and the Committee of the Regions Recommendations to the Member States as Regards their Strategic plan for the Common Agricultural Policy. SWD/2020/384 final. Brussels.
European Commission (2020c) Communication from the Commission to the European Parliament, the Council, the European Economic and Social Committee and the Committee of the Regions Stepping up Europe's 2030 Climate Ambition. Investing in a climate-neutral future for the benefit of our people. COM/2020/562 final. Brussels.
European Commission (2020d) Commission Implementing Decision (EU) 2020/2126 of 16 December 2020 on setting out the annual emission allocations of the Member States for the period from 2021 to 2030 pursuant to Regulation (EU) 2018/842 of the European Parliament and of the Council. (Text with EEA relevance), OJ L 426/2020.
European Commission (2020e) A Renovation Wave for Europe – Greening our buildings, creating jobs, improving lives. Available at: https://eur-lex.europa.eu/legal-content/EN/TXT/HTML/?uri=CELEX:52020DC0662 (15.11.2023).
European Commission (2020f) Commission Staff Working Document, assessment of the final national energy and climate plan of Croatia. SWD (2020) 910 final. Brussels.
European Commission (2020g) Commission Staff Working Document. Impact assessment. Accompanying the document communication from the commission to the European Parliament, the Council, the European Economic and social committee and the Committee of the Regions. Stepping up Europe's 2030 Climate Ambition Investing in a Climate-neutral Future for the Benefit of Our People. SWD (2020) 176 final. Brussels.
European Commission (2020h) 2020 European Semester: Overview of Investment Guidance on the Just Transition Fund 2021–2027 Per Member State (Annex D). Available at: https://commission.europa.eu/system/files/2020-02/annex_d_crs_2020_en.pdf (15.11.2023).
European Commission (2020i) Communication from the Commission to the European Parliament, the Council, the European Economic and Social Committee and the Committee of the Regions. A New Circular Economy Action Plan for a Cleaner and More Competitive Europe. COM/2020/98 final. Brussels.
European Commission (2020j) Department: Energy – In Focus: Energy Efficiency in Buildings. Available at: https://commission.europa.eu/system/files/2020-03/in_focus_energy_efficiency_in_buildings_en.pdf (24.03.2023).
European Commission (2021a) Infringement Decisions. Available at: https://ec.europa.eu/atwork/applying-eu-law/infringements-proceedings/infringement_decisions/ (28.03.2021).
European Commission (2021b) Communication from the Commission to the European Parliament, the Council, the European Economic and Social Committee and the Committee of the Regions, New EU Forest Strategy for 2030, COM/2021/572 final. Brussels.
European Commission (2021c) Sustainable and Smart Mobility Strategy. Available at: www.europarl.europa.eu/RegData/etudes/BRIE/2021/659455/EPRS_BRI(2021)659455_EN.pdf (17.11.2023).
European Commission (2021d) Proposal for a Council Recommendation on Ensuring a Fair Transition towards Climate Neutrality. Strasbourg, COM (2021) 801 final. 2021/0421 (NLE)

European Commission (2021e) Communication "Updating the 2020 New Industrial Strategy: Building a Stronger Single Market for Europe's Recovery". Available at: https://ec.europa.eu/commission/presscorner/detail/en/ip_21_1884 (17.11.2023).

European Commission (2021f) EU Action Plan: "Towards a Zero Pollution for Air, Water and Soil" (and annexes). Available at: https://environment.ec.europa.eu/strategy/zero-pollution-action-plan_en#:~:text=Documents-,Objectives,creating%20a%20toxic%2Dfree%20environment (17.11.2023).

European Commission (2021g) Communication from the Commission to the European Parliament, the Council, the European Economic and Social Committee and the Committee of the Regions Forging a Climate-resilient Europe – the New EU Strategy on Adaptation to Climate Change. COM/2021/82 final. Brussels.

European Commission (2022) Investing in Skills and Jobs for the Green Transition in Croatia. Available at: https://ec.europa.eu/european-social-fund-plus/en/news/skills-and-jobs-green-transition-croatia (17.11.2023).

European Commission (2023a) *Annex 2. ANNEX to the COMMISSION DELEGATED REGULATION (EU) .../...supplementing Regulation (EU) 2020/852 of the European Parliament and of the Council by establishing the technical screening criteria for determining the conditions under which an economic activity qualifies as contributing substantially to the sustainable use and protection of water and marine resources, to the transition to a circular economy, to pollution prevention and control or to the protection and restoration of biodiversity and ecosystems and for determining whether that economic activity causes no significant harm to any of the other environmental objectives and amending Delegated Regulation (EU) 2021/2139 and Delegated Regulation (EU) 2021/2178.* Available at: https://eur-lex.europa.eu/legal-content/EN/TXT/?uri=PI_COM%3AC%282023%293851 (17.11.2023).

European Commission (2023b) Fit for 55. Delivering on the Proposals. Available at: https://commission.europa.eu/strategy-and-policy/priorities-2019-2024/european-green-deal/delivering-european-green-deal/fit-55-delivering-proposals_en#:~:text=Under%20the%20European%20Climate%20Law,fit%20to%20meet%20this%20target (17.11.2023).

European Environment Agency (EEA) (2020) Croatia Country Profile – SDGs and the Environment. Available at: www.eea.europa.eu/themes/sustainability-transitions/sustainable-development-goals-and-the/country-profiles/croatia (15.11.2023).

European Environment Agency (EEA) (2022a) Air Quality in Europe. Available at: www.eea.europa.eu/publications/air-quality-in-europe-2022 (17.11.2023).

European Environment Agency (EEA) (2022b) Economic Losses from Climate-related Extremes in Europe. Available at: www.eea.europa.eu/en/analysis/indicators/economic-losses-from-climate-related (15.11.2023).

European Environmental Agency (EEA) (2023) Croatia – air pollution country fact sheet. Available at: www.eea.europa.eu/themes/air/country-fact-sheets/2023-country-fact-sheets/croatia-air-pollution-country (15.11.2023)

Germanwatch (2020) Global Climate Risk Index 2020. Available at: www.germanwatch.org/en/17307 (17.11.2023).

GRC – Government of the Republic of Croatia (2022) Savjetovanje o Prijedlogu nacrta Strategije pametne specijalizacije do 2029. Available at: https://mzo.gov.hr/vijesti/savjetovanje-o-prijedlogu-nacrta-strategije-pametne-specijalizacije-do-2029-s3/5203 (17.11.2023).

Hopkins, V. (2019). Former Croatian PM convicted of corruption in privatisation case. *Financial Times*. www.ft.com/content/caf797ec-2af2-11ea-bc77-65e4aa615551 (17.11.2023).

Hrvatske vode (2015) Plan upravljanja vodnim područjima 2016-2021. Available at: https://voda.hr/sites/default/files/2022-05/nacrt_plana_upravljanja_vodnim_podrucjima_za_razdoblje_2016._-_2021.pdf

IPCC (2021) Climate Change 2021. The Physical Science Basis IPCC. Available at: www.ipcc.ch/report/ar6/wg1/ (17.11.2023).

IPCC (2022) AR6 Climate change 2022. Impacts, Adaptation and Vulnerability. IPCC. Available at: www.ipcc.ch/report/ar6/wg2/ (17.11.2023).

Jordan, A., Benson, D., Wurzel, R. and Zito, A. (2012) 'Environmental Policy: Governing by Multiple Policy Instruments', in J. Richardson (ed.) *Constructing a Policy-Making State? Policy Dynamics in the EU*. Oxford: Oxford University Press, pp. 104–124.

Jordan, A. and Liefferink, D. (eds.) (2004) *Environmental Policy in Europe: The Europeanization of National Environmental Policy*. London: Routledge.

Kotarski, K. (2022) *The Effect of Long-Term EU Budget 2021–2027 and Recovery Package on Croatia's Post-Pandemic Economic Recovery*. Emerics, KIEP, South Korea.

Ladrech, R. (1994) 'Europeanization of domestic politics and institutions: The case of France', *Journal of Common Market Studies*, 32(1), pp. 69–88.

LTRS (2020) Dugoročna strategija obnove nacionalnog fonda zgrada do 2050. godine. Available at: https://energy.ec.europa.eu/system/files/2021-01/hr_ltrs_2020_0.pdf (17.11.2023).

Mack, S. (2023) 'Get your priorities right. Europe must not underestimate the role of banks for the green transition. Hertie School Gmbh', *Jacques Delors Centre*. Berlin. Available at: www.delorscentre.eu/en/publications/banks-role-for-green-transition (17.11.2023).

McCormick, J. (2010) *Razumjeti Europsku uniju (4th edition)*. Zagreb: Mate.

MINGOR (2022) Popis zahtjeva za izdavanje EO. Available at: https://mingor.gov.hr/UserDocsImages/UPRAVA%20ZA%20ENERGETIKU/Popis%20zahtjeva%20za%20izdavanje%20EO.pdf (17.11.2023).

Ministry of Economy and Sustainable Development of the Republic of Croatia (2021) Low Carbon Development Strategy of the Republic of Croatia until 2030, with a View to 2050 (OG 63/2021). Available at: https://mingor.gov.hr/UserDocsImages/klimatske_aktivnosti/odrzivi_razvoj/NUS/lts_nus_eng.pdf (17.11.2023).

Ministry of Economy, Labour and Entrepreneurship of the Republic of Croatia (2020) Energy strategy of the Republic of Croatia for the period until 2030, with a view till 2050 (OG 25/2020). Available at: https://mingor.gov.hr/UserDocsImages/NASLOVNE%20FOTOGRAFIJE%20I%20KORI%C5%A0TENI%20LOGOTIPOVI/doc/energy_strategy_of_the_republic_of_croatia.pdf (15.11.2023).

Mus, J. (2021) '2030 National Development Strategy of the Republic of Croatia. Deepening integration with the EU', *IES Commentaries*, 334. Available at: https://ies.lublin.pl/en/comments/2030-national-development-strategy-of-the-republic-of-croatia-deepening-integration-with-the-eu/ (17.11.2023).

Official Gazette of the Republic of Croatia (2017) Nature Protection Strategy and Action Plan of the Republic of Croatia for the period 2017–2025 (OG 72/2017). Available at: https://narodne-novine.nn.hr/clanci/sluzbeni/2017_07_72_1712.html (17.11.2023).

Official Gazette of the Republic of Croatia (2019) Law on Climate Activities and Protection of the Ozone Layer (OG 127/2019). Available at: https://narodne-novine.nn.hr/clanci/sluzbeni/2019_12_127_2554.html (17.11.2023).

Official Gazette of the Republic of Croatia (2020) Strategy for Adaptation to Climate Change in the Republic of Croatia for the Period to 2040 with a View to 2070 (OG 46/2020). Available at: https://narodne-novine.nn.hr/clanci/sluzbeni/2020_04_46_921.html (17.11.2023).

Official Gazette of the Republic of Croatia (2021a) Law of Renewable Energy and High Efficiency Cogeneration (OG 138/2021). Available at: https://narodne-novine.nn.hr/clanci/sluzbeni/2021_12_138_2272.html (17.11.2023).

Official Gazette of the Republic of Croatia (2021b) National Development Strategy of the Republic of Croatia until 2030 (OG 13/2021). Available at: https://narodne-novine.nn.hr/clanci/sluzbeni/2021_02_13_230.html (17.11.2023).

Official Gazette of the Republic of Croatia (2021c) Zakon o tržištu električne energije / Electricity Market Law (OG 111/21). Available at: https://narodne-novine.nn.hr/clanci/sluzbeni/2021_10_111_1940.html (15.11.2023).

Official Journal of the European Union (2018) Regulation (EU) 2018/841 of the European Parliament and of the Council of 30 May 2018 on the Inclusion of Greenhouse Gas Emissions and Removals from Land use, Land use Change and Forestry in the 2030 Climate and Energy Framework, and Amending Regulation (EU) No 525/2013 and Decision No 529/2013/EU. OJ L 156, 19.6.2018, pp. 1–25. Available at: https://eur-lex.europa.eu/legal-content/EN/TXT/?uri=CELEX%3A32018R0841 (17.11.2023).

Official Journal of the European Union (2021) Regulation (EU) 2021/1119 of the European Parliament and of the Council of 30 June 2021 Establishing the Framework for Achieving Climate Neutrality and Amending Regulations (EC) No 401/2009 and (EU) 2018/1999 ('European Climate Law'). OJ L 243, 9.7.2021, pp. 1–17. Available at: https://eur-lex.europa.eu/legal-content/EN/TXT/?uri=CELEX%3A32021R1119 (17.11.2023).

Official Journal of the European Union (2022) Decision (EU) 2022/591 of the European Parliament and of the Council of 6 April 2022 on a General Union Environment Action Programme to 2030. *OJ L 114*, pp. 22–36.

Official Journal of the European Union (2023) Regulation (EU) 2023/839 of the European Parliament and of the Council of 19 April 2023 amending regulation (EU) 2018/841 as regards the scope, simplifying the reporting and compliance rules, and setting out the targets of the Member States for 2030, and regulation (EU) 2018/1999 as regards improvement in monitoring, reporting, tracking of progress and review, *OJ L 107*, 21.4.2023, pp. 1–28. Available at: https://eur-lex.europa.eu/eli/reg/2023/839/oj (17.11.2023).

Petak, Z. (2012) 'Europeizacija javnih politika u Hrvatskoj', in V. Puljiz, S. Ravlić and V. Visković (eds.) *Hrvatska u EU: Kako dalje?* Zagreb: Centar za demokraciju i pravo Miko Tripalo.

Radaelli, C. M. (2002) 'The domestic impact of European Union public policy: Notes on concepts, methods, and the challenge of empirical research', *L'Hartmattan, Politique européenne*, 1(5), pp. 105–136.

Radaelli, C. M. (2004) 'Europeanisation: Solution or problem?', *European Integration Online Papers*, 8, p. 16.

Saurugger, S. (2013) *Teorije i koncepti europske integracije*. Zagreb: Fakultet političkih znanosti.

Standard Eurobarometer 97 (2022) Summer 2022, Country Factsheets in English Croatia. Available at: https://europa.eu/eurobarometer/surveys/detail/2693 (17.11.2023).

Statista (2023) Tourism Sector GDP Share Forecast 2013-–2028. Available at: www.statista.com/forecasts/1153595/tourism-sector-gdp-share-forecast-in-croatia#:~:text=Share%20of%20the%20GDP%20of%20the%20tourism%20sector%20in%20Croatia%202013%2D2028&text=The%20tourism%20sector%20GDP%20share,to%2026.2%20percent%20in%202028 (17.11.2023).

USKOK (2022) Podignuta optužnica protiv devetero okrivljenika. 30.12.2022. Available at: https://uskok.hr/hr/priopcenja/podignuta-optuznica-protiv-devetero-okrivljenika-4 (17.11.2023).

World Bank (2021) Croatia: Circular Economy Approaches in Solid Waste Management. Available at: www.worldbank.org/en/country/croatia/brief/croatia-circular-economy-approaches-in-solid-waste-management (17.11.2023).

World Economic Forum (2021) The Global Risks Report 2021 (15th edition). World Economic Forum.

13 Croatian Social Policy under the Impact of the European Union

Zdenko Babić and Domagoj Račić

13.1 Introduction

This chapter examines the interrelationship between the Croatian social policy and its European Union (EU) context. In the last two decades, Croatia's public policy has been developing under the influence of the EU. The Europeanisation of social policy in Croatia coincided with a more prominent role of social policy objectives and mechanisms in EU policymaking. Member states have traditionally been primarily responsible for their social policies. However, the Stability and Growth Pact, which entered into force in 1998, the Amsterdam Treaty, enacted in 1999, and the Lisbon Strategy from 2000 have engendered a more active role of EU-level institutions, objectives and mechanisms in social policy in member states and candidate countries. New institutionalised hard and soft policy coordination forms were introduced, which promoted budgetary restraint and social policy benchmarking and harmonisation (cf. De la Porte and Madama, 2022).

EU is a polity in which a specific form of policy transfer occurs.[1] Defined as Europeanisation, such policy transfer shapes the relationship between supranational institutions and domestic actors across different contexts (Coman and Tulmets, 2021). The concept of Europeanisation of public policy has had different and evolving meanings (cf. Petak, 2006). It initially encompassed a basic notion of EU influences on national policymaking, which, in the context of candidate and accession countries, could also be associated with the reforms required for EU accession. Moreover, since most of these countries were also undergoing a post-socialist transition, Europeanisation was associated with modernisation or convergence of their governance arrangements and public policies with their EU peers, which were also expected to contribute to their democratic consolidation and market economy. However, as the evidence summarised below indicates, such views have, over time, been challenged, and Europeanisation took on a more complex relational meaning, which assumes an interplay of top-down, bottom-up and horizontal influences on public policies across the EU.

We argue that the Europeanisation of social policy in Croatia can be traced by analysing two main influence channels – regulatory frameworks and EU funding. In its foundation is a discursive dimension of Europeanisation, emphasised by Radaelli (2000) – the construction, diffusion and institutionalisation of shared

DOI: 10.4324/9781003394013-13

beliefs and norms, rules, procedures and policy paradigms. Initial harmonisation of regulation occurred through adopting the *acquis communautaire*, whereas key policy processes were aligned with the EU before the accession. Further, EU influence on the national social policy was extended through the European Semester and Country Specific Recommendations (CSRs) (cf. Munta, 2021). At the same time, the Instrument of Pre-accession Assistance (IPA) and European Structural and Investment Funds (ESIF) provided additional resources to governmental and non-governmental social policy actors in Croatia.

The chapter is organised as follows. A discussion of the Europeanisation of social policy follows this introduction. The third part tackles the EU's impact on Croatian social policy during the pre-accession phase. Policy frameworks in specific social policy domains are subsequently analysed. These include employment, education and lifelong learning, pension system, health and long-term care, poverty, and social exclusion. An analysis of the impact of EU funding follows. In the final segment, some concluding remarks are offered.

13.2 Europeanisation of Social Policy

In the EU context, social policy has traditionally been viewed as a primarily national competence whereby EU-level institutions, objectives and mechanisms play a relatively limited role. Moreover, comparative research demonstrated that implementation problems are much more pronounced in social and environmental policies than in competition or agricultural policies (Knill, 2006). Only with the Amsterdam Treaty, which incorporated the Agreement on Social Policy and was effective from 1 May 1999, has the EU adopted the commitments related to the social dimension of European integration (cf. Puljiz, 2019). These commitments were further reinforced by the Treaty of Lisbon in 2007 and the Treaty on the Functioning of the EU, which came into force on 1 December 2009. Article 151 states the EU's social policy objectives: promoting employment, improving working and living conditions, equal treatment of workers, adequate social protection according to need, social dialogue, developing human resources to achieve a high and sustainable level of employment, and combating exclusion. Strategic documents such as the Lisbon Agenda from 2000 aimed to make the EU the most competitive and dynamic knowledge-based economy and provide more and better jobs and greater social cohesion, whereas Europe's 2020 strategy focused on smart, sustainable and inclusive growth (EC, 2010).

Despite legal enshrinement and strategic commitment to the social policy objectives at the EU level, their implementation is subject to ongoing policy debates and possible conflicts with economic objectives enshrined, e.g., in the Stability and Growth Pact, as well as with the influences of EU bodies promoting the economic objectives (cf. De la Porte and Heins, 2016; Zeitlin and Vanhercke, 2018). Moreover, the EU dimension of social policy is implemented in the context of existing welfare state regimes in each country (cf. Isakjee, 2017). Welfare state regimes are not static and react to their changing environments, so any consolidation of stable institutional features is persistently challenged by the elements of crisis and change (cf. Lendvai and Stubbs, 2015). Furthermore, normative transformations of the EU entail both hard and soft regulatory instruments; soft law can be either a substitute or a complement to hard law, and their interplay is often complex (Saurugger and Terpan, 2021).[2] Although the Europeanisation of post-socialist countries was primarily concerned with economic benefits and institutional stabilisation, social considerations were also important in the enlargement process (Meardi, 2016). Moreover, EU institutions and policies are changing. For example, Zeitlin and Vanhercke (2018) argue that there has been a partial but progressive 'socialisation' of the European Semester of policy coordination, in terms of increasing emphasis on social objectives in its priorities, intensified social monitoring and review of national reforms, and an enhanced decision-making role for EU social and employment actors. The focus on social objectives has subsequently only been strengthened by the Covid-19 pandemic.

Therefore, analysing the Europeanisation of social policy in the context of EU accession of Croatia is challenging due to the lack of the EU social model as a stable or coherent reference point and the complexity and multifaceted nature of the Europeanisation process itself in practice and social policy literature. Early Europeanisation research in the late 1990s analysed how policies, institutional arrangements, rules, beliefs and norms are transferred from the EU to other jurisdictions (Bulmer, 2007). Much of the mainstream scholarship employed a predominantly functionalist framework which examined the impact of the EU within separate and distinct policy domains (Lendvai and Stubbs, 2015). Social policy discussions were usually framed in modernisation, convergence and catching up in post-socialist countries undergoing transition and seeking EU membership. Social policy scholars have also developed the concept of 'cognitive Europeanisation' as a socialisation process through which the EU discourse is incorporated into national policy debates, instruments and activities (cf. Guillén and Álvarez, 2004; Stubbs and Zrinščak, 2009). However, as Lendvai and Stubbs (2015, p. 450) point out: 'Dynamics of "Europeanisation" are not based on an institutional equilibrium or a stable institutional fix; rather, they involve constant reforming, reworking and recalibration'. In other words, Europeanisation is not a one-way top-down process that could be reduced to implementing EU rules on national administrative systems (Lenschow, 2006). According to the same author, there are four distinct aspects of Europeanisation in the realm of public policy: the emergence of the EU-level institutional structures, the impact of the EU on its member states, the horizontal transfer of concepts and policies between member states and the complex interactions (top-down and bottom-up) between the EU and its member states. Such a view contradicts the approaches assuming that Europeanisation is a one-way, expertise-driven process of cumulative policy learning and possibly even convergence. Knill and Lehmkuhl (1999) distinguish three main mechanisms of Europeanisation: institutional compliance ('positive integration'), changing domestic opportunity structures ('negative integration') and mobilising for domestic support ('framing integration'). The first type prescribes institutional models to which domestic policies should be adjusted. The second type changes the domestic rules of the game and/or the distribution of power and resources. The third type operates even more indirectly, by altering domestic actors' assumptions, beliefs and expectations (and thus corresponds to 'cognitive Europeanisation' mentioned above).

The complexity of processes associated with Europeanisation concerning specific countries and policy domains should be addressed by complex and multi-faceted research, which would cover macro-level structural analysis of political economy, meso-level dealing with policy transfer, adaptation and learning, and micro-level of specific interactions. Moreover, specific attention should be devoted to interrelationships of intersecting policy domains, e.g. social and economic policy (cf. Lendvai and Stubbs, 2015). The process-tracing methodology would also be needed to obtain in-depth knowledge of causal influences (cf. Moumoutzis and Zartaloudis, 2016). Such an all-embracing analysis would be outside the scope of this chapter. Munta's (2021) analysis of the domestic policy effects of socio-economic governance in the European Semester on national employment policies in selected Central and Eastern European countries provides an example of such a comprehensive approach. So, while being aware of the challenges mentioned above, the authors restrict their analysis to the evolution of main social policy instruments – regulatory frameworks and funding mechanisms – before and after Croatia joined the EU.[3] In Knill and Lehmkuhl's (1999) framework, changes in the regulatory framework primarily correspond to institutional compliance. However, they may also entail a degree of framing integration. In contrast, EU funding mechanisms change domestic opportunity structures by providing additional resources and increasing the autonomy of domestic social policy actors.

13.3 The EU's Impact on Croatian Social Policy during the Pre-accession Phase

In the 1990s, the first decade of Croatia's independence was marked by war and reconstruction efforts. This state-building occurred in a context of tendencies towards political authoritarianism, clientelism and 'crony capitalism' (cf. Bičanić and Franičević, 2003). In the social policy, a 'crisis welfare state' model was employed, which was focused on the immediate needs of the existential needs of vulnerable groups, whereas reforms were being postponed (Bežovan, 2019b). However, such context also engendered clientelistic tendencies in social policy, influencing its future developments (Stubbs and Zrinščak, 2015). Europeanisation of Croatian public policy in general and social policy, in particular, began with the election of a reform-oriented coalition government in January 2000. However, the break with the previous decade should not be overstated. A broad political and societal consensus viewed the pursuit of EU membership as crucial for democratic consolidation and economic progress (Stubbs and Zrinščak, 2009).

Stubbs and Zrinščak (2015) argued that social policy developed in the post-war period in the context of the nation-state's formation and delayed Europeanisation. The focus of social policy on war victims and veterans (defenders) happened in parallel with the relatively low level of rights of most other users of social policy measures. In the area of social policy Croatia in the 2000s displayed 'welfare parallelism' (Stubbs and Zrinščak, 2007), in which there was little coordination between either the central and local state or between state and non-state actors. In a centralised state like Croatia, the national social policy level defines the scope and standards of public service provision, pensions, social benefits and rights, income taxation and subsidies. Local and regional self-government units decide on the application of social rights, which gives them partial autonomy and the possibility of creating additional social programmes, their own networks and exchange relations, which may also include elements of clientelism (cf. Račić, 2021).

Each level and/or set of social policy actors had their objectives, programmes and projects, whereas some policy actors (e.g. NGOs) operated in different environments and at multiple levels. For instance, some NGOs were simultaneously engaged in advocacy at the national level and in concrete projects at the local level. In that context, the influence of the EU has been occasional, fragmented and mediated (cf. Stubbs and Zrinščak, 2010) rather than systematic and coherent. On the other hand, social policy reforms such as the pension system reform initiated in 2002, or employment legislation reform from 2003 were more influenced by the World Bank and other policy actors (Puljiz, 2019).

Before the institutionalisation of EU policy concerns in the national social policy, the initial incorporation of EU discourse into national policy debates was primarily promoted by NGOs concerned with human rights, gender equality and the rights of national minorities. These NGOs sought support from EU institutions to pressure Croatian authorities to address the tangible issues and problems in the areas mentioned above. At the same time, core social policy concerns, such as poverty and social exclusion, employment, pensions and healthcare, did not receive much EU attention (Stubbs and Zrinščak, 2010).

Europeanisation of the social policy in Croatia was intensified from 2004 onwards, in the context of stable economic growth and preparations for the EU accession negotiations (Puljiz, 2019). Systematic policy harmonisation between Croatia and the EU in the areas of social and employment policy began in late 2005 when Croatia joined the 'open method of coordination' process, which led to the elaboration of two key pre-accession documents in collaboration with the European Commission and consultation with a wide range of stakeholders (ministries, government agencies, social partners, NGOs, regional and local authorities). The first document, the Joint Inclusion Memorandum (JIM), dealt with poverty and social exclusion and was signed in March 2007. The second document, the Joint Assessment Paper (JAP), dealt with employment policy issues and was signed in May 2008. JIM and JAP established policy commitments which were monitored in subsequent years. The fulfilment of these commitments and other obligations led to the provisionally closing of Chapter 19 of the *acquis communautaire*, which deals with social policy and employment, on 21 December 2009.

JIM articulated a clear social policy agenda based on evidence and reflecting the thinking and influence of experts, civil servants and wider stakeholders obtained through a process which had more of a technical and professional than political nature. Stakeholder dialogue and open consultation initiated a new practice which was substantively different from the previous 'closed door' strategy development practices. Subsequent activities entailed not only a more comprehensive data collection and research activities into social issues but also the strengthening of the EU discourse within social policy, which now included not only discrimination against minorities and gender equality but also more core social policy and employment issues, as well as emerging topics such as deinstitutionalisation, decentralisation and lifelong learning (Stubbs and Zrinščak, 2009, 2010).

However, despite some improvements, the EU influence was much more strongly felt in the social policy processes related to the requirements ('benchmarks') of Croatia's EU accession than in the actual budget, content or impacts of social policy. On the one hand, there was no EU influence on national expenditures on social welfare. Direct EU assistance through the Human Resource Development component of the IPA was limited in scope and size, largely employment-focused and very much 'projectized', so the impacts on policy direction have been weak (Stubbs and Zrinščak, 2010). Instead of a comprehensive social policy reform supported by specific projects, the overall approach emphasised a combination of top-down projects and grant schemes supported by technical assistance.[4] The total allocation for the IPA Human Resource Development Operational Programme (HRD OP) was EUR 111,084,756, of which IPA provided the amount of EUR 94,422,000 and EUR 16,662,756 came from the Croatian public contribution.[5]

Ex-post evaluation undertaken in 2015 (Ecorys, 2015) emphasised several lessons learned and recommendations for future policymaking. The operations should be better aligned with the policies and the needs of potential beneficiaries. Investments in awareness raising, stakeholder consultation and capacity building are needed to do so. Partnerships between the public and private sectors and civil society should be supported to improve capacity for implementing larger projects with higher potential for sustainable results to the target groups. Innovative approaches in providing support to the target groups should be strengthened. Finally, monitoring and reporting mechanisms should be simplified and digitised to collect up-to-date and comprehensive data sets as a tool for future policymaking. IPA has contributed to knowledge acquisition, expansion of financing opportunities and strengthening of non-state actors in social policy, but its influence was fragmented and its impacts limited. Furthermore, the long recession from 2009 until 2014 and the related austerity measures overshadowed the effects of IPA and exposed the vulnerabilities of the social welfare system in Croatia. According to Bežovan (Bežovan, 2019b), IPA funding did not help Croatia's fragmented and deprofessionalised social sector to transfer knowledge, skills and experiences from other EU member states and build more efficient and effective social institutions that would cope with growing new social risks.

During accessing negotiations, Croatia adopted the *acquis communautaire*, thereby achieving a formal harmonisation of its regulation with the EU. Europeanisation of social policy has gained momentum when Croatia joined the EU on 1 July 2013. Social policy is defined mainly by national laws, regulations and funding mechanisms, which the EU has influenced. The sources of EU influence include not only the relevant directives adopted in the European Parliament, which are obligatory for the member states, but also sources such as EU strategic documents, CSRs (issued by the Council of the EU within the European Semester), advisory committees, and funding provided from EU sources.[6] The analysis in subsequent parts of the chapter is structured under specific social policy domains – employment, education and lifelong learning, pension, health and long-term care, and poverty and social exclusion. The focus of the analysis on soft law instruments (embedded in the European Semester) and EU funding mechanisms is grounded in the specificity of their design. They are designed, communicated and implemented to tackle specific social policy issues in Croatia. Croatian policymakers may or may not respond to such stimuli, but their reactions (or the lack thereof) and the corresponding social policy evolution can be discerned and analysed.

13.4 Employment, Education and Lifelong Learning

Employment policy coordination within the EU usually operates under the 'open method of coordination' framework (Munta, 2017). Hereby the EU institutions define common goals and propose instruments for their achievement, which, however, are not binding for member states, and there are no sanctions for non-compliance. European Semester framework strengthened the employment policy coordination, as employment guidelines and objectives are defined every five years, and member states annually receive recommendations on their National Reform Programmes. In the area of employment policy and labour market, Croatia received several CSRs within the European Semester, which are discussed below. In June 2013, Croatia's Labour Act reform was amended in order to harmonise it with the relevant directives and practices of the Court of Justice of the EU.[7] The amendments primarily tackled the issues of fixed-term contracts and collective dismissals, identified problems concerning termination of the employment contract during the probationary period and informing and consulting with workers at the transnational level, i.e., through the European Work Council.

Since 2014, Croatia has received several CSRs related to employment, labour market and education policy. The focus was on flexibilisation of employment, developing capacities to implement active labour market policies (ALMPs), including outreach to vulnerable groups, modernising the qualification systems and vocational education and training and tackling undeclared work.[8] Other issues that received attention in CSRs in 2016 and 2017 are up- and re-skilling and adult education to increase the employability of target groups, including the low-skilled, the long-term unemployed and older workers. Therefore, the new Labour Act was enacted in 2014, but without a consensus among social partners, resulting in dissatisfaction from employers' associations and trade unions. Labour Act reforms implemented in 2013 and in 2014 increased the overall flexibility of the Croatian labour market, whereas the mechanisms for protecting the most vulnerable workers were not adequately developed. According to Eurostat, the share of fixed-term employment in total employment increased from 14.5% in 2013 to 17% in 2014. The Minimum Wage Act was also adopted in 2013 to improve the protection of workers' earnings exposed to the risk of poverty. The Act introduced the obligation of setting the minimum wage annually through a process led by the Government and in consultations with social partners.

Moreover, ALMPs were expanded with co-financing from the European Social Fund (ESF) (please also see below). Furthermore, the implementation of the Youth Guarantee from 2014 onwards has provided the primary reform which tackled the position of youth in the labour market. Most implemented Youth Guarantee measures were ALMPs, while most others have been implemented partially and/or with delays. Implementing the Youth Guarantee eased young people's pathway to integration into the labour market (cf. Babić and Račić, 2017). However, some drawbacks have also been identified in specific ALMPs. Youth Guarantee was too focused on the activation measures (e.g. Traineeship for work without employment) and much less on improvements in the NEET youth tracking system and outreach (Munta, 2017, 2021). Furthermore, highly educated youth disproportionately benefited from these activation measures (Ipsos, 2016).

Education system reform, focusing on quality improvement and labour market relevance, has not been directly driven by Europeanisation. However, the reform was often facilitated by competitiveness concerns in the context of the EU market, whereas the adopted policy measures were usually similar to other EU countries. An example is the Croatian Qualifications Framework, adopted in 2013 and implemented ever since.[9] The competitiveness of the national economy significantly depends on the quality and productivity of its human capital, which is eventually determined by investments in education and the quality of the education system (cf. Hanushek and Kimko, 2000). Low PISA results of Croatian students and low participation in lifelong learning indicated a need for quality improvements at all education levels. In October 2014, the Croatian Parliament adopted the Strategy for Education, Science and Technology (MSES, 2014), which set a long-term development framework for five main areas: lifelong learning, early and preschool, primary and secondary education, higher education, adult education and science and technology. Its implementation has been fragmentary, subject to the political will and consent of the affected stakeholders. For example, in January 2015, comprehensive curricular reform in primary and secondary schools was initiated as a cornerstone reform of the education system, but after the change of Government in late 2015, political support became questionable, and the process was first slowed down and then effectively stopped (cf. Babić and Račić, 2017). Although investments into educational institutions (such as kindergartens, vocational schools and tertiary education institutions) were secured from the ESIF in 2014–2020, they were rarely accompanied by significant reforms. According to Matković and Buković (2022), institutional changes in the Croatian vocational education and training sector also occur slowly; possible explanations include (i) path dependence (dominant position of the central state obtained in the early 1990s has not engendered appropriate policymaking capacity), (ii) the lack of interest and capacity of non-state actors to play a more prominent role and (iii) structural factors, i.e. abundance of qualified labour force, hindering employers' investment in human capital and innovation. Croatia belongs to the countries with a less developed system of early and preschool education (cf. Dobrotić, 2022). Significant regional differences in the availability of early and preschool education facilities and services were addressed through several rounds of investments co-financed from the ESF, which enabled the construction or renovation of 200 kindergartens.[10]

Education system reform has received an additional impetus from implementing the Recovery and Resilience Plan for Croatia (RRP, 2021), which combines investments and reforms. One example in lifelong learning and adult education is vouchers for upskilling, focused on green and digital skills and introduced at the end of 2021. The voucher system is to be used to finance participation exclusively in the educational programmes developed on the basis of the Croatian Qualifications Framework and implemented through accredited institutions in accordance with the adopted new Adult Education Act.

13.5 Pension, Health and Long-Term Care

Since 2002, the Croatian pension system consists of three pillars. In addition to the pay-as-you-go scheme with defined benefits, there are compulsory and voluntary defined contribution schemes based on individual accounts financed by contributions and investment returns. Given the ageing population, emigration, widespread occurrence of early retirement and a high share of privileged pensions, the pension system's sustainability depends on budgetary transfers. Moreover, pension adequacy is low, and the poverty risk among pensioners is high. These circumstances have often been emphasised in the CSRs from 2015 to 2018[11] (CEU, 2015, 2016, 2017, 2018). As early as 2013, the Government of Croatia, led by the Social Democratic Party, announced a pension reform aimed at ensuring long-term fiscal sustainability, which included the extension of the retirement age to 67 in the period 2030–2038, stricter penalties for early retirement and allowing retired persons to work part-time while retaining their pension. However, the implementation of the reform was slow and partial, as the long-lasting recession created unfavourable conditions for the proposed restrictions; at the same time, the European Commission was not entirely satisfied with the pace of announced changes and created pressure to intensify the reform of the pension system towards financial sustainability (cf. Munta, 2021). The next attempt to implement a pension system reform was carried out by the centre-right Government of Croatia, led by the Croatian Democratic Union, and was made in 2018 when the pattern of economic growth was restored. They have announced a comprehensive pension reform planned for 2019, aiming to increase sustainability by increasing the retirement age, increasing penalties for early retirement and reducing some rights. That was done due to the influence of the European Semester and repeated recommendations of the European Commission and as a means to advance broader economic policy goals such as ending the Macroeconomic Imbalance Procedure and entering the ERM II mechanism to introduce the euro.[12] However, trade unions mobilised citizens and collected enough signatures to hold a referendum against it. To prevent such an outcome, the Government abandoned most planned interventions and accepted many provisions requested by the trade unions.[13] Moreover, to decrease poverty among the elderly, a basic income benefit for older people was introduced in January 2021. The benefit targets citizens aged 65, who have resided in Croatia for 20 years, do not fulfil minimum conditions for a regular pension, and whose income is at most EUR 105 per monthly household member. Since average family pensions paid out in 2021 were significantly below the poverty line, from 2023, the family pension model was amended, enabling the payment of a part of the family pension of deceased spouse/partner together with the use of old-age, early old-age or disability pensions, leading to the expected increases of average family pensions (between 10% and 15%).

The healthcare system in Croatia is mainly financed through contributions. However, health insurance provides almost universal coverage, leading to financial sustainability issues and reliance on budgetary transfers to cover losses. According to self-reported access to healthcare, based on EU-SILC data, Croatia still performs well. However, the difference between the highest and the lowest income groups is significantly high, amounting to more than 6 to 1 (Stubbs and Zrinščak, 2018). However, ensuring an equal availability of health services to patients throughout the country has also been challenging. The inefficient organisation of the system, financial issues and, increasingly, the lack of medical staff (due to ageing and emigration to other EU countries) have resulted in unequal access to primary care, emergency care and long waiting lists for many specialist procedures. The National Health Development Plan from 2021 to 2027 (MHRC, 2021) stated that a priority in healthcare should be improving healthcare services for vulnerable groups. However, they are not visible through the set measures and indicators of the implementation of measures (Šimunković and Babić, 2022). Several reform waves have sought financial stabilisation of the healthcare system and a balance between resources, rights and performance, but they have not been successful (Zrinščak, 2019). Despite these complex structural challenges, which are still unresolved, the European Semester healthcare sector was only mentioned in 2015, when CSR no. 2 recommended tackling its fiscal risks.

The demand for long-term care in Croatia is increasing due to the ageing of the population, in addition to other risk groups such as children and persons with disabilities. The long-term care system is fragmented among several ministries (responsible for social policy, health and war veterans), central and regional/local administration, and public and private providers. The occasional policy debates about long-term care challenges involve issues such as the balance between cash benefits and services, financing models, employment of persons who provide services, quality standards or the issue of unequal access to services in different parts of Croatia. Despite being one of the least developed parts of the healthcare and social care system in Croatia (Bežovan et al., 2020), long-term care has never been explicitly mentioned in CSRs for Croatia.

13.6 Poverty and Social Exclusion

Poverty is still an issue in Croatia, but there are also some recent positive trends due to economic growth and increased employment prospects. Croatia's at-risk-of-poverty (AROP) rate was 19.2% in 2021, 2.6 percentage points above the EU27 average in the same year (16.6%). Between 2017 and 2021, AROP for women was 2–3 percentage points higher than AROP for men. The at-risk-of-poverty or social exclusion (AROPE) in 2021 was 20.9%, somewhat below the EU27 average (21.7%) and significantly below the AROPE rate of 23.7% in 2017. The rate of severe material and social deprivation in 2021 was also lower in Croatia, 3.5%, than in the EU27 (6.3%), and it had been steadily declining since 2017, when it was 7.1%.

A central open issue in addressing poverty is the low adequacy of Croatia's minimum income (MI). The net MI of beneficiaries in 2019 was only 43.9% of the poverty threshold for single-person households (compared to 58.4% in the EU27). Only the Czech Republic, Hungary, Latvia, Portugal, Romania and Slovakia had lower MI adequacy than Croatia in that year. Croatia's guaranteed minimum benefit (GMB) scheme has low adequacy and relatively low coverage of the poor. Low coverage and low benefits lead to limited poverty alleviation effects (Babić, 2008; World Bank, 2014; Nguyen and Rubil, 2021). The value of GMB depends on an arbitrary decision made by the Government. There are no reference budgets to set benefits levels, and no indexation is implemented. GMB base is set very low; in 2020, the GMB base for a single adult person was EUR 106 per month, and the relative poverty threshold for single-person households was EUR 385 per month. Moreover, strict means of testing lead to the exclusion of some of the actually poor. The adequacy of MI schemes has been emphasised in several EU policy papers and CSRs and was often linked with the recommendations to consolidate social benefits, eliminate overlaps and improve the adequacy of unemployment benefits.[14] However, the adequacy level, coverage rate and system of activation for unemployed GMB beneficiaries still need to be satisfactorily addressed.

The adequacy of unemployment benefits has only been mentioned cursorily in CSRs. Such benefits should play a significant role in preventing poverty and social exclusion. However, the Croatian unemployment benefit system is relatively stringent, resulting in low replacement and coverage rates for the unemployed, leading to diminished poverty alleviation effects. In the period after the first three months of unemployment, the benefits are regularly lower than the poverty threshold.[15] The coverage rate is also low and oscillates around 20%, and young graduates and school leavers without sufficient work experience are completely excluded (CES, 2023).

As for the consolidation of social benefits, the National Reform Programs for 2017 and 2018 emphasised the need to continue the implementation of the reform of the social protection system, protecting the most vulnerable groups in society and achieving a more just and efficient social protection system. To facilitate the process, the project Harmonization of Local Social Benefits Using the ESSPROS Methodology within the European Commission's Structural Reform Support Program framework was implemented, which improved statistical data collection and analysis of social benefits at regional and local levels. All social benefits provided at the local level are recorded, and the data are available in a new database.

13.7 The Impact of EU Funding

Croatia became a beneficiary of sizable EU financial assistance when it joined the EU. For the second half of 2013, additional financial allocation was provided within the HRD OP (please see endnote 2). ESF funding was later distributed through the Operational Programme Efficient Human Resources (OPEHR), developed and implemented in 2014–2020. Further support was provided by the Youth Employment Initiative (YEI), which contributed to employment, education and training of the vulnerable young population and Priority Axes 8 and 9 within the Competitiveness and Cohesion Operational Programme (funded by the European Regional Development Fund – ERDF), which provided investments into social, health and education infrastructure and pilot interventions into five deprived smaller cities. As outlined above, the Fund for European Aid to the Most Deprived (FEAD) financed school meals for the deprived children and food and toiletries for other beneficiaries.

The total value of the OPEHR 2014–2020 amounts to EUR 1.89 billion, of which 1.62 billion is financed from EU funds (ESF and YEI), while the rest was national funding (WYG, 2021a). As with pre-accession assistance, the main focus was on employment, primarily through expansion and additional funding provided for ALMPs. Almost EUR 930 million was allocated to five investment priorities related to access to employment and strengthening labour mobility, integration of young people into the labour market, improvement of access to social and health services, tertiary education and lifelong learning, whereas EUR 328 million was allocated for the social inclusion of vulnerable groups.[16] When it comes to the social policy domains analysed in this chapter, it can be observed that, as in the case of pre-accession assistance, most funding has been allocated to the domain of employment, education and lifelong learning. Poverty and social exclusion are also mainly tackled through support to employability and vulnerable groups, but there are also interventions related to the provision of social services and active citizenship of target groups. On the other hand, the pension system and long-term care have not been tackled (except for some support for deinstitutionalisation). In contrast, the health sector has been supported by the investments in infrastructure, promotion of healthy lifestyles and education and training of health professionals.

The analysis of the impact of EU funding on social policy is primarily based on mid-term evaluations of OPEHR priority axes, which were completed in 2021 and 2022 (cf. Ernst and Young, 2021; WYG, 2021a, 2021b, 2021c, 2022). These evaluations assessed the relevance, effectiveness, efficiency and impact of the interventions undertaken within these priority axes or more specific areas, such as social entrepreneurship. Although it is too early to formulate any definitive conclusions about the effects of EU funding, some systemic features of social policy facilitated by the EU and enabled by additional financial resources have already been observed and embedded in the relevant practices and institutions. This analysis attempts to identify some such features.

The relevance of the undertaken interventions is assessed reasonably highly, as OPEHR priorities were well-aligned with the relevant EU and national strategies and priorities and based on needs assessments and stakeholder dialogue. Some of the interventions were later adjusted to the changing needs of relevant target groups and/or to the changes in the sizes of these groups (cf. WYG, 2021a), but this has yet to be a general practice. In the case of employment policy, in 2014, the focus was on increasing employability and integration into the labour market, emphasising the young, elderly, long-term unemployed, low-skilled, and inactive persons and women. Croatia's socio-economic situation subsequently improved. Increased employment and decreased unemployment levels were combined with intensive migration, leading to labour shortages in some sectors. Consequently, changes in interventions were introduced in 2017 to ensure more financial sustainability, improve profiling and segmentation of the unemployed, and open up access to the ALMPs (WYG, 2021a).

The situation is more complex when it comes to the effectiveness and efficiency of the implemented policy measures and projects. Due to the complexity of decision-making and administrative procedures associated with designing and implementing calls for proposals and project evaluation, contracting and implementation, delays have been frequent, whereas bridging mechanisms from national sources were usually not provided. The capacity of some beneficiaries to successfully implement projects was also occasionally an issue, further exacerbated by the gaps mentioned earlier in funding. Consequently, achieving immediate results and meeting programme objectives have also usually been delayed and sometimes challenging to achieve (cf. Ernst and Young, 2021; WYG, 2021a, 2021b, 2021c). In the case of social entrepreneurship, most planned interventions still needed to be implemented (WYG, 2022). The efficiency and effectiveness of interventions were more easily attainable when the measures were based on the revision and expansion of existing (or previously implemented) national measures and embedded in the accompanying practices and institutions, as in the case of many ALMPs and some social services (WYG, 2021a, 2021b). However, even in those cases, uncertainties and gaps in financing have occurred, as in the case of Zaželi – Women's Employment Programme, the most significant intervention in social inclusion (cf. WYG, 2021b). Moreover, the complexity of interventions negatively affected efficiency and effectiveness, e.g., subsidies as opposed to grant schemes (projects), let alone reforms supported by technical assistance and/or grant schemes.

Successful public policies engender strong and sustainable impacts. The issues mentioned earlier related to relevance (e.g. changing needs), effectiveness and efficiency (e.g. design and implementation issues) have limited the impacts achieved by social policy interventions supported by OPEHR. Moreover, the focus on maximisation of EU funds absorption may lead to supporting a range of beneficiaries that is wider than optimal, thereby reducing impact. In the case of employment, only three measures (YEI, general employment subsidies and self-employment support) experienced a net positive effect of the intervention concerning the control group. Further research might uncover additional deadweight losses due to subsidising employment of those who would have found a job anyway. Furthermore, positive impacts have been observed in capacity building in the Croatian Employment Service, improved visibility, planning and revision of ALMPs, developing tools for labour market analytics and improving procedures through simplified cost options and online submission of applications (WYG, 2021a).

In the area of social inclusion, educational impacts are positive, and social impacts are more robust than the impacts on employment; there were also positive impacts on the availability of social services (WYG, 2021b). There is an important difference between grants to specific educational institutions that are considered sustainable in education and training, as they enable the beneficiaries to expand and improve their activities. Moreover, many projects have contributed to networking, strengthening communication and cooperation between actors in the education system, which should positively affect the educational process and outcomes. However, it was considered unlikely that the results of direct support to target groups would be sustainable without further EU co-financing (Ernst and Young, 2021). Despite discernible improvements, evaluations also identify recommendations for possible improvements of social policy measures design and delivery in the context of EU funding. The recommendations revolve around flexibility and stakeholder involvement (to facilitate relevance in a changing world), capacity building and administrative simplification (to facilitate efficiency and effectiveness) and more emphasis on achieving sustainable impacts.

During the Covid-19 pandemic, the EU implemented the European instrument for temporary Support to mitigate Unemployment Risks in an Emergency (SURE) to help member states protect jobs and workers' incomes. Croatia disbursed EUR 1.02 billion from SURE (EC, 2022). To facilitate post-pandemic economic and social recovery and resilience, the Resilience and Recovery Plan for Croatia (RRP, 2021) defined a policy mix of reforms and investments that aim to facilitate socio-economic recovery aligned with the green and digital transitions. Its components (3) education, science and research, (4) labour market and social protection and (5) health address the challenges related to social policy, including those which EU-supported policy measures have not tackled. Such examples include ensuring adequate social protection (including improving pensions adequacy), improving health system governance and reduction of health inequalities and reforming the education system by introducing the whole-day school, modernising tertiary education and widening access to lifelong learning. In other words, many deep-rooted socio-economic challenges should finally be tackled through reforms and investments co-financed and monitored by the EU. In the current programming period, Efficient Human Resources Program 2021–2027 has been developed and adopted for the utilisation of funding from the ESF+. The ESF+ integrates the former ESF, the YEI, the FEAD and the EU Programme for Employment and Social Innovation (EaSI). With national co-financing, the total financial value of the OPEHR 2021–2027 amounts to almost EUR 2.268 billion. To reach its objectives, which have been set under the goals of the European Pillar of Social Rights, the program entails the concentration of investment in four key areas: investment in employment and increasing the level of skills, social inclusion, education and lifelong learning, and investments in health and long-term care. The program is based on the National Development Strategy of the Republic of Croatia until 2030 (NDS, 2021), experiences of OPEHR 2014–2020, reports and recommendations received within the European Semester, and stakeholder consultations. ESF interventions will also have a pronounced local/regional dimension in order to address the specific needs of beneficiaries and facilitate a more balanced regional development.[17]

13.8 Conclusion

This chapter has concisely presented and analysed some of the main facets of the EU's influence on social policy in Croatia. Although more in-depth research would be needed to conclude the topics analysed, some preliminary findings can already be outlined here. Europeanisation of social policy in Croatia has corresponded with increasing importance given to social policy objectives and mechanisms at the EU level. Although member states are still primarily responsible for their social policies, during the last two decades, EU bodies have been increasingly aware and concerned with social policy issues – and these concerns have provided inputs and feedback into national policymaking (and vice versa). Although its economic integration roots and concerns still prevail, the EU has been accepting its social dimension as a necessary component of its policy landscape. In 2017, the European Parliament, the Council and the Commission proclaimed the European Pillar of Social Rights framework despite its patchy implementation.[18] This framework may serve as a vehicle of social cohesion and development in the EU. Its importance has only been exacerbated by the Covid-19 pandemic and the renewed emphasis on recovery and resilience. Suppose we view social policy as a response to social issues and challenges. In that case, we can observe that both the dominant challenges and the corresponding policy responses in Croatia have been reasonably stable, although with some modifications (e.g. changes in the labour market after 2015, which led to revision of ALMPs). The most considerable challenge that has not been tackled is the loss of human capital (including younger and well-educated persons) to more developed EU countries, particularly pronounced between 2014 and 2018 (Babić and Račić, 2018). Between 2011 and 2021 Croatia lost 9.64% of its population, which caused profound effects on the labour market, pension system, healthcare and other social policy domains.

Europeanisation of social policy in Croatia has been tackled through an analysis of regulatory frameworks such as the European Semester (which facilitated policy transfer through institutional compliance) and EU funding (which expanded the pool of available resources and affected their distribution). From its onset in 2004 in the context of accession negotiations onwards, social policy domains and instruments influenced by the EU have been expanded and differentiated. However, soft law and financial assistance have also demonstrated their weaknesses as tools of Europeanisation, as they are often used strategically by domestic policy actors and beneficiaries. The pre-accession focus was on policy processes supported by limited IPA funding, leading to weak impacts on the policy direction. Later on, European Semester in general and CSRs in particular have affected social policy reforms, although often with quite uneven results. In this chapter, we have analysed three policy domains, each of which exemplifies a relatively coherent range of issues, institutions and instruments of social policy and an implicit approach to the social dimension of society.

In the domain of employment, education and lifelong learning, which has been the dominant sphere of EU influence and funding in Croatia, social policy effectively supports economic policy through increased employability, skills endowments and job creation and retention. Hereby direct influence was modest, but indirect effects were substantial, often due to creative appropriation of the European Semester and EU funding for domestic political objectives (cf. Munta, 2021). In the domain of poverty and social exclusion, the social policy serves as a means of social cohesion (which comes through participation in the economy and society). However, the need for intervention in this domain often arises from the negative social externalities of the prevailing economic paradigm. Hereby EU influence on core concerns such as poverty has been minimal; for example, recommendations to revise the MI scheme and improve the adequacy of unemployment benefits were not heeded. Furthermore, social inclusion was facilitated through project-based support to employability and vulnerable groups and the provision of social services, with positive educational and social impacts and limited impacts on employment (cf. WYG, 2021b). In the domain of pension, health and long-term care, social policy is treated as management of social risks and costs. Hereby EU influence has been the least observable; until recently, it was often reduced to emphasising the need to improve the financial sustainability of pension and healthcare systems. Only recently, there has been more emphasis on health and long-term care investments.

Gradual differentiation and expansion of size and scope led to the current variety of funding instruments influenced and/or supported by the EU. Although EU funding has enormously contributed to the resources available for social policy instruments, its impacts have been limited by the changing needs of beneficiaries, design and implementation issues and other issues. In many cases, the results and impacts may only be sustainable with further EU co-financing. Moreover, organisations implementing projects and the beneficiaries (vulnerable groups) would enormously benefit if bridging mechanisms from the national budget could be implemented to prevent uncertainty and discontinuity of support.

Notes

1 Dolowitz and Marsh (2000, p. 5) define policy transfer as '…the process by which knowledge about policies, administrative arrangements, institutions and ideas in one political system (past or present) is used in the development of policies, administrative arrangements, institutions and ideas in another political system'. Policy transfer operates on a continuum whose poles are voluntary (e.g. lesson-drawing) and coercive transfer (e.g. direct external imposition), with most cases being somewhere in between.

2 According to Saurugger and Terpan (2021), hard law corresponds to a situation where hard obligation and hard enforcement are connected. In contrast, non-law entails the lack of both obligations and enforcement mechanisms. All other regulations on the continuum between these two 'ideal types' can be considered soft law, with different forms and degrees of 'softness'.

3 Where necessary, some political economy context is also provided to shed light on the drivers that influenced the evolution of social policy mechanisms and the use of EU funds.
4 The assistance was distributed across priority axes focused on supporting access to sustainable employment and adaptability of the labour force, reinforcing social inclusion and integration of people at a disadvantage, enhancing human capital in education, research and development, and strengthening the role of civil society for better governance and technical assistance.
5 In the second half of 2013, when Croatia joined the EU, additional financial allocation was provided within the HRD OP, and the total for 2007–2013 reached EUR 179,309,591.
6 Some role is also played by advisory committees (Employment Committee and Social Protection Committee), harmonisation of statistical indicators and peer review process and learning from best EU practice.
7 Labour Act was harmonised with the Directive 2009/38/EC on the establishment of a European Works Council, as well as with the Directive 20018/104/EC, Council Directive 98/59/EC.
8 For example, CSR no. 3 from 2014 stated:

> Implement the second phase of the labour law reform, following consultation with the social partners, particularly regarding conditions for dismissals and working time, and to prevent further labour market segmentation including for young people, by March 2015. Review the wage-setting system to align productivity developments and wage conditions better. Present the conclusions of this review by the end of 2014. Strengthen the effectiveness and reach of active labour market policies by reinforcing the administrative capacities of the public employment services, including at the regional level, and by increasing the coverage of the young, long-term unemployed and older workers. Prioritise outreach to non-registered youth and mobilise the private sector to offer more apprenticeships, in line with the objectives of a youth guarantee – outline plans by the end of 2014 to address undeclared work. Implement measures to improve the labour market relevance and quality of education outcomes by modernising the qualification systems, implementing quality assurance mechanisms and improving school-to-work transitions, mainly through strengthening vocational education and work-based learning.
>
> (CEU, 2014)

9 It includes the development of educational programmes which consider the needs of employers, who, in defining specific occupation standards, outline the key competencies that a person employed in that occupation must have. Based on occupational standards, qualification standards are defined, which specify the content and structure of a particular qualification. Finally, educational curricula are defined and/or revised. The ultimate objective is that students and other trainees acquire the knowledge and skills needed for successful performance in the context of specific occupations and jobs related to them.
10 www.esf.hr/uruceno-75-ugovora-u-vrijednosti-vise-od-177-milijuna-kuna-za-unaprjedenje-usluga-ranog-i-predskolskog-obrazovanja/
11 CSR from 2015 states: 'Discourage early retirement by raising penalties for early exits. Improve the adequacy and efficiency of pension spending by tightening the definition of arduous and hazardous professions. Tackle the fiscal risks in healthcare' (CEU, 2015). CSR from 2016 states: 'By the end of 2016, take measures to discourage early retirement, accelerate the transition to the higher statutory retirement age and align pension provisions for specific categories with the rules of the general scheme…' (CEU, 2016).

12 Croatia was monitored under the Macroeconomic Imbalance Procedure from 2014 until 2022 and introduced the euro on 1 January 2023.

13 The pensionable age remained at 65; the early retirement age returned to 60 years, cancelling the increase to 62. Long-term insured persons with a 41-year contributory period will be entitled to an old-age pension at 60, cancelling the increase in the required age to 61 (Bežovan, 2019a). The permanent reduction (penalisation) of early retirement pensions was reduced from 0.3% to 0.2% per month, lowering the reduction cap for early retirement from 18% to 12%. The transitional period for applying equal conditions to women and men for entitlement to an old-age pension and early retirement pension was extended from 2026 to 2029. At the same time, remaining employed longer will be stimulated with an increase of 0.34% per month of earning the right to old-age pension after the prescribed age and 35 years of insurance.

14 CSR number 3 for 2015 and 2016 stated: 'Based on the 2014 review, carry out the reform of the social protection system and further consolidate social benefits by improving targeting and eliminating overlaps' (CEU, 2015, 2016). After that, new CSR number 2 for 2018 and 2019 stated: '...Consolidate social benefits and improve their poverty reduction capacity' (CEU, 2018, 2019), while CSR number 2 for 2020 specifically demanded minimum income adequacy improvements: 'Strengthen labour market measures and institutions and improve the adequacy of unemployment benefits and minimum income schemes…' (CEU, 2020).

15 Unemployment benefit is calculated based on the last three months of earnings before the termination of employment. The average unemployment benefit in 2022 was 372 EUR monthly, while the poverty threshold for a person household in the same year was 431 EUR monthly (CES, 2023).

16 www.esf.hr/europski-socijalni-fond/razdoblje-2014-2020/

17 https://esf.hr/esfplus/esf/

18 The European Pillar of Social Rights Action Plan was only adopted in 2021 (please see https://op.europa.eu/webpub/empl/european-pillar-of-social-rights/en/).

References

Babić, Z. (2008) 'Redistribucijski učinci sustava socijalnih transfera u Hrvatskoj', *Revija za socijalnu politiku*, 15(2), pp. 151–171.

Babić, Z. and Račić, D. (2017) *Croatia: Labour Market Policy Thematic Review 2017: An In-Depth Analysis of the Impact of Reforms on Inequality*. Brussels: European Commission, DG Employment, Social Affairs and Inclusion.

Babić, Z. and Račić, D. (2018) *Croatia: Labour Market Policy Thematic Review 2018: An In-Depth Analysis of the Emigration of Skilled Labour*. Brussels: European Commission, DG Employment, Social Affairs and Inclusion.

Bežovan, G. (2019a) *Trade Unions Mobilise Citizens Support for Referendum against Recent Pension Reform*. ESPN Flash Report, European Social Policy Network (ESPN). Brussels: European Commission.

Bežovan, G. (2019b) 'Hrvatska socijalna politika u vremenu globalizacije i europeizacije', in G. Bežovan, V. Puljiz, Z. Šućur, Z. Babić, I. Dobrotić, T. Matković and S. Zrinščak (eds.) *Socijalna politika Hrvatske*. Zagreb: Faculty of Law, University of Zagreb, pp. 59–108.

Bežovan, G., Šućur Z. and Babić, Z. (2020) *ESPN Thematic Report: Contribution to the 2021 SPC-COM Report on Long-Term Care for Older People in the EU: Croatia.*.

In: *Long term care report. Trends, challenges and opportunities in an ageing society. Country profiles.* Volume II, pp. 167–181. Joint Report prepared by the Social Protection Committee (SPC) and the European Commission (DG EMPL). Available at: https://ec.europa.eu/social/main.jsp?catId=738&langId=en&pubId=8396

Bičanić, I. and Franičević, V. (2003) *Understanding Reform: The Case of Croatia.* The WIIW Balkan Observatory Working Paper, 33. Available at: https://wiiw.ac.at/understanding-reform-the-case-of-croatia-dlp-3287.pdf (03.04.2023).

Bulmer, S. (2007) 'Theorizing Europeanization', in P. Graziano and M. Vink (eds.) *Europeanization. New Research Agendas*. Basingstoke: Palgrave Macmillan, pp. 46–58.

CES (2023) *Godišnjak 2022.* Zagreb: Croatian Employment Service. Available at: www.hzz.hr/app/uploads/2022/09/GODISNJAK-2022-2.pdf (03.07.2023).

CEU (2014) *Council Recommendation of 2 June 2014 on the National Reform Programme 2015 of Croatia and Delivering a Council Opinion on the Convergence Programme of Croatia*. Brussels: The Council of the European Union.

CEU (2015) *Council Recommendation of 15 July 2015 on the National Reform Programme 2015 of Croatia and Delivering a Council Opinion on the Convergence Programme of Croatia*. Brussels: The Council of the European Union.

CEU (2016) *Council Recommendation of 18 May 2016 on the National Reform Programme 2016 of Croatia and Delivering a Council Opinion on the Convergence Programme of Croatia*. Brussels: The Council of the European Union.

CEU (2017) *Council Recommendation of 22 May 2017 on the National Reform Programme 2017 of Croatia and Delivering a Council Opinion on the Convergence Programme of Croatia*. Brussels: The Council of the European Union.

CEU (2018) *Council Recommendation of 23 May 2018 on the National Reform Programme 2018 of Croatia and Delivering a Council Opinion on the Convergence Programme of Croatia*. Brussels: The Council of the European Union.

CEU (2019) *Council Recommendation of 5 June 2019 on the National Reform Programme 2019 of Croatia and Delivering a Council Opinion on the Convergence Programme of Croatia*. Brussels: The Council of the European Union.

CEU (2020) *Council Recommendation of 20 May 2020 on the National Reform Programme 2020 of Croatia and Delivering a Council Opinion on the Convergence Programme of Croatia*. Brussels: The Council of the European Union.

Coman, R. and Tulmets, E. (2021) 'Policy transfer within the European Union and beyond: Europeanization in times of stability and crises', in O. Porto de Oliveira (ed.) *Handbook of Policy Transfer, Diffusion and Circulation.* Cheltenham: Edward Elgar, pp. 337–363.

De la Porte, C. and Madama, I. (eds.) (2016) *The Sovereign Debt Crisis, the EU and Welfare State Reform.* Basingstoke: Palgrave Macmillan.

De la Porte, C. and Madama, I. (2022) 'Researching social Europe on the move', in K. Nelson, R. Niewenhuis and M. A. Yerkes (eds.) *Social Policy in Changing European Societies: Research Agendas for the 21st Century.* Cheltenham: Edward Elgar, pp. 136–153.

Dobrotić, I. (2022) 'The (In)equality Dynamic of Childcare-Related Policy Development in Post-Yugoslav Countries', *Journal of European Social Policy*, 32(3), pp. 270–286. Available at: https://doi.org/10.1177/09589287221088167 (14.11.2023).

Dolowitz, D. P. and Marsh, D. (2000) 'Learning from Abroad: The Role of Policy Transfer in Contemporary Policymaking', *Governance: An International Journal of Policy and Administration*, 13(1), pp. 5–24.

EC (2010) *EUROPE 2020: A Strategy for Smart, Sustainable and Inclusive Growth*. Communication from the Commission. COM (2010) 2020. Brussels: European Commission.

EC (2022) *SURE: Two Years On*. COM (2022) 483 Final. Brussels: European Commission.

Ecorys (2015) *Evaluation of Previous IPA HRD OP Assistance: Final Report*. Available at: www.esf.hr/wordpress/wp-content/uploads/2015/12/Zavrsno_izvjesce_Evaluacija-prethodne-IPA-pomoci.pdf (04.04.2023).

Ernst and Young (2021) *Vrednovanje djelotvornosti, učinkovitosti i učinka Operativnog programa Učinkoviti ljudski potencijali 2014. – 2020. – Prioritetna os 3 "Obrazovanje i cjeloživotno učenje" – Završno izvješće*. Zagreb: Ministry of Labour, Pension System, Family and Social Policy of the Republic of Croatia & Ernst and Young. Available at: www.esf.hr/wordpress/wp-content/uploads/2021/09/Zavr%C5%A1no-izvje%C5%A1%C4%87e_evaluacija_PO3_Obrazovanje-i-cjelo%C5%BEivotno-u%C4%8Denje_2021.pdf (01.04.2023).

Guillén, A. and Álvarez, S. (2004) 'The EU's Impact on the Spanish Welfare State: The Role of Cognitive Europeanization', *Journal of European Social Policy*, 14(3), pp. 285–299.

Hanushek, E. and Kimko, D. (2000) 'Shooling, Labor-Force Quality, and the Growth of Nations', *American Economic Review*, 90, pp. 1184–1200.

Ipsos (2016) *Vanjska evaluacija mjera aktivne politike tržišta rada 2010. – 2013. Sumarno evaluacijsko izvješće*. Zagreb: Croatian Employment Service & Ipsos. Available at: www.esf.hr/wordpress/wp-content/uploads/2016/04/sumarno-evaluacijsko-izvjesce-maptz.pdf (01.07.2023).

Isakjee, A. (2017) *Welfare State Regimes: A Literature Review*. IriS Working Paper Series, No. 18/2017. Birmingham: University of Birmingham, Institute for Research into Superdiversity. Available at: www.birmingham.ac.uk/Documents/college-social-sciences/social-policy/iris/2017/IriS-WP-18-2017UPWEB18.pdf (01.04.2023).

Knill, C. (2006) 'Implementation', in J. Richardson (ed.) *European Union: Power and Decision-Making*. 3rd edition. London: Routledge, pp. 351–375.

Knill, C. and Lehmkuhl, D. (1999) 'How Europe Matters: Different Mechanisms of Europeanization', *European Integration Online Papers*, 3(7). Available at: https://papers.ssrn.com/sol3/papers.cfm?abstract_id=302746 (07.07.2023).

Lendvai, N. and Stubbs, P. (2015) 'Europeanization, Welfare and Variegated Austerity Capitalisms – Hungary and Croatia', *Social Policy & Administration*, 49(4), pp. 445–465.

Lenschow, A. (2006) 'Europeanisation of public policy', in: Richardson, J. (ed.) *European Union: Power and Decision-Making*. 3rd edition. London: Routledge, pp. 55–71.

Matković, T. and Buković, N. (2022) 'Croatia: Impact of Europeanization on skill formation', in V. Tūtlys, J. Markowitsch, S. Pavlin and J. Winterton (eds.) *Skill Formation in Central and Eastern Europe. A Search for Patterns and Directions of Development*. Frankfurt: Peter Lang, pp. 265–290.

Meardi, G. (2016) 'The fate of the 'hard' and 'soft' acquis communautaires in the new member states', in V. Delteil and V. Nikolaev Kirov (eds.) *Labour and Social Transformation in Central and Eastern Europe: Europeanization and beyond*. London: Routledge, pp. 1–26. Available at: https://dx.doi.org/10.4324/9781315682112 (14.11.2023).

MHRC – Ministry of Health of the Republic of Croatia (2021) *Nacionalni plan razvoja zdravstva za razdoblje od 2021 do 2027. godine*. Zagreb: Ministry of Health of the Republic of Croatia. Available at: https://zdravlje.gov.hr/UserDocsImages/2022%20Objave/Nacionalni%20plan%20razvoja%20zdravstva%202021.-2027..pdf (10.04.2023).

Moumoutzis, K. and Zartaloudis, S. (2016) 'Europeanization Mechanisms and Process Tracing: A Template for Empirical Research', *Journal of Common Market Studies*, 54(2), pp. 337–352. DOI:10.1111/jcms.12294

MSES (2014) *New Colours of Knowledge: Strategy for Education, Science and Technology*. Zagreb: Ministry of Science, Education and Sports. Available at: https://mzo.gov.hr/UserDocsImages//dokumenti/Obrazovanje//Strategy%20for%20Education,%20Science%20and%20Tehnology.pdf (10.04.2023).

Munta, M. (2017) 'The Influence of the European Semester on Employment Policy in Croatia, 2013–2016', *Anali hrvatskog politološkog društva,* 14(1), pp. 187–211. DOI:10.20901/an.14.09

Munta, M. (2021) *EU Socio-Economic Governance in Central and Eastern Europe: The European Semester and National Employment Policies*. Abingdon, NY: Routledge. DOI:9780367697532

NDS (2021) *Nacionalna razvojna strategija Republike Hrvatske do 2030. godine*. Official Gazette 13/2021. Available at: https://narodne-novine.nn.hr/clanci/sluzbeni/2021_02_13_230.html (11.04.2023).

Petak, Z. (2006) 'Europeanization and Policymaking in the National Context: The Work of Policy in Croatia', *Politička misao*, 43(5), pp. 61–75.

Puljiz, V. (2019) 'Socijalna politika Hrvatske', in G. Bežovan, V. Puljiz, Z. Šućur, Z. Babić, I. Dobrotić, T. Matković and S. Zrinščak (eds.) *Socijalna politika Hrvatske*. Zagreb: Faculty of Law, University of Zagreb, pp. 1–58.

Račić, D. (2021) 'Od jedine partije do stožerne stranke: kontinuitet zarobljavanja države u Hrvatskoj', *Politička misao*, 58(3), pp. 39–76.

Radaelli, C. (2000) 'Whither Europeanization? Concept Stretching and Substantive Change', *European Integration Online Papers*, 4(8). Available at: www.eiop.or.at/eiop/texte/2000-008.htm (01.04.2023).

RRP (2021) *ANNEX to the Council Implementing Decision on the Approval of the Assessment of the Recovery and Resilience Plan for Croatia*. Brussels: Council of the European Union.

Rubil, I. and Nguyen, N. T. V. (2021) *Fiscal Policies, Inequality, and Poverty in Croatia*. Working Paper No. 04 / 2021. Zagreb: The Institute of Economics. Available at: www.eizg.hr/UserDocsImages/publikacije/serijske-publikacije/radnimaterijali/Fiscal%20Policies%20_Inequality_and%20Poverty%20in%20Croatia.pdf?vel=807438 (05.04.2023).

Saurugger, S. and Terpan, F. (2021) 'Normative Transformations in the European Union: On Hardening and Softening Law', *West European Politics*, 44(1), pp. 1–20. DOI:10.1080/01402382.2020.1762440

Šimunković, G. and Babić, Z. (2022) 'Koncept socijalnih investicija u zdravstvenom sustavu', *Revija za socijalnu politiku*, 29(3), pp. 367–392.

Stubbs, P. and Zrinščak, S. (2007) 'Croatia', in B. Deacon and P. Stubbs (eds.) *Social Policy and International Interventions in South East Europe*. Cheltenham: Edward Elgar, pp. 85–102.

Stubbs, P. and Zrinščak, S. (2009) 'Croatian Social Policy: The Legacies of War, State-Building and Late Europeanisation', *Social Policy and Administration*, 43(2), pp. 121–135.

Stubbs, P. and Zrinščak, S. (2010) 'Social protection and social inclusion from Lisbon to Europe 2020', in V. Samardžija and H. Butković (eds.) *From Lisbon Strategy to Europe 2020*. Zagreb: Institute for International Relations, pp. 164–181.

Stubbs, P. and Zrinščak, S. (2015) 'Citizenship and Social Welfare in Croatia: Clientelism and the Limits of 'Europeanisation' ', *European Politics and Society*, 16(3), pp. 395–410.

Stubbs, P. and Zrinščak, S. (2018) *ESPN Thematic Report on Inequalities in Access to Healthcare: Croatia*. Brussels: European Commission, Directorate DG Employment, Social Affairs and Inclusion.

The Council of the European Union (2014) *Council Recommendation of 8 July 2014 on the National Reform Programme 2014 of Croatia and Delivering a Council Opinion on the Convergence Programme of Croatia*. Brussels: The Council of the European Union.

World Bank (2014) *Croatia – Public Finance Review: Restructuring Spending for Stability and Growth*. Report No. 78320-HR. Washington: World Bank. Available at: http://bib.irb.hr/datoteka/814323.783200REVISED00PFR0final0report0ENG.pdf (10.03.2023).

WYG (2021a) *Vrednovanje Prioritetne osi 1 "Visoka zapošljivost i mobilnost radne snage" uz vrednovanje učinka mjera aktivne politike zapošljavanja. Završno izvješće o provedenom vrednovanju*. Zagreb: Ministry of Labour, Pension System, Family and Social Policy & WYG. Available at: www.esf.hr/wordpress/wp-content/uploads/2021/06/Zavrsno-izvjesce_evaluacija-PO1-i-MAPZ_OPULJP_final_lipanj_2021.pdf (01.04.2023).

WYG (2021b) *Vrednovanje Prioritetne osi 2 "Socijalno uključivanje". Završno izvješće o provedenom vrednovanju*. Zagreb: Ministry of Labour, Pension System, Family and Social Policy & WYG. Available at: www.esf.hr/wordpress/wp-content/uploads/2021/06/Zavrsno-izvjesce_evaluacija_PO2_final_lipanj_2021.pdf (01.04.2023).

WYG (2021c) *Vrednovanje društvenog poduzetništva. Završno izvješće o provedenom vrednovanju*. Zagreb: Ministry of Labour, Pension System, Family and Social Policy & WYG. Available at: www.esf.hr/wordpress/wp-content/uploads/2021/11/Zavrs%CC%8Cno-izvjes%CC%8Cc%CC%81e_vrednovanje-dru%C5%A1tvenog-poduzetni%C5%A1tva.pdf (01.04.2023).

WYG (2022) *Vrednovanje Prioritetne osi 4 "Dobro upravljanje". Završno izvješće*. Zagreb: Ministry of Labour, Pension System, Family and Social Policy & WYG & MAP. Available at: www.esf.hr/wordpress/wp-content/uploads/2022/03/Zavr%C5%A1no-izvje%C5%A1%C4%87e_finalna-verzija-1.pdf (01.04.2023).

Zeitlin, J. and Vanhercke, B. (2018) 'Socialising the European Semester: EU Social and Economic Policy Coordination in Crisis and Beyond', *Journal of European Public Policy*, 25(2), pp. 149–174.

Zrinščak, S. (2019) 'Zdravstvena politika', in G. Bežovan, V. Puljiz, Z. Šućur, Z. Babić, I. Dobrotić, T. Matković and S. Zrinščak (eds.) *Socijalna politika Hrvatske*. Zagreb: Faculty of Law, University of Zagreb, pp. 159–194.

Index

Note: Page numbers in *italics* refer to figures, **bold** page numbers refer to tables and page numbers followed by n. are in a note.